AMERICAN
CARTEL

AMERICAN CARTEL

INSIDE THE BATTLE TO BRING DOWN
THE OPIOID INDUSTRY

SCOTT HIGHAM and SARI HORWITZ

TWELVE

NEW YORK   BOSTON

Twelve

Hachette Book Group

1290 Avenue of the Americas, New York, NY 10104

twelvebooks.com

twitter.com/twelvebooks

First Edition: July 2022

Twelve is an imprint of Grand Central Publishing. The Twelve name and logo are trademarks of Hachette Book Group, Inc.

The publisher is not responsible for websites (or their content) that are not owned by the publisher.

The Hachette Speakers Bureau provides a wide range of authors for speaking events. To find out more, go to www.hachettespeakersbureau.com or call (866) 376-6591.

Library of Congress Cataloging-in-Publication Data
Names: Higham, Scott, author. | Horwitz, Sari, author.
Title: American cartel : inside the battle to bring down the opioid industry / Scott Higham and Sari Horwitz.
Description: First Edition. | New York : Twelve, [2022] | Includes index.
Identifiers: LCCN 2021053699 | ISBN 9781538737200 (hardcover) | ISBN 9781538737194 (ebook)
Subjects: LCSH: Pharmaceutical industry—United States. | Opioid abuse—United States. | Drug control—United States. | United States.
Drug Enforcement Administration.
Classification: LCC HD9675.O643 U64 2022 | DDC 338.4/76153—dc23/eng/20220106
LC record available at https://lccn.loc.gov/2021053699

ISBNs: 978-1-5387-3720-0 (hardcover), 978-1-5387-3719-4 (ebook)

Printed in the United States of America

LSC-C

Printing 1, 2022

For the victims and their families

Contents

Cast of Characters   *xi*

PART ONE: THIS IS WAR

     Prologue   *3*

1.   Joe Rann   *7*
2.   Dr. Evil   *15*
3.   Lightning Strike   *21*
4.   The Alliance   *25*
5.   "We Will Not Get Fined Again!"   *29*
6.   The Blue Highway   *34*
7.   "Just Like Doritos"   *37*
8.   Follow the Pills   *41*
9.   "Pillbillies"   *46*
10.   Broward County North   *50*
11.   "Game, Set, Match"   *54*
12.   A Betrayal   *58*
13.   Cardinal Knowledge   *63*
14.   "Because I'm the Deputy Attorney General"   *68*
15.   Imminent Danger   *74*
16.   "At the Corner of Happy & Healthy"   *81*
17.   "Crisis Playbook"   *86*
18.   Marsha and Tom   *90*
19.   Playing Games   *95*
20.   "Tom Marino Is Trying to Do That?"   *99*
21.   "Be Zen"   *103*

22. "You're Being Paranoid" *106*

23. "The Best Case We've Ever Had" *109*

24. The Mushroom Treatment *120*

25. An Expensive Speeding Ticket *124*

26. Banjo *129*

PART TWO: THE RECKONING

27. A Public Nuisance *135*

28. "Our Allies" *142*

29. "They're Gonna Get Hammered" *148*

30. On the Road *152*

31. Field of Dreams *157*

32. "The Hunt Is On" *161*

33. "Make Them Pay" *163*

34. Legal Titans *166*

35. The Drug Czar *173*

36. Jumped the Gun *178*

37. "This Is Horrific" *185*

38. "Tear Each Other Up" *191*

39. A Perry Mason Moment *197*

40. The Death Star *203*

41. The Digital Detectives *209*

42. The Magician *214*

43. The 60 Minutes Man *220*

44. A Lone Lawyer *226*

45. My Cousin Vinny *234*

46. RICO *237*

47. "We Have a Deal" *244*

48. "This Can't Be Real" *254*

49. "Every Nineteen Minutes" *258*

50. "We're Going to Trial" *267*

51. Death Threats *277*

52. "A Stunning Claim"   *285*

53. "Are You Ready?"   *294*

54. "Magic or Tragic"   *305*

    Epilogue   315

    Acknowledgments   *331*
    A Note on Sources *337*
    Index   *387*

Cast of Characters

The Drug Enforcement Administration

D. Linden Barber, associate chief counsel; drug company lawyer
Ruth Carter, diversion investigator and program manager
Kathy Chaney, diversion supervisor
Jack Crowley, supervisory investigator; Purdue Pharma executive
Jim Geldhof, supervisor, Detroit field division
Michele Leonhart, administrator
John J. Mulrooney II, chief administrative law judge
Imelda "Mimi" L. Paredes, executive assistant, Office of Diversion Control
John Partridge, executive assistant, Office of Diversion Control
James Rafalski, diversion investigator, Detroit field division
Joseph T. Rannazzisi, deputy assistant administrator, Office of Diversion Control
Clifford Lee Reeves II, associate chief counsel
Jack Riley, acting deputy administrator
Chuck Rosenberg, acting administrator
David Schiller, assistant special agent in charge, Denver field office

The Department of Justice

James M. Cole, deputy attorney general
James H. Dinan, associate deputy attorney general
Stuart M. Goldberg, chief of staff to James Cole
Jamie Gorelick, deputy attorney general; lawyer for Cardinal Health, Inc.
Eric H. Holder Jr., attorney general

Craig Morford, deputy attorney general; legal affairs for Cardinal
Health, Inc.

Randolph D. Moss, assistant attorney general; lawyer for Cardinal
Health, Inc.

The Plaintiffs' Attorneys

Jayne Conroy, Simmons Hanly Conroy

Paul T. Farrell Jr., Farrell Law

Richard W. Fields, Fields PLLC

Michael J. Fuller Jr., McHugh Fuller

Paul J. Hanly Jr., Simmons Hanly Conroy

Anthony Irpino, Irpino Avin Hawkins

Evan M. Janush, Lanier Law Firm

Eric Kennedy, Weisman Kennedy & Berris

Anne McGinness Kearse, Motley Rice

Mark Lanier, Lanier Law Firm

Mike Papantonio, Levin Papantonio Rafferty

Mark P. Pifko, Baron & Budd

Amy J. Quezon, McHugh Fuller

Joe Rice, Motley Rice

Pearl A. Robertson, Irpino Avin Hawkins

Hunter J. Shkolnik, Napoli Shkolnik

Linda Singer, Motley Rice

The Defense Attorneys

Mark S. Cheffo, Dechart LLP, representing Purdue Pharma

Geoffrey E. Hobart, Covington & Burling, representing McKesson
Corporation

Enu A. Mainigi, Williams & Connolly, representing Cardinal
Health, Inc.

Robert A. Nicholas, Reed Smith, representing AmerisourceBergen Corp.

Brien T. O'Connor, Ropes & Gray, representing Mallinckrodt

Paul W. Schmidt, Covington & Burling, representing McKesson
Corporation

Kaspar J. Stoffelmayr, Bartlit Beck, representing Walgreens

The Drug Manufacturers

Actavis, Davie, Florida (purchased by Teva)
Victor Borelli, national sales manager, Mallinckrodt
Cephalon, Inc., Fraser, Pennsylvania (purchased by Teva)
Endo Pharmaceuticals, Malvern, Pennsylvania
Johnson & Johnson, New Brunswick, New Jersey
Mallinckrodt Pharmaceuticals, St. Louis, Missouri
Purdue Pharma, Stamford, Connecticut
Burt Rosen, vice president, government affairs, Purdue Pharma
Teva Pharmaceuticals, Jerusalem, Israel
Watson Laboratories, Corona, California (purchased by Teva)

The Drug Distributors

AmerisourceBergen Corp., Valley Forge, Pennsylvania
Cardinal Health, Inc., Dublin, Ohio
Harvard Drug, Livonia, Michigan
H.D. Smith, Conshohocken, Pennsylvania (purchased by
AmerisourceBergen Corp.)
Healthcare Distribution Alliance ("The Alliance")
John Gray, president, The Alliance
KeySource Medical, Cincinnati, Ohio
Masters Pharmaceutical, Forest Park, Ohio
McKesson Corporation, San Francisco, California (now in Irving, Texas)
Sunrise Wholesale, Broward County, Florida

The Pharmacies

CVS Health Corporation, Woonsocket, Rhode Island
Rite Aid Corporation, Camp Hill, Pennsylvania
Walgreens, Deerfield, Illinois
Walmart, Bentonville, Arkansas

Congress

U.S. Representative Tom Marino, Republican of Pennsylvania
U.S. Senator Marsha Blackburn, Republican of Tennessee

U.S. Senator Orrin G. Hatch, Republican of Utah
U.S. Senator Sheldon Whitehouse, Democrat of Rhode Island

The Courts

Judge David A. Faber, U.S. District Court, Charleston, West Virginia
Judge Dan Aaron Polster, U.S. District Court, Cleveland, Ohio
Judge Reggie B. Walton, U.S. District Court, Washington, D.C.

PART 1

THIS IS WAR: 2005–2016

The Opioid Supply Chain

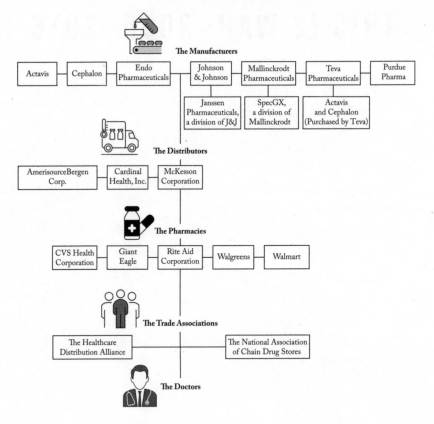

The Manufacturers

Actavis	Cephalon	Endo Pharmaceuticals	Johnson & Johnson	Mallinckrodt Pharmaceuticals	Teva Pharmaceuticals	Purdue Pharma

			Janssen Pharmaceuticals, a division of J&J	SpecGX, a division of Mallinckrodt	Actavis and Cephalon (Purchased by Teva)	

The Distributors

AmerisourceBergen Corp.	Cardinal Health, Inc.	McKesson Corporation

The Pharmacies

CVS Health Corporation	Giant Eagle	Rite Aid Corporation	Walgreens	Walmart

The Trade Associations

The Healthcare Distribution Alliance	The National Association of Chain Drug Stores

The Doctors

Prologue

DEA Headquarters, Arlington, Virginia, October 2015

Late on his last day as a DEA agent, Joe Rannazzisi grabbed a mailroom cart and wheeled a few boxes with personal belongings to his midnight blue Ford Excursion in the parking lot outside. He had turned in his badge earlier—a day without a formal goodbye lunch that was now an evening without farewell drinks. Almost everyone had already cleared out of the Drug Enforcement Administration's sleek office complex in Arlington, Virginia, and the silent corridor was a numbing coda to a career that for all its accolades seemed to have ended in defeat.

It was an unusual feeling for the muscled, tough-talking New Yorker who had spent a storied thirty years bringing down bad guys. Most recently, as head of the DEA's division responsible for policing the drug industry, Joe and his agents had pursued corrupt doctors, pharmacies, and the nation's largest drug manufacturers and distribution companies, who were pouring powerful and highly addictive opioids into communities across the country. Righteous investigations, Joe believed. But he and his team had been crushed, their struggle to stop the destructive flow of pain pills snuffed out by a secret, well-financed campaign. It was led by a coalition of drug company executives and lobbyists with close ties to members of Congress and high-ranking officials inside the Department of Justice, including some who had jumped from the DEA to the fat payrolls of the drug companies and the law firms that represented them.

Washington at its worst.

Joe's friends had known for months that he was being ostracized at the DEA—no longer a welcome crusader—and that he had finally been forced from the job that gave him a daily jolt of purpose. His buddies called him at home, gently probing to see if he was safe. Could someone as obsessive and wounded as Joe transition to retirement? "Don't worry, I'm not going to off myself," he told them. Still, some wondered whether they should take his Walther PPK .380, just to be sure. Joe was just a little bemused by the concern. He may have lost his job, but he was no quitter. He had two daughters at home to take care of and, he noted with a smile, a new coonhound mutt from the pound named Banjo.

The fight, he hoped, would go on in some form. Addiction to opioids was an epidemic. People were dying from overdoses by the hundreds of thousands. The companies would eventually choke on their greed. Citizens would eventually demand that their government stop it all. There had to be a reckoning. The shape of that reckoning, however, was not visible to Joe Rannazzisi on the dreary Friday he was finally cut loose from the DEA.

But other forces, just a state away, in the deadlands of the overdose epidemic, were beginning to stir. A few short years, and tens of thousands of deaths later, they would combine to expose the inner workings of the opioid industry and bring the drug companies to account.

In Huntington, West Virginia, Paul T. Farrell Jr., a small-town lawyer, sat at the kitchen table in his parents' home. A local news story in the *Charleston Gazette-Mail* was the talk of the town. It reported that several drug companies, including some of the largest in the nation, had sent 780 million prescription pain pills to West Virginia within six years, while 1,728 people in the state overdosed. The shipments were enough to supply 433 pain pills to every man, woman, and child in the state.

Paul's family had lived in Huntington for generations, Irish Catholic immigrants who arrived in New York's Hell's Kitchen during the nineteenth century and made their way to West Virginia. Huntington once prospered from the coal mines. But those boom years were long gone, and Paul's town had descended into something resembling a zombie movie—shells of human beings wandering downtown, empty syringes and needles in public parks, parentless children, an entire generation raised in foster homes or by grandparents.

The 2016 newspaper story led to the shocking realization that the blame didn't lie with Mexican drug cartels or any of the usual suspects, but instead with American companies, some of them household names, others obscure distribution outfits, all of them profiting from the misery on the streets outside.

These corporations were earning unprecedented profits in the billions of dollars while, to Paul's mind, his neighbors were being exterminated by opioids such as OxyContin, Percocet, and Vicodin. The disclosures in the story infuriated Paul's mother, Charlene. She and her family had seen too many deaths, gone to too many funerals. "Someone should do something," she said as her husband stood over the stove, frying up bacon for the Sunday morning family breakfast.

Paul's younger brother, Patrick, a fighter pilot during the Iraq War, chimed in. "Isn't that what you do for a living?" he asked Paul.

Paul's journey into the corrupt labyrinth of America's opioid industry began with that Sunday morning challenge. Soon he would collaborate with some of the most colorful and high-profile plaintiffs' lawyers in the nation. Along the way they would call as a star witness a former DEA agent named Joe Rannazzisi.

By 2018, this sprawling coalition of lawyers and investigators had launched the largest and most complex civil litigation in American history on behalf of thousands of counties, cities, and Native American tribes. The coalition won access to a confidential pill-tracking database and millions of internal corporate emails and memos during courtroom combat with legions of white-shoe law firms defending the opioid industry.

One breathtaking disclosure after another—from emails that

mocked addicts to sales reports chronicling the rise of pill mills—showed the indifference of big business to the epidemic's toll. The revelations open a horrifying panorama on corporate greed and political cowardice. They also highlight the efforts of community activists, DEA agents, and a coalition of lawyers to stop the human carnage.

The records include once-confidential communications inside corporate boardrooms, DEA headquarters, and the marbled corridors of Capitol Hill. The documents would eventually find their way into thousands of lawsuits filed in federal courthouses across the country and form the basis of a legal battle without precedent in American jurisprudence—a bruising, complex, and unfinished quest for justice.

A modern-day opium war has been fought on American soil over the last twenty years and it has claimed five hundred thousand lives—more than the U.S. military lost during World War II. The death toll from overdoses continues to rise as the opioid epidemic takes new forms.

Over time, it became apparent to Paul that the companies that comprised the opioid industry were not behaving like any corporations he had ever seen.

They aren't, Joe would say one day. They are an American cartel.

Chapter 1

Joe Rann

DEA Headquarters, 2006

Joseph T. Rannazzisi was furious, his anger teetering toward rage as he stepped into a DEA conference room to meet with several executives from the McKesson Corporation, the largest drug distribution company in America. For months, he and his team of investigators on the sixth floor of the agency's headquarters in Arlington had been demanding that the company follow the law. A bear of a man at six foot two and 205 pounds, Joe quickly commanded attention. It was January 3, 2006, and time for a come-to-Jesus.

Headquartered in San Francisco, with seventy-six thousand employees around the world, McKesson had $93 billion in annual revenues, making it the eighteenth-largest corporation in the country. The firm had been shipping copious amounts of hydrocodone—a highly addictive opioid laced into the popular pill commonly known as Vicodin—to just six pharmacies in Tampa, Florida. Between October 10 and October 21, 2005, McKesson distributed more than two million doses of hydrocodone to those drugstore clients. The pharmacies then sold the pills over the internet to just about anyone with a credit card.

As the chief of the DEA's Office of Diversion Control, the unit responsible for policing the pharmaceutical industry, Joe saw prescription opioids as a threat far more deadly than the crack and meth epidemics of the 1980s and '90s. Euphoria-inducing, heroin-like pain pills such as Vicodin and OxyContin and their generic cousins, hydrocodone and oxycodone, were killing ten to fifteen thousand people a year—almost as many as the U.S. military lost in Vietnam in 1968, the bloodiest year of the war. Joe's job was to make sure prescription drugs were not diverted from the legitimate supply chain to the black market.

Joe couldn't blame transnational cartels for smuggling the drugs into the country, like he did when he was a special agent based in Detroit battling heroin, cocaine, and crystal meth. He didn't hold the Playboy Gangster Crips or the Black Mafia Family or MS-13 responsible for selling them on the street. He faced a far more formidable foe: the executives who ran some of the nation's most respected Fortune 500 corporations—the drug manufacturers, the pharmacies, and the little-known distributors that serve as the middlemen in the supply chain of prescription pain pills. Three distributors— companies that purchase the pills from manufacturers wholesale and ship them to their pharmacy clients on the retail level—transport nearly 95 percent of all pharmaceuticals in the United States: Cardinal Health, Inc., AmerisourceBergen Corp., and McKesson, the last the focus of Joe's fury on this first Tuesday of 2006.

Joe had summoned the executives to Arlington to make good on a threat. The shipments to Tampa were clearly suspicious. Why would six small drugstores need two million tablets of hydrocodone over eleven days? The DEA had already warned McKesson that the outlets were pushing pain pills to the internet; the agency had shown McKesson's executives paperwork cataloging the vast quantities of pills the stores had been requesting and demanded that the corporation stop filling the orders. Under the law—the Controlled Substances Act of 1970—Joe told the executives that it was up to them to figure out why the stores wanted so many doses. If McKesson didn't get a plausible explanation, the company was obligated to stop the shipments and report the pharmacies to the DEA. Instead, McKesson had been shipping the pills to its drugstore customers without saying a word—a practice it continued after the DEA warnings.

Joe and his team sat down at the conference table across from three McKesson executives and their lawyer from a Washington law firm, Hyman, Phelps & McNamara, which specialized in representing drug industry clients. One of the executives was McKesson's leader of Six Sigma, an elite business training program. Another held dual undergraduate degrees in biology and pre-med. The third held an MBA from Carnegie Mellon. The lawyer from Hyman had worked as an attorney in Joe's division at the DEA before going into private practice to represent drug industry clients.

The McKesson executives worked for John H. Hammergren. At forty-seven, boyish and bespectacled, Hammergren was a quiet yet intensely ambitious businessman, the son of a traveling salesman, who rose through the ranks of McKesson to become one of the highest-compensated corporate executives in the United States. He owned a 23,000-square-foot mansion in Orinda, California, nestled in the hills east of Berkeley. The 3,100-square-foot Tudor-style carriage house on his nine-acre estate was filled with high-end sports cars, including a pair of Ferraris and a rare Ford GT40. He also owned a 3,456-square-foot summer home near Lake Winnipesaukee, not far from the White Mountains of New Hampshire. McKesson's shareholders covered his $66,000 round-trip flights between California and New Hampshire aboard the company's Dassault Falcon 900 jet.

Hammergren was a quarry far different from the targets Joe pursued in the early years of his career. Joe realized that his life was far less complicated when he was a special agent in Detroit. He missed the camaraderie of working the streets, the informants, the undercover buys, the all-night surveillance in "beater" cars that blended into the background. Street drug cases had a rhythm. Leads, interviews, wiretaps, controlled buys, court appearances, and if it all went well, convictions. There were good guys and bad guys, he believed, and not much in between.

A life in law enforcement was not an unexpected choice for Joe, but it strained his relationship with his father, who had hoped his son would take a different career path. Joe worked his way through college and had a pharmacy degree from Butler University in Indiana, and his father anticipated that would be a stepping-stone to medical school. Stephen Rannazzisi was a high school chemistry and biology teacher on Long Island, and he wanted Joe to rise above the family's modest Victorian home in a working-class Freeport neighborhood on Long Island's unfashionable South Shore.

Joe loved Freeport. During the 1960s, he lived an idyllic *Wonder Years* kind of life there, a tableau of minibikes and slot cars, baseball cards and go-carts. Cops and firefighters lived on every block, and Joe wanted to be one of them. They had a sense of purpose, and they knew how to have fun, drinking beers in the blue-collar bars and catching bands at the raucous Oak Beach Inn near Jones Beach.

Joe thought that med school was for the kids who grew up on the North Shore, the sons and daughters of doctors and lawyers, Wall Street traders and hedge fund managers. His father couldn't understand why Joe studied pharmacology only to become a cop. But Joe longed for a job that would combine his fascination with science and law enforcement.

While attending Butler, Joe volunteered as a firefighter. He basked in the brotherhood. To stay in fighting form, he liked to box and jogged more than forty miles a week. A rock and roll fan, he played guitar and worshipped Neil Young. Weekends, he went to downtown cop bars, hanging with a law enforcement crowd. "Joe Rann," as everyone called him, had found his second home.

His life choices bewildered his father. "Why are you spending all of this money to go to pharmacy school just to be a cop?" his father asked during a phone call in Joe's senior year, his voice a mixture of anger and disappointment. "Why don't you go to med school? Why are you wasting your time?"

"Well, that's what I want to be," Joe said. "It's a noble profession and I can't see myself doing pharmacy or doing medicine the rest of my life. I just can't see it."

What about a master's degree? his father asked. What about a research position?

"Dad, I'm tired," he replied. "I gotta go to sleep."

The line went dead. His father had hung up. It would be a year before they spoke again.

After graduating, Joe joined the DEA in 1986 as a diversion investigator before becoming a special agent two years later in the Indianapolis field office and then in Detroit. With his educational background, passion for the work, and propensity to put in twelve- to fourteen-hour days, he was quickly seen as an agent with a big future. He won a promotion to supervise a task force of federal and local officers to solve drug-related murders, nicknamed Redrum, "murder" spelled backwards. He then became coordinator of the clandestine lab group in Detroit, knocking over meth labs in hazmat suits. In his spare time, he attended the Detroit College of Law at Michigan State University, adding a law degree to his qualifications in 1999.

By 2006, at age forty-five, Joe had secured a post at DEA headquarters as head of the Office of Diversion Control, where he managed a staff of 320. The office had long been derided as a backwater inside the agency, pursuing prescription pill cases—ridiculed as "kiddie dope" prosecutions—not prestige takedowns of the big drug rings that peddled cocaine and heroin. But now kiddie dope was killing tens of thousands of Americans, as much or more each year than heroin or cocaine.

The carnage had to stop. DEA leadership expected Joe's division to lead the charge. He began by targeting unscrupulous doctors and small-town pharmacies illegally selling massive quantities of opioids on the internet. But he soon realized that he needed to move higher up the chain and target the drug distribution companies to choke off the supply. Less than a year into his new job, Joe and his colleagues launched the "Distributor Initiative," shifting the DEA's focus to some of the biggest corporations in America, companies such as McKesson.

Joe didn't care that the McKesson executives sitting across from him at the conference table had highly specialized training in the pharmaceutical world. To him, they were little more than drug dealers dressed in suits.

"How did this happen?" Joe erupted. "All of these kids are going on the internet and collecting hydrocodone like baseball cards."

The executives seemed taken aback, but they shouldn't have been. For months, Joe and his team had been warning McKesson and dozens of other drug companies that they were violating the law and in danger of losing their DEA registrations to sell controlled substances like hydrocodone. He had sent every drug company in the nation letters outlining their responsibilities to report unusually large orders of drugs from their customers and prevent them from being diverted to the streets. If a distributor receives an order from a pharmacy that is unusually large, unusually frequent, or deviates substantially from previous orders, the distributor is required under federal law to "maintain effective controls" to prevent the drugs from reaching the black market and to notify the DEA, he told them. The same rules apply to drug manufacturers who receive suspicious orders from drug distribution companies like McKesson.

Joe and his team had briefed seventy-six companies in total, warning them that they were breaking the law by funneling huge amounts of pain pills to online pharmacies that were nothing more than fronts for corrupt doctors and drug dealers.

Four months earlier, on September 1, 2005, McKesson had received one of those briefings. The DEA told the company about the proliferation of internet pharmacies that were selling—"diverting" in DEA parlance—prescription pain pills to the black market. The following month, a DEA investigator contacted the head of McKesson's cavernous drug distribution center in Lakeland, Florida, warning him that the company was still filling large orders for suspicious customers in Tampa. Throughout the fall of 2005, Joe and his team monitored an internal DEA database that traces the path of every single pain pill sold in America. By the end of the year, when Joe saw that McKesson had sent another two million pills to the online pharmacies in Tampa in an eleven-day period, he blew up. "It's like we never spoke to them," he told his team.

Their audacity was part of what filled Joe with rage as he sat across from the McKesson executives at that conference table in Arlington. He glared at the executives. One smiled and tried to lighten the mood with a joke. "Well, I guess you got us," he said. "Is there anything we can do to make this right?"

Joe had heard that question before, but never from a corporate executive. It usually came from a street drug trafficker who had been arrested and was looking for a deal. Joe glanced over at his second in command, Supervisory Special Agent Gary Boggs. Joe shook his head in disbelief.

The McKesson executives and their lawyer weren't really interested in making it right. If the online drugstores were such a big problem, why didn't the DEA shut them down, they countered? They argued that they were not in the enforcement business, that they were simply middlemen delivering a legitimate product legally prescribed by a doctor. They also said they didn't have the same data as the DEA.

To Joe, the excuses were pathetic. People are becoming addicted, he thought, people are dying, and this is all they have to say? There are sixty-six thousand pharmacies in the United States and only three major drug distribution companies, he told the McKesson executives. His division couldn't go after every dishonest pharmacy, but he could go after their company. Joe reiterated that the distribution companies are required to police or "know their customers" under federal law, and the data the DEA used to track the shipments had come from McKesson's own sales reports.

"I would like you to surrender your registration," Joe told them.

In the pharmaceutical world, to lose a DEA registration is

equivalent to losing a business license. The revocation can cost a company like McKesson millions every day that one of its warehouses, some of them the size of Amazon fulfillment centers, is shut down. It can cost millions more in attorney's fees to fight the DEA to reinstate the registration.

"I'm done here," Joe said, rising from the table. "I don't have time to fuck around. I gave you an opportunity to fix your issues and you just sent more drugs downstream."

Chapter 2

Dr. Evil

Dallas, Texas, 2007

Inside a Dallas conference hall, the lights dimmed and Dr. Evil from the movie *Austin Powers: International Man of Mystery* appeared on a large screen.

It was about 9 a.m. and the hall at the Gaylord Texan Resort & Convention Center was packed with sales representatives for Cephalon, a pharmaceutical manufacturer headquartered in Frazer, Pennsylvania, just northwest of Philadelphia. The salesmen were in town for a rah-rah retreat. Their work, encouraging doctors to prescribe opioids, had catapulted Cephalon, founded just twenty years earlier, onto the Fortune 1000 list of U.S. companies. In 2006, it posted $1.7 billion in revenue, a 46 percent increase over the previous year. The sales reps were not in Texas just for a collective pat on the back. Cephalon wanted more revenue, much more—and it wanted it from a new opioid tablet the company had brought to market.

The voice of comedian Mike Myers, who played Dr. Evil in the *Austin Powers* movies, was dubbed over by a Cephalon executive. The parody opened with ominous music and the subtitle "Somewhere outside Frazer, Pa." Dr. Evil—bald, scarred, and wearing a gray Nehru suit—was seated at the head of a conference table, addressing his nervous acolytes while stroking his white cat. "I want to go over some problems we are having with Fentora," the dubbed voice said, referring to the new fentanyl tablet Cephalon had created. The company had introduced Fentora the previous year with a corporate stage show that included fireworks and the U2 song "Beautiful Day" blasting in the background. Cephalon wanted Fentora to be a bestseller.

Dr. Evil said he was unhappy with the child-resistant packaging the Cephalon team had designed for its version of fentanyl—a synthetic opioid that is fifty times more powerful than heroin and typically used for anesthesia and cancer pain. "It's a pain in the butt to open," Dr. Evil said. He then pushed a button, causing one of those sitting around the table, the executive responsible for the packaging, to plunge into a pit of fire. "Let this be a reminder to you all that this organization will not tolerate failure," Dr. Evil said, before urging his executives to push Fentora as a treatment for lower back pain—a radical reorientation of the drug's use. Fentora had been approved by the Food and Drug Administration to treat what is called "breakthrough pain" from cancer, but the company now was pitching it to doctors to treat everyday ailments.

"Tell the Street," Dr. Evil said, "a billion in sales this year!"

The use of opium to relieve pain dates back thousands of years. Opium poppies were cultivated in 3400 BC in lower Mesopotamia, where the Sumerians called them "joy plants"; Greek and Roman physicians used opium to induce sleep and soothe pain. In the United States, from the Civil War through the early 1900s, doctors treated pain with opium gum and morphine, without fully understanding their potential for addiction. By then, there were about three hundred thousand morphine addicts, many of them war veterans originally treated with the drug for their injuries. They were said to have the "soldier's disease."

In 1914, the federal government passed the nation's first drug enforcement law, the Harrison Narcotics Tax Act, regulating the production and distribution of opioids. During congressional hearings before its passage, Donald McKesson, an executive of the company, founded in 1832, testified in favor of the legislation. He told the House

Ways and Means Committee, "We have been ever since against the sale of habit-forming drugs and all that kind of thing. Orders which have come to us from suspicious people, we have put in the hands of the proper authorities for tracing and prosecution if necessary."

Ten years later, the use of heroin was outlawed. The opioid was first introduced in 1898 by the German pharmaceutical company Bayer as a cough suppressant and headache treatment. For much of the twentieth century, opioids were reserved for late-stage cancer patients and short-term, in-hospital treatment after major surgery. American doctors would not prescribe powerful opioids for chronic ailments; the fear of addiction outweighed pain management gains. Doctors instead sought to provide relief for their patients with other therapies. It wasn't until 1970 that Congress passed the Controlled Substances Act to regulate dangerous and addictive drugs, including opioids. Three years later, it created the Drug Enforcement Administration.

Even though opioids were heavily regulated and had earned a reputation as dangerously addictive, a movement started to gather strength in the early 1990s to use them for pain management. It was led by doctors such as Russell Portenoy at New York City's highly prestigious Memorial Sloan Kettering hospital, who pushed for the wider use of opioids. Portenoy argued that many patients were suffering needlessly and the risk of opioid addiction was low, bolstering his claims with reports and data that were discredited years later.

But it was the pharmaceutical company Purdue Pharma, based in Stamford, Connecticut, that changed the culture of prescribing opioids in the United States and rewrote the narrative around pain management. Purdue, owned by the Sackler family, introduced Oxy-Contin in 1996. Its main ingredient was oxycodone, an opioid first synthesized by German researchers in 1916. Purdue added a time-release feature and promoted OxyContin as a wonder drug for continuous pain relief with the slogan "The One to Start With and the One to Stay With." So many people started and stayed with OxyContin that it became one of the most sought-after opioids on the street.

In a promotional video Purdue sent to fifteen thousand doctors in 1998, a doctor trumpeted that "the rate of addiction amongst pain patients who are treated by doctors is much less than 1 percent."

The new uses of fentanyl, like Cephalon's Fentora tablets, and other painkillers grew out of that industry-wide pitch: *Less than 1 percent of people prescribed opioids become addicted.* It was a falsehood, but a beguiling one. The lie permitted both the drug makers and the doctors to jettison a century of medical caution in the United States about addiction to painkillers.

The false statistic that would launch a thousand marketing campaigns—and seed the epidemic that has killed half a million Americans—emerged from a one-paragraph letter to the editor of the *New England Journal of Medicine* in 1980. The 104-word note was written by Hershel Jick, a doctor and drug specialist at Boston University School of Medicine, and Jane Porter, his assistant. They reported their observations on hospital patients who were provided opioids. Their finding was summed up in the headline that accompanied their letter: "ADDICTION RARE IN PATIENTS TREATED WITH NARCOTICS." Jick and Porter reported that they had observed only four cases of addiction out of 11,882 patients.

In interviews more than thirty years later, Jick said that he put his findings in the letter because they couldn't be considered a study. The claim that pain pills carried a small risk of addiction for all patients was "not in any shape or form what we suggested in our letter," he said. He said he was "amazed" that the drug companies had used his letter for "pushing out new pain drugs." No one from Purdue or the other companies that later used the less-than-1-percent statistic had ever asked him about his letter or its use in their advertising.

"I'm essentially mortified that that letter to the editor was used as an excuse to do what these drug companies did," Jick said.

The 1 percent statistic spread and mutated in pain literature and the general media. At one point, *Time* magazine called the Jick letter "a landmark study." But the real rate of addiction was far higher—at least 8 to 12 percent of patients prescribed opioids for chronic pain became addicted.

By 2007, other drug manufacturers had taken a page from the highly successful Purdue playbook. The companies paid doctors, who often cited the 1 percent claim, to speak at medical conferences and continuing medical education seminars as well as on national television and professional society dinners. Portenoy, the New York pain doctor, served as a spokesman for Purdue. And the companies quietly funded advocacy groups that encouraged wider use of opioids for pain patients.

The Joint Commission on Accreditation of Healthcare Organizations—a nonprofit that evaluates hospitals and medical programs—urged the medical community in 2001 to consider pain as the "Fifth Vital Sign" along with body temperature, blood pressure, and respiration and pulse rates. Doctors, nurses, and other health care providers were encouraged to ask their patients to rank their pain from 1 to 10—and not to be concerned about treating these self-diagnosed pain levels with opioids.

Aggressive sales reps who visited doctors' offices to pitch their wares were the linchpin of the marketing strategy. Like most drug reps, they wined and dined doctors. They also showered them with little gifts of coffee mugs, golf balls, and fishing hats. But the reps pushing pain pills were particularly aggressive and cavalier. Some handed out stuffed toy gorillas wearing blue OxyContin T-shirts, as if the drug they were hawking was a plaything instead of a potential killer. The companies dangled big bonuses for sales reps who sold the most pain pills at the highest doses and rewarded the best performers with Caribbean cruises and expensive watches.

Between 1996 and 2001, the annual number of prescriptions for OxyContin soared from three hundred thousand to six million; the number of oxycodone-related deaths increased 400 percent during the same period. There was some pushback from concerned doctors, and even warnings from a handful of Purdue sales representatives, but their voices were drowned out by the marketing deluge and the intoxicating profits Purdue and other drug companies were posting.

Drug manufacturers also paid movie stars to promote more aggressive pain treatment. One was Jennifer Grey, famous for her role in the 1987 romantic drama *Dirty Dancing*. After she suffered a severe neck injury in a car crash, Purdue hired Grey as a spokeswoman for its "Partners Against Pain" campaign. She appeared on television programs to urge people in pain to become advocates for themselves. She later said she didn't know she was being used to "potentially advance a darker agenda."

Joe Rannazzisi was incensed by what he was witnessing, but powerless to address misleading marketing; that was the purview of the Food and Drug Administration. What he could speak out about—and what he knew from his training as a pharmacologist—was the addictive power of opioids. Joe and his team of investigators put together a slide show on the history of opioid addiction and the advent of the internet pharmacies. He began to present the slide show to medical boards, law enforcement officers, community organizations, pharmacy associations, congressional committees—anyone who would listen—to counter the messaging of the drug companies.

"All of a sudden the whole medical community says, 'Oh, you know what, they're not as addictive as we thought they were,'" Joe said during his presentations. "That's crazy because we have had a hundred years-plus of addiction here based on these drugs."

Someone always stood up and asked, "What about the study that shows that less than 1 percent of people get addicted to opioids?"

"That's ridiculous," Joe told his audiences. "I just want to see some evidence other than somebody saying that they're not as addictive as we once thought they were. I want somebody to show me some peer-reviewed articles with a large population of patients. Not a letter to the editor in the *New England Journal of Medicine*."

He left these meetings wondering if anyone was listening.

Chapter 3

Lightning Strike

DEA Headquarters, 2007

When his warnings to executives went unheeded, Joe Rannazzisi went on the offensive, launching a series of strikes against the opioid industry. It was the first time the DEA had gone after Fortune 500 companies. He began with McKesson. He decided to deploy one of the agency's most potent weapons against the company, an Order to Show Cause, compelling McKesson to explain why some of its operations shouldn't be shut down for violations of federal drug law. If McKesson couldn't satisfy the DEA, it would lose its registration to sell narcotics at the offending warehouses, forcing it to forfeit millions in profits.

McKesson's executives pleaded with Joe, pledging to pay closer attention to the volume of pain pills the company was sending to its customers. But little had changed. The flow from McKesson's warehouses to the online pharmacies had turned into a torrent.

"The time for talk is over," Joe told his staff.

The operation was code-named "Lightning Strike." Joe dispatched DEA raid teams across the country to choke off the supply of pills to the pharmacies. Agents and investigators shut down one of McKesson's largest drug distribution warehouses, in Lakeland, Florida, between Tampa and Orlando, from where the company had sent the two million pain pills to the six pharmacies.

For many major corporations, Lakeland was a strategic transportation hub, providing easy access to points east and north along Interstate 4 and Interstate 75 to Appalachia, a region that was quickly becoming the epicenter of the pain pill epidemic. There is so much congestion at the Tampa interchange, much of it from the thousands of trucks pulling in and out of the warehouses operated by companies like Best Buy, Advance Auto Parts, Publix, and Pepperidge Farm, it's derided by locals as the "Malfunction Junction." The interchange had also become known for something else: a transshipment point for the nation's opioid distributors. Not only did McKesson maintain one of its largest warehouses in Lakeland, but so did Cardinal, the nineteenth-largest company in America.

Joe's teams struck five other McKesson warehouses in 2007. One of them, in Maryland, had shipped 3 million pain pills to a single pharmacy in Baltimore. Another, in Texas, had sent 2.6 million pills to a pair of pharmacies in Houston. Inside the enormous warehouses, the DEA agents and investigators sifted through the company's computers and filing cabinets, seizing tens of thousands of order forms, invoices, memos, emails, and drug distribution records.

On April 24, 2007, Joe's teams raided the third-largest drug distribution company in the nation—AmerisourceBergen, based in Valley Forge, Pennsylvania, the twenty-ninth-largest corporation in America. As he had done with McKesson, Joe warned the company about its online-pharmacy customers. Joe targeted AmerisourceBergen's warehouse in Orlando, Florida, with the DEA's most severe sanction, an Immediate Suspension Order. It was seen by drug industry executives as a death sentence. The DEA deemed the company's conduct to be so egregious, it posed an "imminent danger" to the public. The order prevented AmerisourceBergen from distributing any more narcotics from the location. AmerisourceBergen capitulated to avoid the wrath of the DEA. Within five months, the company announced that it had designed a monitoring system to detect and halt huge and suspicious orders of pills. The DEA lifted its order.

Joe next trained his sights on Cardinal, a Fortune 500 company based in Dublin, Ohio, with revenues of $87 billion. Joe's DEA team had warned Cardinal that its drug shipments were a serious concern and pills were being diverted from the supply chain and winding up on the street. The DEA stormed three Cardinal warehouses between November 28 and December 7, 2007—in Auburn, Washington; Swedesboro, New Jersey; and Lakeland. At each warehouse, Joe's team served the company with Immediate Suspension Orders for shipping massive amounts of opioids to pharmacies that the company "knew or should have known" were diverting them to the black market.

In Florida, pharmacies typically dispensed an average of 8,400 tablets of hydrocodone each month. Cardinal supplied one of its pharmacy customers in Tampa with an average of 242,000 pills in four months and another in the same city with 287,000 pills inside of three months. The DEA ordered Cardinal to cease distribution of all narcotics at each of the warehouses, which served hundreds of Cardinal's retail pharmacy clients.

Inside of a year, Joe had moved against the largest opioid distribution firms in the country, known in the industry as the "Big Three."

Maybe they'll finally get the message, he thought.

In the midst of the raids, in May 2007, Joe received an unexpected late-night call on his private line at DEA headquarters. It was from an old colleague at the Department of Justice, John L. Brownlee, a career federal prosecutor now serving as the U.S. attorney for the Western District of Virginia. Brownlee, normally unflappable, was upset. He told Joe that his superiors at the Justice Department were pushing him to settle the case he had worked so hard to build against Purdue Pharma in exchange for a $634 million fine for misbranding its blockbuster OxyContin pill as safer and less addictive than other painkillers. As part of the deal, three company executives would plead guilty to misdemeanor charges. No one would go to jail. Joe knew that the Justice Department had amassed a mountain of evidence, enough to

bring felony counts against Purdue and its top executives for a litany
of fraud charges. He also learned that the company had hired several
high-powered former Justice officials, now in private practice, to lobby
the department on behalf of Purdue. They included former U.S. attorneys Mary Jo White and Rudy Giuliani, who had formed his own
consulting and lobbying firm after serving as the mayor of New York
City.

Brownlee told Joe he didn't want to settle, but the pressure from
outside and inside the Justice Department had become unbearable.

"John, you know, there's no shame in taking a settlement," Joe
told him, trying to comfort a friend. "I'm sorry you can't finish what
you started, but you should be proud of what you accomplished."

Purdue had lit the fuse with the introduction of OxyContin, but
by 2007, many more companies were fueling the opioid epidemic,
turning it into a conflagration.

Joe knew he might have to eventually target the other opioid
manufacturing companies such as Mallinckrodt Pharmaceuticals, a
giant in the industry that had so far managed to escape scrutiny. In
2006, Purdue manufactured 130 million pain pills. That same year,
Mallinckrodt, headquartered in St. Louis, manufactured 3.6 billion
generic pills—twenty-seven times more than Purdue. It costs drug
makers pennies to manufacture a 5mg oxycodone pill. At the pharmacy, twenty of those pills sell for $13. On the street they go for $100.
But for now, Joe wanted to stay focused on the distributors. One day,
he thought, an executive from McKesson or Cardinal or AmerisourceBergen might see the inside of a prison cell. That would chasten
the industry.

"Guys in business suits don't do well in prison," Joe liked to say.

Chapter 4

The Alliance

Arlington, Virginia, 2007

Four miles from DEA headquarters in northern Virginia stands a nondescript beige concrete-and-glass office building that is home to one of Washington's powerful trade associations. The Healthcare Distribution Alliance was the nerve center for the nation's opioid distributors, the institution that made sure Congress and regulators did not mess with the profitable nexus between the drug makers and the pharmacies. The Alliance, as it was called, served as their lobbyist, crisis manager, and legal adviser. Few people beyond the boardrooms of the drug companies and the corridors of Capitol Hill knew that The Alliance even existed.

Top corporate officers from each of the Big Three distributors—McKesson, Cardinal, and AmerisourceBergen—formed its executive council, each company paying $1 million in annual dues. Midsized and smaller drug distribution companies also belonged to The Alliance, a nonprofit organization. They worked with the manufacturers and chain pharmacies. Even though many of the companies were fierce competitors, the raids had given them a common purpose, and a common enemy—Joe Rannazzisi and the DEA. Their profits and stock prices were being threatened. So was their ability to distribute prescription pain pills without more aggressive oversight by government agencies that could no longer ignore the magnitude of the companies' misdeeds following Joe's raids. To settle the cases with the DEA, the companies would have to pay fines and install costly systems to identify and stop dubious orders of pills.

Joe viewed The Alliance with deep suspicion—a well-financed shield for illegal behavior. In Joe's mind, the members of The Alliance didn't want to obey the law. "They just want to do what they want to do," he liked to tell his staff, "and what they want to do is make money." He thought that their zeal for massive profits had made them willing to dismiss any concern for the human costs of the drugs they were peddling.

With Joe's raid teams fanning out across the country, serving warrants and seizing company records, members of The Alliance were becoming increasingly alarmed. They began to exchange a flurry of urgent emails. On September 25, 2007, a senior Alliance director, Anita T. Ducca, alerted her colleagues in a confidential memo that the DEA was threatening their multibillion-dollar business.

Ducca urged The Alliance's members to craft a "comprehensive DEA strategy" and explore all options to protect their businesses from further enforcement actions. Ducca knew her way around Washington. Before joining The Alliance five years earlier, she had served on the staff of the FDA, which has oversight over the pharmaceutical industry. She also worked for the White House's Office of Management and Budget and the Environmental Protection Agency.

"Develop a strategy for outreach to appropriate decision makers, such as DEA staff, the Hill, other federal agencies who may be supportive, e.g., OMB or the Small Business Administration," Ducca wrote to her colleagues. "What, if any, legal options do we have?"

Two and a half weeks earlier, Ducca, accompanied by the general counsel for The Alliance and a veteran outside attorney who specialized in DEA regulatory matters, met with the DEA. Four DEA staffers from Joe's team walked them through the same PowerPoint that had been provided earlier to drug company executives. The DEA staffers stressed that the companies were required under federal law to maintain "effective controls" over the narcotics they distributed, and they needed to set up systems to detect and stop enormous and clearly illicit orders of pain pills. They also demanded that the distributors "know their customers" and be on the lookout for telltale signs that pills were being diverted to the streets through illegal channels, such as pharmacies filling prescriptions from patients who lived in different parts of the country.

"DEA's expectations are clearly heightened," Ducca and the two attorneys noted in an internal memo. Their concerns were echoed by one of The Alliance's key members, Cardinal Health. Stephen J. Reardon, a vice president of the company, wrote to his team in a confidential email following The Alliance's meeting with the DEA. Reardon said he was worried by the agency's aggressiveness. He noted that AmerisourceBergen had already set up a suspicious order monitoring system to try to avoid losing its DEA registration, and the agency was now calling that system "the new industry standard." Reardon wrote that he had learned McKesson executives were working on a similar system as part of a settlement it was negotiating with the DEA.

Under AmerisourceBergen's system, orders of unusual size or frequency needed to be red-flagged, stopped, and examined. The company promised to conduct "due diligence" investigations to figure out why a customer had ordered so many pills. If the company couldn't resolve the red flag, the shipment was to be canceled and reported to the DEA. AmerisourceBergen also agreed to install a computer system that would flag giant orders that exceeded thresholds of pills each of its customers was allowed to order every month.

As head of quality and regulatory affairs for Cardinal, Reardon was responsible for ensuring that there were no interruptions in the supply chain. He warned his colleagues about the costs of setting up a more sophisticated system similar to the one at AmerisourceBergen. That system, he told them, "is not customer friendly." If put into place at Cardinal, he said, it would delay the "delivery of controlled substance orders to the customer."

On December 7, three months after the Alliance meeting with the DEA, Jack Crowley, a former DEA supervisor who had joined Purdue Pharma as executive director of compliance, wrote an email to one of his counterparts at Cardinal to commiserate about the agency's enforcement actions.

For nearly thirty-one years, Crowley was with the DEA, working his way up to head its international drug unit before becoming a supervisory investigator handling pharmaceutical cases. A rotund man with a jovial manner and intimate knowledge of the inner workings of the DEA, Crowley was widely respected by his colleagues at the agency—until he switched allegiances and accepted the post at Purdue in 2003. He was one of many DEA officials to leave the agency for high-paying jobs with the companies they once regulated, or with the Washington, D.C., law firms that did the companies' bidding.

"I see our friends are at it again. I wanted to say hello and I'm sorry that DEA is being so aggressive with this Suspicious Orders stuff," Crowley wrote. "I wish there was something I could do to help in this situation—we are all in the same boat."

The DEA, in other words, was bad for business.

Chapter 5

"We Will Not Get Fined Again!"

Washington, D.C., 2008

With each warrant, each raid, and each fine, executives at the nation's major drug companies were becoming angrier and angrier. Joe Rannazzisi's enforcement actions had rankled the drug industry, and now the companies' practices were attracting attention on Capitol Hill. The days when just about anyone could purchase pain pills over the internet were drawing to a close.

In 2008, Congress shut down the online pharmacies by overwhelmingly passing the Ryan Haight Online Pharmacy Consumer Protection Act, named after an eighteen-year-old La Mesa, California, teenager who had overdosed on Vicodin pills he ordered online without ever seeing a doctor or obtaining a prescription. His death became a clarion call for parents terrified that their children could order deadly narcotics from their computers and have them delivered to the family's front door. The bad publicity was so intense, longtime supporters of the drug industry in Congress did not have sufficient political cover to oppose the bill.

As one major source for illicit drugs was shut off, Joe had to shift his focus to another: pain management clinics—little more than "pill mills"—that were springing up around the country, particularly in Florida, where state regulations were lax. Palm Beach, along with

Broward and Dade counties, home to Fort Lauderdale and Miami, were quickly becoming the epicenter of these storefront operations run by unprincipled doctors and pharmacists who wrote and filled prescriptions with few questions asked. The clinics began to resemble open-air drug markets. Long lines of customers lingered in parking lots filled with cars from multiple states: Tennessee, West Virginia, Alabama, Ohio. Signs in the windows demanded "cash only." Inside, some owners had installed bulletproof partitions and kept pistols and attack dogs in the back.

As Joe's teams raided the pill mills in 2008, he again targeted the drug distributors that were supplying them—the same companies that had shipped hundreds of millions of painkillers to the online pharmacies. He once again put the drug manufacturers on notice.

Inside the drug companies, executives were trying to figure out how to fight back. On March 19, 2008, Jack Crowley, the former DEA official and executive director of compliance for Purdue Pharma, sent an email to the head of his company's supply chain. Crowley said that the time had come to arrange a meeting with the Big Three drug distributors, along with some in-house corporate investigators, "to talk about DEA's latest plans to squeeze the wholesalers and distributors on 'pain clinics.'"

Crowley said he had been hearing that the DEA was shifting its enforcement efforts to the pill mills. "They will call distributors into Headquarters and read them the riot act, etc. 'We don't need all these pain meds on the street,'" Crowley wrote. "I think we're going to have some potential problems with patient access and making sure our product is available to our patients."

Crowley worried that the DEA might shut down another marketplace for opioids if the manufacturers and distributors didn't come together and push back. "We really do have to partner with our own customers to help them in their business with pharmacies catering to 'pain clinics.' Otherwise, they will cut them off based on some kind of threshold. We need to convince them they should talk to us when our product is involved and make it a joint decision," he said.

Crowley was articulating a growing industry-wide perception: The DEA had to be stopped.

On March 20, a day after Crowley warned colleagues about a growing DEA problem, Kristen Freitas, a lobbyist for The Alliance, sent out an alert to members of her organization. She crafted a "confidential draft political strategy" designed to defang the DEA. It contained nine tactics. In one, Freitas proposed that The Alliance seek out pain patient advocacy groups, many of them funded by the drug industry, and enlist them in a public relations campaign against the DEA. In another, she said The Alliance should contact executives in the pharmacy community, including her former employer, the National Association of Chain Drug Stores, which represented some of the biggest names in the retail pharmacy industry, including CVS and Walgreens. She wanted to warn them about the impact the DEA's actions could have on their businesses.

Most critically, it was time to get Congress involved. She proposed that The Alliance contact members of the House and Senate appropriations subcommittees, which were responsible for approving the DEA's budget, and the House and Senate judiciary committees, which oversaw the agency's operations, to persuade lawmakers to compel the agency to curtail its operations. The purpose of enlisting Congress was clear: If the DEA didn't back off, its oversight committees could squeeze the agency by threatening its budget or blocking appointees.

Over the years, The Alliance and the pharmaceutical industry had cultivated close ties with sympathetic members of Congress, including U.S. senator Orrin G. Hatch, a powerful Republican from Utah, and contributed generously to their campaigns. As part of her political strategy, Freitas crafted twenty questions those lawmakers could ask DEA officials when they came to Congress to testify.

The practice of lobbyists writing questions for members of

Congress and drafts of legislation is an open secret in Washington, but not widely known outside the Beltway. Freitas began her career as an aide to Representative Dick Chrysler, a Republican from Michigan, before moving to the National Association of Chain Drug Stores and later joining The Alliance. She urged her colleagues to keep the practice a "close hold." The public might not warm to such naked special interests.

Most of the questions Freitas wrote for the lawmakers were designed to shift blame away from the drug companies and place it on disreputable doctors and pharmacies and the DEA itself. One question she suggested: "Can or should a wholesale distributor be asked to determine the appropriateness of a validly-licensed pharmacy's practice?" Another question: "Isn't your initiative overly broad and not focused specifically enough on the rogue pharmacies?"

A lawmaker could be particularly helpful if he or she were to read an Alliance talking point during a congressional hearing. Freitas proposed that a senator or representative could say from the dais during a hearing, "It seems to me at the end of the day, this prescription drug abuse is caused by inappropriate prescribing and inappropriate dispensing, neither of which wholesalers are authorized or capable of regulating or enforcing."

"Tactic 8" was perhaps the most important piece of Freitas's DEA political strategy: "Identify high-level Congressional 'champion' who will request a meeting with DEA to discuss concerns." Freitas listed the status of that tactic as "In development."

Two months later, on May 2, 2008, McKesson settled its case with the DEA. The agency had alleged that three of the company's warehouses were filling extremely large orders from its online pharmacy customers and neglecting to report them to the DEA. McKesson paid a $13.25 million fine, the largest levied against a drug distributor. "By failing to report suspicious orders for controlled substances that it received from rogue Internet pharmacies, the McKesson Corporation fueled the explosive prescription drug abuse problem we have in this country," DEA administrator Michele Leonhart said in a statement. As part of the settlement, McKesson promised to install a system to flag and report all unusual orders of opioids to the DEA. Joe was not pleased by the settlement, negotiated by agency leaders and the Justice Department. He thought that the fine was pitiful compared to the company's annual revenues of more than $93 billion. He also questioned whether McKesson would actually stop sending excessively large orders of opioids to its customers, including the emerging pill-mill industry.

John Hammergren, McKesson's president, signed the settlement on behalf of the company. Nineteen days after the settlement, one of Hammergren's top corporate officers sent a cautionary note to McKesson employees. "With the recent fines and ongoing attention being paid to this issue, it is quite possible that wholesalers will be under scrutiny for quite some time," Tracy Jonas, the company's director of regulatory affairs, wrote in a May 21, 2008, email. "All communications regarding controlled substances will therefore be subject to subpoena and discovery.

"Write information as if it were being viewed by the DEA (it just might be)," Jonas continued. "Refrain from using the word 'suspicious' in communications. Once we deem an order and/or customer suspicious, McKesson is required to act. This means all controlled substances sales to that customer must cease and the DEA must be notified."

Using the word "suspicious" could hurt the bottom line.

Jonas said there were "13.3 million reasons" to follow his advice, referring to the dollar amount of the DEA fine. "We will not get fined again!"

Chapter 6

The Blue Highway

St. Louis, Missouri, 2008

The route between the pill mills of South Florida and the Appalachian and Ohio River valley regions went by many nicknames, none more fitting than the "Blue Highway." As 2008 drew to a close, Purdue Pharma's OxyContin tablets were no longer the most highly sought-after prescription painkillers being doled out by doctors, pill mills, and pharmacies and winding up on the streets. A generic pill manufactured by a company that most Americans had never heard of—Mallinckrodt—was becoming the opioid of choice on the black market.

Powder blue in color and stamped with the company's trademark "M" logo, the pills packed a euphoric punch. Containing 30 milligrams of oxycodone, each pill was the equivalent to a hit of heroin. Drug users and dealers simply called them "blues." Unlike OxyContin, blues didn't need to be crushed to neutralize the time-release formula Purdue had so successfully pioneered as a marketing tool during the previous decade. The delay device had been designed to provide continuous pain relief. But one popped blue, on the other hand, brought an instant rush of pure oxycodone. It was enough to sustain four hours of opioid bliss, leaving users relaxed, happy, and feeling no pain—before the sickening pangs returned and they needed to take another and then another to stave off the ravages of withdrawal.

With the internet pharmacies decimated by the DEA and Congress, pill mills acting under the guise of pain management clinics—many of them set up in the seemingly endless strip malls of Palm Beach, Broward, and Dade counties in South Florida—quickly took their place. On one street in Broward County alone, there were thirty-one pain clinics. Drug users and dealers hopped from one location to the next, shopping for doctors who would sell them painkillers in exchange for a few hundred dollars. On the street, each thirty-count bottle of oxycodone 30mg pills went for $900. Florida lacked a prescription drug monitoring system, enabling the pill seekers to obtain and fill multiple prescriptions. South Florida became an opioid wonderland. Billboards along I-75 and I-95 advertised the pain clinics with toll-free numbers and promises of easy access to prescription narcotics. "Walk-Ins Welcome," read signs outside.

Drug dealers organized buying trips to South Florida from Huntington, West Virginia, Portsmouth, Ohio, and other towns reeling from opioid overdoses and deaths. They piled into cars, vans, and buses, bringing back bottles filled with Mallinckrodt's pills and other favored brands of oxycodone and hydrocodone. Some eschewed the rigors of the road and took in-and-out flights to Fort Lauderdale. The route became known as the "Oxy Express."

Founded in 1867 in St. Louis, Mallinckrodt started out as the world's leading supplier of chemicals for the emerging photography industry. The company went on to score a series of scientific breakthroughs—inventing contrast chemicals for X-rays; providing purified uranium oxide for the Manhattan Project and enabling the U.S. government to create the world's first self-sustaining nuclear chain reaction. It also worked in the drug trade. In 1898, Mallinckrodt entered the lucrative opioid business, creating chemicals for the production of morphine and codeine.

The company became a generous benefactor for the renowned Washington University in St. Louis. The medical school's radiology institute is named after Mallinckrodt. So is the building that houses the student union and the performing arts center. Two members of the family, Edward Mallinckrodt Sr. and Edward Mallinckrodt Jr., were on the board of trustees of the university.

By 2008, Mallinckrodt was manufacturing more painkillers than any other company in the United States. That year, it produced 4.3 billion doses, many of them the 30mg blues. Mallinckrodt executives maintained that they had no way of determining where the pills went after they left their factory in Hobart, New York, seventy miles west of Albany. They said their customers—the drug distribution companies—knew where the pills wound up. They insisted they couldn't follow the path of the pills from their factory to the retail pharmacies.

Mallinckrodt capitalized on the market Purdue had once dominated by churning out generic versions of oxycodone in what was becoming an increasingly competitive arena. That year Actavis in New Jersey produced 3.6 billion pills. Following the federal fine and convictions, Purdue tried to remain competitive. It reformulated its blockbuster OxyContin, but its numbers were dwarfed by those of its competitors.

Mallinckrodt made more than ten times as many pills as Purdue in 2008, yet it hadn't received nearly the same public attention and scorn. Members of the Sackler family, who controlled Purdue Pharma, were becoming pariahs. Their name would later be stripped from the wings of some of the world's most iconic institutions, including the Louvre in Paris, the Serpentine Gallery in London, and New York's Metropolitan Museum of Art.

The Mallinckrodt name had no such negative connotation. That was about to change.

Chapter 7

"Just Like Doritos"

Reisterstown, Maryland, 2008

Victor Borelli was a driven national salesman for Mallinckrodt. One of his biggest clients was a drug distributor named Key-Source Medical based in Cincinnati. In May 2008, Borelli sent an email to Steve Cochrane, the vice president of purchasing for Key-Source, telling Cochrane to order more pain pills—whether he needed them or not.

"If you are low, order more. If you are okay, order a little more. Capesce?" Borelli then joked, "destroy this email...Is that really possible? Oh Well..."

In another email, Borelli told Cochrane that twelve hundred bottles of oxycodone 30mg tablets had just been shipped to KeySource.

"Keep 'em coming!" Cochrane wrote back. "Flyin' out of here. It's like people are addicted to these things or something. Oh, wait, people are..."

"Just like Doritos," Borelli wrote back. "Keep eating, we'll make more."

In his career, Borelli, ruddy-faced with short brown hair, had peddled everything from toothpaste to shampoo to coffee. By age forty-six, he had stints with some of the biggest consumer goods companies in the world: Unilever, a British-based multinational; H. J. Heinz, the famous ketchup company; and Sara Lee Corporation, best known for its buttery pound cake.

And then, in 2005, Borelli began selling opioids. He was hired as a district manager for Mallinckrodt, winning promotions to regional and then national sales manager, working out of a home office in Reisterstown, Maryland. He handled some of Mallinckrodt's biggest drug distribution customers. Unlike Purdue, which pitched its wares directly to doctors, generic manufacturers didn't need to market their products. They sold generic hydrocodone and oxycodone to drug distributors. Generic drugs are typically far less expensive than branded versions, requiring manufacturers to sell large volumes to turn a profit. There were only a half dozen national sales managers at the company, creating lucrative opportunities for people like Borelli, who could move tens of millions of tablets of oxycodone and bring home big bonuses.

Borelli, who graduated from Northeastern University in 1984 with a degree in business management, had seen the news stories about the opioid epidemic and how it was wrecking communities across America. He knew that companies like Mallinckrodt were under strict requirements to monitor suspiciously high orders of narcotics from their customers. But other company officials were supposed to watch for unusual ordering patterns among his distributor clients. He had only one responsibility, and that was to sell. Or as he wrote in an email to another Mallinckrodt official, "Ship, ship, ship."

Borelli's drive for sales and the extraordinary orders of oxycodone his company was moving unsettled some of his colleagues. In the spring of 2008, Brenda Rehkop, a Mallinckrodt customer service representative, wrote a note to Borelli about a new customer, Sunrise Wholesale, just outside Fort Lauderdale. Sunrise had placed an enormous order for 252,000 tablets of 30mg oxycodone.

"Were you expecting Sunrise to place such a large order??" Rehkop asked Borelli in an email. "And do they really want 2520 bottles of OXYCODONE HCL 30 MG TABS USP, 100 count each??"

Another executive forwarded the email to one of Mallinckrodt's senior compliance officers with a note: "FYI—the customer service reps all state that Victor will tell them anything they want to hear just so he can get the sale..." The compliance officers, despite their obligation to scrutinize suspicious orders, did nothing to rein in Borelli.

Sunrise Wholesale was sending oxycodone by the bucketload to a doctor based in Delray Beach in Palm Beach County, Barry Schultz. On July 7, 2009, a Tennessee task force investigating drug trafficking in the state seized several 100-tablet bottles of Mallinckrodt-made oxycodone in a sting operation—and all of the prescriptions had been written by Schultz. The task force alerted Mallinckrodt because the company's lot numbers were stamped on the bottles. Three days later, after checking its records, Mallinckrodt told the Tennessee authorities that Sunrise had sent the bottles of oxycodone to Schultz—20,400 tablets in the previous year.

At the same time, the Florida Department of Health filed an administrative complaint against Schultz for prescribing inordinate amounts of oxycodone. On one day, Schultz had prescribed 1,000 tablets to a single patient. He prescribed 20,000 over ten months to another. Schultz later said he had only been trying to relieve the pain of the patients who came to his clinic for help. But even after the seizure and the complaint against Schultz, Borelli kept shipping to Sunrise. In the six weeks after the task force notified Mallinckrodt about the Tennessee sting in July 2009, the company shipped another 2.1 million oxycodone tablets to Sunrise, and the company continued to supply Schultz. The doctor was later arrested on drug trafficking charges and sentenced to 157 years in prison.

In 2009, an executive at Mallinckrodt sent Borelli several news stories about the opioid crisis in Florida, including one chronicling how Broward County had become the pill-mill capital of the United States. The first line of another article read, "South Florida has become the largest supplier of illegal prescription drugs in the country."

"Interesting article," Borelli wrote back in an email.

But whatever concern had led executives to circulate the article did nothing to change the company's practices.

In the seven years that Borelli worked as a salesman at Mallinckrodt, he was well compensated. In 2006, a year after arriving at the company, he received a $26,442 bonus. The next year, it jumped to $35,904. In 2008, when Mallinckrodt's sales of oxycodone were skyrocketing, Borelli's bonus soared as well, to $119,096. He twice received Mallinckrodt's "President's Club" top salesman award, and the company treated him to an all-expenses-paid trip to the Caribbean island of Saint Thomas.

On a single day in 2010, KeySource ordered 12,720 hundred-count bottles—or 1.2 million pills. The company ordered another 12,720 bottles to be delivered the following day. Again, Rehkop, the Mallinckrodt customer service representative, questioned the quantities sent to KeySource. That year, KeySource sent a total of 41 million tablets of Mallinckrodt-made oxycodone to its customers in Florida.

Rehkop sent an email to several people inside Mallinckrodt, including Borelli. "This will undoubtedly show up as a peculiar order," she wrote. "Do you know why they are ordering so much oxy?"

Chapter 8

Follow the Pills

DEA Headquarters, 2010

In the fall of 2010, Joe Rannazzisi summoned hundreds of agents and investigators stationed across the country to DEA headquarters. His deputies had prepared a detailed PowerPoint presentation singling out the companies responsible for shipping the largest quantities of pain pills to Florida. Jim Geldhof, the supervisor in charge of the DEA's Detroit field division, noticed that some of the companies highlighted in the presentation were based in his backyard. He fumed as he took in the staggering numbers and saw how they lined up with the escalating death toll across the country.

Geldhof, a thirty-eight-year veteran of the DEA, grew up in Detroit despising drugs, a hatred he shared with his father, a Chrysler tool and die factory worker. They had seen firsthand how heroin, crack cocaine, and pills hollowed out the once-thriving neighborhoods of the city. But rather than join his father on the factory floor like so many kids of his generation, Geldhof was looking for a way to confront the scourge, and in 1972 he joined the Bureau of Narcotics and Dangerous Drugs, renamed the Drug Enforcement Administration the following year.

A burly man with a shock of white hair, a thick Michigan accent, and little patience for incompetence, Geldhof wanted to be in the middle of the action at the new agency created by President Nixon.

He saw his share, working cases in New York City and Newark during the 1970s and early '80s, a time when syringes littered public parks and pimps and drug dealers populated Times Square.

In 1986, Geldhof was promoted, returning to Detroit as a DEA supervisor of diversion investigators for the Midwest. In the fourteen years he had been away, Detroit had been ravaged. Blocks of abandoned houses and boarded-up storefronts blighted the city. Decimated by the loss of auto industry jobs, Detroit was awash in drugs and guns and murders. Prescription opioids were quickly rising in popularity, joining heroin, crack, and crystal meth. Among the prescription drugs, Dilaudid, an opioid normally prescribed to cancer patients, was the most popular pill on the street, followed by brand-name opioids Percodan, Percocet, and Vicodin.

In 2000, the year Geldhof returned to Detroit, the city recorded 637 homicides, including the deaths of 43 children under the age of sixteen, making it the murder capital of the United States. The deluge of drugs fueled the homicide rate. In the years following the introduction of OxyContin in 1996, the drug scene shifted dramatically in Detroit, as it did in many other cities and towns across the country. Purdue's blockbuster painkiller set off a tsunami of misuse, and OxyContin and generic tablets of oxycodone and hydrocodone swept through the city.

Geldhof directed his three dozen DEA investigators in Detroit, Cleveland, Columbus, Cincinnati, Louisville, and London, Kentucky, to pursue doctors who were writing illegal prescriptions. But his investigators were overmatched. They could hit rogue doctors every day, sending some of them to jail, and not make much of a difference. As soon as one went out of business, another would pop up.

As Geldhof watched Joe's presentation at DEA headquarters, he was happy to see his friend in a position of real power at the agency. He always liked Joe. The two had become friends in Detroit during the '80s and '90s, when Joe was working drug-related murders and knocking over meth labs.

After the presentation, Geldhof returned to Detroit and assigned some of his best investigators to examine the drug distribution companies singled out by Joe. One of them was James Rafalski, who was already on the trail of a company in Michigan called Harvard Drug, which had off-the-charts amounts of business in Florida. (The company had no connection to the university.) Rafalski was the Joe Friday of the Midwest regional office, a just-the-facts DEA investigator with cropped hair, a manicured mustache, and intense brown eyes that never seemed to blink. Nicknamed "Ralph," he loved diving into the minutiae of cases, piecing together disparate bits of information from documents and sources, working the edges, slowly and methodically closing in on the targets of his investigations.

Rafalski had once considered an engineering career in the auto industry and even followed his father to the Ford Motor Company, working on a shock absorber assembly line after high school. But the U.S. auto industry was reeling in the early '80s and Rafalski decided to join some of his friends who had found steady work in law enforcement. Once out of college, he became a guard at a county jail before joining the police department in the town of Romulus, a Detroit suburb. After twenty-one years, Rafalski had risen to the rank of executive lieutenant and could have retired, but he wanted to stay in the game. At forty-nine, he joined the DEA.

Harvard Drug was based in Livonia, another suburb of Detroit. Most of the oxycodone the company was shipping to Florida came from one manufacturer: Mallinckrodt. Rafalski began by looking at the numbers. He was floored by what he found in the DEA database. The Automation of Reports and Consolidated Orders System, a mind-numbing bureaucratic name for one of the DEA's most potent weapons, collects sales data from every drug manufacturer and distributor in the country. Known by the acronym ARCOS, the database revealed that Harvard had distributed thirteen million tablets of oxycodone across the country between March 2008 and March 2010, nearly half of them going to Florida. Rafalski spotted another red flag: Doctors purchased the vast majority of the pills. Normally, drug distributors sent pills directly to pharmacies.

Rafalski knew he had a case and began to dig deeper. He noticed that one of Harvard's biggest customers was the South Florida Pain Clinic in Broward County. It was run by twin brothers, twenty-seven-year-olds Christopher and Jeffrey George. Rafalski quickly learned that the brothers were already under investigation by the DEA and the FBI in South Florida for drug trafficking. The twins had recruited doctors on Craigslist and opened their first pain clinic in Wilton Manors, a small city three miles north of Fort Lauderdale. Customers could visit the clinic, see a doctor, fill their prescriptions, and head back the same day to Kentucky or West Virginia or Ohio, flush with pain pills. The brothers soon expanded, opening a chain of clinics, each bringing in as much as $50,000 a day. They spent their riches on lavish homes, Rolex watches, and fast cars, including a Lamborghini Murciélago worth nearly $400,000.

On June 10, 2010, Rafalski and a team of nine DEA investigators and forensic computer specialists raided the offices of Harvard inside a large warehouse the size of a Home Depot. The seventy-six employees of the company sat in silence as members of the raid team pulled thousands of records documenting every sale of oxycodone—customer files, company notes, and internal order records. They also mirrored Harvard's servers, capturing every keystroke made on a company computer.

When he started to go through the records, Rafalski saw that Mallinckrodt was supplying the company with oxy 30s through its leading salesman, Victor Borelli. He also discovered from internal sales documents that Harvard was supplying other pain clinics run by the George brothers. The case was starting to come together, the targets coming into focus.

Rafalski began to interview employees of Harvard; he was surprised that they answered his questions without lawyering up. Rafalski let his subjects talk, rarely interrupting them. Sometimes they would implicate themselves or unwittingly reveal key pieces of information. He liked to ask deceptively simple questions. Why did you do it? Or, besides you, who else was involved? He was constantly amazed by what people told him, often against their own self-interest. At one point, he sat down with Harvard's top compliance officer, Samir Shah. He asked Shah about the pills the company had purchased from Mallinckrodt and shipped to Florida. Shah told him that Mallinckrodt executives knew exactly where every one of their pills had gone. That was startling news to Rafalski. Drug manufacturing executives had claimed to him and other DEA officials that they didn't know where their pills went once they shipped them.

Rafalski's heart raced, but he tried to remain impassive. "How do they know?" he asked. Shah told him his company and other drug distributors provided their sales information to Mallinckrodt in exchange for a rebate on drug purchases. It was called a "chargeback," a term Rafalski had never heard before. In other words, Mallinckrodt was aware of—or should have been—the identities of all of Harvard's customers, including the George brothers.

Chapter 9

"Pillbillies"

Valley Forge, Pennsylvania, 2011

The parody was of the theme song from the 1960s CBS sitcom *The Beverly Hillbillies*:

"Come and listen to a story about a man named Jed," it began. "A poor mountaineer, barely kept his habit fed, / Then one day he was lookin at some tube, / And saw that Florida had a lax attitude. / About pills that is, Hillbilly Heroin, 'OC' [oxycodone].

"Well the first thing you know ol' Jed's a drivin South," the parody continued. "Kinfolk said Jed don't put too many in your mouth, / Said Sunny Florida is the place you ought to be / So they loaded up the truck and drove speedily. / South, that is. / Pain Clinics, cash 'n carry. / A Bevy of Pillbillies!"

At the height of the opioid epidemic, executives at Amerisource-Bergen sent around an email with this takeoff of a show that reinforced the worst stereotypes of people from places like Appalachia—slow-talking, dirt poor, and uneducated. "Saw this and had to share it," wrote Joseph Tomkiewicz, an AmerisourceBergen corporate investigator, in an April 22, 2011, email.

Two of Tomkiewicz's colleagues then forwarded it to others, including Julie Eddy, director of state government affairs for Ameri-sourceBergen. She wrote back to one of them, Chris Zimmerman, the vice president of regulatory affairs for the company: "I sent this to you a month or so ago—nice to see it recirculated." She closed her email with a smiley face emoji.

In 2011, nearly sixteen thousand people died from prescription opioid overdoses. Appalachia, including West Virginia, Tennessee, Kentucky, Ohio, and southwestern Virginia, had become the epicenter of the nation's opioid crisis. That year alone, AmerisourceBergen distributed 1.7 billion pain pills in the United States. In April, as AmerisourceBergen employees were getting a laugh out of the "Pillbillies" parody, the company shipped 291,400 pills of hydrocodone and oxycodone to just one county in West Virginia—Cabell County, population 96,612—in the heart of Appalachia.

One of the world's largest pharmaceutical service companies, AmerisourceBergen ranked twenty-seventh on the Fortune 500 list with $77 billion in annual revenue. It was headed by South African native Steven H. Collis, who joined the company in 2011. His annual compensation package was worth $4.6 million.

AmerisourceBergen was one of the companies that had received a letter from Joe Rannazzisi outlining its responsibility to stop and report outlandish drug orders. In 2007, when Joe and his DEA team had been investigating illegal opioids sales over the internet, they raided and shut down the company's Orlando distribution center and temporarily suspended its license, alleging that AmerisourceBergen had distributed 3.8 million doses of hydrocodone products in one year to rogue online pharmacies.

The same year the company executives circulated the "Pillbillies" parody, AmerisourceBergen and other drug companies were trying to block legislation being debated by the Florida Legislature to curb the explosion of the pill mills and subject drug distribution companies to strict reporting requirements for all shipments of pain pills to the state. After several media investigations into the pill mills, the state legislature was forced by growing public concern to consider a law that would police the industry and stop the drugs being moved along the Blue Highway and on the Oxy Express.

The legislation required companies to submit monthly drug distribution reports of controlled substances to the Florida Department of Health. Improper distribution and false reporting would now be felonies. The law also barred most doctors from dispensing narcotics from their offices or clinics and allocated $3 million to law enforcement to investigate and target pill mills suspected of violations. To prevent doctor shopping, a state prescription monitoring system would identify how often a person was prescribed pain pills, which doctors prescribed them, and which pharmacies dispensed them.

In a series of private emails, executives for McKesson, Cardinal Health, and AmerisourceBergen mapped out a lobbying strategy to defeat or amend the legislation. On April 21, 2011, Ann Berkey, a senior vice president in charge of public affairs for McKesson, wrote an email to the top lobbyists for Cardinal Health and AmerisourceBergen. The subject line: "Florida Pill Mill."

"We are very concerned about the pending state pill mill bill and could really use your help on the ground in Tallahassee next week," Berkey wrote. She said that three McKesson executives and a lobbyist were working the state House of Representatives, but they needed help with the Senate. "Looks like outright defeat is no longer a viable option. Any way you can persuade some of your execs to come to Tallahassee next week? We are much stronger as a group!"

The lobbyist for AmerisourceBergen, Rita Norton, wrote back on April 25, noting that Julie Eddy—the same executive who added the smiley face emoji to the "Pillbillies" email—was flying to Florida to help with the lobbying effort to defeat the bill.

The push to kill the legislation, however, failed; it passed the following month. Lawmakers could not ignore the spotlight that had been put on their state by the DEA and journalists. Republican Florida governor Rick Scott signed the pill mill legislation in June 2011. There was an element of karma to the governor's signature. He had been personally singled out in the "Pillbillies" parody.

"Well now it's time to say Howdy to Jed and all his kin," read the last stanza. "And they would like to thank Rick Scott fer kindly invitin them. / They're all invited back to this locality / To have a heapin helpin of Florida hospitality / Pill Mills that is. Buy some pills. Take a load home. Y'all come back now, y'hear?"

Chapter 10

Broward County North

Portsmouth, Ohio, 2011

On a warm June night in 2011, Jim Geldhof sat down on a folding chair inside a high school gymnasium in Portsmouth, Ohio. Two weeks earlier, the DEA had shut down a string of pill mills in the city and arrested several doctors. Outside the pill mills in Portsmouth, crowds cheered the raids. Geldhof and one of his supervisors in the state capital, Columbus, Kathy Chaney, were invited that night to a town hall on the opioid crisis with the city's police chief, federal officials, and community residents.

Hundreds filed into the gymnasium. After a few people spoke, the police chief turned off the lights and the room grew dark. A large screen flickered with photographs of Portsmouth's dead. One by one, twenty-eight bright young faces flashed across the screen. A high school cheerleader. A football player. A boy wearing a red toboggan hat. A teenage boy sporting a tie in his senior-year photo. Another teenager smiling on the beach. A young nurse.

People sitting in the rows behind Geldhof began to sob.

They were parents, siblings, relatives, and friends of the faces on the screen. Practically everyone in Portsmouth had been touched by an overdose death. The Appalachian city of 20,000 on the north bank of the Ohio River, just across from Kentucky, was saturated with opioids. It had acquired the nickname "Broward County North."

Located almost as far south as one could travel in Ohio before reaching Kentucky, Portsmouth in Scioto County had once been a booming blue-collar industrial city known for its shoe factories and its enormous steel mill, the Portsmouth Steel Company. During World War II, it became a large producer of bombs. But the mill had closed long ago, along with the shoe factories. As unemployment climbed, abandoned buildings scarred the city. Pain clinic after pain clinic opened in Scioto County. With them came an underground economy. Residents, many on disability, used their insurance to cover the cost of opioid prescriptions and sold the pills on the street for thousands of dollars.

As the photos flashed across the screen, the sobs behind Geldhof became louder. It was gut-wrenching. Sons and daughters and grandsons and granddaughters in graduation pictures. They were dead before they had a chance to live.

The hardened DEA supervisor thought about his daughter and two sons. He had seen the stats about addiction and drug arrests and seizures. But the young faces on the screen and the weeping in the gym resonated with him in a way that no DEA report or investigation ever could.

Soon, Geldhof was in tears, too. "I'm not sure I'm going to be able to get through this," he said, leaning over to Chaney.

Chaney was crying, too. For her, it was a particularly difficult night. She had joined the DEA because of a deeply personal loss: Her mother became addicted to Percocet after a car crash and died of an accidental overdose.

The faces on the screen were mostly White. Portsmouth was 90 percent White, as were many other epicenters of the epidemic, which in the early to mid-2000s disproportionately affected White communities. Addiction experts theorized that White people, especially those on disability insurance, had more access to doctors who were willing to prescribe opioids. Racial bias appears to have led some doctors not to prescribe painkillers to Black or Latino patients as indiscriminately as they did with Whites. Some doctors with conscious and unconscious bias deemed that minority patients would be more likely to abuse the drugs or sell them. But they didn't have to look far to see that the vast majority of people selling and abusing pain pills were White.

One of the speakers that night was Lisa Roberts, a nurse who had worked for the Portsmouth City Health Department for twenty-two years. She was active in SOLACE—Surviving Our Loss And Continuing Every Day—a support group created a year earlier to raise awareness about how opioids were ravaging the city and to pressure local and state officials to take action. The group, which had helped to create the video, had Scotch-taped many of the same photographs from the town hall in the display window of an abandoned department store on Portsmouth's main thoroughfare.

Roberts, born and raised in Scioto County, understood the torment of the parents around her. Her own teenage daughter had become addicted to pain pills. So had the children of some of her colleagues. Her daughter survived. Many of her friends' children did not.

Geldhof had met Roberts several years earlier while he and his team were investigating Ohio pain clinics run by unscrupulous doctors. One of the most notorious in Portsmouth was Margaret Temponeras, a forty-six-year-old family physician who owned a clinic called Unique Pain Management. A billboard advertising the facility stood at the entrance to the city. "Legitimate Pain Care," it read. Over six years, beginning in 2005, Temponeras ordered 1.6 million pain pills. Eight of her patients died.

Temponeras and her eighty-four-year-old father, who also worked as a doctor at her clinic, saw more than twenty patients a day from Ohio, Kentucky, and West Virginia. They were paid cash for each exam, starting at $200. When pharmacies concerned about Temponeras's practices stopped filling her prescriptions, she opened her own dispensary. She often prescribed a combination of opioids, muscle relaxers, and anti-anxiety drugs, known as "the Holy Trinity" or the

"Scioto County Cocktail." She would later plead guilty to drug conspiracy and be sentenced to seven years in prison.

Vying with Temponeras for most dangerous doctor in Portsmouth was Paul Volkman, who had been investigated by Geldhof's group in Cincinnati for illegally prescribing millions of painkillers. Four of his patients overdosed and died. Volkman operated out of three pain clinics in Portsmouth and one in Chillicothe, Ohio. He, too, asked his patients to pay cash and opened his own dispensaries. The DEA discovered that Volkman purchased more oxycodone than any other doctor in the nation between 2003 and 2005, prescribing millions of pills. He later received four consecutive life sentences.

When the town hall ended, Geldhof and Chaney drove to a nearby diner. They were shaken.

"That was horrible," Chaney said

"Really rough," Geldhof said. "Let's get these sons of bitches."

Chapter 11

"Game, Set, Match"

South Florida, 2011

The bodies were piling up in the Sunshine State. By the summer of 2011, eleven people were dying every day from drug overdoses. Between 2005 and 2010, Florida had recorded a staggering 346 percent increase in fatalities, most of them from pain pills, and the numbers kept climbing.

It was clear from the DEA's pill-tracking ARCOS database that a handful of drug distribution companies based in Jim Geldhof's region were responsible for fueling the Florida death toll.

Geldhof saw that one of the worst offenders was Masters Pharmaceutical, a midsized drug distribution company with outsized ambition based in Forest Park, Ohio, eighteen miles north of Cincinnati. Between 2007 and 2011, the company distributed 86 million tablets of oxycodone 30mg pills to Florida.

Masters was already well known within the DEA. In 2009, the agency had fined the company $500,000 for shipping "extraordinarily large amounts" of hydrocodone to rogue internet pharmacies. Masters signed a settlement agreement with the DEA that year, promising to monitor drug orders and report them to the agency. But it was clear to Geldhof that the company was reneging on its commitments.

Geldhof's go-to investigator in Detroit, James Rafalski, began to dig into Masters. Poring over documents the DEA had collected on the company, Rafalski spotted a common thread that tied Masters to another much larger entity already on his radar: Mallinckrodt. The drug maker was selling massive amounts of its 15mg and 30mg tablets of oxycodone to Masters as well as Harvard Drug, KeySource, and Sunrise Wholesale in Florida. All of them were shipping to clients in South Florida, many of them doctors and pharmacists working for the booming pill-mill indus-try. Rafalski recognized another name in the documents: Victor Borelli. As Mallinckrodt's national sales manager, Borelli was involved in many of the oxycodone sales to the distributors. They were among his most loyal customers and a reason why he continued to receive six-figure bonuses.

In April 2011, Rafalski served a subpoena on Mallinckrodt, demanding corporate emails, sales order forms, and thousands of other internal records relating to the manufacturer's business relationship with Masters. Rafalski knew the subpoena would rattle Mallinck-rodt. He wasn't surprised to hear a month later that the company had reached out to his superiors at DEA headquarters, frantically try-ing to arrange a meeting. Rafalski suspected that Mallinckrodt was attempting to get ahead of the investigation, but he was confident in the strength of his case. He thought he had the company cold.

Rafalski's sleuthing paid off. He discovered that between 2009 and 2010, Mallinckrodt manufactured more than one billion oxy-codone 30mg tablets—the highly sought-after "blues"—and nearly half of them went to pharmacies in Florida. He also examined how many of the pills went directly from distributors to doctors, a warn-ing sign that those doses might end up on the black market. He found that there were 409 physicians in the entire country who ordered Mallinckrodt-made 30mg oxycodone. Ninety-four percent of them—383—were based in Florida. Together, they had received twenty-seven million tablets. Rafalski also determined that many of those doctors worked for the pill mills, like the ones run by the George brothers in Palm Beach and Broward counties. He looked up their DEA registration numbers and traced their pill orders directly back to the distributors and Mallinckrodt.

While the numbers were damning, Rafalski and the DEA had another powerful piece of information: the existence of the sales rebate program at Mallinckrodt. The DEA now knew that the company had the ability to trace the path of every one of its pills to individual pharmacies and doctors' offices through the chargeback rebate program it had set up with its network of drug distributors.

On August 23, 2011, Rafalski and a team of DEA supervisors and investigators met with Mallinckrodt executives at the agency's headquarters in Arlington. They filed into a windowless sixth-floor conference room and took their seats. Patricia Duft, Mallinckrodt's legal counsel, led the presentation on behalf of the company. Accompanied by compliance managers and company investigators, she told the DEA team that Mallinckrodt also was concerned about some of its drug distribution customers. She said the company had set up a system to flag suspicious orders and promised to be more vigilant in the future. Still, she believed Mallinckrodt was not responsible for what happened to its pills once they went to the drug distributors.

Barbara Boockholdt, chief of the DEA's regulatory division, walked the Mallinckrodt executives through their legal responsibilities and what she and Rafalski had seen in the ARCOS database. "Fifty percent of your product is going to Florida," she told them. Mallinckrodt executives said they would cut their production of oxycodone and stop shipping the drug to Masters. Rafalski sat in silence. He knew Mallinckrodt was in serious legal trouble. Regardless of whether they cut production or stopped sending oxycodone to certain distributors, the damage had been done. The DEA was sitting on file folders full of evidence. *They're in for an ass whooping*, he thought to himself.

After the meeting, Rafalski and the other DEA team members rode an elevator up to Boockholdt's tenth-floor office, where they were joined by Leslie Wizner, an assistant U.S. attorney in Detroit assigned to the Mallinckrodt investigation. As they discussed the meeting and plotted their next moves against Mallinckrodt, including hitting the company with another, much more expansive subpoena, the building began to shake and sway.

"Holy cow, did you feel that?" Wizner asked.

It was a rare 5.8-magnitude earthquake in the mid-Atlantic region, the epicenter a hundred miles southwest of Arlington. It cracked the marble and granite blocks of the Washington Monument and broke off three of the four spires that soar above the Washington Cathedral. It was felt as far north as Quebec and as far south as Atlanta. DEA headquarters, like so many buildings in the Washington region, was evacuated. Standing outside, Rafalski tried to lighten the mood. "Maybe it's because we finally made a decision on Mallinckrodt," he said.

Three weeks later, Mallinckrodt notified forty-three of its distributors that they would no longer receive rebates from the company if they continued to supply certain pharmacies whose orders appeared to be suspiciously large. But by then, the DEA and Wizner had decided to intensify their investigation. On November 30, 2011, the DEA served another subpoena on Mallinckrodt, demanding documents relating to sixteen of the largest distributors of the company's oxycodone pills to Florida. The list included Harvard, KeySource, and Masters. It also included the Big Three distributors: McKesson, Cardinal, and AmerisourceBergen.

The subpoena delivered a gold mine of information. Buried in the hundreds of thousands of memos, sales orders, and emails was the "Doritos" exchange between Steve Cochrane at KeySource and Borelli at Mallinckrodt. Rafalski was sickened. He tucked a printout of the email into his jacket. He showed a copy to Wizner and Geldhof.

"No way," Wizner exclaimed.

"This is game, set, match," Geldhof said.

Chapter 12

A Betrayal

DEA Headquarters, 2011

Joe Rannazzisi called her the "Puzzle Master." A diminutive lawyer with a cherubic face and long dark hair, Imelda L. Paredes was a disarming but demanding presence as she walked the halls of the DEA. "Mimi," as everyone called her, was one of Joe's secret weapons in his battle to bring the nation's largest drug companies to account for the opioid epidemic.

At her desk inside DEA headquarters, Paredes pored over spreadsheets of pill numbers and internal drug company documents, finding patterns as she built cases and crafted the legal arguments for Joe's biggest investigations. Over time, she would become one of Joe's closest legal advisers—his warrior, he called her—as he went after the rogue internet pharmacies, doctors, pill mills, and drug distributors. Paredes was calm. She was analytical. But she could be brutally honest about what was needed to make a case, snuffing out any investigative shortcuts. She was never wrong, Joe realized. Not once.

Paredes's route to the DEA had been a circuitous one. She grew up in Virginia Beach, next to the largest U.S. naval base in the world, where her parents settled after immigrating from the Philippines. Her father was a Navy mess chef for the sailors living aboard aircraft carriers. In 1981, Paredes, as a sixth-grade student, was inspired to become a lawyer after watching Sandra Day O'Connor ascend as the first woman on the U.S. Supreme Court.

In high school, she and her close friend, a handsome star athlete named Alton Grizzard, worked hard and dreamed big. She went west to the University of California at Berkeley, while he entered the U.S. Naval Academy in Annapolis. He became captain of the Navy's football team and one of the best quarterbacks in the Academy's history. They remained close.

In 1993, three years after he graduated, Grizzard was shot to death in a murder-suicide at the Naval Amphibious Base in Coronado, California, where he was a Navy SEAL, a member of the Navy's elite commando team. He was at the apartment of a friend from the Academy when her twenty-four-year-old estranged fiancé, a Navy officer distraught about their recent breakup, burst into her room and shot both of them before turning the gun on himself. Paredes was devastated when her father called her with the news.

After graduating from George Washington University Law School, Paredes joined the Navy as a lawyer, known as a judge advocate general. As a member of the JAG Corps, she asked to be assigned to San Diego. She found it comforting to be on the base on Coronado near the SEALs. Paredes served as a military lawyer and legal counsel to the commander of the Navy SEAL training center, which included BUD/S, the Basic Underwater Demolition/SEAL school. She advised the commander on courts-martial, and she also taught ethics, rules of engagement, and law-of-war classes to staffers and students.

Eventually, she was ready to move on. After several years in San Diego and a stint at the Navy Yard in Washington, D.C., she started looking for a new challenge. A professor from law school connected her with a DEA lawyer and she joined the agency in 2002.

Paredes was impressed with the close-knit group of attorneys at DEA headquarters. The esprit de corps reminded her of the camaraderie she had found in the Navy. She felt part of a team dedicated to protecting the public. One colleague stood out—a tall, lean graduate of Notre Dame Law School. With his shaved head and broad smile, he reminded her of the actor Woody Harrelson. His name was D. Linden Barber. Everyone called him Linden.

Barber was cool and outgoing in a way she had never been. He had married his childhood sweetheart, a girl he met in the fourth grade. Both had become creatures of Washington; his wife was the deputy assistant secretary of defense for communications at the Pentagon. Barber, casually stylish and oozing self-confidence, cut a striking figure at DEA headquarters.

Like Paredes, Barber had served as a JAG lawyer. He was an officer in the Army and deployed to Iraq, where he was awarded the Bronze Star and Combat Action Badge in 2004. As serious as he could be in the office, Barber had a playful side. He acted and sang in skits at agency parties. He was a fun-loving fan of Frank Sinatra. In 2006, he was promoted to associate chief counsel of the DEA and for the next four years headed the agency's diversion litigation division, providing Joe and his team with legal advice. Paredes was assigned to work for him. She saw herself and Barber as the white hats dedicated to the DEA's mission: the smart, tough, former military JAGs who were going to hold drug companies accountable. They frequently talked of the horror of the opioid epidemic, but they also argued over legal theory. Barber at times seemed uncomfortable with the aggressive tactics of Joe's team.

Still, it stunned Paredes and her colleagues when Barber announced in October 2011 that he was leaving the DEA. He joined a law firm, Quarles & Brady, in Indianapolis and carved out a "DEA litigation and compliance" practice. He would defend the companies he once pursued with Joe and Paredes.

In a video for his new law practice, Barber promoted himself as someone who could help companies in trouble with the DEA. "If you have a DEA compliance issue or you're facing a government investigation or you're having administrative or civil litigation involving the Controlled Substances Act, I'd be happy to hear from you," he said.

Paredes felt betrayed. But Barber's path to the other side was well-worn. Dozens of top officials from the DEA and the Justice Department—which oversaw the DEA—left for high-paying posts at the drug companies or the law firms that protected them. It was the way of Washington, even at the DEA, where there was a constant revolving door between the agency and the companies it regulated.

The pattern was a win-win for the government employees and the drug companies. The employees could triple or quadruple their salaries by going to Fortune 500 companies like McKesson or the law firms that represented them. And the companies were hiring high-ranking DEA and Justice officials who had intimate knowledge of how the agency and the department operated, and how they could be short-circuited. The public was the only one sold short.

Joe understood that these former civil servants wanted to make a better living, but he saw the passage of people like Barber to the drug industry as a con on the American people. It was all about money and power, not public service, and it was at the core of everything that he saw as wrong with Washington. He and his staffers at the DEA didn't have the same influence as those with deep pockets and close connections to Capitol Hill and the Justice Department. He saw too many officials at Justice and the DEA who hungered for the same paychecks, the same perks as their former colleagues who were making high six-figure salaries working for the drug industry. He wondered whether some government employees were pulling punches, not being as aggressive as they could be, because they didn't want to upset a future employer like McKesson or Cardinal, or a high-powered law firm on K Street. It was a carousel of greed, he thought, one that was oblivious to the country's full-blown public health crisis and rising death toll.

Joe knew that with a law degree, a pharmacy degree, and all his years with the DEA, he could cash out. But he had joined the agency to be an agent, not a lobbyist or a corporate executive. When he saw people like Barber standing on the other side of his cases, defending what he saw as the indefensible, he wondered how they had lost their way.

Chapter 13

Cardinal Knowledge

Sanford, Florida, 2011

The phone calls haunted Joe Rannazzisi. Mothers and fathers sobbing, barely able to breathe as they told him that they had just lost a son or daughter to an opioid overdose. They pleaded with Joe to make sense of it all. What was the DEA doing? How could so many lives be destroyed so easily? Who's to blame? Sometimes Joe cried, too. As a parent, he understood. But he still had his two daughters at home and three grown sons; the grieving parents on the other end of the line no longer did.

Over the years, Joe had met hundreds of parents at meetings the DEA had set up in communities torn apart by opioids. He always handed out his business card at the end of each gathering, dozens at a time. Still, he dreaded the days when his office phone would ring with an unrecognizable out-of-state number. "Hi," they told him, "I met you at a town hall," and then the story of another death would unfold, the body found on the street, or in a stairwell. And the parents invariably blamed themselves. Joe felt like a priest hearing confession, but without the gift of absolution.

Despite all the warnings to the drug companies—the briefings, the PowerPoint presentations, the phone calls, the civil cases, and the fines—he could not stop the carnage. As soon as he shut down the internet pharmacies, the pill mills sprouted up, seemingly overnight.

Rapacious doctors kept writing prescriptions. Unprincipled pharmacists kept filling them. The drug companies kept supplying them.

It was so bad, the Florida surgeon general declared a public health emergency on July 1, 2011. Dr. Frank Farmer reported that ninety-eight of the top hundred physicians writing prescriptions for oxycodone in the nation were based in his state. In 2010, 100 pharmacies in the state filled prescriptions for 126 million pills. "More oxycodone is dispensed in the state of Florida than in the remaining states combined," Farmer said as he announced the emergency.

Joe dispatched one of his best investigators to Florida, Ruth Carter, a twenty-three-year veteran of the DEA with shoulder-length blonde hair and hazel eyes who spoke with a soft Texas twang. Joe admired her tenacity and ability to close cases. He could give her an assignment and know that she would find something—or nothing—and not waste anyone's time. If the case wasn't there, Carter would tell Joe, and they would move on. If he didn't hear back, he knew she was making progress and soon would be asking for permission to secure a search warrant and start taking witness statements.

Joe had one drug company fixed firmly in his sights: Cardinal Health. The numbers kept by his data team enumerated how Cardinal had saturated Florida with narcotics, and which pharmacies had purchased them from the distributor and doled them out by the tens of millions. The numbers revealed that Cardinal's warehouse in Lakeland, Florida, by the Malfunction Junction near Tampa, was distributing 22 percent of all oxycodone in Florida—132 million doses in 2010 alone. It was the same warehouse the DEA had shuttered three years earlier for supplying the internet pharmacies. But it was now shipping monstrous amounts of opioids to brick-and-mortar pharmacies.

Joe had had it with Cardinal and its executives. "They either don't want to understand, or they just don't give a shit," he told Carter. "We're just going to have to hit them harder."

Cardinal had a banner year in 2011. The company posted revenues of \$102.6 billion, up 4 percent. The company paid its chairman and chief executive, George S. Barrett, \$10.2 million, which included a \$2 million bonus.

The numbers in the DEA's ARCOS database led Carter to Sanford, Florida, a historic town about twenty miles north of Orlando on the banks of Lake Monroe. The town served as a U.S. Army outpost during the Seminole Wars of the 1830s before becoming the gateway between South Florida and the rest of the booming state. By the time Carter arrived in Sanford, the town had become a conduit for something else: the Blue Highway. After obtaining prescriptions from the pill mills, drug users and dealers stopped at pharmacies in Sanford to fill them on their way home. The pharmacies were perfectly situated, just off Interstate 4, with easy access to Orlando International Airport and Interstates 75 and 95. They were also at the start of Amtrak's auto train to points north.

Two CVS pharmacies in Sanford, along with two independent pharmacies on the west coast of Florida, stood out for the eye-popping amounts of oxycodone they were dispensing. Carter swung by the CVS stores. *How could pharmacies in one of America's biggest chains be running up street gang numbers?* What she saw stunned the seasoned investigator. Parking lots filled with cars and trucks bearing out-of-state license plates. Long lines of customers spilled out the door. Many customers paid cash for their pills. Queues at the drive-through windows curled around the stores. Most prescriptions were written for 30mg oxycodone tablets, the "blues" manufactured by Mallinckrodt.

Carter studied the distribution numbers and discovered that Cardinal sent 3.1 million tablets of oxycodone to six of the sixteen pharmacies within the Sanford city limits in 2011. That was enough to supply every man, woman, and child in the city, population 53,570, with 58 doses of the drug.

"I knew it was bad," Carter told Joe. "But it's a lot worse than I thought."

On October 18, 2011, she executed search warrants on the two CVS stores and the two independent pharmacies. Eight days later, on October 26, Carter served the Cardinal warehouse in Lakeland with a similar warrant. Squads of agents and investigators, clad in windbreakers with "DEA" in yellow emblazoned on their backs, swarmed the warehouse and the stores. CVS store no. 219 in Sanford, Carter discovered, was Cardinal's biggest customer in Florida. Between 2008 and 2011, the company sold more than 5 million pills to that one CVS. The store, in turn, accepted cash payments for 42 percent of the oxycodone pills it sold, a tell that the pills were destined for the black market.

Material turned up in the search showed how Cardinal kept raising the ceiling on how many oxycodone pills its customers could purchase—without ever asking for an explanation as to why sales were skyrocketing. Between 2009 and 2010, Cardinal increased its monthly oxycodone distribution to the top-selling CVS by 63 percent—from 1.2 million to 2 million pills. Carter noted that the average yearly sales of oxycodone for pharmacies in Florida was 112,000 tablets.

Ten days after serving the warrants on the CVS pharmacies, Carter interviewed the pharmacist-in-charge of CVS store no. 219, Paras Priyadarshi. He acknowledged that most of his customers were requesting "blues" or "M's" when they were filling their prescriptions. He also knew that his store was filling more prescriptions for oxycodone than any other store in the region. But he said "no one from CVS corporate had said anything to him about the high volume," Carter later noted in a DEA document, and he didn't find the conduct of his customers suspicious. He told Carter, "If a customer asked for a particular brand name, he would fill the prescription with that brand name if the pharmacy had that brand in stock."

Carter then traveled to Cardinal's second-biggest customer, CVS store no. 5195, also in Sanford. Cardinal had sold that store 2.2 million oxycodone tablets between 2008 and 2011. Carter discovered that 58 percent of the pills were purchased by cash-carrying customers between 2010 and 2011. The DEA database revealed that Cardinal had increased its monthly oxycodone sales to that store by 748 percent between 2009 and 2010.

Carter interviewed the pharmacist-in-charge, Jessica Merrill. She was surprisingly candid. Merrill was so forthcoming that Carter called one of her supervisors over. She wanted a witness because she thought no one would believe what Merrill was telling her.

Merrill said she could fill oxycodone prescriptions "all day long," but she decided to set a limit. Once that limit was reached, customers were told the store was out of stock. Glassy-eyed customers would begin staggering to the pharmacy the next morning to stand in line for their doses of oxycodone.

Merrill told Carter she was "between a rock and a hard place" because she believed she had to fill prescriptions written by doctors— even though pharmacists are required to turn away customers if they suspect laws are being broken. "It's very time consuming," she told Carter, "to call the doctors' offices and verify each prescription."

Merrill then said something Carter would always remember: Once the pharmacy reached its self-imposed limit of oxycodone sales, Merrill disclosed that she always kept a reserve supply on hand.

Why? Carter asked.

For my "real pain patients," Merrill told her.

When Joe read Carter's report, he was livid. He directed his team to prepare Immediate Suspension Orders against the Cardinal warehouse, the CVS stores, and the two independent pharmacies.

Time to shut these motherfuckers down, Joe said to himself.

Chapter 14

"Because I'm the Deputy Attorney General"

Department of Justice, Washington, D.C., 2011

On November 22, 2011, two days before Thanksgiving, Joe Ranazzisi was racing to leave work when his office line lit up. It was late, the end of another long day. His daughter had just called, asking him to hurry home. Joe's father had fallen ill and might not be able to make the trip down from Long Island for the holiday. With so much going on, Joe almost passed on picking up the call, but he glanced at the incoming number. It was from Main Justice, as insiders call the department's headquarters in D.C.

"Hi, Joe. It's Jim Dinan."

Joe sensed trouble. James H. Dinan headed the Organized Crime Drug Enforcement Task Force program at the Justice Department. More important, he served as a top aide to the second-ranking law enforcement officer in the country, Deputy Attorney General James M. Cole, known at the department as the "DAG."

"Joe, what are your guys doing in Florida?" Dinan asked.

"What do you mean?"

"Are you executing warrants in Florida?"

"We did already," Joe said.

When the call came in from Dinan, the DEA was preparing

orders to immediately suspend the ability of the Cardinal warehouse, the two CVS stores, and the two independent pharmacies to sell narcotics. The agency determined that their conduct was so egregious, they posed an "imminent danger" to the public's health and safety.

Dinan cautioned Joe. "Former Justice Department people are calling the DAG's office," he said.

"So?" Joe said.

"So, the DAG told me to tell you, 'Don't do anything that can't be undone,'" Dinan said.

"Well, Jim, we're in the process of gathering evidence. What do you expect me to do?" Joe asked.

"What are your plans?"

"My plans are, we're investigating crimes. We're investigating drug crimes here."

"Don't do anything," Dinan ordered. "The DAG wants to be briefed."

The call angered Joe. It was highly unusual. He had never been called over to Main Justice to brief top department officials about an ongoing investigation. He knew the industry was ranging its forces against him. Clearly, powerful people were putting pressure on the Justice Department to slow him down. He already knew that a high-powered Cardinal executive, Craig S. Morford, who served as the deputy attorney general during the George W. Bush administration, had sent a three-page memo three weeks earlier to Joe's boss, DEA administrator Michele Leonhart. After leaving government, Morford had taken a senior position at Cardinal as its chief of legal affairs. In the memo, he told Leonhart that his company wanted to cooperate with the DEA and had stopped shipping pills to dozens of disreputable pharmacies. He copied Joe and attached a handwritten note to Leonhart that began with first-name-basis familiarity: "Michele: We are committed to working with DEA to address the challenging problem of diversion and welcome the opportunity to meet with you and your team to address these issues in a non-adversarial way. Craig."

The implication was clear: Joe was not working this out as old pals and lawyers should.

Joe called Leonhart. How should we handle this? he asked her.

"Figure out how to deal with it," she replied. Leonhart trusted Joe and said she would back him up. "Just be careful."

Joe was at heart a cop. Why should he talk to the lawyer representing the target of his investigation? If he was investigating a drug operation in Detroit or D.C., would the DEA or the Justice Department give them the same consideration?

"Michele, I don't think we deal with it at all," Joe told her. "We have an ongoing case on this company and we just issued warrants. So, we're in the throes of our investigation at this point in time and anything you say to him will be problematic because you can't confirm or deny the existence of an investigation."

Leonhart seemed to agree. Joe thought he had managed the Morford problem. But he wondered what else was headed his way. He had handled hundreds of these enforcement cases and never received a call like this. What else was going on?

Several hours earlier, Jamie Gorelick, one of the most influential attorneys in Washington, had privately reached out to Cole. It was reminiscent of how former U.S. attorney Mary Jo White and Rudy Giuliani had intervened at the Justice Department on behalf of Purdue in 2007. Gorelick was one of the city's star lawyers for the rich and powerful. During the Clinton administration, she had held the same job at the Justice Department as Cole and Morford. Now she was a partner at WilmerHale, a powerhouse firm located two blocks from the White House, with a thousand lawyers in cities around the globe. It represented Cardinal, and Gorelick was able to get a memo outlining her client's concerns into the hands of the deputy attorney general.

Gorelick told Cole she had received a tip that the DEA was about to prevent Cardinal's Lakeland warehouse from distributing narcotics. She denied that the company's behavior constituted an "imminent danger" to the public. Instead, she insisted that any DEA action against Cardinal would "cause significant harm to the public health and to our client." Cardinal had already halted the shipment of pills to certain pharmacies, she wrote, and it pledged to stop filling dubious orders. The company was adhering to the 2008 agreement it had signed with the DEA to settle allegations that it was fueling the black market in opioids, she argued. "Immediate suspension is a drastic and punitive enforcement tool that is not appropriate for these circumstances," Gorelick wrote to Cole. "We would appreciate the opportunity to discuss this urgent matter with you prior to the initiation of any action by DEA."

Apart from that first phone call from Dinan, Main Justice was silent. Thanksgiving and Christmas passed without further comment from Cole. Joe thought the outside pressure might have ended with Morford's memo. But he didn't know about Gorelick's letter.

Joe's team had sifted through the evidence it obtained from the warrants and was preparing to move against Cardinal when he received another call from Dinan on February 1, 2012, but he didn't answer it. Early the next morning, at 1:36 a.m., Dinan sent Joe an email: "Please call me in the morning," he wrote. "I want to make double sure nothing happens that can't be reversed before the DAG is briefed as we talked about at Thanksgiving."

Dinan said that Cole wanted a briefing on the Cardinal case and told Joe to be at the deputy attorney general's office that afternoon.

Joe was being sandbagged. The previous night, Gorelick had privately reached out to Cole's chief of staff, Stuart M. Goldberg, to discuss the issue and let him know that Randolph D. Moss, a lead WilmerHale lawyer for Cardinal, also was available to discuss the issue with Cole's staff.

Like Gorelick, Moss had served at the Justice Department during the Clinton administration, holding a series of senior posts in the Office of Legal Counsel, which acts as the legal adviser to the president and the executive branch.

Moss sent an email to Dinan the following afternoon, about an hour before Joe's arrival at Main Justice. He too struck the tone of old colleagues who could get things resolved. "Following up on Jamie's call with Stu last night," Moss wrote. "I just wanted to let you know that I'm back in DC and available to talk whenever you are."

Moss gave Dinan his direct dial at WilmerHale. "Many thanks," Moss signed off.

Shortly before 2 p.m., Joe arrived at the Robert F. Kennedy Department of Justice Building, an imposing seven-story art deco structure with Greek columns that takes up an entire city block along Pennsylvania and Constitution avenues in downtown Washington. Hundreds of lawyers and staffers occupy its nearly one million square feet of office space. Joe rode the elevator up to Cole's fourth-floor office and stepped into his personal conference room, a formal space framed by large windows, the walls lined with portraits of former Justice Department officials, a fireplace at one end of the room.

Joe took a seat at the long conference table. Cole sat at the head and Dinan and Goldberg and several other Justice Department and DEA officials seated themselves around the table.

Joe enjoyed giving presentations about his investigations. He had briefed several attorneys general and their deputies, and he felt particularly confident about the case against Cardinal. He had just begun describing Cardinal's past conduct, the problem of the pill mills and the scale of overdoses nationally, when he was interrupted.

"What is your endgame?" the chief of staff, Goldberg, asked.

The question rankled Joe. "Before I answer that, I've got to ask you: I've done hundreds of these cases, and I've never been called over to the Justice Department to explain myself. I'm just curious why this case is so important," he said.

Cole jumped in. "Because I'm the deputy attorney general of the United States, and I want to know about it," he said.

"Well, that doesn't really answer the question," Rannazzisi said.

"Joe, we're just trying to help you with your case," Goldberg said.

Joe glared at him. He considering saying, "Dude, I'm the Babe Ruth of these cases. I never lose." But he caught himself.

"I think we're doing pretty well," he said.

The room went quiet.

Joe continued his presentation in the awkward silence. As he showed his charts and graphs documenting pill distribution numbers and overdose deaths, he thought to himself, *I know I'm going to get disciplined for this.*

When he wrapped up his presentation, Joe asked if anyone had questions. No one did. Cole rose from his seat and walked out without saying a word.

On his drive back to DEA headquarters on the other side of the Potomac River, Joe called Mimi Paredes. "Someone has gotten to DOJ and Cole," he said.

"Come on, Joe," Paredes said. "That's not happening."

"No one has ever been interested in what we do in this division. Why are they so interested now?"

"I don't know, Joe. You sound like a conspiracy theorist."

The companies were going over his head; they were trying to go through the Justice Department to shut him down. He was convinced of that, regardless of what Paredes said. But he wasn't going to figure out how to deal. He wouldn't stop until the companies stopped.

Joe summoned his staff to his office and shut the door. "Now this is war," he told them. "We're going after these people, and we're not going to stop. And I don't really give a damn what the department wants."

Chapter 15

Imminent Danger

E. Barrett Prettyman U.S. Courthouse, Washington, D.C., 2012

Joe Rannazzisi kept his word. The day after his meeting with Deputy Attorney General James Cole at the Justice Department, the DEA launched its most powerful weapon against Cardinal Health: an Immediate Suspension Order, halting all shipments of pain pills from the company's warehouse in Lakeland. The DEA executed the same order against the two CVS stores in Sanford, along with the two independent pharmacies, barring them all from dispensing any more narcotics.

Just before Joe struck, Jamie Gorelick learned that an enforcement action was imminent, and she was livid. She sent a scathing email to Stuart Goldberg at the Justice Department on February 2, 2012, at 7:01 p.m., copying James Dinan, the other top aide to Cole. "Stu: I am stunned by the events of the past couple of days as we have tried to interact with the DEA to no avail," Gorelick wrote after Joe's meeting with Cole. "I don't think I have ever seen anything like this."

She gave Goldberg some advice if the DEA intended to shutter Cardinal's warehouse. "I would ask that the Deputy's Office assure itself that the [DEA's] Chief Counsel has found a legal and factual basis for that drastic action," Gorelick wrote.

The veiled warning changed nothing. The DEA was determined

to move against Cardinal. Michele Leonhart, the agency's administrator, had already signed off on a raid. On February 3, at 7:30 a.m., DEA agents and investigators descended on Cardinal's warehouse in Lakeland. Wearing their DEA windbreakers, members of the team fanned out inside the warehouse, sealing up huge cages and vaults filled with bottles of pain pills with red-and-white adhesive tape emblazoned with the agency logo. Stunned employees, some of them driving forklifts or standing at their stations next to long conveyor belts that stretched to the truck bays, watched in silence as the DEA team locked up Cardinal's inventory of opioids.

That afternoon, nine hundred miles to the north, Randolph Moss, the Justice Department official now representing Cardinal, rushed to the E. Barrett Prettyman U.S. Courthouse in Washington, D.C., for an emergency hearing before U.S. district judge Reggie B. Walton. Moss told the judge he tried to contact lawyers for the DEA but he had no luck. He argued that Cardinal's conduct was not causing an "imminent danger" to the public, the legal standard the DEA needed to show before shutting down a distribution center. The DEA was the one causing the imminent danger. Hospitals, nursing homes, and thousands of patients in Florida served by Cardinal would soon be forced to go without "critically important" drugs if the order remained in place.

Moss said Cardinal had already stopped doing business with the two independent drugstores and suspended all shipments of oxycodone to the two CVS pharmacies in Sanford. How could there still be an "imminent danger" to the public if the pharmacies no longer had access to oxycodone? Moss asked Walton to issue a temporary restraining order, known as a TRO, to lift the DEA suspension until a full-blown court hearing could be held.

Walton, a former public defender, prosecutor, and D.C. judge before his appointment to the federal bench by George W. Bush, was skeptical. "These are extremely dangerous drugs," the judge said.

"And if they are not being appropriately disseminated and they go out into the public without the appropriate authorizations by medical personnel, obviously that can cause severe harm."

"We agree entirely with that," Moss replied. "This is a company that is extremely committed to doing what it can to avoid diversion of controlled substances."

"Have there been any other allegations of inappropriate distribution by the plaintiff [Cardinal]?" Walton asked.

"There have never been any allegations today or previously of improper diversion by this company itself," Moss said.

That was not accurate. The DEA had accused Cardinal of the same conduct in 2007 and the company paid a $34 million fine the following year to settle the case. As part of the settlement, Cardinal promised to prevent pain pills from reaching the black market by installing systems to red-flag dubious drug orders at its warehouses, including the one in Lakeland.

Without hearing from the DEA, Walton issued the TRO and scheduled another hearing.

After the ruling, Gorelick sent Goldberg a told-you-so email. "Stu—To keep you apprised re the Cardinal Health matter we discussed, here is the TRO issued by Judge Walton," she wrote.

"Thanks Jamie for the information," Goldberg replied.

That afternoon, the DEA agents and investigators were ordered back to the Lakeland warehouse to remove the tape from Cardinal's drug vaults and cages. The company was free to ship pain pills from the warehouse for twenty-six days, until February 29, when lawyers from Cardinal, the DEA, and the Justice Department appeared in Walton's courtroom.

The judge used the intervening period to read the DEA records detailing the amounts of pills Cardinal had sent to the four pharmacies. He also read the 2007 case the agency had filed against the company for sending similarly vast quantities of pills to the online pharmacies and the 2008 agreement it had signed to settle that case.

Walton began the hearing in the case—*Cardinal Health, Inc. v. Eric H. Holder Jr.*—by addressing Moss. Moss was accompanied by three other attorneys for Cardinal, including Craig Morford, the former deputy attorney general who had reached out to Leonhart the previous fall.

"Their position is that, well, there's been a history of problems with your client in reference to diversion, or not having in place appropriate controls to make sure diversion isn't taking place," the judge told Moss. "Now, we've got a significant distribution of a large amount of this substance compared to what is being distributed by other companies.

"And we've got this major problem in this part of the world where this distribution is taking place," the judge concluded, noting that the opioid black market was centered in Florida.

The order signed by Leonhart said Cardinal was in violation of that 2008 agreement, Walton noted, and that's why the DEA was going after the company a second time. "She's saying, I guess, that 'We've got this history. We've got the current situation and therefore, under those circumstances, we believe immediate action has to be taken. Otherwise you're going to have a significant problem as far as loss of life and significant addiction problems that we need to address immediately,'" Walton said.

This time around, Moss acknowledged that Cardinal had been in trouble with the DEA before. But he brushed it off. The past was the past. That case had nothing to do with this one. "The events from that period of time cannot possibly support today an imminent danger to the public," Moss argued. "But indeed, back then when that occurred, that dealt with a circumstance in which the company stood up to it, recognized it had to do something about it and made very substantial changes."

Walton pushed back. "If you had a distributor of pharmaceuticals and it was the only distributor in this particular area and you had a high death rate from that substance and a high addiction rate from that substance, I think those factors, coupled with volume, would be sufficient to show that there's an imminent danger," he said.

"Well, Your Honor, it would depend, I think, on what type of patients were in the area," Moss offered. "Is there a hospital there? Is it, as is the case with respect to one of the examples there, is it something that is adjacent to a large medical complex with many, many, many doctors? Is it a circumstance where you're near a large oncology center? Is it near a nursing home?"

The lawyer representing the government picked apart Moss's arguments. Clifford Lee Reeves II, a career Justice Department attorney, was flanked by two other lawyers from the department, along with two attorneys from the DEA, including Larry P. Cote, who had taken over Linden Barber's job when he left the agency to represent the drug industry.

Reeves told the judge that the DEA had already given Cardinal a chance to change its conduct. Instead, the company just kept shipping more pills. Cardinal, he said, rarely saw an order that was suspicious enough to stop. Most orders sailed through the Lakeland warehouse, saturating Florida with massive amounts of oxycodone. Cardinal's own employees were sounding alarms, but those warnings were disregarded.

"In September 2010, Cardinal's corporate offices expressed concern about Lakeland's oxycodone shipment to the Sanford CVS stores," Reeves told the judge. "So, Lakeland asked CVS 219 for data about its oxycodone sales, and according to Cardinal's own internal emails, their own documents, CVS adamantly refused. It's not in my words. Those are Cardinal's words that appear in its own documents. Does Lakeland do the reasonable thing? Do they do the rational thing? Do they say, 'You provide us this data or we're cutting you off?' No, they do not, Your Honor. They just keep shipping."

"You're saying the pharmacy refused to provide information to Cardinal?" the judge asked.

"Yes, furthermore, according to Cardinal documents, Cardinal contacted CVS chief pharmacist, Paras Priyadarshi, in January 2010 to find out why the oxycodone sales are so large at CVS 219. Mr. Priyadarshi says, quote, 'They are the only pharmacy in the area,' end quote, to carry oxycodone," Reeves said. "It's patently unbelievable that a pharmacist would say that we're the only pharmacy to carry oxycodone. It's like a pharmacist saying: 'We're the only pharmacy in the area to carry penicillin or Band-Aids.' It's just not believable. But setting the credibility aside, Cardinal knows this is false. Why? Because they supply other pharmacies in the area with oxycodone. Yet, faced with this obvious falsehood, they still keep shipping."

Reeves also noted that Cardinal didn't cut off the two independent pharmacies until the DEA executed search warrants the previous October. And Cardinal didn't suspend the CVS stores until the DEA served them with the Immediate Suspension Orders earlier that month, on February 3.

Walton had heard enough. He rejected every one of Moss's arguments: that the DEA action threatened to cripple its business; that its reputation would be badly tarnished; and that patients would be "irreparably harmed." Moss didn't "come close" to documenting significant financial harm to the company, the judge said, noting that Cardinal had posted $102 billion in revenue the previous year. He said the company failed to prove its reputation had suffered after the DEA shut its operations down in 2007, and it would likely not suffer this time around either. He called Cardinal's arguments "exaggerated and uncorroborated." He also ruled that the shutdown would not impact any patients because the pharmacies and hospitals in Florida could be supplied by one of Cardinal's other warehouses in the region.

Noting that Cardinal continued to ship unchecked quantities of pills, he ruled that the company's conduct did constitute an "imminent danger" to the health and safety of the public.

"If Cardinal had been engaging in the level of proactivity to make sure that diversion doesn't occur, then they would have or at least should have become aware of the fact that there was a problem in reference to these particular pharmacies," Walton said. "With that knowledge, [Cardinal] should have taken some steps, considering the volume that was being provided to those pharmacies. It should have taken some action, before it did, in making sure that diversion by these pharmacies was not, in fact, occurring."

It was a stinging defeat, not only for Cardinal, but for the entire opioid drug industry. Cardinal quickly appealed Walton's ruling. The Alliance, on behalf of its thirty-four members, including Cardinal, McKesson, and AmerisourceBergen, drafted a friend-of-the-court brief that argued the DEA had set an impossibly high bar for the industry to meet and failed to give the companies guidance on how to avoid the agency's wrath.

But less than three months after Walton's ruling, on May 15, Cardinal suddenly settled the case with the DEA, saying it wanted "to avoid the uncertainty and expense of litigation." The company grudgingly admitted that its "due diligence efforts for some pharmacy customers," along with its compliance with the 2008 settlement, "in certain respects, were inadequate." Cardinal agreed to suspend shipments of narcotics from its Lakeland warehouse. It again promised to do a better job of flagging and stopping shipments of staggering amounts of pain pills and would ultimately pay a $44 million fine. CVS, headquartered in Woonsocket, Rhode Island, had also filed a legal challenge against the DEA. With seventy-four hundred pharmacies and $123 billion in revenues, CVS was the nation's largest chain drugstore. Larry J. Merlo, its president and chief executive, made $20 million in 2012. The company eventually settled the case by paying slightly more than the equivalent of Merlo's annual salary—$22 million.

"A pittance," Joe said.

Cardinal and the drug industry couldn't win by arguing the law. So at a meeting of drug industry reps at The Alliance's headquarters, they decided to change it.

Chapter 16

"At the Corner of Happy & Healthy"

Oviedo, Florida, 2012

On March 15, 2011, Jeffrey Chudnow, the police chief in Oviedo, Florida, a small city just northeast of Orlando, had written to the top executives at Walgreens, Chairman Alan G. McNally and President and Chief Executive Officer Gregory D. Wasson.

Oviedo, population 33,000, had two Walgreens stores, and Chudnow told the executives he had "seen the parking lots of your stores become a bastion of illegal drug sales and drug use." Once oxycodone prescriptions were filled inside, the chief wrote, "the drugs are sold, distributed as payment, crushed and snorted, liquified and injected, or multiple pills swallowed while in the parking lot of your pharmacies."

Chudnow asked the executives to stop Walgreens pharmacists from accepting orders when customers had more than one prescription for pain pills to fill. "These types of prescriptions overtly denote misuse and possible street sales of these drugs," he told them.

Chudnow got no response.

Instead, over the next four months, the nation's second-largest pharmacy chain shipped another 496,100 pills to one of its drugstores in Oviedo, a quantity far greater than demand in an average pharmacy.

The letter was the culmination of months of frustration with the pharmacies. Chudnow first directed his officers to surveil the Walgreens stores in 2010 after a chorus of complaints from the community. The parking lots appeared to have become open-air drug bazaars. After his officers responded to more than a hundred calls for help and made many arrests in and around the parking lots, Chudnow summoned managers from the two stores to police headquarters. He was concerned not only about the illegal oxycodone sales, but that people were popping pain pills and then getting behind the wheel.

"You can help stop this," he told them.

Nothing changed.

Chudnow also wrote formal letters to the drugstore managers, listing the names of the people his officers had arrested, the drugs they seized, and the doctors who were writing the bogus prescriptions. He again asked the pharmacies for help in "dealing with the prescription medication epidemic." He noted that under the law, if pharmacists suspected that a prescription was fraudulent or being misused, they weren't supposed to fill it.

But the stores kept filling the prescriptions—even for those Chudnow had flagged as chronic offenders. The managers had the audacity to summon the police when the crowds in the parking lot became unruly. But they continued to do nothing to confront the underlying cause and stop filling the prescriptions.

Seriously? Chudnow thought to himself. *You're causing this problem. We've talked to you about the problem. And now you're calling us to help you?*

The chief turned to the DEA. He had a good relationship with the agency's field office in Florida, and one of his officers worked with the DEA on a federal task force.

Joe Rannazzisi and his team opened another front: an investigation into Walgreens and its massive distribution center in Jupiter, Florida, which was selling pain pills to the Oviedo pharmacies and many others in the state.

The Oviedo pharmacies were among the nearly eight thousand drugstores owned by Walgreens Company, founded in Chicago in 1901 by Charles Walgreen Sr. In 2012, the company introduced a new slogan: "Walgreens: At the Corner of Happy & Healthy."

The stores, in fact, were at the corner of addiction and misery.

Between 2006 and 2012, Walgreens sat atop the nation's retail opioid market, selling about thirteen billion pills—three billion more than CVS, its closest competitor. Most chain and independent pharmacies relied on drug distributors like McKesson, AmerisourceBergen, and Cardinal to supply their prescription opioids. Walgreens, however, obtained 97 percent of its pain pills directly from drug manufacturers. In effect, Walgreens, with its twelve warehouses around the United States, was acting as both drug distributor and pharmacy chain. By cutting out the middleman, the company could make more money and had more control over how many pills it sent to its stores. But by acting as its own distributor, Walgreens also had the responsibility to alert the DEA to enormous orders by its own pharmacies and make sure the drugs weren't being diverted to the streets.

On April 4, 2012, the DEA launched its investigation, executing search warrants at six Florida Walgreens pharmacies—in Oviedo, Hudson, Fort Myers, Port Richey, and Fort Pierce. Using the ARCOS database and the records they had seized, DEA investigators discovered that Walgreens's Jupiter warehouse had been the single largest distributor of oxycodone in Florida. Between April 2010 and February 2012, the facility sent 13.7 million oxycodone doses to those six Walgreens stores. While the average pharmacy in the United States ordered about 70,000 oxycodone pills in 2011, the six Walgreens pharmacies in Florida ordered more than a million pills apiece that year. The dispensing of oxycodone at the stores increased by more than 600 percent between 2009 and 2011.

Not everyone at Walgreens was blind to the obvious. On January 10, 2011, Kristine Atwell, who managed distribution of controlled substances at the Jupiter warehouse, wrote an email to Walgreens corporate headquarters with the subject line "High Quantity Stores." She singled out a Walgreens pharmacy in Port Richey, near Tampa.

"I ran a query to see how many bottles we have sent to store #3836 and we have shipped them 3,271 bottles between 12/1/10 and 1/10/11," Atwell wrote. "I don't know how they can even house this many bottle[s] to be honest. How do we go about checking the validity of these orders?"

The month after Atwell raised her alarm, the stores received the same quantity of oxycodone. The indifference at all levels of the organization was illustrated by one incident at the Walgreens in Fort Pierce in 2010. A pharmacist mistakenly dispensed an extra 120 doses of oxycodone to one customer. When he called the customer's home, he was told by the person who answered that the customer was a user and a dealer who had viewed the extra pills as a "pot of gold." He refused to return them. After the mix-up, the store continued to fill the same customer's prescriptions for pain pills.

In September 2012, the DEA shut down the Jupiter warehouse by using an Immediate Suspension Order—the same weapon Joe's investigators had used against the Cardinal warehouse and the CVS stores in Sanford. They said the Walgreens warehouse posed "an imminent danger to the public health and safety." Even when Walgreens employees identified extremely large orders, the warehouse shipped them anyway. The DEA documented similar problems in Colorado, Michigan, and New York.

DEA investigators also discovered that Walgreens's corporate headquarters pushed its stores to increase sales with a program that gave bonuses to pharmacists based on the number of prescriptions filled. That practice seemed to come in conflict with the oath pharmacists take: "I shall always place the needs of all those I serve above my personal interests and considerations."

The soaring sales of opioids caused some alarm at headquarters. Executives there began formulating a pharmacy store survey called "Florida Focus on Profit." Among the survey's proposed questions were some about the legitimacy of pain clinic prescriptions: "Do pain management clinic patients come all at once or in a steady stream?" and "Do you see an increase in pain management prescriptions on the day the warehouse order is received?"

Dwayne Pinon, a Walgreens attorney, balked at including the questions. "If these are legitimate indicators of inappropriate prescriptions, perhaps we should consider not documenting our own potential noncompliance," he wrote in an email to Walgreens officials. The questions were dropped.

In June 2013, Walgreens agreed to pay an $80 million fine to settle allegations that the company committed an "unprecedented" number of violations and filled opioid prescriptions that they knew or should have known were not for legitimate medical use and were being diverted to the black market. The company surrendered its DEA registrations for six Florida Walgreens pharmacies until May 2014.

It was the largest fine and sanction in DEA history, but it had little impact on the company's bottom line. That year, Walgreens posted $72 billion in revenue—$80 million was an easily absorbed cost of doing business.

Chapter 17

"Crisis Playbook"

Orlando, Florida, 2013

Members of The Alliance felt like they'd been knocked to the canvas by a series of quick blows. They had been raided by the DEA and had their opioid distribution operations shuttered. Attempts to lobby the Justice Department had failed and the federal courts had ruled against them. Costs were running into the tens of millions in lost revenue and fines.

To turn things around, the industry deployed a strategy straight from Big Tobacco's playbook: Deceive and deflect.

The Alliance hired APCO Worldwide, a multinational company based in Washington, D.C., with a long history of helping corporations and industries in trouble with the law, the press, or both. With nearly six hundred employees and more than $100 million in annual revenues, APCO was one of the largest crisis communications companies in the world. It started in the 1980s as a spin-off from a large Washington law firm, Arnold & Porter. The company, originally called APCO Associates, would represent controversial clients without sullying the good name of the law firm.

In 1993, APCO took on a damaged brand—the tobacco giant Philip Morris—and created a front group to challenge the science linking tobacco and secondhand smoke to cancer. APCO called the group The Advancement of Sound Science Coalition. An internal plan outlining the mission of the center would surface years later. It was created to "encourage the public to question the validity of scientific studies," and APCO enlisted medical experts and other key opinion leaders or influencers to amplify the tobacco industry's message. Only years later did the public and the press learn that Philip Morris was financing the covert disinformation campaign and pulling every string.

For $515,000, The Alliance would get its own covert makeover. APCO's plan was rolled out in two phases. In the first, the PR outfit set up three focus groups, interviewing key opinion leaders, pharmacists, and law enforcement officials. APCO wanted to identify negative perceptions of the drug industry, figure out how to mitigate them, and test rebranding messages that would resonate with the public, the press, and Capitol Hill. The campaign also sought to determine who the public believed was responsible for drug abuse and the opioid epidemic. "Who's to blame?" APCO asked in its binders of material prepared for The Alliance. The majority of those surveyed said "users," followed by "drug dealers" and then "doctors." Members of The Alliance were relieved to find themselves near the bottom of the list. "Distributors rank very low on the 'who's to blame' list for prescription drug diversion and misuse," the members of The Alliance were informed at an executive committee meeting on June 2, 2013, at the JW Marriott Orlando, Grande Lakes, a luxurious resort.

APCO also created talking points, an "educational tool kit" for the press and the public, and a scale ranking the risks The Alliance faced. At the top was "DEA enforcement actions," followed by "negative and/or inaccurate media coverage of the industry."

In phase two of the project, APCO created a forty-four-page "Crisis Playbook" to repair the image of the drug companies, shift public opinion, and combat the DEA and negative news stories about the industry. The playbook contained several key talking points to repeat to the public and news media: The drug companies protected patient rights and provided unfettered access to legitimate prescriptions.

The DEA was being overly aggressive and preventing patients from obtaining the medicine they needed.

The playbook proposed responses for the industry to deploy, depending upon the situation. If the DEA had suspended the registration of a drug company for shipping excessive orders, the playbook suggested that The Alliance consider using the suspension as "an opportunity" to "push its message of misdirected DEA enforcement with national media." The playbook also proposed informing "relevant members of Congress about the action to head off greater criticism." The playbook included other talking points to use with reporters, such as arguing that the "DEA appears to be pursuing a path of conflict, rather than collaboration with our industry." It also sought to shift the blame for the epidemic to drug users and the DEA itself.

APCO urged The Alliance to repeat the message that its members did not have access to the DEA's ARCOS database. The playbook recommended asking: How are the drug distributors supposed to know how many pain pills are being sold? It left out one important fact: The DEA database is based on sales information provided by the drug distributors themselves.

Six months after the Orlando meeting, on December 11, the Alliance members gathered at their headquarters in Arlington for a "DEA Strategy Task Force Meeting." Executives from McKesson, Cardinal, and AmerisourceBergen were there. So too was Tom Twitty, a senior vice president of H.D. Smith, a midsized drug distributor based in Springfield, Illinois. A director of APCO and an attorney for The Alliance also sat in.

The executives identified "three areas of attack" as part of their DEA strategy. They agreed to form a broader coalition, enlisting more companies and pharmaceutical trade associations. Aside from the drug distributors, it would include Teva Pharmaceuticals, a large opioid manufacturer that had purchased Cephalon—the company that created the *Austin Powers-Dr. Evil* spoof. They also decided to use the material from APCO to conduct a "targeted media outreach" campaign. It was time, they agreed, to push back against the DEA and the proliferation of negative news stories around the country, "rather than making no public statement and letting the public only hear what the media puts out, such as calling us 'pill mills,'" Twitty wrote in an email to the owners of H.D. Smith.

One of the most important elements of the strategy was a classic Washington counterattack: Identify members of Congress who might be willing to introduce legislation to derail the DEA's enforcement campaign. That work, Twitty told his colleagues, was now under way.

Chapter 18

Marsha and Tom

Capitol Hill, 2013

Marsha Blackburn was a former beauty queen, a first runner-up for Miss U.S. Teen and the Oil Festival Queen in Laurel, Mississippi, where her father managed a steel company. Blackburn attended Mississippi State University on a 4-H scholarship and received a bachelor's degree in home economics. In 1975, she moved to Tennessee while working for a marketing company, selling educational material. She also dabbled in politics, founding a local chapter of the Young Republicans. With her staunchly conservative credentials, Blackburn quickly rose through the ranks of the Tennessee Republican Party. She secured a state senate seat and became the minority whip in the statehouse. In 2002, she ran for Congress, crushing her Democratic opponent in a deep red district west of Nashville by a 44 percent margin.

In Washington, Blackburn continued her ascent. Within two years, *Washingtonian* magazine named her one of the three top newcomers to the House. She then tied her political fortunes to the insurgent Tea Party and became a darling of the right. A series of important committee assignments followed in the Republican-controlled Congress, none more consequential than her appointment to the House Energy and Commerce Committee, one of the oldest standing committees in the lower chamber and one of its most powerful. The committee also was one of the largest on Capitol Hill, with jurisdiction over nearly every facet of corporate America—telecommunications, public health, energy, and interstate commerce. The committee also had jurisdiction over food and drug safety, making it one of the most important panels on the Hill for The Alliance and its confederates in the drug industry.

Lobbyists for The Alliance reported back that they had identified Blackburn as a member of Congress willing to take on the DEA. She was one of two potential allies. Ten days after the June 2013 Orlando meeting, a lobbyist for The Alliance told her colleagues that the industry had found another partner on Capitol Hill: Tom Marino, a Republican representative from Pennsylvania. He had reviewed a draft of the legislation designed to stop Joe Rannazzisi and the DEA's aggressiveness and liked what he saw.

"Rep. Marino's office is very open to feedback and additional ideas," Jewelyn Cosgrove, the Alliance lobbyist, wrote in a June 12, 2013, email.

Marino was a second-term congressman from Williamsport, Pennsylvania, the home of the Little League World Series. It was a postcard-perfect town along the banks of the western branch of the Susquehanna River, surrounded by the hills of Lycoming County. Marino began his career as a lawyer there before serving as the district attorney and then the U.S. attorney for the Middle District of Pennsylvania.

Marino's tenure as the top law enforcement official in central Pennsylvania didn't end well. In 2007, he was forced to resign after it was revealed that he had vouched for a convicted felon, Louis DeNaples, who was seeking a casino license. At the time, DeNaples was under investigation by Marino's office. After stepping down, Marino went to work for DeNaples as an attorney for his business interests.

Despite the scandal, Marino won a seat in Congress in 2010. Like Blackburn, he rode the Tea Party wave that upended the balance of power in the House of Representatives that year. Eighty-seven freshman Republicans were elected, resulting in the party's largest gain of House seats since 1938. The election toppled House Speaker Nancy Pelosi and hobbled the agenda of the Obama administration. In 2012, Marino won reelection by a whopping 30 percent margin. Not only was he popular in his district, but his star was rising in Washington, where he was seen as a political firebrand and a friend to big business and the pharmaceutical industry. The nation's third-largest drug distributor, AmerisourceBergen, was based in Pennsylvania. From his perch as a member of the powerful House Judiciary Committee, its leadership in the hands of the Republican Party, Marino was in a prime position to help the drug distributor and other industry giants.

For years, the drug industry could count on key members of Congress to sponsor legislation or attach amendments to bills to improve the industry's bottom line, or to kill amendments that could threaten its finances. In the House, where lawmakers face reelection every two years, raising money had become a full-time job. As soon as a candidate won, the next campaign had already begun. Each day, many members of Congress set aside time for rounds of fund-raising calls. The average cost of running a successful House campaign during the 2012–14 election cycle was $1.5 million; in the Senate it was $9.6 million. Money equaled political survival.

Depending on the issue, lobbyists had their favorite lawmakers, but all companies currying favor worked off a similar approach—throwing fund-raisers, dinners at the finest restaurants in Washington, tickets to Capitals hockey games, or performances at the Kennedy Center. Being a member of Congress had its perks. But it also carried a price. The lobbyists and the companies they represented always wanted something in return. In 2013, it was passage of legislation to stop the DEA. Much like the title APCO had devised for its tobacco-industry-financed "science center," the drug industry created an equally deceptive moniker for its legislation: the Ensuring Patient Safety and Effective Drug Enforcement Act. The three-page bill did nothing to ensure patient safety, nor did it do anything to provide for effective drug enforcement. It was an exercise in newspeak.

What the bill really sought to do was eliminate the language the DEA had relied on for decades to immediately suspend the registrations of companies found to be in violation of the law. Instead of proving that the conduct of a company was creating an "imminent danger to public health and safety," the DEA would now need to demonstrate that the company's actions created "a significant and present risk of death or serious bodily harm." Proving that a company based in Ohio or Pennsylvania was posing a "present risk" to residents of Florida would be an insurmountable legal hurdle, and the drug companies knew it. The bill contained another provision coveted by the drug industry. If a company violated the law, it could present the DEA with a "corrective action plan" before the agency could take any enforcement action.

The legislation was the brainchild of one of the early architects of the DEA's crackdown on the opioid industry—Linden Barber, the agency attorney who had worked alongside Joe Rannazzisi and Mimi Paredes before representing the drug industry. Barber had built an impressive client list, working on behalf of Cardinal Health and others. The legislation also won wide support from the retail pharmacy industry, including the National Association of Chain Drug Stores, which represented CVS and Walgreens, the National Community Pharmacists Association, and the American Pharmacists Association.

In 2013, as they pushed the Ensuring Patient Access and Effective Drug Enforcement Act, the drug companies and industry associations began to contribute to the campaigns of Marino and Blackburn. Marino received $9,000 that year; Blackburn $31,000. It was early seed money. Hundreds of thousands would follow. To attract Democratic support, The Alliance authorized spending $250,000 "to engage a legislative consultant (with significant Democratic connections) to actively recruit Democratic co-sponsor." The Alliance eventually signed up Democratic lawmakers Peter Welch of Vermont and Judy Chu of California.

Patrick Kelly, The Alliance's executive vice president in charge of lobbying, warned his colleagues that the DEA was "adamantly opposed to this legislation and has made their position known to hill staff, as well as to some industry representatives." Kelly said the DEA was cautioning that the bill would tie "the agency's hands to actively and aggressively address diversion and compliance with the CSA (Controlled Substances Act)."

To bolster its efforts against the DEA, The Alliance hired an outside lobbying firm, Thorsen French Advocacy, to help orchestrate a congressional hearing before the House Energy and Commerce Subcommittee on Health. Scheduled to testify: Joe, Barber, and John Gray, the president of The Alliance. On April 3, 2014, the lobbying firm, which was paid $140,000 that year, provided The Alliance with questions for members of Congress to ask during the hearing. The questions were provided to Blackburn and Representative Michael C. Burgess, a Texas Republican who served as vice chairman of the subcommittee.

"This is all so sensitive and anxiety levels are high so we need to have some control over how these questions are shared," Kristen Freitas, the Alliance lobbyist, wrote to Carlyle P. Thorsen, the head of the lobbying firm, four days before the hearing.

Thorsen agreed. He too wanted to stay in the shadows.

"Pls scrub my name and source info before they are forwarded," he replied.

Chapter 19

Playing Games

Rayburn House Office Building, Washington, D.C., 2014

On April 7, an overcast Monday afternoon, Joe Rannazzisi drove across the Potomac River to appear before the House Energy and Commerce Subcommittee on Health. He had testified on the Hill more than thirty times, explaining an array of drug issues to members of Congress. But this time he knew he was walking into hostile territory.

Joe sat down at a long table in Room 2123 and fingered his blue-and-silver club tie. He surveyed the vast hearing room inside the Rayburn House Office Building, named for Sam Rayburn of Texas, the longest-serving House Speaker. Joe wore an orange wristband. "Families Against Narcotics," it read.

Members of Congress took their seats on the dais as the 3 p.m. hearing began. Its title was bland and bureaucratic: "Improving Predictability and Transparency in DEA and FDA Regulation." But the goal was far from anodyne. The drug industry wanted to build support for the legislation that Tom Marino and Marsha Blackburn had introduced on February 18. The industry smoothed the way with tens of thousands of dollars in contributions to several of those who now sat before Joe.

Congressional hearings have their own choreography. Government officials, experts, and representatives of special interests are called to testify at a witness table in the well of the chamber. Members of Congress ask questions, but in their allotted five minutes, they are mostly playing to the television cameras, their constituents, and the companies that donate to their campaigns.

Joe delivered his opening statement. Mimi Paredes, his trusted counsel, sat behind him.

"The DEA's sole interest is protecting the public from harm," Joe said. He explained some of the tools at the agency's disposal. One was the Immediate Suspension Order he had used to bar the Cardinal warehouse and the CVS stores from selling opioids. Without those tools, he said, it "would be tremendously more difficult to protect the public health and safety."

The Alliance had already identified members of Congress who were willing to ask questions on behalf of the industry. Among them was the vice chairman of the subcommittee, Texas Republican Michael Burgess.

"Sometimes it seems that all the DEA cares about is the number of enforcement actions and not real solutions to stop the abuse," Burgess said from the dais.

"That's not correct," said Joe, who tried to explain all the steps the DEA tried to take before issuing a suspension order.

Blackburn took her turn. She said she only had a couple of questions. "I want us to be able to move on so we can get to the second panel." That panel included John Gray, the president of The Alliance, and Linden Barber.

Blackburn looked down at some papers on the dais and started to read her first question. "Let me just ask you if you can list for us what you are doing, articulate what the efforts are that the DEA is engaged in to promulgate some clear standards for the prescribers, for the pharmacies, for the distributors?"

The question, almost word for word, was one written by the Washington lobbying firm hired by The Alliance and passed to Blackburn and other members of Congress for them to parrot.

Joe briefly answered the first part of Blackburn's question about prescribers, in the process citing one of his favorite U.S. Supreme Court cases that ruled doctors must issue prescriptions for legitimate medical purposes as part of their professional practice. He was starting to talk about how pharmacists had a similar responsibility and to address the responsibilities of the distributors when Blackburn cut him off.

"We were looking for a little bit of new information," she said. "And I guess it's kind of a Monday attitude sort of day, so let me move on."

"Well, I'd like to finish," Joe said.

Blackburn cut him off again.

"I guess not," Joe said.

Blackburn moved quickly to her next question—another that had been written by the lobbying firm: "What are you doing to help well-intentioned registrants determine who they can do business with?" Registrants are manufacturers, distributors, pharmacies, and doctors who have been given a DEA registration to handle controlled substances.

"I'm sorry?" Joe responded. "We don't dictate who the registrant does business with." The agency did, however, tell them what red flags to look for to comply with the law prohibiting enormous shipments of narcotics to pharmacies, he said.

"Well, let me move on, then," Blackburn said.

"I mean, we—" Joe said, trying to finish his answer.

The congresswoman cut him off again.

Joe was becoming agitated. "Sixteen thousand six hundred and fifty-one people in 2010 died of opiate overdose, okay, opiate-associated overdose," he said, looking straight at Blackburn. "This is not a game. We're not playing a game."

Blackburn cut Joe off again. "Nobody is saying it is a game, sir," she said testily. "We're just trying to craft some legislation. Let me ask you this."

"Especially in Tennessee—" Joe started to say, trying to point out how many people had died in Blackburn's home state, which had been hit hard by the opioid epidemic.

"What is DEA doing to help registrants identify the prescribers and pharmacies that they should refuse to do business with?" Blackburn asked, repeating another version of the question scripted by The Alliance's lobbying firm.

Joe repeated his answer. The DEA cannot direct a drug company to sell or not to sell to a particular customer, he said. The companies are required to catch and report suspicious orders and not ship them. "That's a due process issue," he said. "We can't direct a wholesaler or distributor or a pharmacy not to sell to a particular person."

"Okay, my time has expired," Blackburn said.

"That's what—" Joe started to say before Blackburn cut him off a sixth time.

"I yield back," she told the committee chairman.

Paredes was appalled by the lack of respect Blackburn showed her boss. After college, she had worked on the Hill as a staffer, assigned to the same congressional committee. She had seen sparring between members of Congress and witnesses, but this exchange seemed particularly rude.

Joe looked up at the dais in dismay. All he could see were mouthpieces for the drug industry. Where were the members of Congress who were on the side of the DEA and the communities being victimized by the epidemic? Hundreds of thousands of Americans were dead.

Where is the outrage? he wondered.

Chapter 20

"Tom Marino Is Trying to Do That?"

Department of Justice, 2014

It was an early afternoon in June 2014, and Joe Rannazzisi was uncharacteristically nervous. He was about to give Attorney General Eric H. Holder Jr. a thirty-slide PowerPoint presentation on his pending opioid investigations and he was having trouble uploading his slides. He turned to a department techie for help. Holder's aides had told Joe and his boss, Michele Leonhart, that the attorney general had little time that day. Keep it tight, they warned.

Joe wanted to leave Holder with one key message: The legislation introduced by Republicans Tom Marino and Marsha Blackburn would deliver a body blow to the DEA's ability to stop the illegal flow of pain pills. Joe knew that Marino had been trying to lobby Holder and others at Justice. The DEA had already warned in a memo that the bill "would constitute perhaps the greatest reduction in the Attorney General's authority under the Controlled Substances Act since the Act's passage in 1970." Joe needed to ram home that message. The DEA wanted Holder to come out publicly against the bill.

Holder was an historic figure: the first African American attorney general. He was the top law enforcement official in the Obama administration. He was a liberal icon, but also a lightning rod on Capitol Hill, where he frequently clashed with conservative lawmakers. Two months earlier, on April 8, Holder had been summoned to a hearing before the House Judiciary Committee, the panel that oversaw the Justice Department. It was a packed, three-hour-and-forty-five-minute session where thirty-four members of the committee grilled Holder on a wide array of national and international issues. Five minutes before the hearing ended, Marino jumped in to ask Holder about prescription drugs. He complained that the Justice Department was treating the drug companies like "illicit narcotics cartels."

Holder had announced that a spike in overdoses from heroin and prescription painkillers was causing "an urgent and growing public health crisis," and he vowed that his department would combat the epidemic. People addicted to pills, struggling to fill prescriptions as the crackdown on opioid companies took hold, had turned to heroin, triggering a second wave of the opioid epidemic. Actor Philip Seymour Hoffman had recently been found dead in his New York City apartment after overdosing on heroin and other street drugs.

"I was troubled by some language that you chose," Marino told Holder. "I inferred you seem to equate legitimate supply chain businesses to illicit narcotics cartels. I found that disappointing. This mindset, it is extremely dangerous to legitimate business."

Marino continued, mischaracterizing the actions of the DEA. "My understanding is the DEA now is going to the drug companies and saying you should have realized that the amount of drugs that you were sending out to this particular individual, you should have made the determination that that individual was abusing drugs. And then these legitimate businesses are being held responsible for that and fined and perhaps put out of business."

Holder gently pushed back, saying he didn't mean to imply any such thing. "I do not want to cast that wide a net," the attorney general said. He told Marino he would welcome another conversation.

"I would love to," Marino replied.

Holder continued, "We cannot in our desire, our legitimate desire and one that I am pushing, to stop opioid use, which potentially leads to heroin involvement. We cannot lose sight of the fact that there are good people, sick people, good companies who employ good people who are trying to do the right thing."

Marino's time had expired, but he had one more thing to say. "If you find yourself not having something to do some evening, which you probably never do, I would love to discuss the issues," he said.

"Okay," Holder said.

Marino followed up three weeks later with a letter to Holder, telling him about his legislation and urging him to set up a meeting with drug industry executives. He added a handwritten note to the attorney general: "It would be great to work together on this.—Tom"

On June 4, Bill Tighe, Marino's chief of staff, wrote to Peter Kadzik, Justice's top congressional liaison officer, thanking him for trying to set up a meeting for Holder with the industry executives. Tighe asked Kadzik to coordinate with the industry's point person: Linden Barber.

Marino's overtures to the attorney general and his efforts to set up a meeting with industry set off alarms and a flurry of emails and memos within the DEA and Justice Department. "Linden Barber used to work for DEA," Jill Wade Tyson, another Justice congressional liaison officer, told Kadzik in an email. "He wrote the Marino bill."

DEA officials believed that it would be improper for the attorney general or others at Justice to meet with industry executives because many of the companies were under active investigation or in settlement negotiations with the department. Leonhart asked for a meeting with Holder to brief him on the agency's drug industry investigations and to add her voice to the internal alarm.

Leonhart and Joe knew Holder had a complicated past. In 2001, in one of the earliest lawsuits against an opioid manufacturer, the state of West Virginia sued Purdue Pharma. Purdue had hired Holder, who was in private practice at Covington & Burling, to represent the company. The case settled in 2004 with Purdue agreeing to pay $10 million over four years while admitting no wrongdoing. Despite that connection, Joe thought Holder would do the right thing. He felt as though he understood Holder, partly because they were both New Yorkers. He believed the attorney general, who himself had experienced the loss of friends from heroin overdoses, would be sympathetic to his cause.

"They are attempting to take away your authority," Joe told Holder, singling out the Marino-Blackburn bill as he began his PowerPoint presentation.

"I don't understand what you mean," Holder said.

The attorney general was juggling a massive number of issues ranging from terrorism to cybersecurity to civil rights violations and a botched gun operation on the southern border dubbed "Fast and Furious." Joe knew Holder couldn't be expected to know the intricacies of every piece of legislation. He explained what the Marino-Blackburn bill would accomplish with the change of a few words, making it nearly impossible for the DEA to issue Immediate Suspension Orders against drug companies. Instead of proving that a company was posing an "imminent danger to public health and safety," the bill would force the DEA to show that the company's actions presented "a significant and present risk of death or serious bodily harm."

"Tom Marino is trying to do that?" Holder asked. "He was a former U.S. attorney."

"Yes, Tom Marino is trying to do that," Joe said.

The attorney general was surprised by something else on one of Joe's slides. From 2010 through 2012, more people had died from prescription drug overdoses than from heroin.

"You're telling me that more people are dying from pharmaceuticals?" Holder asked Joe.

Holder turned to his aides.

"Were we aware of this?" he asked.

Chapter 21

"Be Zen"

Capitol Hill, 2014

The streets of Capitol Hill are lined with finely crafted nineteenth-century town houses, many of them appointed with parlors, libraries, and servants' quarters. The neighborhood began as a community of upscale boardinghouses for members of Congress in the early 1800s. More recently, it had become a fashionable enclave for congressional staffers, political operatives, and journalists.

On June 24, 2014, drug industry executives and lobbyists arrived on Capitol Hill for a fund-raising luncheon in honor of Tom Marino. They gathered in the D.C. offices of AmerisourceBergen, the drug distributor headquartered in Marino's home state. Along with AmerisourceBergen, the sponsors included Cardinal Health, the National Community Pharmacists Association, and the National Association of Chain Drug Stores. The invitation sent to the drug industry representatives listed Marino's committee assignments—Foreign Affairs, Homeland Security, and, most important, Judiciary, which oversees the DEA. It also suggested donation levels to attend: $2,500 for each political action committee; $1,000 for each individual; $500 for each guest.

It was the continuation of the money flowing into the campaigns of lawmakers and the accounts of Capitol Hill lobbyists working to pass the industry-backed Ensuring Patient Safety and Effective Drug

Enforcement Act. By the summer of 2014, The Alliance had spent $233,000 lobbying in favor of the legislation and other issues. In addition, CVS had spent $6.6 million; the National Association of Chain Drug Stores, $2 million; Cardinal Health, $1 million; and Walgreens, $610,000.

A week after the Marino fund-raiser, on July 2, Republican staffers for two committees on the Hill—Judiciary, and Energy and Commerce—requested a conference call with the DEA. They wanted to hear why the DEA was so opposed to the Marino-Blackburn bill. Mimi Paredes didn't want Joe Rannazzisi to join the call. She knew how upset Joe was about the bill and she worried that he wouldn't be able to keep his cool.

"Don't do this, Joe," Paredes pleaded with him in his sixth-floor office. "They're going to bait you. They're going to twist your words."

Joe held a sheaf of printouts, a roll call of overdose deaths in states across the country, including those in Pennsylvania and Tennessee. "I know how to handle this," he said.

"Stay calm," Paredes said. "Be Zen."

Joe sat down at his conference table, flanked by Paredes and John Partridge, a career DEA man who had become one of Joe's most trusted lieutenants. Listening in on the call were congressional liaison officers for the DEA and the Justice Department.

At first, the conversation was cordial. Joe began to read from the printouts, pointing out the number of opioid overdose deaths in Tennessee, Pennsylvania, and other states around the country.

"You know, with all these people dying, why would you write legislation that restricts our enforcement authority?" Joe asked, holding the printouts. "I mean, there's a lot of people dying."

With the invocation of overdose numbers, the tenor of the meeting quickly turned testy. "We just want to understand why you're so opposed to this legislation," one of the staffers said.

Paredes could see Joe's eyes narrow. *Shit*, she thought.

"What problem are you trying to address with this bill?" Joe asked.

"We're not trying to address any problems," the staffer said. "We're just trying to pass a bill."

Paredes could almost feel the heat of indignation coming off Joe. He had already lost his patience with the drug companies and their excuses. Now he was being confronted by congressional staffers who seemed to be willfully clueless about the legislation and what it would do to the DEA. He leaned into the Polycom set up on his conference table.

"Wait a minute. You're not trying to address a problem? What are you trying to do?" Joe asked, his voice rising. "This legislation is tantamount to you guys supporting defendants in our investigation. You'll be protecting criminals."

"Whoa, we're not protecting criminals," one of the staffers said. "I can't believe you just said that."

"If you pass this legislation, a lot of people are going to die," Joe said. "That blood is on your hands, not mine."

The line went dead.

"Oh, fuck," Eric Akers, a DEA congressional affairs officer listening in on the call, said to himself as he sat in his office.

Joe didn't regret what he said. But he asked Paredes to call Jill Wade Tyson, the Justice Department's congressional liaison officer, to assess whether any damage had been done.

She told Paredes not to worry. "It's fine," she said.

Tyson and Akers tried clean up. They called the staffers and apologized, insisting Joe didn't mean what he said. The staffers weren't buying it.

"That was really out of bounds," one said. "I don't like being threatened."

Chapter 22

"You're Being Paranoid"

Washington, D.C., 2014

At a daylong law enforcement conference in Washington on July 31, 2014, Attorney General Eric Holder urged federal agents to start carrying naloxone, a miraculous drug that can revive overdose victims. He told his audience that there had been a "dramatic, 45 percent increase in heroin-related deaths" between 2006 and 2010. "And 110 people die every day from overdoses, primarily driven by prescription drugs. The shocking increase in overdose deaths illustrates that addiction to heroin and other opioids, including some prescription painkillers, represents nothing less than a public health crisis. It's also a public safety crisis. And every day, this crisis touches—and devastates—the lives of Americans from every state, in every region, and from every background and walk of life."

Holder turned to the Marino-Blackburn bill that was pending in the Senate. He began by thanking top Justice Department officials, mentioning Joe Rannazzisi by name.

"I'd particularly like to thank," Holder said, "Deputy Assistant Administrator Joe Rannazzisi, and the dedicated men and women of the Drug Enforcement Administration—for bringing us together this morning." He added, "Every day, you stand on the front lines of our fight to confront an urgent and growing threat to our nation and its citizens."

Holder then brought up Immediate Suspension Orders, or ISOs, saying they "allow DEA to immediately shut down irresponsible distributors, pharmacies, and rogue pain clinics that flood the market with pills prescribed by unethical or irresponsible doctors."

He continued, "Particularly now, at a time when our nation is facing a heroin and prescription drug abuse crisis, law enforcement tools like ISOs could not be more important. And if Congress were to take them away, or weaken our ability to use them successfully, it would severely undermine a critical component of our efforts to prevent communities and families from falling prey to dangerous drugs."

Joe couldn't have been happier. The attorney general's words might have just doomed the Marino-Blackburn bill. *He is standing on the side of the angels*, Joe thought.

Joe was right. The Ensuring Patient Safety and Effective Drug Enforcement Act stalled in the Senate and would die in the 113th Congress that year. Joe also knew he had made some powerful enemies. One afternoon that summer, he told Mimi Paredes that he thought the drug industry and certain members of Congress were out to get him.

"What are you talking about?" she said as they stood in his office.

Forces were aligning against him, Joe said. They wanted to bring him down. Congress. The drug companies. Their lobbyists. The Alliance. He cited the questions that Blackburn had asked him during the congressional hearing. They had to have been written by the industry, he said.

"You're crazy," Paredes teased him. "Come *on*. You're being paranoid."

A few weeks later, Joe brought the subject up again, calling Paredes at home. A source, he said, had told him the industry and their congressional allies were gunning for him.

For years, Paredes had looked up to Joe. She thought he had impeccable judgment. Now she wondered. Paredes didn't believe in conspiracies. Her career as a former Navy SEAL lawyer and now as a DEA attorney was grounded in hard facts that could be proven.

On September 18, the House Judiciary Subcommittee on Crime, Terrorism, Homeland Security, and Investigations called DEA administrator Michele Leonhart to testify. Marino admonished her, demanding that she and her agency collaborate with "legitimate" drug companies "that want to do the right thing."

"Big fines make headlines," Marino said from the dais. "But that is all they do. Press releases do not save lives."

Then he called out Joe, barely able to control his anger. "It is my understanding that Joe Rannazzisi, a senior DEA official, has publicly accused we sponsors of the bill of, quote, 'supporting criminals,' unquote," Marino said. "This offends me immensely."

A week later, on September 25, Marino and Blackburn wrote to the Justice Department's inspector general, Michael E. Horowitz, requesting that he open an investigation into Joe. Horowitz's job was to examine allegations of misconduct and violations of criminal and civil laws by Justice Department employees. The offices of inspectors general were created by Congress, and IGs respond quickly to congressional requests.

In their letter to Horowitz, Marino and Blackburn accused Joe of trying to "intimidate the United States Congress," referencing the ill-tempered July 2 phone call with the congressional staffers. "We believe an accusation of this nature from a DOJ official is totally unacceptable," they wrote.

Paredes now understood. They *were* coming after Joe.

Chapter 23

"The Best Case We've Ever Had"

Denver, Colorado, 2015

David Schiller was a rock star at the DEA. He had worked airport drug interdiction operations at LAX; helped crack a smuggling ring of FedEx drivers and managers that resulted in fifty-six arrests and the seizure of thirty thousand pounds of marijuana and $4 million in cash; and duped international drug lords from nations without extradition treaties with the United States to enter the country, where they were promptly arrested by the DEA. Working alongside the agency's elite Special Operations Division, he had chased cocaine and heroin kingpins around the globe.

But none of those cases felt as important to him as the one he was building against McKesson. He could understand the motivations of international drug trafficking rings. He couldn't understand how a U.S. company could be involved in what he saw as one of the largest drug rackets in America.

As the assistant special agent in charge of the DEA's Denver field office, Schiller, a Southern California native, had spent two years investigating the drug distribution giant. He had assembled a national investigative team comprising nine DEA field divisions that worked alongside a dozen U.S. attorneys' offices across eleven states. He wanted to revoke McKesson's registrations to distribute narcotics at some of its twenty-eight warehouses across the country, several of them supplying regions that were being ravaged by the opioid epidemic. Schiller hoped to fine the company $1 billion. More than anything, he anticipated the first-ever criminal case against a drug distributor, maybe even a perp walk of an executive out of McKesson's towering San Francisco headquarters, TV cameras rolling. That would send a message to the rest of the industry.

Schiller and his lead investigator, Helen Kaupang, believed that they could prove the company had failed to report suspicious orders involving hundreds of millions of highly addictive painkillers. Schiller and Kaupang came to think of McKesson as the Sinaloa Cartel of corporate America.

But as 2014 drew to a close, the case was going sideways. Schiller's requests to prosecutors and DEA lawyers for large civil fines and criminal charges were languishing. He was hearing whispers from colleagues that the agency's own lawyers were secretly negotiating a settlement with the company. He had even heard that lawyers for the DEA had quietly flown into Denver—Schiller's own turf—to meet with representatives of McKesson, and hadn't invited him.

DEA lawyers from headquarters were, in fact, in serious talks with a high-powered lawyer hired by McKesson, Geoffrey E. Hobart. He was a former Justice Department prosecutor who now specialized in defending drug companies at Covington & Burling, an influential D.C. law firm with $1 billion in annual revenue.

Schiller couldn't get a straight answer about the status of his case. Why wasn't he being included in the discussions over whether to settle in the first place? Instead of getting answers, he was being ghosted by his own agency.

McKesson first appeared on Schiller's radar in 2012, when state and local law enforcement officers were investigating oxycodone sales at the Platte Valley Pharmacy in Brighton, Colorado, a suburb of Denver on the Platte River. Only thirty-eight thousand people lived in the town, but the pharmacist at Platte Valley, Jeffrey Clawson, was dispensing nearly two thousand pain pills every day. DEA agents soon learned that Clawson's most loyal customers belonged to a notorious Denver-based drug ring. A grand jury indicted Clawson and the head of the ring, along with thirteen others, for illegally distributing oxycodone in Colorado and Oklahoma. The grand jurors made special mention of McKesson's role.

"The Grand Jury learned of evidence demonstrating that Clawson's Platte Valley Pharmacy engaged in the regular purchase of Oxycodone from McKesson that was either unusually large, unusually frequent, and/or which substantially deviated from the normal pattern typically observed for comparable pharmacies in the area in and around Brighton, Colorado," the grand jurors wrote in their indictment. "From 2008–2011, the percentage increase for Oxycodone 30 mg orders supplied by McKesson to Platte Valley Pharmacy was approximately 1,469%."

As he did with every investigation, Schiller began to build a timeline. It helped him keep the facts straight, to see the strengths and weaknesses of his case, and where he needed to train the DEA's firepower. The timeline began in 2008, when McKesson paid its $13.25 million fine for failing to report the massive orders of hydrocodone it was shipping to internet pharmacies. The company signed an agreement with the DEA, promising to flag those kinds of orders in the future, using a sophisticated monitoring system. The company also promised to report all unusually large orders to the DEA and stop those shipments. The Platte Valley case suggested that McKesson had not only violated that agreement, he believed the company had flat-out ignored it.

McKesson supplied Platte Valley from its enormous warehouse in Aurora, Colorado, ten miles east of Denver. Schiller discovered that between signing the 2008 agreement and 2012, McKesson had shipped 1.6 million orders of prescription narcotics from the Aurora facility to drugstores in the region. It reported just 16 of those to the

DEA as suspicious, none of them involving Platte Valley. After the DEA began its investigation, the company filed 2,447 suspicious order reports with the agency. The sudden and huge correction was damning. Even more damning: Schiller and his team tied nine over-dose deaths to pharmacies that were receiving off-the-charts quantities of painkillers from the Aurora warehouse.

Schiller contacted other DEA field offices around the country. They were seeing the same pattern at a dozen different McKesson warehouses: in Livonia, Michigan; Washington Courthouse, Ohio; Landover, Maryland; and Lakeland, Florida, among others. Huge orders for pain pills were being shipped to drugstores, but McKesson reported few, if any, to the DEA as suspicious. Schiller also learned that two more pharmacies, in addition to Platte Valley, were supplying drug rings with oxycodone shipped from McKesson's warehouses.

Schiller called Joe Rannazzisi to update him on the investigation. "Joe, it's the best case we've ever had," he told him.

The two had worked together a decade earlier, shortly after Joe arrived in Washington from Detroit to head the diversion control office and Schiller was running the undercover and special operations section at headquarters. From the start, the two hit it off. They were both intensely serious about the work, logging insanely long hours, often neglecting their families as they pursued cases. Schiller saw Joe as a straight shooter, a rare find in Washington. If someone didn't like what Joe told them, he would say, "Well, if you don't like the truth, then don't ask me for the truth."

In 2014, two years into the investigation, Schiller had asked the agency's Chief Counsel's Office to bring McKesson before a DEA administrative law judge. Those judges hear cases involving agency enforcement actions. If the company couldn't explain why it was shipping so many doses of painkillers, the judge could suspend McKesson's registrations to distribute drugs. Schiller wanted a judge to issue an Immediate Suspension Order against McKesson but he was told he needed more proof. He noted that he had already sent eight boxes of evidence to the Chief Counsel's Office at headquarters. It wasn't enough, they said.

A week before Christmas in 2014, Schiller was invited to Washington. McKesson wanted to show the DEA the steps it had taken to flag unusually large orders of drugs from its warehouses. It was a bid at contrition to avoid losing its registrations. The meeting was supposed to be held at DEA headquarters. The lawyers in the Chief Counsel's Office, which provides legal advice to the entire agency, consented to moving the meeting to the D.C. offices of Covington & Burling. The decision was made while Schiller was flying from Denver to Washington. He couldn't understand why the agency agreed to it. To him, Covington was enemy territory. Why cede ground to McKesson? *It's like going to a crook's house to talk to the suspect before you arrest him,* he thought.

As Schiller waited to pass through security at the firm, a few blocks from the Justice Department, he spotted an old colleague, Gary Boggs, Joe's top lieutenant who had helped to bring the earlier cases against McKesson and Cardinal.

"Gary, what are you doing here?" Schiller asked.

Boggs said he had joined McKesson as its director of regulatory affairs.

"You're kidding me," Schiller said.

"They brought me in to change things," Boggs said.

"They haven't done anything right since 2008," Schiller told him.

"They didn't know what they were doing. I got a phone call, and they were looking for somebody to run their compliance program, and they told me they would let me actually run it and not be a front man. We're holding everyone accountable now," Boggs said.

"You know they're not compliant. They're never going to be," Schiller said. "They're there to make money."

"Well, until they prove to me that they're not willing to do the right thing from this point forward, I'll run their compliance section," Boggs said.

Schiller didn't believe the McKesson executives, but he didn't want to get into an argument in the black-striated marble lobby of the law firm. He boarded an elevator and the doors opened onto a vast conference room—one designed to project power and intimidate.

Joe had decided to shun the sit-down. He didn't think a DEA assistant administrator should cross the threshold of a law firm that represented a company he saw as a defendant, a repeat offender at that. Instead, he sent one of his top executives, John Partridge, to monitor the meeting, with instructions to leave if he didn't like what he was hearing.

Partridge, an unflappable twenty-five-year veteran of the agency, took a seat near the back of the conference room. He was incensed by how the case was being handled. He, too, had heard about the meetings between the Chief Counsel's Office and McKesson, and how the agents, investigators, and supervisors were frozen out. As McKesson executives enumerated the steps they said they were taking to prevent the mistakes of the past, with a slick PowerPoint presentation and colorful graphics, Partridge thought to himself that none of it mattered. What mattered was that McKesson had violated the terms of its 2008 agreement, the company had flooded the nation with pain pills, thousands of people had died, and the company should pay a high price. He also believed that some of McKesson's executives, including its president, John Hammergren, should be prosecuted.

As Partridge listened to the McKesson executives and their attorneys drone on, he asked himself, *Why am I here? Whatever they say doesn't change what happened. They were given a second chance and they broke the law.* McKesson, he thought, should be telling this to a judge, not a room full of DEA lawyers. About an hour into the daylong meeting, Partridge recalled what Joe had told him before he headed over to Covington. He was busy that day. He took Joe's advice. He stood up and walked out.

In Detroit, Jim Geldhof, also working the McKesson case, had a sickening feeling as he sat in his sixth-floor office overlooking the federal courthouse. He had been with the DEA for nearly forty-three years. He was close to retirement, reflecting on his legacy and calculating all the time he had spent away from home. He looked around his office, the photos of his family displayed on a wooden credenza, plaques and awards hanging on the walls. In the corner was a small wooden table where he and his colleagues had spent countless hours mapping out strategies to pursue hundreds of cases across the years. He thought the case against McKesson would be a fitting capstone.

Two of McKesson's largest warehouses were located in Geldhof's region, one in Livonia, Michigan, the other in Washington Courthouse, Ohio. Both of them, he believed, had helped to fuel the opioid epidemic in Ohio, West Virginia, and Kentucky. Yet he was left to wonder why the leadership of the DEA and its Chief Counsel's Office were retreating in the face of the agency's biggest fight against the drug industry. Why were they refusing to back up the cases his office and DEA field divisions across the country were bringing to headquarters, he wondered? Was someone at Justice putting pressure on the DEA?

Geldhof traced the start of the problem to 2013, after a new lawyer was named to the Chief Counsel's Office. Clifford Lee Reeves II, the career Justice Department attorney who argued the Cardinal case, became the associate chief counsel of the DEA the previous year. DEA program managers, agents, and investigators watched as their once-promising cases hit a wall of resistance at Reeves's office. They were having difficulty winning approval for search warrants, for court orders to force companies in front of judges, and for requests to immediately suspend the DEA registrations of drug companies that were failing to follow the law. Every request Geldhof made turned into a confrontation. Before Reeves's arrival, DEA investigators had to show that they had amassed "a preponderance of evidence" before moving forward with their civil cases. After Reeves's arrival, DEA investigators and lawyers said they were told that the standard was being changed to "beyond a reasonable doubt," a heavy burden reserved for criminal cases. Lawyers working under Reeves thought he was afraid of losing. One of those lawyers, Jonathan P. Novak, couldn't convince Reeves to bring cases against the drug companies. He thought the cases were ready to file and he couldn't understand why he kept getting shut down. Reeves became overly cautious and too deferential to the large teams of attorneys from law firms representing the companies under DEA investigation. The days of bold moves against the drug companies were coming to a close. A new era of cooperation between the DEA and the opioid industry had begun.

"What are you doing?" Geldhof asked Reeves during one heated exchange. "All we have had is wins in every case. I don't get it."

In Washington, the DEA's chief administrative law judge, John J. Mulrooney II, who oversaw the agency's enforcement actions, also began to question the plummeting cases against the drug industry. Mulrooney wrote in a June 2013 report that there was "a significant drop" in the number of "orders to show cause." Four months later, he noted "a free fall in the numbers of charging documents." For the first time since records had been kept, no charging documents had been filed for an entire month. The judge noted that the number of civil case filings against distributors, manufacturers, pharmacies, and doctors reached 131 in 2011, before dropping to 40 within three years. The number of Immediate Suspension Orders plummeted from 65 to 9 during that same time.

"There can be little doubt that the level of administrative Diversion enforcement remains stunningly low for a national program," Mulrooney wrote in his report.

The flow of cases had turned to a trickle.

"Assuming also that opioid-related deaths remain at over 20,000 per year," the judge wrote, "this would mean that the Agency is on course to institute one administrative enforcement action for every 625 fatalities."

Toward the end of 2014, Mulrooney reported that the caseload was so low, his judges had little left to do at the DEA. In response,

Mulrooney farmed them out to hear cases at other federal agencies, like the Bureau of Prisons and the Treasury Department.

By 2015, some of the DEA's biggest cases against the drug industry were withering. DEA lawyers and federal prosecutors kept negotiating with the drug companies, and they stopped talking to the field agents and investigators and their supervisors like Geldhof and Joe. It was as if they were working for the other side, not the DEA, Geldhof thought.

On the final day of March 2015, Schiller sent an urgent message to one of the few people he trusted at DEA headquarters, Mimi Paredes. Schiller was losing control of the McKesson case. He and an assistant U.S. attorney, M. J. Menendez, had prepared a memo outlining a possible criminal case and presented it to the U.S. attorney in Denver, John Walsh. He rejected it. Walsh thought it would be too difficult to prove that McKesson intended to illegally distribute oxycodone or knew its narcotics were winding up in the hands of criminal pharmacies and drug gangs. Walsh and the other U.S. attorneys involved in the case decided to proceed against McKesson with civil penalties, just as the DEA had done in 2008. The fate of the case now rested with the Justice Department and the DEA's Chief Counsel's Office—and they wanted to settle.

Schiller was apoplectic. "If Chief Counsel and the 12 U.S. Attorneys Offices do not want to go [to] court, we need to at least hold McKesson and the industry as a whole accountable," he wrote to Paredes on March 31, 2015. "Past agreements with Cardinal and others continue to let the industry operate with reckless abandon, and they continue to laugh at DEA as they continue to knowingly violate their responsibilities as a DEA registrant. They only care about the mighty dollar."

"David, I totally agree with you," Paredes responded. "I'm totally against settling, but how do we hold their feet to the fire if counsel refuses to litigate. Our attorneys have us over a barrel with their refusal to go to court."

It got worse. Schiller and Paredes thought the DEA and the Justice Department were being too deferential to McKesson during the settlement talks that spring. At every step, the government lawyers ceded to McKesson's demands. At first, the government lawyers proposed that McKesson lose its DEA registrations to distribute controlled substances for four years at its warehouses in Ohio, Michigan, and Colorado. They also wanted McKesson to lose its registrations for two years at its warehouses in Massachusetts and Florida.

But Hobart, McKesson's attorney, called those requests dealbreakers. He said McKesson would consent to having its DEA registrations temporarily "suspended." If the company lost its registrations—as distinct from having them suspended for a short period—it would have to reapply to the DEA and state regulatory boards, a costly and time-consuming process.

Hobart also demanded a special reprieve be included in the settlement that would permit McKesson to keep sending controlled substances to the Veterans Administration, federal prisons, and the Indian Health Service from its warehouses in Michigan and Ohio. McKesson had lucrative contracts with the federal government, including a $31 billion deal to supply the nation's VA centers. Losing those would be a huge blow to the company's bottom line and its stock price.

Paredes was unsympathetic. "Their bad acts continued and escalated to a level of egregiousness not seen before," she wrote in a memo to the government lawyers negotiating the settlement. "They were neither rehabilitated nor deterred by the 2008 [agreement]."

McKesson had already received the benefit of a similar reprieve in its 2008 settlement, Paredes pointed out. Why should the company get a second chance? The former Navy lawyer also chafed at McKesson still being able to supply America's veterans. It was an insult. The company was not good enough to serve the public, but was "'good enough' to serve veterans?" she asked in her memo.

McKesson responded that disrupting the flow of drugs would

hurt veterans. Paredes dismissed that argument, too. Companies like Cardinal and AmerisourceBergen would be more than happy to take over McKesson's multibillion-dollar contracts.

"Find other distributors," Paredes wrote.

Not only was the McKesson case going up in flames, but the biggest case the DEA had ever brought against a drug maker— Mallinckrodt, the largest manufacturer of generic oxycodone in America—was about to blow up.

Chapter 24

The Mushroom Treatment

DEA Headquarters, 2015

At the end of August, Joe Rannazzisi received a call from a colleague who asked if he was retiring.

"No," Joe said. "Why?"

"Well, they just announced a guy who's going to be taking your job."

Three months earlier, President Obama had named Chuck Rosenberg as the DEA's acting administrator, following the retirement of Michele Leonhart, Joe's longtime boss and ally at the agency. Rosenberg had been a U.S. attorney in Virginia and Texas. As soon as Rosenberg arrived at DEA headquarters that May, Joe had an uneasy feeling. After their first meeting, he thought Rosenberg was standoffish. Soon he heard that Rosenberg was questioning his colleagues about him. "How do you think Joe Rannazzisi runs his division?" he would ask.

One DEA official warned Joe to be careful. "He's got a thing about you," the official said.

Shortly after Joe received the call and learned that he was being replaced, he got another, from one of his friends at the DEA, James Soiles, who was running global operations for the agency.

Soiles told Joe that Rosenberg's number two, Acting Deputy Administrator Jack Riley, wanted to see both of them. Riley, the former special agent in charge of the Chicago field division, was known for his efforts to hunt down Sinaloa Cartel drug kingpin Joaquín "El Chapo" Guzmán, who was caught on wiretaps offering to pay for Riley's assassination. When Rosenberg first arrived at the DEA, Riley told him that the most important task the agency faced was repairing its fractured relationship with Congress. Riley advised Rosenberg to meet with lawmakers and ask them for help. Rosenberg took Riley's advice and began meeting with numerous members of Congress.

Soiles met Joe outside an elevator on the twelfth floor of DEA headquarters near Riley's office. He urged Joe to stay calm.

"Jimmy, what do you mean don't get upset?" Joe said. "I just heard that I don't have a job."

"Dude, don't lose it on this guy," Soiles said.

They walked together into Riley's office and sat down.

"Joe, there's going to be some changes," Riley told him. "They've got a guy coming in to replace you."

Joe couldn't believe what he was hearing. "Jack, I'm not retiring," he said.

"We'll figure that out. Just find a place to sit," Riley told him, ordering him to vacate his office and find a new desk.

"Well, how long do I have?" Joe asked.

"Boss wants you out immediately, so just find a place," Riley said.

"What is my role?" Joe asked.

"I don't know, but right now you've just got to find a place until we can figure out what we're going to do," said Riley.

"So, that's it?" Joe said.

"That's what the boss wants," Riley said. "He's the administrator."

"*Acting* administrator," Joe said to Riley.

As they walked out, Soiles turned to Joe. "Dude, that was impressive."

Joe stopped. "Jimmy, do you honestly think for one second that I'm not burning up inside?"

Joe was disgusted that Rosenberg had tasked Riley with sacking a DEA veteran, one of the highest-ranking senior executive service officials at the agency. He didn't have the guts to do it himself. "The guy sitting in the front office is such a coward, he can't even look me in the eye and tell me he's removing me," Joe told Soiles.

Joe returned to his office. He told Mimi Paredes, John Partridge, and other members of his team what had happened. He was visibly crushed.

It had worked, he told them. The drug industry had finally got what it wanted. When he went home that night, Joe taped his hands with boxing wraps and threw punches at the heavy bag hanging from the rafters in his garage. He pounded the bag for an hour. In the days that followed, his investigators went from room to room to find an empty office for him. They finally found one on the tenth floor in an area nicknamed "The Hinterlands" because it was barren.

After thirty years at the DEA, leading some of the highest-profile nationwide investigations, Joe was being given what was known at the DEA as the "mushroom treatment." He was stuck in a dark office with no people, the equivalent of bureaucratic exile, in the expectation that he would give up and retire. In late September, he submitted his papers.

During his last weeks, Joe packed up boxes of all of the plaques and awards and the coffee mugs he had been given by police departments across the country. He had one last presentation to make to DEA employees. He also had to introduce the man named to replace him, Louis J. Milione, a lawyer, former theater and film actor, and eighteen-year veteran of the agency. It was a painful moment, but Joe wanted to be professional. He tried to hide his feelings as he turned the stage over to Milione, whom he saw as a sycophant who would do Rosenberg's bidding. He took a seat in the front, but he really wanted to walk out the door and not look back.

Taking Joe off the board was good news for the companies that manufactured, distributed, and dispensed opioids; the $12.4 billion opioid market was that much more secure. It was also good news for The Alliance and members of Congress urging passage of a new iteration of the Marino-Blackburn bill, now called S.483. Joe's last line of defense at the Justice Department, Attorney General Eric Holder, had stepped down and returned to private practice at Covington & Burling. President Obama named Loretta E. Lynch to take his place.

The latest version of the bill went even further in its efforts to undermine the DEA: The agency would now have to show that a drug company's practice posed an "immediate" threat before issuing a suppression order—a standard that Joe knew the DEA could never meet. The bill also retained the built-in second chance for companies, allowing them to take corrective action when caught and avoid DEA penalties.

Within days of Joe submitting his retirement papers, John Gray, The Alliance's president, said during a board of directors meeting that the organization's executive committee had agreed on several priorities.

Item Number 1: "Exhaust all efforts to secure passage of S.483."

Chapter 25

An Expensive Speeding Ticket

Detroit, Michigan, 2015

By September 25, 2015, within weeks of Joe Rannazzisi's removal, the DEA and the Justice Department reached a settlement with McKesson. Mimi Paredes's arguments against a deal had been rejected by the DEA's Chief Counsel's Office and the Justice Department.

McKesson would not lose its registrations to distribute narcotics. Instead, the registrations would be suspended in Colorado for three years, in Ohio and Michigan for two, and in Florida for one. The company would get the reprieve it demanded and keep supplying the Veterans Administration, the Indian Health Service, and federal prisons. There would be no criminal charges. No perp walks. No $1 billion fine. Instead, McKesson would pay $150 million to settle the allegations. The fine was $50 million more than the annual compensation package of CEO John Hammergren. For a company with annual revenue of nearly $200 billion, about the same as ExxonMobil, it once again amounted to an expensive speeding ticket, David Schiller thought.

Jim Geldhof was in his office in Detroit when he heard the news. He had once thought the McKesson case would set an example to the rest of the drug industry. No other company would want to endure the pain of prison sentences, registration revocations, crippling fines, and plummeting stock prices. Instead, McKesson prevailed over the DEA and Geldhof thought his agency had become a paper tiger.

Other major DEA cases against the industry were in trouble as well. The case that Geldhof's top investigator, James Rafalski, had built against Masters Pharmaceutical was in serious legal jeopardy. Masters had appealed the agency's decision to file the Immediate Suspension Order and the case was pending before the U.S. Court of Appeals in Washington, D.C., the second most influential judicial panel in the nation. A loss there would make it nearly impossible for the DEA to continue its aggressive enforcement campaign against the drug industry. The stakes couldn't be higher. The industry had lined up an impressive legal team in an all-out effort to secure a win in the Masters case. It included Gregory G. Garre, the solicitor general under President George W. Bush, who had been retained by The Alliance and the National Association of Chain Drug Stores, which filed a brief supporting Masters. Larry Cote, the former DEA lawyer who had joined Linden Barber's private practice, also filed a brief. Cote was representing the Generic Pharmaceutical Association.

Rafalski's other big case was also going sideways. He had been investigating Mallinckrodt for nearly four years. At every turn, Rafalski believed the giant drug maker was dragging out the production of documents that he and Leslie Wizner, the assistant U.S. attorney assigned to the case, were filing with the company. Eventually, Mallinckrodt turned over a quarter million records. As Rafalski and Wizner sifted through the emails, order forms, and client lists, they were astonished by the volume of pills they saw. The Blue Highway between Florida and points north was paved with Mallinckrodt's oxycodone 30mg tablets. Reading the documents, Rafalski believed that people like Victor Borelli, the company's national sales manager who wrote the "Doritos" email, should be under criminal investigation. Internally, Wizner and other federal prosecutors began to formulate the arguments they could make against Mallinckrodt before a jury one day.

"We will argue that thousands of orders from the distributors as well as tens of thousands of orders from these down-stream customers were suspicious because of the pattern of distribution to Florida," they wrote in one internal prosecution memo. They singled out Mallinckrodt's oxycodone shipments to Sunrise Wholesale, the Florida distributor, which then supplied Barry Schultz, the Delray Beach doctor who was later convicted of drug trafficking and sentenced to 157 years in prison. The prosecutors said they had documented a pattern of behavior that was so egregious it could result in civil conspiracy charges against Mallinckrodt.

"Mallinckrodt did knowingly, intentionally and unlawfully combine, conspire, confederate and agree with Sunrise and Barry Schultz to commit offenses against the United States," the prosecutors wrote in a draft complaint against the company. "That is, to knowingly, intentionally and unlawfully distribute, dispense or prescribe controlled substances, including but not limited to the Schedule II drug oxycodone 30 mg."

But the complaint was never filed.

Mallinckrodt had assembled a sophisticated legal team to fend off the allegations. It included Brien T. O'Connor, a former federal prosecutor in Boston who specialized in fraud and corruption cases. O'Connor had an important ally, Linden Barber, who was working on the case.

On July 10, 2015, Wizner sent a proposed settlement to O'Connor. She said the U.S. attorney's office in Detroit had completed its review of the evidence and concluded that Mallinckrodt could face as much as $2.3 billion in fines. She noted that 222,107 orders of oxycodone to Florida were "excessive" and should have been reported as suspicious to the DEA. She also said the federal government could hit the company with a $1.3 billion fine because 217,022,834 of the company's 30mg oxycodone pills had been sold for cash in Florida in 2009 and 2010.

"As you are aware, significant cash sales are an indication of diversion," Wizner wrote in her settlement letter.

She also asserted that Mallinckrodt knew where its pills were going because of the chargeback rebate program Rafalski had uncovered while investigating Harvard Drug five years earlier.

O'Connor countered that there was nothing in the Controlled Substances Act that required Mallinckrodt to determine where its pills went after it shipped them to its distributors. Wizner understood that the debate over how much responsibility a drug maker had for its pills once they went to the retail level presented legal risks for both sides. Jurors could agree with the government, finding that the company knew what was happening to its drugs and should have done something to stop the shipments. But a jury could also return a verdict clearing Mallinckrodt, finding that the law was vague when it came to drug manufacturers. The entire case could fall apart. Wizner proposed settling in exchange for a $70 million fine.

O'Connor argued that it was impossible to monitor all of the fifty-five thousand retail outlets where its drugs had been delivered. He noted that the DEA was aware of the company's increased sales of oxycodone and could have reduced the amount of narcotics the company was permitted to make. Rafalski thought the argument was specious. The DEA sets quotas for the quantities of controlled substances that can be manufactured. Under the law, the agency was required to increase the quota for controlled substances to meet the demand of the prescriptions being written by doctors and the amounts requested by the scientific and research communities. For years, manufacturers had been complaining to Congress that they needed the DEA to increase the quota even more or they would deprive legitimate patients from getting their prescriptions filled.

Negotiations dragged on that summer, with offers and counteroffers over money, and arguments over whether Mallinckrodt had a responsibility to tell the DEA what it knew about its pills that were going downstream and saturating the black market. Threats of setting trial dates came and went without any visible progress in the case.

By the fall, Geldhof was losing his patience. He was planning to retire on January 2, just a few months away, and he wanted to know what was happening with one of his biggest cases. He frequently patrolled the sixth floor of the DEA offices in Detroit, stopping by Rafalski's pod and towering over his desk.

"What's going on? What's taking so long?" Geldhof boomed.

"I haven't heard a thing," Rafalski replied.

It was as if the Mallinckrodt case had fallen into a black hole.

Chapter 26

Banjo

DEA Headquarters, 2015

There is a long-standing tradition at the DEA: When agents retire, one of the agency's top two officials presents them with their retirement credentials. The credentials—a badge and ID enshrined in a leather case—are handed to the retiring agent in a brief but emotional ceremony, capping off a long career. That did not happen for Joe Rannazzisi, who had served the agency for twenty-nine years and six months.

On the morning of his last day, October 30, 2015, Joe received a call from Mark Mazzei, an official in DEA's security programs branch. He asked Joe who should present his credentials—Acting Administrator Chuck Rosenberg or Acting Deputy Administrator Jack Riley?

They were the last two people Joe wanted to touch his credentials.

"Why don't you come over to my office, Mark, and let's talk," Joe said. "And let me see the retirement credentials because I've never seen them before."

When Mazzei arrived at Joe's desk in "The Hinterlands" and showed him his credentials, Joe looked at him. "Mark, I have no respect for Jack Riley. And I have a lot less than that for Chuck Rosenberg. I don't want them touching my credentials. But you're a working agent. I've known you for a long time. I want you to give them to me."

"That's not protocol, Joe," Mazzei replied, noting that Joe was his superior officer.

"Mark, give me my fucking credentials," Joe said. "Hold out your hand. Say, 'Joe, congratulations on a job well done.'"

Mazzei handed Joe the leather case and shook his hand.

"Now I've got my credentials," Joe said.

"What am I going to tell them?" Mazzei asked.

"Tell them I left," Joe said. "I'm done."

Joe saw himself as a casualty of the way Washington worked. Key members of Congress were caving to the drug industry, which helped to finance their campaigns. The lawmakers were putting enormous pressure on DEA administrators to fall in line. If they didn't, Congress could cut the agency's funding and demand leadership changes.

Joe's friend Jimmy Soiles stopped by his desk at two that afternoon. Soiles had decided that under the new regime it was also time for him to retire. This would be his last day as well. No one had organized a formal farewell lunch for Joe. He and Soiles went to the Athena Pallas in Arlington, Joe's favorite Greek restaurant and hangout. At particularly stressful times, he would grab a corner table, order chicken Mediterranean, a house specialty, and quietly ponder his cases. The Athena Pallas lunch with Soiles would have to suffice as Joe's retirement celebration.

The next day, Joe took his two daughters, Rachel and Gabby, and two of their friends to adopt a rescue coonhound mutt that had been brought to a PetSmart in Centreville, Virginia. He drove his Ford Excursion to pick up the puppy, one of seven siblings who had been badly abused. When he arrived at the PetSmart, he saw that the puppy he picked out had mange and was blind in one eye. Someone at PetSmart suggested that he name him Banjo. Joe, a big music fan who plays the guitar, thought the name was perfect.

Driving home, Joe glanced in his rearview mirror to see Banjo cowering in the backseat. He looked hurt and scared.

"Don't worry," Joe said. "I feel the same way."

The days and weeks after leaving the DEA were monotonous and depressing. For nearly thirty years, Joe had gone full throttle, working twelve- to fourteen-hour days, fueled by a constant adrenaline rush. Now there was little to do except train the dog. He would take Banjo on long walks in the woods, trying to nurse the puppy—and himself—back to health.

But Joe couldn't stop thinking about his cases at the DEA. He reread the old cases—Cardinal, McKesson, Masters, Amerisource-Bergen, Mallinckrodt, Walgreens, CVS. *What more could we have done?* he wondered. Were there other steps that he and his team could have taken to protect the public?

Over and over, he listened to a recording of the oral arguments in his favorite Supreme Court case—*United States v. Moore*. He traced his life's work back to this landmark 1975 case—it was the linchpin to all the cases Joe had built against the industry. In *Moore*, an appeals court had overturned the conviction of a Washington, D.C., doctor who unlawfully prescribed methadone. The doctor sold prescriptions for large quantities of the narcotic to his patients. On one day, he wrote 271 prescriptions without performing a single physical exam.

In his October 7, 1975, oral argument, Assistant Solicitor General Paul L. Friedman said that the evidence was overwhelming that the doctor had acted no differently than a street-corner drug pusher. The lawyer for the doctor said his client was protected from being prosecuted because he was registered to sell the drugs by the DEA. But Justice Thurgood Marshall noted that under the Controlled Substances Act, licensed doctors or drug companies are not protected when they act illegally.

"A wholesaler can sell a million dollars' worth of methadone to the Mafia and he can't be convicted?" Marshall asked rhetorically.

Joe was struck by how Marshall seemed to anticipate what would happen in the future. The case was argued thirty years before the opioid epidemic. The Supreme Court ruled unanimously in favor of upholding the doctor's conviction.

One day, Joe's daughter Rachel saw him rereading the cases. "Dad," she said. "You're not with the DEA anymore. Why do you keep doing this?"

"These cases were my life," Joe told her.

As he continued reading, Joe was struck by something else. With each drug company he investigated, a voluminous number of court documents had been produced. Joe and his investigators had left a bright trail for any attorney to bring a civil action. Where were all the mass tort lawyers?

That question also haunted Jim Geldhof. On Christmas Day 2015, he and his family gathered at his home in Lake Orion, Michigan, an hour north of Detroit. They sat around the dining room table, platters of Beef Wellington, mashed potatoes, and vegetables spread out before them. Geldhof was one week away from retirement after his forty-three-year career—and feeling morose. The McKesson case had been settled without serious consequences for the company. The future of the Masters case remained uncertain. The Mallinckrodt case was in limbo. Joe had been removed from his job. The Marino-Blackburn bill was hurtling through Congress. Geldhof remembered the grieving families he had met. It was hard to give himself over to the holiday celebration. Toward the end of dinner, the conversation turned to his retirement. His youngest son, Matt, perhaps sensing his father's mood, asked an unexpected question.

"Dad, what's the most disappointing thing that happened in your career?"

"That's an easy one," Geldhof said. "That the American people will never know what these companies did to our country. They'll never know."

PART 2

THE
RECKONING: 2016–2022

Multi-District Litigation Trial Locations

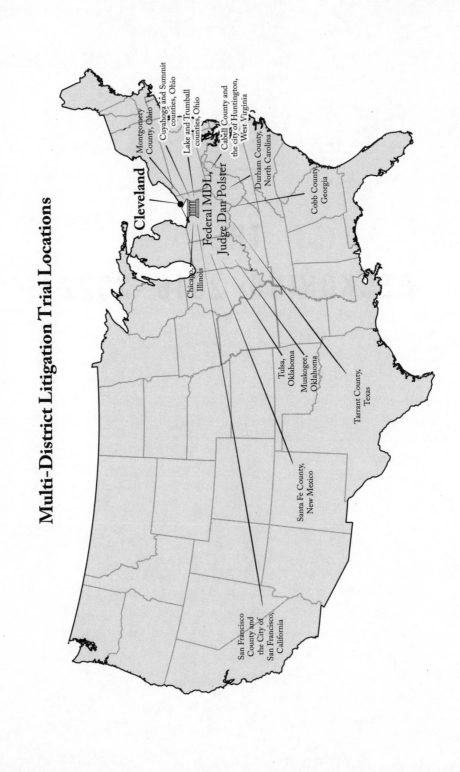

Montgomery County, Ohio

Cuyahoga and Summit counties, Ohio

Lake and Trumball counties, Ohio

Cabell County and the city of Huntington, West Virginia

Cleveland

Federal MDL, Judge Dan Polster

Durham County, North Carolina

Cobb County, Georgia

Chicago, Illinois

Tulsa, Oklahoma

Muskogee, Oklahoma

Tarrant County, Texas

Santa Fe County, New Mexico

San Francisco County and the City of San Francisco, California

Chapter 27

A Public Nuisance

Washington, D.C., 2017

On February 10, 2017, Paul T. Farrell Jr., a small-town lawyer from Huntington, West Virginia, climbed into his Chevy Silverado pickup shortly before dawn and drove six hours to Arlington. The forty-two-year-old pulled into a parking spot near DEA headquarters and walked to the marbled lobby of the towering black-and-tan glass and steel building across the Potomac River from Washington. Built like a linebacker and sporting a soldier's buzz cut, Paul was an intimidating figure. He didn't have an appointment. And he didn't care. He was determined to speak with the DEA agent in charge of the D.C. field office, which happened to oversee his home state. Even if he couldn't see the agent, Paul wanted to make sure the high-ranking law enforcement official was aware of his presence.

Ever since his younger brother had challenged him during Sunday breakfast two months earlier to do something about the opioid epidemic in West Virginia, Paul had been trying to determine if there was a civil case to be made against the drug industry. After reading an investigative report in his local newspaper, he had concluded that ARCOS, the agency's pill-tracking database, held crucial information that could be the foundation of a potential case. If he got lucky and the DEA supervisor he had come to see, Karl

Colder, was willing to talk to him, he might find out how he could get access to ARCOS. The database, he believed, would reveal the identities of the companies that had hollowed out his hometown and thousands of other communities across the country. It would show precisely how many pills each company had shipped, where they had shipped them, and which pharmacies had parceled them out.

Paul also planned to go to the Library of Congress during his Washington field trip, hoping to find a friendly researcher who would guide him through the archives. Paul had read that the drug companies had objected to some of the reporting requirements contained in the Controlled Substances Act prior to its passage in 1970. If he could find their statements in old copies of the *Federal Register*, he might be able to use them to reinforce his case. How could the companies say they didn't know they were obliged to stop shipping enormous orders of pain pills when they had objected to those very same requirements five decades earlier?

But more than anything else that day, Paul wanted to find Joe Rannazzisi. He had read about the DEA agent turned whistleblower, and his fierce but futile battle against the drug companies, in an investigative series published by the *Washington Post* the previous fall. Paul imagined Joe as his star witness one day, telling rapt jurors about his decade-long fight to hold the drug industry accountable.

Two months before Paul's trip to Washington, the *Charleston Gazette-Mail* in West Virginia had published a blockbuster investigation into the opioid industry. The paper's star investigative reporter, Eric Eyre, obtained partial access to ARCOS and discovered that drug distributors had dumped 780 million doses of oxycodone and hydrocodone into the state between 2007 and 2012. McKesson, Cardinal, and AmerisourceBergen were responsible for shipping more than half of those pills. The DEA provided the ARCOS data to the attorney general of West Virginia, who had sued the drug distributors. (Eyre's newspaper had won access to this data after filing suit.)

Cardinal and AmerisourceBergen settled with the attorney general, paying a combined $36 million. Paul thought the amount was a pittance and none of the money would ever reach his hometown. He had a strategy for a bigger payday that would benefit all of the towns and counties in the state.

After Eyre's story appeared, Paul filed fifteen Freedom of Information Act requests with the DEA seeking agency documents about the drug companies, as well as access to ARCOS. He received nothing but pro forma acknowledgments. He also left numerous messages for Colder, to no avail. He was tired of being stonewalled. Time to doorstep the DEA agent.

"Hi, I'm Paul Farrell and I'm here to see Karl Colder," Paul told the receptionist in the lobby of DEA headquarters.

"I'm sorry. Who are you?" she asked.

"I'm Paul Farrell. I'm a lawyer from West Virginia and I'm here to see Karl Colder."

"Hold on," she said.

Fifteen minutes later, the receptionist summoned Paul back to the front desk. "I'm sorry, Mr. Farrell," she said. "He's not available."

"Can I speak to his assistant?" Paul asked.

"Can I take a message, Mr. Farrell?"

"The message is, I'd like to speak to Karl Colder."

"I'm sorry, Mr. Farrell. You're going to have to make an appointment."

Farrell knew he wasn't going to have much success at DEA headquarters that morning. But that wasn't the point. He wanted to fire a warning shot: The lawyer from West Virginia wasn't going away. Paul had been raised to be relentless, told by his mother, Charlene, from an early age that God had a plan for him. As a good Catholic who went to Our Lady of Fatima most Sundays and said grace before dinner every night, Paul believed that his mother might be right. He doted on her and admired her commitment to their town, where she had founded a hospice care facility three decades earlier. She also volunteered for the Red Cross and raced to New

York in the aftermath of the 9/11 terror attacks and to New Orleans following Hurricane Katrina. The need to do some good was a family trait.

Sometimes it seemed like there were as many Farrells as pickups in Huntington, a small city of forty-eight thousand people on the banks of the Ohio River that had boomed during the best coal mining years in West Virginia and eastern Kentucky. The Farrells had arrived in the United States from Ireland. Paul's great-grandfather settled in New York's Hell's Kitchen and worked as a police officer before dying from pneumonia during the 1918 flu pandemic. Paul's grandfather was a flight surgeon in World War II and went to work as a doctor at the VA hospital in Huntington after the war ended. The family found a region full of economic promise—and they thrived. One of the downtown buildings is named for the family. For decades, the building was occupied by the law firm of Farrell, Farrell & Farrell. It was run by his uncles and his father, Paul Sr., who started out as a prosecutor in Huntington. Paul Sr. went on to help coordinate federal drug task forces in the region and became a West Virginia circuit court judge. Paul followed his father in the field, graduating from the West Virginia University College of Law in Morgantown in 1997 after attending Notre Dame.

At first, Paul joined the family firm, defending doctors and health care organizations in medical malpractice lawsuits, known as "med mal" cases, before striking out on his own. He signed on to a firm in Morgantown, where he switched and began to represent patients harmed or killed by defective medical devices. In 2011, he became one of the lead attorneys in national litigation against manufacturers of transvaginal mesh, a surgically implanted device that caused serious injuries to thousands of women. Two of Paul's cases resulted in $20 million jury verdicts.

While he chased big paydays, Paul also had an idealistic streak. In 2016, he ran a quixotic campaign in his home state as a Democratic candidate for U.S. president. He was not a cautious person. He signed on to causes, always confident of his success. He was a pushy, fearless doer—arrogant and romantic in equal measure.

Paul came in third in the state, surprising everyone but himself. He hoped to bring national attention to the economic ruin in West Virginia following the collapse of the coal industry. He even beat Hillary Clinton in one of the hardest-hit counties in West Virginia, Mingo; the county is site of the legendary feuds between the Hatfields and McCoys, and the bloody labor clashes in the 1920s between coal miners and the Pinkerton cops their bosses had hired to crush the rebellion in the town of Matewan.

The day after his brother's challenge to do something about the epidemic, Paul had an epiphany: What if the conduct of the drug distributors was treated as a public nuisance? He knew that West Virginia had created a law decades earlier to clean up illegal trash dumps, and later to demolish crack houses and shut down strip clubs. It had seldom been used, even though it conferred broad powers to counties in the state to eliminate hazards to the public health and fine those who created them. Paul began to envision using the same tool designed to address a municipal nuisance, like dumping trash, to prove that the drug distributors had created a public hazard by dumping enormous amounts of oxycodone and hydrocodone into his community. He unearthed an obscure passage deep in the West Virginia code, the sort of lines that most law students would have breezed past in search of more exciting material. He only needed to absorb the first section of Chapter 7 to know that he was on to something. It gave county commissioners the power to eliminate "hazards to the public health and safety and to abate or cause to be abated anything which the commission determines to be a public nuisance."

Tie the wanton dumping of pills to the nuisance statute and liability could follow. It was a novel theory. Some lawyers had started to test it in other cases against the drug industry. How many other states or counties around the country had similar statutes on their books, he wondered?

Paul started poring over cases. Anything to do with pills. That's when he spotted what he was looking for: *Cardinal Health, Inc. v. Eric H. Holder Jr.*, the 2012 investigation that pitted Joe Rannazzisi against James Cole, the deputy attorney general of the Justice Department. He read and reread the thirty-four-page declaration Joe had filed in the case. It was a blow-by-blow account of how Cardinal had ignored its legal obligations to halt blatantly suspicious drug orders and report them to the DEA. It also detailed how the company had shipped vast amounts of oxycodone to a string of pharmacies in Florida, including the two CVS stores in Sanford, Florida. Paul also found the case the DEA had brought against Masters Pharmaceutical, the Ohio-based company that flooded Florida with 30mg oxycodone "blues" made by Mallinckrodt. Finally, he turned up the DEA cases against McKesson and AmerisourceBergen, two companies he had never heard of before. He downloaded every document he could find—every motion, affidavit, and hearing transcript in the cases against the companies. By accepting fines and promising to change their practices, it seemed to Paul that each of these companies had essentially pleaded guilty to unlawful conduct on a national scale.

Paul also discovered another organization he never knew existed, the Healthcare Distribution Alliance—a group that appeared to be at the center of the fight between the DEA and the drug industry. In both the Cardinal and the Masters cases, The Alliance had filed friend-of-the-court briefs supporting the companies. To Paul, the briefs read like industry claims of blanket immunity from DEA oversight.

His head was swimming with the minutiae of those cases on the day he made his unannounced visit to DEA headquarters. After he'd been rebuffed, he headed over to the Library of Congress, the grand building across the street from the U.S. Capitol. He stepped into the opulent reading room and was impressed by its majesty, the soaring domed ceiling with ten-foot-high statues representing religion, philosophy, art, poetry, commerce, science, history, and the law.

"Hi, I'm Paul Farrell and I'm looking for the legislative history of these documents," he said to the librarian, handing her a copy of the *Federal Register* from 1970. During the public notice period a year before, he told her, there had been objections to drug distribution measures under consideration by Congress, and he would like to see them.

"Well, you'll have to file a request for that," she said.

"I already have," Paul replied. "Where can I find these types of documents?"

"Well, they're certainly not here," she said.

"Do you know where they are?"

The librarian left her post and returned a few minutes later. "My understanding is, if these documents exist, they'll be in a warehouse maintained by the DEA in Virginia. Have you tried the DEA?"

Paul had one final stop to make that February day. He drove across town to the W hotel near the White House where he was staying and walked a few blocks to meet with two reporters for the *Washington Post* who had written the investigative series about Joe. Paul said he had some documents he wanted to share; he was really hoping to obtain Joe's unpublished phone number.

"Hey, do you guys have a phone number for Joe Rannazzisi?"

They did, but they told him they couldn't give it out without Joe's permission. They told Paul they would pass along his contact information.

If Joe wanted to talk, he'd give Paul a call.

Joe never did.

Chapter 28

"Our Allies"

Washington, D.C., 2017

There was a reason Joe Rannazzisi didn't call Paul Farrell in February. Three months earlier, he was walking to dinner at P.F. Chang's off the Las Vegas Strip when he felt a throbbing ache in his stomach. *Probably indigestion*, he thought. It was December 2016, a little over a year after Joe had been pushed out of the DEA.

When Joe first left the agency, a former colleague, Jimmy Craig, often called to check on him. "What are you going to do? Sit around and mope all day? Why don't you get a job?"

Joe said he wasn't ready. Craig persisted. "We've got to talk," he said. "Dude, I'm worried about you sitting there all day. You and that stupid dog of yours."

Joe laughed. Craig worked at a software company that contracted with government agencies and was developing a system that identified anomalies in drug ordering patterns. They were looking for someone with Joe's skills.

"Why don't you apply?" Craig asked him.

Joe was hired.

One day, after he began his new job in 2016, Joe received an unexpected call from Richard W. Fields, a lawyer who was representing the Cherokee Nation in Oklahoma, the largest federally recognized tribe in the country. The Cherokee were going to file the first tribal lawsuit against the opioid industry. Fields had read about Joe and the DEA cases he brought against the drug distributors. He also had a personal experience with opioids: Fields's own brother became addicted to opioids after suffering back injuries as a sheet metal worker. Fields found Joe through a mutual acquaintance at the DEA. Would he be interested in helping? Fields asked.

Joe agreed to meet. Prescription pain pills had ravaged the Cherokee Nation, Fields told Joe. The social services, medical, law enforcement, and foster care systems were overwhelmed by families struggling with addiction. He needed Joe's expertise. Joe was moved by the plight of the Cherokees and said he would like to help. But he had just started his new job and needed to concentrate on his work. He told Fields to stay in touch.

That December, Joe, along with Craig's son, Dustin, who also worked for the software company, flew to Las Vegas to staff the company's booth at the American Society of Hospital Pharmacists at the Mandalay Bay Resort. The convention drew twenty thousand people, and Joe was so busy, he didn't have time to leave the resort. He grabbed lunch and dinner at the hotel's overflowing buffet tables. Too many questionable buffet items were probably causing his indigestion, he thought. On his last night, he and his colleagues met at P.F. Chang's for dinner. Joe felt worse after dinner. As he left the restaurant, the pain in his stomach became so unbearable he had to stop walking.

"You okay?" Craig asked.

"I'm fine," he said.

Joe flew home early the next day, still feeling ill. When he landed, he called his doctor, who told him to come to his office immediately.

"You don't have indigestion," he told him. "You might be having a slow-onset heart attack."

Joe couldn't believe it. "I'm not showing any symptoms of a heart attack," he said. "I don't have shooting pain. There's no chest pressure."

Joe's skepticism—and stubbornness—kept him from going to a

cardiologist for several days. When he finally saw the specialists, one doctor performed a heart catheterization; Joe had blockages in three arteries.

"I'll see you in recovery," the doctor said.

Just before surgery, a nurse asked Joe if he needed anything. He asked for a priest. As he was wheeled into the operating room, a priest came by and blessed him.

While recovering in the hospital following seven-hour open-heart triple bypass surgery, Joe thought back on everything that had happened over the previous year. How could he be jogging forty miles a week and end up under the knife? It was the damned DEA, he concluded. Leaving the agency hadn't ended the seething resentments, and he was affronted by new slights that he felt just as keenly from afar. The new officials running the DEA had exiled his top supervisors. His senior deputy, John Partridge, was transferred to Colorado. His executive assistant, John Scherbenske, was told he was going to be transferred to Dallas. He retired instead. His most trusted legal counsel, Mimi Paredes, was demoted into irrelevancy. At forty-eight, her career was now in jeopardy. She had taken a six-month maternity leave around the time Joe left. Upon returning, DEA officials gave Paredes the same "mushroom treatment" they gave to Joe. They stripped her of her drug diversion work and assigned her to an office with nothing to do. At night, she would come home to her baby daughter, put her to bed, and cry.

Paredes reached out to Joe for support. He felt that he was to blame. His team had become collateral damage.

On March 17, 2016, four and a half months after Joe left the agency, Kentucky Republican Mitch McConnell, the Senate majority leader, brought the latest version of the Marino-Blackburn bill to the Senate floor. By then, the DEA had dropped its opposition. Behind-the-scenes lobbying had weakened the ability of the agency to resist. A senior DEA official said that the agency had battled the bill for years in the face of growing pressure from key members of Congress and the industry. He said the agency was forced to accept a deal it didn't want, one that made it nearly impossible to issue Immediate Suspension Orders. "They would have passed this with us or without us," he said. The final bill defined "imminent danger" as "a substantial likelihood of an immediate threat that death, serious bodily harm, or abuse of a controlled substance will occur in the absence of an immediate suspension of the registration." The second chance "corrective action" provision remained intact.

It passed by unanimous consent, a parliamentary procedure reserved for bills considered to be noncontroversial. Because no senator objected, a recorded vote was unnecessary. On April 12, 2016, the House passed the bill using the same procedure. It was the crowning achievement of a two-year-long campaign by the drug industry to weaken the DEA's aggressive enforcement efforts. Joe was livid. He also felt a kind of despair at how much of his work had been undone.

The drug industry had spent $60 million lobbying Congress on the bill and other legislation between 2014 and 2016. Political action committees representing the industry contributed at least $1.5 million to the campaigns of the twenty-three lawmakers who sponsored or cosponsored various versions of the bill. Tom Marino collected $93,500, Marsha Blackburn $128,850, and Republican senator Orrin G. Hatch of Utah, a longtime friend of the drug industry, received $197,700. Hatch was one of the key sponsors of the bill in the Senate, along with Democratic senator Sheldon Whitehouse of Rhode Island, home to CVS. Hatch's office handled negotiations with the DEA and the Justice Department over its final language.

Hatch had also worked on the final language with representatives of the drug industry, including lobbyists for Purdue Pharma. The night the House approved the bill, Burt Rosen, Purdue Pharma's vice president for government affairs, applauded its passage in an email to colleagues. In another sign of how closely the industry was collaborating, Rosen noted that for two years he had been working to pass the bill with members of The Alliance and the National Association of Chain Drug Stores.

"Purdue was very active in influencing the ultimate definition of an 'imminent danger to the public health or safety,'" Rosen boasted in the email.

With Joe, most members of his team, Attorney General Eric Holder, and DEA administrator Michele Leonhart all gone from government service, there were no high-level officials left to oppose the bill. Neither Chuck Rosenberg, the new acting DEA chief, nor anyone in power at the Justice Department pushed back. With no objections, President Obama signed it into law on April 19, 2016.

On June 22, Rosenberg testified on Capitol Hill before the Senate Judiciary Committee. Hatch praised him from the dais. "I've been told the DEA's relationship with supply chain stakeholders has improved since you've taken the helm at DEA," Hatch said. "I want to just say I applaud your efforts on this front." The senator asked Rosenberg how he saw the "partnership" between the agency and the drug industry "evolving."

"Thank you for that," Rosenberg replied. He noted that there were 1.6 million health care professionals and drug companies with DEA registrations, allowing them to manufacture, prescribe, sell, or distribute controlled substances.

"The overwhelming majority, 99-plus percent, are our allies in this thing. Historically, we've done a very good job of alienating them. I'm being sarcastic. What we need is them as partners," Rosenberg said. "I think we've been slow. I think we've been opaque. I think we haven't responded to them."

He promised to repair the relationship between the DEA and the drug companies. Rosenberg told Hatch that he had hired a new chief of the division Joe once supervised. "I have a new head of diversion, and actually he is a star," Rosenberg said.

Joe was watching the hearing on C-SPAN. Joe's name hadn't been mentioned. But Rosenberg's diss was obvious. Several of his former colleagues called.

"Rosenberg just bitch-slapped you," one said.

"Are you watching this?" another asked.

"No," Joe lied. "What hearing?"

Months later, while recovering in the hospital, Joe would wake up to find a friend from the DEA sitting by his side. DEA administrative law judge John Mulrooney had dropped by to cheer him up. Joe opened his eyes and saw Mulrooney sitting in a chair, looking at his phone.

"It's about time you got up," Mulrooney said. "I was about to leave. It's kind of rude that I came all this way to see you and you're asleep."

Joe smiled. He looked up at the day board next to Mulrooney. A nurse had written her name and listed Joe's goal for the day: Walk three loops around the ward. But next to it, someone had added more goals in different handwriting: "Run a 10K. Invent a better mousetrap. Write a novel."

Joe started laughing so hard his chest hurt.

A nurse walked in. "Stop!" she told Mulrooney. "You have to stop making him laugh." She looked at Joe with alarm. "You're going to split your sternum!"

When Joe returned home in the first week of January 2017, there was a message on his answering machine from the man who had sidelined him. "Joe, this is Chuck Rosenberg. I heard you got heart surgery. And I was just worried about you. I wanted to check up on you."

That was another call Joe didn't return.

Chapter 29

"They're Gonna Get Hammered"

Huntington, West Virginia, 2017

Paul Farrell settled into his windowless law office in an old bank building in downtown Huntington and fired up his computer. He clicked on a link to the website of the U.S. Court of Appeals in Washington and began listening to a recording of the January 12 oral arguments in a case that could well determine his own ability to take on the opioid industry.

During his weeks of research, Paul had come across the efforts of DEA supervisor Jim Geldhof and his investigator, James Rafalski, to sanction drug distributor Masters Pharmaceutical. After a seven-year odyssey, the matter was finally before a three-judge panel on the U.S. Court of Appeals for the District of Columbia Circuit.

Richard T. Lauer, an attorney based in Cincinnati who served as the general counsel for Masters, was trying to convince the judges that the DEA had no authority to require drug companies to monitor orders of narcotics, report suspiciously large shipments, or work to keep painkillers out of the hands of the pill mills. If Lauer prevailed, any civil litigation would be stopped in its tracks. The ruling would set a precedent for the industry and the DEA.

Lauer began by telling the judges that the DEA had saddled the drug industry with new regulations without going through the federal government's rule-making process. Under the law, he argued, drug distributors like Masters were not responsible for what happened to the pills once they reached the pharmacies. The DEA, he said, was not only demanding that distributors monitor their customers and withhold suspiciously large orders, it was also requiring that the companies conduct "due diligence" investigations when there was reason to believe the pills were being siphoned off to the black market.

"Do you agree that there was a duty in place already to disclose suspicious orders?" U.S. district judge Sri Srinivasan asked Lauer.

"There is a duty to identify and report suspicious orders, yes," Lauer conceded.

"So, a lot of the things that you've ticked off sound like they're just commensurate with the duty to identify and report suspicious orders," noted the judge, who served as principal deputy solicitor general and argued two dozen cases before the U.S. Supreme Court before being named to the bench by President Obama.

Lauer countered that the DEA had crafted "an entirely new definition of suspicious orders, which has to do with the pharmacy placing the order. It is simply not a reasonable—"

"I'm not entirely following what you're saying," Srinivasan interrupted.

It was still early in the forty-six-minute-long hearing, but Paul sensed that Lauer was in trouble. The judges' questions were sharp and skeptical and Lauer was rowing against a bad set of facts.

Masters had paid a $500,000 fine in 2009 for supplying the internet pharmacies with "extraordinarily large amounts" of hydrocodone, the highly addictive opioid contained in pain pills such as Vicodin. To settle that case, Masters promised the DEA that it would track its shipments and set limits for how many pills its pharmacy customers could order. The company also pledged to set up a suspicious order monitoring system to flag and stop dangerously large orders of drugs. But a year after paying the fine, Masters shipped another thirty-eight million tablets of oxycodone across the country, twenty-five million of them to its Florida customers. Rafalski discovered during his investigation that oxycodone 15mg and 30mg pills accounted for 60 percent of the narcotics Masters distributed in 2009 and 2010—and forty-four of its top fifty customers were based in Florida. He also found that Masters ignored the customer limits it had set. He noted in legal filings that the company had deleted or edited excessive orders to make them appear to fall below the limits.

Lauer tried to stay on message. The DEA was requiring his company to monitor and stop large orders of pain pills, he told the judges. The agency was also demanding that companies like Masters investigate the conduct of their customers. Lauer countered that the agency was being "unreasonable" and misinterpreting existing laws. If the DEA wanted to go that far, it should have given notice to the drug companies and sought their input.

Judge Cornelia T. L. Pillard interjected, asking a question that dripped with skepticism: Did Lauer really think companies had no duty to investigate if they knew pharmacies were engaging in illegal practices?

"I'm just trying to understand your position," she told him.

Lauer agreed there was a duty. But he maintained that his client didn't know its customers were engaged in illegal activity, an argument the DEA dismissed as disingenuous. The company had to know—or should have known—that the pharmacies were not following the law because of the enormous amounts of oxycodone tablets it was pouring into Florida, many of them the 30mg "blues" made by Mallinckrodt.

The attorney representing the Justice Department in the case, Nicolas Y. Riley, urged the judges to look at the facts the DEA had uncovered. Rafalski had examined twenty-one of Masters's pharmacy customers and found glaring violations at eight of them in Florida and Nevada. Riley highlighted one of the stores for the judges, Englewood Specialty Pharmacy near Fort Myers on the west coast of Florida. Between April 1, 2009, and September 30, 2010, Masters had shipped 1.2 million pills to Englewood. Masters had set a 50,000 monthly limit for that store, but was sending it 70,000. Riley told the judges that Masters reduced that number on paper to 50,000, and then shipped 20,000 additional pills to Englewood without recording the additional sales in a way that would have flagged them under reporting requirements. It was straight-up deceit.

Riley told the judges that Masters had been warned by Joe Rannazzisi in the letters he sent to the drug distributors in 2006 and 2007. He also noted that the DEA had met one-on-one with Masters executives in 2009. During that meeting, the DEA warned that some of their shipments appeared to violate the law. Despite the warnings, Masters kept shipping—even when it became clear to the company itself that the orders were suspect.

"Masters," Riley noted, "believes some of these orders were suspicious."

"And, therefore, should have been reported?" Srinivasan said.

"And, therefore, should have been reported," Riley responded. "Exactly."

Listening to the hearing at his office, Paul was exhilarated. He thought the arguments by Lauer were "tone deaf" and made no sense. The company had agreed in its settlement with the DEA to follow the reporting requirements—the same requirements it was now challenging in federal court.

Paul couldn't have hoped for a better hearing. He played back the arguments over and over, before signing out of the court's website. He would have to wait months for the appellate panel to hand down its decision.

But he was confident of how the judges would interpret what Masters had done.

They're gonna get hammered.

Chapter 30

On the Road

Williamson, West Virginia, Spring 2017

The commissioners in Mingo County, West Virginia, had an urgent problem—no heat. Unhappy employees were coming to work in the courthouse in Williamson, the county seat, in winter coats and mittens. And the thousands required to buy a new boiler was more than the county's depleted budget could easily sustain.

Located along the Kentucky border, in the middle of a web of interstate highways, Mingo County had become a hot spot for opioid users and dealers in the Appalachian Mountains and the Ohio River valley. Between 2006 and 2014, drug distributors such as McKesson, AmerisourceBergen, and Cardinal Health shipped more than 43 million opioid pills into Mingo, enough for 179 tablets per person per year. Each day, hundreds of people would line up at the doors of the two pharmacies in Williamson, waiting for hours to fill their hydrocodone and oxycodone prescriptions, many of them written by physicians at the pill mills of South Florida.

To meet the demand, drug distributors shipped 9.8 million pills to Tug Valley Pharmacy on Second Avenue in Williamson's tiny downtown between 2006 and 2014. They sent another 9.8 million to the second pharmacy, Hurley Drug Company. The two drugstores were two-tenths of a mile apart—in a town of just twenty-nine hundred.

Paul Farrell sat in the back of the courthouse meeting room, where county commission meetings were held. He had requested time to pitch the commissioners on joining his public nuisance lawsuit. The busted boiler might be a godsend for him. He was offering the impoverished county the possibility of winning a significant cash judgment.

"As you've read in the newspapers, the volume of pills is unforgivable," he began. He told the commissioners that a recent multimillion-dollar settlement between the West Virginia attorney general and several drug distributors would leave little money for forgotten places like Mingo. Much of it would go to legal fees and state projects that had nothing to do with addressing the epidemic.

Paul said he planned to file his lawsuits in federal court, and counties like Mingo would be the clients; individual counties could recover the millions they had spent fighting the epidemic. For Paul, it was a deeply personal cause. He knew so many families in Huntington who had lost a relative or a friend to the opioid epidemic.

"I have a plan," he told them, detailing his public nuisance theory. "You can pull up a chair to the table and have your own voice in this discussion."

At first the commissioners were skeptical. Some said the epidemic was the fault of drug users, not the companies. "Isn't this an individual's choice, these drug users who are overdosing?" one asked.

"Look, we're not bringing this case on behalf of the people that are addicted," Paul responded. "We're bringing this case on behalf of those of us that have to pay for the damage."

"We're almost bankrupt paying for the jails," another commissioner said. "We're spending all this money on emergency rooms, ambulance drivers. We can recoup that money?"

"Yes," Paul said. "I'll do it on contingency. If I win, then I get my expenses back and get paid. If I lose, I eat all the expenses and you owe me nothing."

Paul left the meeting without sealing the deal. But he was making progress. While the Mingo lawmakers were debating among themselves whether to hire him, he was signing up a handful of other counties as winter turned to spring. With his West Virginia roots and passion for the cause, Paul was becoming a successful salesman. On March 9, 2017, he filed his first suit in U.S. district court in Charleston, West Virginia, on behalf of his own county, Cabell. It was a thirty-eight-page public nuisance complaint against the Big Three distributors, as well as CVS, Walgreens, Rite Aid, Walmart, Kroger, and H.D. Smith, a small drug distribution outfit with a large presence in West Virginia. Paul initially figured he would find additional counties willing to join his fledgling civil action, file a few more lawsuits, and start fighting the companies in court. He soon began to realize that he needed allies.

That spring, he ran into a lawyer he had worked with years earlier, Michael J. Fuller Jr. A college tennis star and former Florida prosecutor who owned his own plane, Fuller co-ran a successful law firm in Mississippi, McHugh Fuller. He made his living suing nursing homes for negligence on behalf of patients who had died or been badly abused. The cases were horrific. They seemed to be everywhere, and Fuller was a serial winner of large judgments. Paul had worked on a West Virginia case with him in which they secured a $91 million judgment, one of the largest in the state's history.

Paul called Fuller, figuring he could use his expertise as well as the deep pockets of his law firm to help underwrite the litigation.

"I've got enough on my plate," Fuller told him. "I'm still killing these nursing home cases."

"C'mon, you gotta be kidding me," Paul said.

"Sorry. Good luck."

Paul, as always, wouldn't take no for an answer. He went around him, contacting a trial lawyer he knew in Fuller's firm, Amy J. Quezon. He pitched his idea to her. Intrigued, she asked Fuller if she could pursue Paul's public nuisance theory and see where it might lead her and the law firm.

"Knock yourself out," Fuller told her.

As Quezon dug deeper into public nuisance statutes and the

potential for a large civil action, she briefed Fuller. He began to change his mind.

Fuller gave Paul a call. "Are you interested in taking this show on the road?" he asked. "There are way more communities out there than the ones in your corner of West Virginia."

"Sure," Paul said.

Fuller suggested they team up with a law firm in Charleston—Hill, Peterson, Carper, Bee & Deitzler. The firm was known for its work on the DuPont Teflon case that was later depicted in the movie *Dark Waters*. Lawyers for the plaintiffs argued that DuPont knew that C8—the key chemical it used to manufacture Teflon—was highly toxic and could cause cancer. Starting in the 1950s, the company dumped huge amounts of C8 into the Ohio River from one of its plants near Parkersburg, West Virginia. In 2017, DuPont settled the case for nearly $671 million.

Hill Peterson served as the local counsel in that case. It was brought by one of the largest mass tort litigation law firms in the nation, Levin Papantonio Rafferty, based in Pensacola, Florida. Paul knew one of its partners, Mike "Pap" Papantonio, the lead attorney in the DuPont case. Paul was beginning to see the makings of a powerhouse national team. He also knew Russell W. Budd, the partner of another large plaintiffs' firm in Dallas, Baron & Budd, which had made its name by winning billions in asbestos-related mesothelioma lawsuits.

Paul began to imagine the possibilities. His tiny stream of cases could turn into a flood. With a who's who of the nation's top plaintiffs' lawyers on his side, he saw himself leading the way and becoming the field general in the battle against the drug industry and its legions of lawyers working for the nation's most prestigious law firms. The consortium he was trying to build would be able to contribute millions toward working up the case—taking depositions, filing discovery demands, reviewing millions of pages of documents, locating and interviewing witnesses and experts. It would also have hundreds of young associates at its disposal, hungry to handle whatever work came their way.

Paul crafted an ambitious plan to pinpoint opioid hot spots around the nation. He wanted to overlay three data sets on a map of the United States: pill distribution numbers, overdose deaths, and the distribution of benzodiazepine pills such as Xanax, which users took to boost the potency of painkillers. After identifying the hot spots, he planned to appear before local governments in those regions and pitch his public nuisance idea. They could crisscross Appalachia in Fuller's four-seat Cessna 335 twin-prop plane.

With Hill Peterson and Levin Papantonio Rafferty on board, Paul reached out to Budd, the Dallas lawyer who could add millions more to the war chest. He sketched out his idea for Budd.

"Are you interested?" he asked.

"I'm in," Budd said.

Chapter 31

Field of Dreams

Huntington, West Virginia, July 1987

Fifteen-year-old Paul Farrell stood with his father on a grassy hill that served as the outfield bleachers for the All-Star Little League game in downtown Huntington. It was a muggy July evening and the ballfield was buzzing. Hundreds of fans from town had turned out to watch the game and the star of the team, Mark Zban, the latest sensation to emerge from a legendary local family of athletes. His uncle had played football at Marshall and was drafted by the New York Giants. Another uncle played basketball for the university. One of Zban's brothers was a star player on three high school state championship baseball teams. Another brother won a full scholarship to play quarterback for Virginia Tech.

As the youngest of six, it was Mark's turn. He was only twelve, but he had quick wrists, a powerful swing, and the presence of a much older, seasoned player. Down a run, with a runner on base, Zban stepped into the batter's box. Spectators lined the fences along the baselines. Zban's bat sliced across home plate as he effortlessly launched a fastball high into the early evening sky.

For Paul, it was a slow-motion, cinematic experience as he watched the ball sail over the outfield fence and clear the small metal scoreboard. Zban ran the bases like a gazelle as the crowd roared. When he trotted around third, his teammates streamed out of the dugout and mobbed him when he reached home. His two-run shot had won the game.

Paul looked up at his father. "Wow," was all he could say.

Paul's family knew Zban's family through church, youth soccer, and Little League, and the two later became friends in high school. Zban looked up to Paul and he was enormously proud of Zban, particularly when the Ohio State University signed him in 1993 as a top quarterback prospect and later when he transferred to Marshall to play alongside future Hall of Fame wide receiver Randy Moss. At six foot five and 220 pounds, Zban was built for the NFL. But hobbled by serious knee injuries at Ohio State and Marshall and a blown disc in his back from years of wear, his dreams of turning pro faded.

By the time he reached his early thirties in 2006, with six children of his own and a high-stress job selling medical supplies, Zban's pain from his sports injuries had become unbearable. Doctors prescribed low doses of hydrocodone, then higher doses of oxycodone. He started to take OxyContin 80mg tablets, sometimes two and three times a day. When he couldn't convince doctors to write him prescriptions, he bought pills on the streets of Huntington.

"I got sick as hell when I didn't take it," Zban said. "I couldn't work. I couldn't be a father. I couldn't do anything. But when I took it when I was withdrawing, I was a completely different person."

Getting high became his daily routine. Nothing else mattered.

"I was so embarrassed and ashamed of what I was doing. I really isolated myself," Zban said. "It got so bad that it became more important than my kids. I'm embarrassed to say that."

Paul was heartbroken when he heard about Zban's descent into opioid oblivion from Zban's wife and his friends. For years, he tried to help. He gave Zban money and legal advice, but he couldn't save his friend.

As his addiction deepened, Zban blacked out one day and crashed the family's GMC Acadia into the brick wall of a local barbershop. He eventually lost his house, his job, his twelve-year marriage, and his children. Two stints in rehab ended in relapses. In 2012, Zban lost his freedom when he was arrested for stealing money to buy pills while working in North Carolina. He spent five months in the Watauga County Detention Center, where he kicked his habit, cold turkey.

"I knew that once I got out of there, I never wanted to go through that again," Zban said. "I wanted to just stay clean for me. I wanted to prove a lot of people wrong."

A year after his release, Zban traveled back to Huntington, where his children were living with their mother. One afternoon, he was standing at the edge of the fence near the outfield wall of the baseball field, watching one of his sons play. His son wasn't speaking to him, and his wife asked him to stay away from his twin girls. They were in the stands, and when they saw him, they ran down the baseline to hug him. His ex-wife was not happy to see Zban at the ballfield. But Paul was. He walked down the fenceline, put his arm around him, and patted him on the back.

"Looks like you're doing well, buddy," Paul said.

"Yeah, I guess," Zban replied.

"Just keep doing what you're doing," Paul said. "Just keep doing your own thing and time will heal."

Zban remarried. He landed a solid job as a salesman for Honeywell. He began to put his family back together, reestablishing a relationship with his children. As Paul started to develop his public nuisance case against the drug companies four years later, his thoughts kept returning to his friend. Huntington was filled with people who had lost their way and never returned. He had grown numb to the carnage. But Zban was different. Watching Zban's life unravel became a deeply emotional experience for Paul. He wondered if he should include people like Zban in his case to put a face on the dry legal arguments and federal regulations. But he worried that personal stories like Zban's might leave the plaintiffs open to attack from drug company lawyers. They could easily place the blame on users like Zban, rip him apart during depositions and on the witness stand, and deflect attention away from their own conduct.

It will be a rabbit hole, Paul thought.

As he prepared his cases for court, Paul interviewed Zban. How did you get the pills? Who were the doctors? Where did they work? Who ran the clinics? How were you able to doctor shop and get so many prescriptions? And how were you able to fill all of them?

"This is the true essence of the epidemic," Paul realized. "How do I tell this story without telling the story of people like Mark Zban?"

Paul decided that Zban would never see the inside of a court-room. But he held his story close, a reminder of why he was bringing this fight, that even the best can fall. He needed to figure out how the doctors, clinics, and pharmacies that supplied Zban were able to get so many pills from the drug manufacturers and distributors. And he knew that gaining access to ARCOS—the DEA's pill-tracking database—would provide the answer.

Chapter 32

"The Hunt Is On"

Lewiston, Michigan, June 30, 2017

One week into his retirement from the DEA, James Rafalski was puttering around the garage of his getaway lake house on the Lower Peninsula of Michigan when his old boss, Jim Geldhof, called his cell.

"I've got some good news. The Masters decision is in," Geldhof said. "I could kiss you."

In a scathing thirty-eight-page opinion, the D.C. Court of Appeals ruled that Masters Pharmaceutical had failed to follow federal law when it poured millions of pills into Florida and Nevada and disregarded clear warning signs that its drugs were winding up on the street. Rather than hold the orders for closer examination, Masters shipped them.

"Most strikingly, in lieu of reporting all held orders, Masters's employees deleted some and edited others so that they appeared to be of a normal size and pattern, and then proceeded to fill them," the appellate panel wrote.

It was a stinging rebuke to the opioid industry, and thunderous vindication for Rafalski, Geldhof, Joe Rannazzisi, and their other DEA colleagues. Rafalski had spent nearly seven years working the case—investigating pill shipments, interviewing witnesses, filing field reports, testifying in court.

When his call with Geldhof ended, Rafalski stood in the silence of his garage, its walls adorned with award plaques and logos from the DEA and the Romulus Police Department. He was overcome by emotion, an unfamiliar feeling for the just-the-facts DEA man. He wiped away some tears and savored the moment. "It's not every day you win a case in the Court of Appeals," he said.

The ruling was unanimous by the three-judge appellate panel, its opinion written by judge Cornelia Pillard. The panel rejected nearly every argument made by Masters, The Alliance, and the rest of the drug industry, which had filed friend-of-the court briefs in the case. The appellate court ruling would become key to future cases against the opioid industry. The judges obliterated Masters's main line of defense—the company had claimed that the DEA unfairly imposed new regulations on them. Instead, the court declared that existing federal law already required the distributors to maintain "effective controls against diversion" and design systems to "identify suspicious orders of controlled substances." If the distributors couldn't obtain a satisfactory answer, they were required to hold back those orders and report them to the DEA.

"Once a distributor has reported a suspicious order, it must make one of two choices: decline to ship the order, or conduct some 'due diligence,'" Pillard wrote in the opinion.

The judges noted that Masters had repeatedly failed to examine irregular orders and looked the other way in the face of clear warning signs that its narcotics were being diverted to drug users and dealers. Some of those signs, they said, included long lines at pharmacies during odd times, or multiple cars in drugstore parking lots bearing out-of-state license plates.

In Huntington, West Virginia, Paul Farrell's phone was blowing up. He began to read the decision on his laptop.

"Holy shit," he said to himself as he scrolled through the opinion. *"They nailed it."*

Paul was turning forty-five the next day. It was an early birthday present, but he kept his celebrations in check.

This isn't the kill, he thought. *But the hunt is on.*

Chapter 33

"Make Them Pay"

Charleston, West Virginia, July 2017

The dining room was in the secluded Italianate mansion that housed the Charleston law firm of Hill, Peterson, Carper, Bee & Deitzler. Dinner, prepared by Jim Peterson, a partner in the firm, was ossobuco with a veal demi-glace. The wine was from Falcor, a vineyard in California's Napa Valley owned by Peterson, who on this hot August evening was pouring one of his finest cabernet sauvignons into James Rafalski's glass.

Damn, Rafalski thought. *This ain't like the DEA where you get a warm bottle of water.*

Rafalski, along with Jim Geldhof and Kathy Chaney, the DEA investigator who had been with Geldhof in the Portsmouth, Ohio, gymnasium filled with grieving parents six years earlier, had been invited by Paul Farrell to discuss the possibility of acting as expert witnesses in the developing civil litigation against the opioid industry.

Rafalski was reluctant to travel from Northville, Michigan, to Charleston. He retired six weeks earlier and was exhausted after years of trench warfare with the drug companies. He was sickened that the government had not done more to stop the flood of pain pills but felt he had done everything he could. He won the Masters case. His case against Mallinckrodt settled for $35 million, an unsatisfactory finale. The federal prosecutor Leslie Wizner had once threatened the company that it could face as much as $2.3 billion in fines. He had had enough. He wanted to relax, travel, maybe go to Europe with his wife. He also was leery of lawyers, unsure of their motives and skeptical that lawsuits would alter the trajectory of the opioid epidemic.

But Paul pressed him to make the trip. "Why don't you come down," Paul said during a phone call with Rafalski. "It's just a get-together and you don't have to commit to anything."

Rafalski figured he could combine his trip south with a visit to his grandson in Maryland, where his stepson worked as a police officer in Montgomery County. He set out on the morning of July 18 on the six-hour drive from his Michigan home. He pulled off the highway as he crossed into West Virginia from southern Ohio. He was hungry and had spotted a Golden Arches. Inside, he saw disheveled customers stumbling around. They were rail-thin, with vacant, bloodshot eyes. Some were shaking. He knew the look of addiction, but it was unsettling to witness it so plainly inside a rural McDonald's. These forgotten parts of the country were blighted.

The scene stuck with Rafalski as he listened during the lavish dinner to the lawyers laugh and talk about their big cases. Joining Paul and the partners from Hill Peterson were Mike Fuller and Amy Quezon from Mississippi, and Mike Papantonio and Peter J. Mougey from Florida. Rafalski knew they were trying to charm him. Still, he felt his hesitancy slipping away. He was enjoying himself.

After dessert, the group gathered on a broad veranda shaded by trees. It was a perfect summer evening. The wine flowed as they sat around a big round patio table. Their stomachs and glasses were full.

It was time for Paul to make his pitch. Suing the opioid manufacturers like Purdue was not their priority, he told Rafalski, Geldhof, and Chaney. They were focused on the distributors, such as McKesson, AmerisourceBergen, and Cardinal Health. They were also considering cases against the nation's largest pharmacy chains such as CVS and Walgreens. Most Americans, he said, didn't know about the companies that had flooded the country with opioids and fueled the worst drug epidemic in its history.

"This is a chance to make them pay," Paul said.

He recounted his Sunday family breakfast story and told his prospective witnesses that his mother and brother had challenged him to do something for the people of West Virginia. Paul said the drug companies would never change their behavior without people like Rafalski, Geldhof, and Chaney taking a stand. They would continue to send pills into poor communities like his. They would continue to pay whatever paltry fines the DEA and the Justice Department negotiated with drug company lawyers. No one would ever be held to account. Paul told them they could make a difference in the lives of tens of thousands of people from places like Huntington.

Paul appealed to their sense of duty, their lingering regrets. He knew they could have cashed in by taking high-paying jobs with the industry but had rejected the revolving door of Washington. He knew they still seethed over the disposition of their most important cases.

"I want to pick up your cause," he told them. "I promise that I will put the resources into finishing the fight."

Before the evening ended, Rafalski knew how he'd answer. They'd talked him into it. And he realized that, all along, he'd been hoping they would. His colleagues were sold, too. Now, he just needed to make sure his wife, Linda, would be okay with him going back to war so soon after leaving the battlefield.

He called her on his way home.

She didn't hesitate.

"Do it," she told him.

Chapter 34

Legal Titans

North Carolina, 2017

At 11 a.m. on November 15, Paul was waiting in a hallway at the headquarters of the North Carolina Association of County Commissioners in Raleigh. The commissioners had heard about Paul's lawsuit and invited him to give a presentation.

A door swung open. Out walked a man dressed in a bespoke broad pinstriped suit, tailored shirt, two-tone handmade shoes, and colorful socks. Paul J. Hanly Jr., a big-time Manhattan trial attorney.

Motherfucker, Paul thought.

Hanly and Paul were chasing the same clients. Both men knew the wreckage the drug companies had visited upon North Carolina. Between 1999 and 2017, more than thirteen thousand North Carolina residents had died from opioid overdoses. In 2017 alone, more than two thousand residents died, a 32 percent increase over the previous year.

Hanly was Paul's opposite in almost every way—dapper, polished, and, at sixty-six, a veteran litigator. The scion of a colorful political family, Hanly had studied analytical philosophy at Cornell University, where he played center on the varsity football team. He earned a master's degree at Cambridge University and a law degree at Georgetown in 1979. He then clerked for a federal judge in New Jersey who was close to his maternal grandfather, John V. Kenny. He had been one of New Jersey's most powerful politicians. Hanly grew up admiring Kenny, who served as mayor of Jersey City from 1949 to 1953. He later went to prison in the 1970s for tax evasion.

Hanly had been working opioid cases for more than a decade. In the early 2000s, along with his partner, Jayne Conroy, he had been one of the first lawyers to take on Purdue Pharma. Tall, with streaks of gray hair, fifty-nine-year-old Conroy was another New York powerhouse. Like Hanly, she dressed stylishly, favoring vintage couture from the 1940s. One of five sisters, she had grown up in Woburn, Massachusetts, outside Boston. She was exposed to the world of mass torts at an early age. Her father, William Joseph Heimlich, was an inventor and a mechanical engineer whose skills in the leather industry were legendary. He spent more than thirty years dismantling U.S. tanneries, shipping them in pieces, and reassembling them in many developing countries. He also was the chief engineer for the John J. Riley Tannery that was a defendant in the high-profile litigation memorialized by the bestselling book and movie *A Civil Action*. The book documented a lawyer's quixotic fight against the tannery, W. R. Grace, and Beatrice Foods, for allegedly causing cancer deaths in Woburn.

Conroy grew up sailing on Cape Cod and skiing in New England. She graduated from Dartmouth College and New England Law and married the owner of a Newton, Massachusetts, funeral home. She raised her two daughters upstairs from the parlor on the main floor and the embalming room in the basement.

Conroy began her legal career as a corporate defense attorney. She met Hanly in the mid-1980s when her office in Boston joined forces with his New York firm to represent the largest asbestos manufacturer in the world, England-based Turner & Newall. Workaholics with a shared sense of the law as vindicator, they hit it off from the start. Despite his sense of high style, Hanly could have a reserved and detached demeanor. Conroy, effortlessly winning, managed the social graces.

For years afterward, Conroy and Hanly made their living defending asbestos lawsuits. In 2002, they formed their own firm, New

York–based Hanly Conroy, and switched sides to become plaintiffs' lawyers, handling complex legal cases. They won hundreds of millions of dollars in settlements for families and victims of the 9/11 terrorist attacks, along with $60 million for 170 Haitian boys who were victims of alleged sexual abuse by a convicted pedophile at a Jesuit-sponsored orphanage in Haiti. They won billions of dollars for businesses and people harmed by the BP *Deepwater Horizon* oil spill. They were part of the legal team that secured a $14.7 billion global settlement for owners of Volkswagen vehicles following the 2016 emissions scandal. On behalf of the 9/11 victims, they also sued to ban the sale of tanzanite, a gem used to support Osama bin Laden's terrorist network.

On the day after Christmas in 2002, while Hanly and his family were visiting Conroy's family at her ski home in Mount Snow, Vermont, he received a call from a Washington, D.C., attorney. The attorney's father was a doctor who had seen an alarming increase in addiction among pain patients. They had all been prescribed OxyContin. Could there be a lawsuit and was Hanly interested?

Hanly and Conroy began investigating a possible case against Purdue Pharma. They talked to medical experts, lawyers, and with addicted patients, who came from all walks of life—lawyers, doctors, truck drivers, longshoremen. After hearing their stories, Hanly and Conroy became convinced they had a case. But it was going to be too expensive for a five-person law firm to take on a major drug company. They needed a partner who could help provide money and resources.

They reached out to John Simmons, a successful Illinois attorney. Simmons had often been on the opposing side of the early asbestos cases. He had made tens of millions a year suing companies on behalf of victims.

On a snowy day in February 2003, Hanly and Conroy flew to St. Louis, rented a car, and drove across the Mississippi River to the tiny community of Edwardsville, Illinois. Simmons's office was housed in an old Kroger grocery store. It was filled with dozens of lawyers. Hanly and Conroy, in formal dark suits, were ushered into one of the few offices in the aircraft-hangar-sized building to meet Simmons, clad in blue jeans, a lumberjack shirt, and construction boots.

Simmons grew up in nearby East Alton. He joined the U.S. Army, served as a combat engineer, and returned home to work with his father, building houses, before going to law school. He wanted to live and work where he grew up. But just because he wanted to live in a small town didn't mean he did not have big ambitions. He wasn't just relentless—he was ruthless. In the sea of plaintiffs' lawyers, Simmons was a great white shark.

Conroy and Hanly laid out their case against Purdue. They planned to file about five hundred cases across the country in the next year—and they needed financial help. Would Simmons and his firm be interested in joining forces? Simmons listened intently. They had come highly recommended, and Simmons was impressed by their work on behalf of the 9/11 victims.

"Well, how much money do you think you're going to need?" Simmons asked.

"For the next three to four months, we're going to need a million dollars," Hanly said.

Simmons pulled open the drawer of his desk, took out a checkbook, and wrote a check for $1 million. He handed it to Hanly. The pair sat poker-faced as Simmons asked if they needed anything else. Ten lawyers from your firm, Hanly replied.

Within weeks, a team of Simmons lawyers and staffers joined Hanly and Conroy as they embarked on their lawsuit against Purdue. They launched a television advertising campaign, urging people who had been lawfully prescribed OxyContin and had become addicted, or who knew of someone who had become addicted or died, to call an 800 number. They drove around the country from small town to small town, taking depositions from Purdue sales reps. They eventually filed about fourteen hundred cases in thirty states on behalf of five thousand patients who alleged Purdue had misled them about the risk of addiction from OxyContin.

In 2007, Purdue settled the lawsuits for $75 million. The Justice Department subpoenaed Hanly and Conroy's firm for millions of pages of Purdue's documents they had obtained during discovery. The department brought its own case against the company that resulted in the criminal convictions of three executives and the $634 million fine. In his Manhattan office, Hanly kept a souvenir from the case—a black stuffed gorilla in a blue T-shirt emblazoned with the word "OxyContin," a gift that company reps once gave to doctors as a marketing ploy.

Seven years later, Hanly and Conroy joined forces with Simmons to create Simmons Hanly Conroy, headquartered in Alton, with offices in New York, Chicago, and other cities. They took on high-profile cases involving defective drugs and medical devices. They secured a $1 billion verdict against Johnson & Johnson subsidiary DePuy Orthopaedics over its metal-on-metal hip implant, and a $894 million settlement of cases against Pfizer for its Bextra and Celebrex painkillers.

In the summer of 2015, Conroy received a letter from Suffolk County attorney Dennis Brown on Long Island, where there had been an explosion of opioid overdoses and deaths. Would the firm consider bringing another lawsuit, this one representing a county instead of individuals, he asked?

By this time, Hanly had a personal experience with the dangers of OxyContin: His son Jake had become addicted, and like a lot of parents, Hanly was oblivious. Jake was first prescribed the drug at fourteen when he broke his arm while skateboarding. Over the next three years, Jake broke his arm two more times, again on his skateboard. Each time, he was prescribed OxyContin.

Early one morning in 2011, Hanly received a frantic call from Jake. He was crying. His girlfriend had overdosed and been rushed to the hospital. Jake confessed to his father that he had been addicted to pain pills for years. The girlfriend survived, and Hanly enrolled his son in a treatment program. Jake eventually recovered, and Hanly's animosity toward Purdue intensified.

In August 2015, Hanly and Conroy drove to Long Island to meet with Lynne A. Bizzarro, the chief deputy county attorney in Suffolk County. There had only been two lawsuits in the country filed against opioid manufacturers by municipalities, and it was still a largely untested area of law. But they took the case.

About a year after meeting with Bizzarro, on August 31, 2016, Hanly and Conroy filed a complaint on behalf of Suffolk County against Purdue and other opioid makers, including Teva Pharmaceuticals, Cephalon, Johnson & Johnson, and Endo Pharmaceuticals. They also sued several physicians, including Russell Portenoy, the pain management doctor at New York City's Memorial Sloan Kettering hospital who had advocated for the wider use of opioids. By then, Portenoy had recanted. He told the *Wall Street Journal* in December 2012 that he had unwittingly provided incorrect information about opioids. "We didn't know then what we know now," he said. In a video cited by the *Journal* and made by the Physicians for Responsible Opioid Prescribing, Portenoy said: "Clearly, if I had an inkling of what I know now then, I wouldn't have spoken in the way that I spoke. It was clearly the wrong thing to do."

Hanly compared his lawsuit to the landmark tobacco litigation of the 1990s that alleged tobacco companies knew smoking caused lung cancer and cigarettes were addictive. For the next year, Hanly and Conroy were flooded with inquiries from other cities, towns, and counties around the nation interested in suing. It was that deluge of inquiries that eventually brought Hanly and Conroy into competition with Paul Farrell.

On November 16, 2017, the day after Hanly ran into Paul in Raleigh, Hanly traveled to Charlotte, North Carolina, to meet with county officials at the Charlotte-Mecklenburg Government Center. As he left the meeting on the center's top floor, he ran into Paul, who was waiting in the wide marble hallway to pitch his lawsuit against drug distributors.

Son of a bitch, Paul thought. It was the second day in a row that Hanly had beaten him.

Hanly's lawsuit against the manufacturers was different than Paul's case against the distributors. Hanly didn't know much about the distribution system for opioids. His case centered on how drug makers deceptively marketed painkillers to doctors and patients. But in North Carolina, as with everywhere they both went, the local officials had to choose between the two Pauls.

"I just want you to know that I will say only good things about you to them," Farrell told Hanly. "I'll tell them you're a great lawyer. You're focused on manufacturers. We're focused on distributors. They can't go wrong whoever they choose."

Hanly looked at Paul and laughed. He had heard about this smart-aleck lawyer from West Virginia.

"Well, I would only say good things about you if I knew you," Hanly said. "But I don't."

Chapter 35

The Drug Czar

Washington, D.C., October 2017

Shortly after Donald Trump was inaugurated as the forty-fifth president of the United States in January 2017, he pledged to make combating the opioid epidemic a top priority. He named Tom Marino, the champion of The Alliance and one of the first members of Congress to back his nascent presidential campaign, as the nation's next drug czar. Whatever elation drug industry executives may have felt following Marino's September 1, 2017, nomination quickly dissipated.

Weeks later, The Alliance and its members learned that the *Washington Post* and *60 Minutes* were preparing to publish a joint investigative report into the role the industry had played in the passage of the Marino-Blackburn bill, blunting the DEA's enforcement efforts. To confront the impending public relations crisis, The Alliance crafted talking points for the news media and members of Congress. Among them: Drug distributors were "logistics companies," they did not drive the demand for opioids, and the bill was a bipartisan effort "to address abuse and misuse" of opioids.

The prospect of a damning joint report by two of the country's leading news outlets led to a flurry of emails by industry officials. The communications chief for AmerisourceBergen, Gabriel Weissman, wrote to his colleagues on October 10 that he had "synched up" with his counterparts at Cardinal Health and McKesson. Together, they had decided to let The Alliance take the lead and defend the industry's role in the Marino-Blackburn bill—a move that would keep the Big Three drug distributors out of the public spotlight. "I've been screaming for [The Alliance] to take the bullet for us," Weissman wrote.

Five days later, on Sunday, October 15, the *Post* published the joint investigative report under the headline "The Drug Industry's Triumph over the DEA." That evening, *60 Minutes* correspondent Bill Whitaker introduced the broadcast version of the report. "In the midst of the worst drug epidemic in American history," Whitaker began, "the U.S. Drug Enforcement Administration's ability to keep addictive opioids off U.S. streets was derailed—that according to Joe Rannazzisi, one of the most important whistleblowers ever interviewed by *60 Minutes*."

Halfway through the interview, Whitaker leaned in and asked Joe to tell the American public what he had witnessed while running the DEA's diversion division. "You know the implication of what you're saying," Whitaker said, "that these big companies knew that they were pumping drugs into American communities that were killing people, and they went out of their way to try to stop legislation, or to put in legislation that would allow them to keep doing this, almost with no concern about the impact that it was having on Americans."

"That's not an implication, that's a fact," Joe said. "That's exactly what they did. They felt that their best interests to preserve the way they do business, their business model, to preserve their profits, was to spend a little money and get a bill passed that takes away DEA's authority and helps them continue on their merry way towards, you know, distributing drugs. And if people die, well, too bad. That's exactly what happened."

Joe's stunning statement was the culmination of a long internal process. Since retiring, he had been reluctant to go public. But the year before he'd agreed to speak on the record to the *Washington Post* for a series on opioids. Those stories won awards but were mostly drowned out by presidential campaign coverage. Joe's appearance on *60 Minutes* as part of the *Post*'s collaboration with the revered news magazine landed at a better moment in the news cycle. Suddenly the story got traction. Other news outlets picked it up. It was getting amplified— big time.

Several members of Congress admitted that they didn't understand the ramifications of the bill. One of those was Democrat Joe Manchin III, who represented Paul Farrell's home state of West Virginia in the Senate. "They made it and camouflaged it so well, all of us were fooled," Manchin said. "All of us. Nobody knew." Marsha Blackburn tried to back away from the bill she cosponsored, saying it may have had "unintended consequences."

Marino's nomination was doomed. The joint *Washington Post*/*60 Minutes* investigative report detailed the industry's efforts to secure passage of the bill. It documented how the industry helped to write the legislation, lobbied members of Congress, wrote hostile questions for lawmakers to ask Joe and other DEA officials when they testified on the Hill, and poured hundreds of thousands of dollars into the political campaigns of the sponsors and cosponsors of the bill. The report also noted that John Mulrooney, the DEA's chief judge, had just written a blistering 115-page article about the Marino-Blackburn bill for the *Marquette Law Review*. He said the new law represented a "dramatic diminution of the agency's authority." It was "all but logically impossible" for the DEA to immediately suspend a drug company's operations for failing to comply with federal law. "If it had been the intent of Congress to completely eliminate the DEA's ability to ever impose an immediate suspension on distributors or manufacturers, it would be difficult to conceive of a more effective vehicle for achieving that goal." Mulrooney also criticized the provision allowing drug companies to submit corrective action plans before they could be sanctioned by the DEA. He compared it to allowing bank robbers to "round up and return ink-stained money and agree not to rob any more banks."

The day after the report appeared, several lawmakers called the White House to demand that Marino's nomination be pulled.

Manchin told reporters that he was "horrified" by the findings and couldn't "believe that the [Obama] administration did not sound the alarm on how harmful that bill would be for our efforts to effectively fight the opioid epidemic."

The Democrat from West Virginia also wrote to Trump, noting that the drug companies that had sent millions of pain pills into his state were the same companies behind the Marino-Blackburn bill. "As the report notes, one such company shipped 20 million doses of oxycodone and hydrocodone to pharmacies in West Virginia between 2007 and 2012. This included 11 million doses in one small county with only 25,000 people in the southern part of the state: Mingo County," the senator said. "As the number of pills in my state increased, so did the death toll in our communities, including Mingo County."

Neither Manchin nor any of his ninety-nine colleagues in the Senate had objected to the bill, ensuring that it passed without a recorded vote.

Two days after the report appeared, Marino withdrew from consideration for the drug czar post. Trump made it official on his Twitter feed on October 17, adding, "Tom is a fine man and a great Congressman!"

In the days that followed, the industry and its allies on Capitol Hill pushed back. Republican Orrin Hatch of Utah, who had guided the bill through the Senate, took to the floor of the Senate to excoriate the reporting.

"I think we need to be candid about what's going on here," Hatch said. "Opponents of the current administration are trying to derail the president's nominee to be head of the Office of National Drug Control Policy, Representative Tom Marino, by mischaracterizing and trying to rewrite the history of a bill that he championed."

A group calling itself the Academy of Integrative Pain Management issued a letter of support for the legislation and Hatch's floor remarks. It was one of several pain patient advocacy groups to come forward to back the bill, many of them funded by drug companies.

"We felt that some balance in enforcement actions needed to be struck, and that the Ensuring Patient Access and Effective Drug Enforcement Act did just that," the Academy of Integrative Pain Management said in its letter. What the academy didn't disclose: It had received more than $1.2 million from opioid manufacturers between 2012 and 2017.

The counterattacks continued, but with little impact on the political reality: Marino was out and Joe had taken on the mantle of whistleblower.

Chapter 36

Jumped the Gun

St. Louis, Fall 2017

Paul Hanly was walking down a street in Manhattan in the fall of 2017 when his cell phone rang. It was Joe Rice, a legendary South Carolina trial lawyer at Motley Rice, one of the nation's largest plaintiffs' litigation firms. Rice and his partner, Ron Motley, had made a fortune suing the asbestos and tobacco industries. They were among the lawyers who secured the largest civil settlement in U.S. history—$246 billion against cigarette companies in 1998. Motley, who died in 2013, was portrayed in *The Insider*, a movie about a tobacco company whistleblower—played by Russell Crowe—who took his story to *60 Minutes*.

Rice also had turned his sights on the opioid industry. He would become one of the most powerful figures in the nascent litigation.

"Paul, did you know about this?" Rice asked Hanly.

"What?" Hanly replied.

"Paul Farrell just filed for an MDL," Rice said.

An "MDL" is shorthand for multidistrict litigation, a special federal procedure designed to manage many similar civil cases filed in different U.S. courthouses. The procedure consolidates them in one courthouse under one judge, whose rulings are binding on each of the cases, no matter where they were filed.

"What the hell?" Hanly said, stopping on the street.

A few minutes earlier, the online news service Law360 had reported that Paul and his consortium of law firms just filed a petition with the Judicial Panel on Multidistrict Litigation to pull more than a hundred opioid cases into one massive lawsuit.

"How would I know about this, Joe?" Hanly said. "I don't know this guy, Farrell. I mean, I only met him once."

"This is not good," Rice said. "Bad idea."

To the two veteran litigators with years of MDL experience, the timing was all wrong. It was way too early to consolidate the opioid cases, they thought. Paul Farrell wasn't an experienced player in their world. They didn't think he understood the intricacies of highly complex civil cases involving multiple defendants.

Hanly and Rice wanted to test their cases by filing them individually in different state and federal courts. There, they could begin discovery—the formal process of obtaining documents, emails, and internal corporate reports, and taking depositions of potential witnesses. Their idea was to divide and conquer, forcing the companies to defend multiple lawsuits in a host of jurisdictions, many of them in communities decimated by the epidemic. When plaintiffs file for an MDL, courtroom activity in the different cases across the country virtually ceases while a judicial panel decides whether to consolidate the lawsuits and who will oversee them. Paul didn't bother to ask for the permission of the other major litigants—in fact he didn't want it. With the opioid epidemic entrenched well beyond the Ohio River valley and more lawsuits being filed, he feared he would be marginalized by lawyers like Hanly and Rice who would bring cases in New York, Chicago, and other cities. The MDL was a gambit to keep control of the litigation and carve out a central role. Paul had already signed up Mike Papantonio and Russell Budd, two lawyers who had successfully litigated high-profile MDL cases. If the judges created an MDL, the judicial panel would appoint lead attorneys for the litigation, and Paul wanted that role for himself and his allies.

On November 30, 2017, the plaintiffs' lawyers gathered in a

packed courtroom on the twenty-eighth floor of the Thomas F. Eagle-
ton U.S. Courthouse in St. Louis for a 9:30 a.m. hearing before the
Judicial Panel on Multidistrict Litigation.

As Conroy approached the courthouse, she saw Paul for the first
time. He was surrounded by a film crew, led by Clay Tweel, an award-
winning director who was following Paul for a documentary. *Who does
this guy think he is?* Conroy wondered. She had seen her share of lawyers being interviewed outside courthouses, but this Hollywood-style
entourage seemed self-indulgent. This hearing was the first step in a
very long legal process.

Insanely premature, Conroy thought.

Conroy didn't know that Paul had a personal connection to Tweel,
whose father had worked with Paul in the same law firm in West Virginia. When Tweel heard about the opioid litigation, he asked Paul if
he could embed with him and document his every move. Paul agreed.
Still, the trailing crew—just like the unilateral decision to seek an
MDL—spoke to Paul's sense of himself as the rising star lawyer in
this drama.

The multidistrict litigation panel has considered creating MDLs
in more than six hundred thousand cases since its creation by Congress in 1968—everything from airplane crashes, train wrecks, and
hotel fires to mass torts involving asbestos, pharmaceutical drugs,
data security breaches, and securities fraud.

Every two months, the panel hears cases in a different federal
courthouse. If it determines that cases should be centralized in an
MDL, it then chooses a judge to oversee the litigation. On November
30, Paul's request to consolidate all the opioid manufacturing, distributing, and dispensing lawsuits was one of twenty-two scheduled to
be heard that day. It was formally called MDL 2804, *In Re: National
Prescription Opiate Litigation.*

The panel of judges, appointed by the chief justice of the Supreme
Court, listened to the arguments of seventeen lawyers on whether
to consolidate the opioid cases. The first to speak on behalf of Paul's

consortium was Roland K. Tellis of Baron & Budd, which represented the city of Cincinnati. Tellis said there were 155 cases filed in 25 different districts. At the heart of all the claims, he said, was "the duty to report and stop suspicious transactions."

"Manufacturers and distributors together have that duty," Tellis said.

"Does the manufacturer have a different way of carrying out that duty than a distributor does, or do they do the same thing?" the chairman of the panel, district court judge Sarah S. Vance, asked.

"I think they do the same thing," Tellis replied.

District court judge R. David Proctor of the Northern District of Alabama said he was concerned that an MDL could make the litigation unwieldy as more and more cases were included. "We get it, that there's a common issue as to the duty to make sure that there was not an overprescription of these medications," Proctor said. But creating an MDL and adding more cases "make[s] this a tangled web that's very difficult to manage."

Several of the attorneys argued against creating an MDL. Jeffrey B. Simon, whose Dallas law firm was suing the manufacturers and distributors on behalf of eight Texas counties, said each of his clients opposed bringing the cases together. "We can coordinate with the defendants on our own in Texas," Simon told the panel.

Hunter J. Shkolnik, who represented about sixty counties and cities across the country, including three cities in Ohio, said he didn't want to get "tied up in a massive MDL." He said, "I'm a proponent of MDLs, but we also know that some MDLs take too long to help communities."

One of the last to speak was Enu A. Mainigi, a partner at Williams & Connolly, a venerable Washington, D.C., law firm. A Harvard Law School graduate, the fiery litigator specialized in defending health care companies, pharmacies, hospitals, nursing homes, and pharmaceutical firms. Mainigi appeared on behalf of the Big Three distributors—AmerisourceBergen, Cardinal Health, and McKesson,

Paul's three largest targets. She joined Paul in his request and supported consolidating the cases into an MDL. Industry lawyers had no desire to fight on more than two hundred different legal fronts; an MDL offered predictability and the possibility of eventually resolving the litigation all at once.

Mainigi said there were many critical questions to be resolved, including the claim that drug distributors are responsible for opioid deaths and whether a city or county could legally bring these kinds of cases.

One of the judges wasn't following her argument. "But then doesn't that argue for non-centralization so that these things can be litigated where we leave them where God flung them and let those issues be litigated in separate courts?" Third Circuit Court of Appeals judge Marjorie O. Rendell asked.

"We cannot have 150 different rulings," Mainigi replied.

Paul had calculated that if he filed an MDL before anyone else, he would become the lead attorney in the litigation, partly because he had held that kind of position before. He filed the first forty transvaginal mesh cases in the country. In 2012, his lawsuits were consolidated with nearly eighty thousand other cases into an MDL in Charleston, West Virginia. Paul was named to the executive committee of the panel and won a multimillion-dollar verdict for his clients. He also believed that an opioid MDL might be transferred to a judge in the Southern District of Ohio. In his petition, Paul had recommended that the panel send it to Edmund A. Sargus Jr., the chief judge of the Southern District of Ohio, appointed by President Bill Clinton in 1996. Paul had already filed twenty cases in that district, and Sargus consolidated them in his courtroom. He felt confident that the other lawyers would chose him to lead the MDL if it went to Sargus, who was presiding over many of Paul's cases.

Conroy thought Paul had jumped the gun. She knew that these cases are seldom assigned to the judge you want. An MDL could wind up anywhere in the country. It could just as easily be assigned to a judge whom the defendants believed would be more sympathetic to their case.

Paul was willing to take that chance. He also believed that he had reached critical mass, signing up close to forty towns, cities, and counties while Rice, Hanly, and Conroy had enlisted just a handful. Paul had the cases, the others didn't. Simple as that.

Mark S. Cheffo, an attorney for Purdue Pharma and other opioid manufacturers, asked the panel to send the case to Chicago, where one of the first opioid cases against manufacturers was filed in 2014. But a lawyer suing Purdue argued against creating an MDL, saying it would delay her lawsuit. Linda Singer, who worked with Rice, told the panel she was almost a year into discovery in Chicago and they would have to relitigate issues that had already been "painfully negotiated." Meanwhile, "defendants continue to engage in the same practices," she said.

Twelve days after the hearing, on December 12, 2017, the panel issued its decision. For Paul, it was a victory. But only a partial one. He got the MDL he wanted. But crucially, his big bet hadn't gotten the MDL placed in a courtroom where he believed he'd have the upper hand. Instead of sending the MDL to his favored judge, the panel assigned it to Dan Aaron Polster, a federal judge for the Northern District of Ohio in Cleveland. The MDL judges said they chose northern Ohio because the area had been hard-hit by the epidemic and was centrally located for the lawyers who were spread across the country. They said they sent the case to Polster, a Cleveland native who graduated from both Harvard College and Harvard Law School, because of his previous MDL experience. They specifically cited his time presiding over several hundred cases involving the toxic medical contrast dye containing gadolinium.

While Conroy was not happy with the creation of an MDL, she was "thrilled" that the cases would be heard by Polster. She had been involved in the gadolinium litigation and was impressed by the judge.

But Paul Farrell was deeply disappointed. He and his consortium knew little about Polster or how he might rule on key aspects of the case. Shkolnik's case, from Cuyahoga County in Ohio, would be the first in line to come before Polster, not Paul's, from West Virginia.

We've lost our venue. We've lost our momentum, Paul thought. *We've lost control of the litigation.*

Chapter 37

"This Is Horrific"

Cleveland, Ohio, December 2017

Downtown Cleveland was decked out for the holidays. A fifty-foot Christmas tree, swathed in bands of colorful lights, towered over Public Square. But two blocks away, the 150 super lawyers with super egos from ninety-seven law firms who had gathered in a cavernous conference hall at the Hilton hotel were not in a festive mood. It was two weeks before Christmas and the assembled attorneys were trying to decide who among them should lead the multidistrict litigation. There were only three co–lead counsel slots and sixteen openings on the plaintiffs' executive committee. Simple math said a lot of people in the convention center would be leaving Cleveland without much of a role in the litigation.

Jayne Conroy had seen her share of these MDL conferences, but nothing like this. There were so many cases—206 and counting. With two dozen drug companies named as defendants and hundreds of millions in legal fees at stake, the conference was turning into a knife fight. Conroy watched the jockeying and the backstabbing with dismay. Lawyers formed factions. Some faced off against one another like contestants in a TV game show. They promoted some attorneys to take leadership positions. They trashed others as undeserving, untrustworthy, or worse.

This is horrific, Conroy thought.

Judge Polster had ordered the attorneys to pick a slate to lead the litigation and sit on the plaintiffs' executive committee. The committee was a "superstructure" of lawyers. It would be responsible for assigning law firms to manage every aspect of the case, filing legal briefs, and carrying out the crucial discovery process—issuing demands for corporate documents and emails, taking depositions of key witnesses, and preparing the mountains of material for trial.

Each week, more and more cases were being added to the MDL and more and more lawyers were demanding a piece of the action. Several law firms had already invested enormous amounts of time and money. Others had done next to nothing, aside from filing complaints in their local courthouses, many of them based on Paul Farrell's public nuisance theory. Lawyers jousted on the convention center floor for leadership positions. The politicking threatened to upend the conference.

Mike Papantonio, who had been through numerous multidistrict litigation fights, tried to calm the packed hall. He stood before his colleagues and pleaded with them to put their self-interests aside.

"This is an epidemic unlike anything we've ever seen," Papantonio began. "It affects the families of everyone in this room, the communities of everyone in this room, and this is an opportunity for us to do some public good. There'll be room for everyone to join the fight."

That was not entirely true. There would be winners and losers, and the attorneys from some of the nation's most feared plaintiffs' law firms were not accustomed to losing. Everyone wanted to be a part of the historic case. And everyone wanted a cut of the billions in damages that they hoped they would see one day.

"We need to check our egos at the door," Papantonio told them.

One of the biggest egos in the hall belonged to Paul. What he lacked in MDL experience he made up for with a supreme confidence that sometimes veered into arrogance.

Paul was unimpressed by the sea of lawyers. They were businessmen, not litigators, signing up clients, aggregating cases, and leveraging them to score lucrative settlements. They didn't want to go to trial; they didn't want to do the work involved in a protracted and successful litigation. And Paul was certain they had no feeling for the magnitude of the epidemic and the individual, family, and community misery it had wrought. Paul was convinced that he knew the case better than any other lawyer in Cleveland that day. This was about people like Mark Zban. This was about places like Huntington. This case was *his*.

He viewed lawyers like Paul Hanly and Joe Rice as aging athletes, past their prime but still trying to stay in the game. He saw himself as the young phenom, and he didn't care who he offended—other lawyers on his team, opposing counsel, even judges. *I don't give a shit if the judges get mad*, he thought.

Shortly before Christmas, a faction that included members of the old guard emerged with a partial framework for the litigation team, and they appeared to have significant support in the hall. Hanly, with his long and successful record of litigating mass torts, would serve as one co–lead counsel. Rice, who helped to negotiate a settlement with the tobacco industry, would serve as another. There was one remaining slot, and nothing was final. Some lawyers, reading the writing on the wall, stormed out of the conference hall and flew home from Cleveland, furious they had not been considered for a leadership position. Others continued to lobby for themselves and members of their own consortiums.

On Christmas Eve, Hanly received a call from Russell Budd, the lawyer from Dallas who had teamed up with Paul Farrell and Papantonio. "Look, we have to have one of our consortium as a co-lead," Budd told Hanly. "If you support that, we will support you and Joe."

"Who's that going to be?" Hanly asked.

"Paul Farrell."

Both Budd and Papantonio believed that Paul deserved a leadership role because he had developed the public nuisance theory for the drug distribution litigation and had filed a batch of cases before the rest of the team.

Hanly scoffed at the suggestion. "He doesn't have any MDL experience," he said.

"Yeah, I know. But I'm going to be here and we have a big team," Budd said. "He's our choice."

Hanly called Rice. They reluctantly agreed. They knew Paul had worked tirelessly to develop the cases in West Virginia and southern Ohio. They also worried about the political fallout if they excluded him. The last thing they wanted was a negative story in the *Wall Street Journal*, portraying them as money-hungry interlopers, bigfooting the case and taking it away from the man from the state with the highest opioid death rate in the nation. The lifestyles of high-profile plaintiffs' lawyers—splendid beach houses in Miami, hundred-foot yachts, and private Gulfstream jets funded by the billions in settlements they had scored over the years—would feed into the narrative of trial lawyers hijacking the case for personal profit. They didn't think that was true, but the optics would be disastrous. They realized they had to put Paul on the leadership committee. And Paul was prepared to fight for what was rightfully his. It was his legal theory. He had the largest number of clients. And he had assembled the litigation consortium. For Paul, it had become personal.

Under no circumstances am I going to relinquish control, he thought.

With the litigation slate set and dozens of law firms involved in the MDL, the lawyers devised a war plan. No weekends off. No vacations. Twelve-hour days, probably more. They divided the case along three tracks: drug distributors, manufacturers, and pharmacy chains. Each firm would be responsible for "burning to the ground" different companies: unearthing every detail about the firm, its executives, its employees, and its drug distribution and manufacturing networks. They would also determine which drug company employees to depose, which documents to seek, and who would review them and catalog them. Paul would oversee all of the distributor cases; Hanly and Conroy, the manufacturers; Papantonio and his firm, the pharmacies. Some lawyers were assigned to investigate specific companies.

Papantonio's firm took McKesson. Mike Fuller and Amy Quezon would dig into Cardinal Health and The Alliance. Budd and his lawyers would handle AmerisourceBergen and the lobbying efforts behind the Marino-Blackburn bill. Settlement negotiations would be handled by Rice and Paul J. Geller, the managing partner of a Boca Raton, Florida, law firm. Geller had earned a national reputation by notching numerous wins, including a $265 million judgment against Massey Energy, a West Virginia coal company found liable for a mine explosion that killed twenty-nine people in 2010. Also on the negotiation team were Elizabeth J. Cabraser, who had founded one of the country's largest plaintiffs' law firms, and Christopher A. Seeger, who had negotiated a $1 billion settlement on behalf of NFL players who had suffered concussions and brain injuries. Peter Mougey, a lawyer from Levin Papantonio Rafferty, joined the negotiation team.

The lawyers assembled constituted a dream team of litigation talent, one of the best ever, if not the best, one of broad and deep experience that had won tens of billions in settlements and jury verdicts against some of the biggest industries in the country.

Rice and the two Pauls had agreed on the lineup of attorneys and responsibilities, but Hanly still wasn't completely happy. He thought his less experienced co-counsel didn't appreciate the complexities of multidistrict litigations and was unwilling to learn. They were vastly different than the med-mal cases Paul had pursued. Those cases usually involved one defendant—a hospital or a pharmaceutical company—and one patient or a number of patients who were seriously harmed by a doctor or a product. They were straightforward and easier to prove, and the defendants were backed by deep-pocketed insurance firms willing to settle for big money, albeit reluctantly. The opioid litigation was becoming the most complex case Hanly had ever seen. Not only did it involve two dozen defendants, but they had different roles in the opioid supply chain—manufacturers, distributors, and pharmacies. Payouts by the publicly traded drug companies and pharmacies could lower their stock prices. The companies would be loath to let

that happen. Adding to the complexity was that numerous government agencies regulated the drug industry—the DEA, the FDA, and
pharmacy boards in every state. What role did they play in the epidemic, and would the drug industry try to raise their shortcomings as
a defense?

Hanly didn't know if Paul was ready. He had seen lawyers like
him before. *He's just a gunslinger*, Hanly thought.

Hanly also understood that West Virginia had been wrecked by
the epidemic and Paul wanted revenge. But as a co-counsel of the
MDL, Paul would now be representing hundreds of communities
across the country, not just a handful in Appalachia.

He's taking this way too personally, Hanly thought.

Chapter 38

"Tear Each Other Up"

Cleveland, January 2018

On the morning of January 9, Judge Polster summoned nearly two hundred defense and plaintiffs' attorneys in the opioid litigation to his wood-paneled courtroom, its windows covered with heavy, teal-colored draperies, to hear an urgent request. Put aside your differences, the judge told them, and settle the case for the sake of the country. The lawyers sat shoulder-to-shoulder in the eighteenth-floor courtroom in the Carl B. Stokes U.S. Courthouse, an imposing skyscraper of gleaming concrete and glass, the fourth-tallest courthouse in the country. It is named for the first Black mayor of a major American city. Polster alternated between cajoling, chastising, and ultimately warning the lawyers against turning the litigation into an all-out legal battle. No one would win, he said, particularly the public.

There was too much at stake. Too many people were dying. Too many people could not find treatment. Too many communities were suffering from the worst drug epidemic in American history. Polster was relentless as he upbraided the lawyers, perhaps because he knew his words would not appear in any news reports. He had barred the press from attending the first hearing of the MDL. He called it a "settlement conference," not a hearing, and he believed he had every right to conduct it behind closed doors.

Polster began his meeting by noting that the MDL created to

handle the opioid cases was unique. Usually, multidistrict litigations address a past wrong—the parties figure out how it happened and who should be held responsible.

The opposite was taking place now, he said. "What's happening in our country with the opioid crisis is present and ongoing," he noted. "I did a little math. Since we're losing more than 50,000 of our citizens every year, about 150 Americans are going to die today, just today, while we're meeting.

"And in my humble opinion, everyone shares some of the responsibility, and no one has done enough to abate it. That includes the manufacturers, the distributors, the pharmacies, the doctors, the federal government and state government, local governments, hospitals, third-party payors, and individuals. Just about everyone we've got on both sides of the equation in this case."

The lawyers sat in stunned silence.

"I don't think anyone in the country is interested in a whole lot of finger-pointing at this point, and I'm not either. People aren't interested in depositions, and discovery, and trials. People aren't interested in figuring out the answer to interesting legal questions," Polster continued. "So my objective is to do something meaningful to abate this crisis and to do it in 2018.

"And we have here—we've got all the lawyers. I can get the parties, and I can involve the states. So, we'll have everyone who is in a position to do it. And with all of these smart people here and their clients, I'm confident we can do something to dramatically reduce the number of opioids that are being disseminated, manufactured, and distributed. Just dramatically reduce the quantity, and make sure that the pills that are manufactured and distributed go to the right people and no one else, and that there be an effective system in place to monitor the delivery and distribution, and if there's a problem, to immediately address it and to make sure that those pills are prescribed only when there's an appropriate diagnosis, and that we get some amount of money to the government agencies for treatment.

"Because sadly, every day more and more people are being addicted, and they need treatment."

Paul Farrell couldn't believe what he was hearing. He looked around the crowded courtroom at "all these lawyers with buckles on their shoes." They were mostly trial attorneys, not negotiators, and they were among the finest in the country. No one was ready to concede a thing. Why would drug company executives and their lawyers suddenly surrender and voluntarily pay out billions in damages, after repeatedly denying that they played any role in the epidemic? It didn't make much sense, and he couldn't imagine that anyone in the courtroom would bend to the judge's will.

Paul didn't know that the epidemic also was deeply personal for Polster. The judge had grown up in Cleveland, a city ravaged by opioids, addiction, and death. One of his friends had lost a daughter.

Outside of work, Polster tutored a third-grader at a nearby elementary school and taught mediation at the Cleveland-Marshall College of Law. As a member of two Jewish congregations, he led a confirmation class on ethical decision making. A former assistant U.S. attorney in Cleveland before President Clinton named him to the federal bench in 1998, Polster cared deeply about his city and wanted the devastation of his community and so many others around the country to stop.

Polster told the lawyers that the alternative to settling was protracted, expensive, uncertain, and bruising litigation. If that's what they wanted, he acknowledged, there was little he could do to stand in their way, but he reminded them he wasn't powerless.

"If I've got to do it in a traditional way—and I guess I'll have no choice—I'll admit failure and I'll say, 'All right. We've just got to plow through this, and, you know, if we can't accomplish something like what I've talked about then, you know, I'll talk to everyone,'" he said. "I'll turn the plaintiffs loose on the defendants; I'll turn the defendants loose on the plaintiffs. You'll, you know, tear each other up way down in 2018 for discovery. You can go after the federal government, full discovery there, too. You know, FDA, DEA, have at it, and in 2019, I'll try the Ohio case myself and see what happens, after dealing with whatever motions, and I'm sure some of the claims and theories are going to be knocked out and some will survive. And I'll try the case that I have jurisdiction over, which is the Northern District of Ohio group. What that will accomplish, I don't know. But I'd rather not do that. So that's really what I want to talk to everyone [about] today, and if we can get some agreement on both sides [then] that's what we ought to do."

Settlement—or at least an attempt at settlement that included a new way to limit the distribution and prescribing of opioids—was a moral imperative, he argued.

"I think we have an opportunity to do it, and it would be an abject abdication of our responsibility not to try it," he said. "And if we can get some general agreement that we should try it, then we'll figure out today how do we organize that effort."

One by one, the key lawyers for both sides addressed the judge. Most spoke in platitudes as they tried to remain deferential to the judge's wishes, but also to be realistic about what they saw as an inevitable courtroom confrontation.

"Thank you for your comments," Joe Rice began. "I think I can say on behalf of all the plaintiffs that we share your feeling of urgency. And I can tell you that all of our clients are dealing with this every day at the city, county level, everybody. So we are here to give you the time and the talents that we can have to try to bring something together as quickly as possible."

Paul Hanly then stood before the judge. The plaintiffs were in favor of reaching a resolution, he said, but they wanted to proceed on a litigation track at the same time because some drug company lawyers were far more interested in fighting than settling.

"I understood that, Paul," Polster replied. "But the resolution I'm talking about is really—what I'm interested in doing is not just moving money around, because this is an ongoing crisis. What we've got to do is dramatically reduce the number of the pills that are out there and make sure that the pills that are out there are being used properly. Because we all know that a whole lot of them have gone walking and with devastating results. And that's happening right now. So that's what I want to accomplish. And then we'll deal with the money. We can deal with the money also and the treatment. I mean, that's what— you know, we need a whole lot—some new systems in place, and we need some treatment. Okay? We don't need a lot of briefs and we don't need trials."

Mark S. Cheffo, the lead lawyer representing Purdue Pharma and other drug manufacturers, told Polster that he recognized there were "issues in this country" and he wanted his company to be part of the solution. "We welcome the opportunity to kind of sit down with the court, hear your ideas and try to be as productive as we can," he said. "We want to participate with Your Honor and at least try to explore some of these ideas."

Toward the end of the meeting, Polster said he wanted to divide up the lawyers, put them in different unused courtrooms, and let them start to figure out a way to settle the cases quickly.

"I read recently that we've managed in the last two years, because of the opioid problem, to do what our country has not done in fifty years, which is to for two consecutive years, reduce, lower the average life expectancy of Americans," the judge concluded. "And if we don't do something in 2018, we'll have accomplished it for three years in a row, which we haven't done since the flu epidemic a hundred years ago wiped out 10 percent of the population. And this is 100 percent man-made. Now, I'm pretty ashamed that this has occurred while I've been around. So, I think we all should be."

Like many lawyers, Kaspar J. Stoffelmayr, a partner with the Chicago-based Bartlit Beck law firm and the lead counsel for Walgreens, listened in on a conference line. A lawyer for twenty years, Stoffelmayr had participated in several sprawling MDLs, defending major corporations such as DuPont and Bayer in product liability cases. He thought Polster had planned to hold a case management conference that morning to discuss logistics—which lawyers would be part of the leadership structure and who would serve as liaisons to several special masters appointed to help the judge.

Stoffelmayr was taken aback when Polster announced that he wanted the parties to settle rather than litigate. How could the judge say on day one that he was less interested in the legal dispute? Stoffelmayr had never been involved in any litigation that worked that way.

Certainly unusual, Stoffelmayr thought.

As the lawyers left the courtroom, they groused in whispered exchanges.

"Pollyanna," one said.

"Over his head," said another.

Paul had a different take.

There ain't no fucking way this thing is going to settle like that, he thought.

Chapter 39

A Perry Mason Moment

Cleveland, February 2018

On February 26 at three in the afternoon, Paul Farrell made his first appearance before Judge Polster as the co–lead counsel in the most complex civil action in the history of American jurisprudence. As he looked around the courtroom, he knew it was a moment to savor. It also was time to launch a carefully orchestrated surprise attack on his courtroom adversaries.

Lawyers for the drug companies and the Justice Department had come to the federal courthouse in Cleveland that day to urge Polster to keep the ARCOS pill-tracking database secret. The lawyers for the companies and the Justice Department had argued in motions that disclosing it could reveal trade secrets and compromise criminal investigations. Perhaps worst of all, it could put the nation at risk if the precise locations of drug distribution centers were divulged, making them easy targets for opioid-seeking gangs.

It's all bullshit, Paul thought.

But he needed to prove it in court. ARCOS was the key to his case. He knew the data would provide a detailed road map to the epidemic. He also knew that ARCOS would enable his team to train its firepower on the companies responsible for manufacturing and distributing the largest volumes of pills. If he won, the plaintiffs might be able to convince the companies to settle, forgoing a costly and time-consuming trial—one of Polster's main objectives. Paul had a figure in mind: $20 billion.

As he sat in Polster's eighteenth-floor courtroom that afternoon, Paul waited for the right moment. James R. Bennett II, a Justice Department lawyer based in Cleveland, began his career as a local prosecutor in Ohio after graduating from Case Western Reserve University Law School and Marshall University in Paul's hometown. He stepped to the podium and told Polster that the plaintiffs should request the ARCOS data from the drug manufacturers and distributors, not the government. "They are the better source of information," Bennett said.

Paul was tired of hearing that argument. Yet again, the federal government was siding with the drug industry and trying to keep critical information away from the public. Paul had been trying to gain access to ARCOS for nearly a year, ever since he unsuccessfully doorstepped DEA supervisor Karl Colder in Washington the previous February. The Justice Department continued to dig in. As the hearing proceeded, Polster began to lose his patience with Bennett.

"The important thing is to track whose pills went where specifically," Polster told him. "There are certain areas of the country where there are hundreds and thousands of pills per person, per year, for every man, woman, and child. Everyone knows that was wrong, it shouldn't have happened.

"The question is, whose pills?"

Bennett lamented the toll the epidemic had taken on the country. The Justice Department, he said, had made combating illegal diversion of pills to the black market a top priority.

"However, the Department of Justice and the DEA must also protect its ongoing and its future investigations, and it must also protect the privacy and the commercial interests of innocent businesses," Bennett argued. "In addition to the law enforcement interests, there are also trade secret interests for the individual manufacturers and distributors."

"There are no trade secrets here," Polster snapped back. "This is a controlled substance, they're pills. We're not going to ask [for] the formulation of any pills. That shouldn't be in the data. Where the pills went is not a trade secret."

Bennett refused to relent. "It also would allow individuals to look and see the marketing and the strategic plans the businesses have by showing how they have had growth in certain areas," he said.

"They obviously know which pharmacies they're selling to and which they aren't," Polster countered, "and I think they probably have a darned good idea which of their competitors are supplying the pharmacies."

Bennett tried a different tack. The ARCOS data, he said, contained the addresses of the drug distribution warehouses. Disclosing those locations could be dangerous and lead to even more pills hitting the black market if the facilities were burglarized or robbed.

"Your Honor, knowing the city, county, and state of where those warehouses are in many situations would allow identification of that warehouse," Bennett said. "It might be very easy for criminals to figure out where these warehouses are located."

Paul had already studied the motions the Justice Department had filed, laying out this argument. He was ready to pounce.

"I don't mean to interrupt, but I think I have something critical to say on this very matter," he said, standing in the courtroom.

"All right," Polster said.

"The address for these warehouses is publicly available."

"It is?" Polster asked.

"Yes, sir. May I approach?"

"Yes," the judge said.

"Cardinal Health in its manufacturer reference manual actually has a table that identifies each of its distribution facilities as well as the address," Paul said.

"May I also have a copy?" Bennett asked.

"I also brought the administrative memorandum and agreement

that the DEA [and] DOJ had with McKesson, and in it, it identifies—I
lost count—maybe fifteen or twenty of the warehouses that were subject to the McKesson fine, and in it this public document identifies
the exact street address for each of the warehouses," Paul said. "In
addition to that, if you get on all three of the companies' websites,
they have job application sections where they post the warehouse that
has job opportunities by city and state. Many of their public statements, for instance, AmerisourceBergen recently announced in June
of 2007, they put out a press release talking about the opening of a
new distribution center in Orlando, Florida."

Polster turned to Bennett. "It looks like, Mr. Bennett, a lot of
these companies don't seem to care about disclosing the exact street
address of their warehouse," the judge said.

"Which I think, Your Honor, is more reason why we need to not
disclose the actual transactions, because now that the information of
where these warehouses [are] located, knowing when they're receiving
shipments and how much, and which are getting big shipments—"

Polster cut him off. "No, we are not going to do that. The companies are so lax they're letting everyone know, it's too bad for them,"
the judge said. "I'm not so worried about the warehouses anymore,
because sadly it looks like the companies themselves haven't bothered
to keep them confidential."

Paul felt like he was in a scene from one of his favorite courtroom
TV shows, *Perry Mason*.

Bennett was flailing. "With the Privacy Act concerns, with the
trade secret concerns, with the law enforcement concerns, the burden
on the agency, with the ability to use this information—" Bennett
started to say before Polster cut him off again.

"I'm not trying to burden the agency," the judge said. "Just turn it
over."

Lawyers representing the drug distributors scrambled to their feet
in the courtroom as they took turns trying to convince the judge to
keep ARCOS secret. Steven M. Pyser, an attorney for Williams &

Connolly representing Cardinal Health, said he worried that the data could disclose the locations of pharmacies in areas where there were large volumes of opioid prescriptions being filled. That might encourage other pharmacies to move into those areas and compete for the business.

"Quite frankly, there shouldn't be a lot of competition for distributing opioids," Polster said.

"Your Honor, in no way was I implying the pharmacies are trying to distribute extra opioids," Pyser said.

"That is what it sounds like," the judge said.

"But it is a standard for how busy a pharmacy is in general," Pyser offered.

"Yeah, but if it's real busy for opioids, that could be a signal that there's something wrong. All right?" Polster said. "That's my point, and that's the plaintiffs' point. And if a distributor knows that, then maybe the distributor should have done something."

Alvin L. Emch, a Charleston, West Virginia, lawyer representing AmerisourceBergen at the hearing, warned that disclosing the database would give the plaintiffs an unfair advantage. It would reveal pill distribution patterns by other companies, allowing the plaintiffs to add even more defendants to their case. He also noted that the drug distribution companies had never seen each other's data. Why should the plaintiffs gain access? "Plaintiffs want this information so that they can take that data and use it against us, data we never had," Emch said.

Polster brushed the argument aside, noting that ARCOS was based on sales information provided by the companies themselves. "Obviously, if they get it, you get it, and the point is you know where every one of your pills went because you supplied the data for your company," the judge said. "I'm saying your client supplied the data for its company. So, you know something they don't know, which is you know where all of your pills went."

"We do," Emch conceded.

Polster had heard enough. He ordered the DEA to turn over the ARCOS data spanning nine years, from January 1, 2006, through December 31, 2014. As a former prosecutor, he understood the importance of keeping ongoing criminal investigations confidential. The judge withheld the last three years of pill distribution numbers, which he said should protect those investigations. He also said the data would be provided to both sides under a protective order, sealing it from the public. It was an incentive for the drug companies to settle.

"Nothing is going to be revealed to the media unless there is a trial," Polster said.

Chapter 40

The Death Star

Washington, D.C., July 2018

Covington & Burling is one of the most prestigious law firms in America, with more than thirteen hundred lawyers and staffers across the globe, from D.C. to Brussels to Beijing. Its roster of past and current partners reads like a who's who in Washington, with former top federal government officials ranging from Dean Acheson, President Truman's secretary of state, to President Obama's former attorney general, Eric Holder. Like Holder, many leave Covington to serve in high-level government positions and then return. Covington is also home to some of the best civil litigators in the country.

The firm's modern office complex occupies more than 450,000 square feet in two twelve-story towers connected by stairs and bridges in the heart of downtown D.C. Natural light pours through the full-length glass windows on every floor and the interior glass walkways. The plaintiffs' lawyers in the opioid litigation jokingly call Covington "the Death Star," a *Star Wars* reference to the Empire's moon-sized space station that can destroy entire planets.

On July 31, 2018, Paul Farrell arrived at Covington to take the first of what would be hundreds of depositions. He was joined by three top lawyers from the Pensacola firm Levin Papantonio Rafferty.

Paul walked into the conference room where the deposition was to take place. The table went from one end of the room to the other. Lawyers from other firms representing the drug manufacturers, distributors, and pharmacies occupied nearly every seat on both sides. Some stood along the back wall of the room. More lawyers listened in on a conference line.

"Man, this place is *fancy*," Paul said to the lawyers. "I wonder if they'll hire me." The joke was met with stony silence.

Paul sat down across from Nathan J. Hartle, the vice president of regulatory affairs and compliance for one of the Big Three distributors, McKesson. Representing Hartle was Covington lawyer Emily Johnson Henn, a Georgetown University Law Center graduate who had clerked for Supreme Court justice Sandra Day O'Connor. Henn had been named one of the top female lawyers in California by *The Daily Journal*, a legal publication. Paul figured that she and the other lawyers on the Covington team had been prepping Hartle for weeks, assuring him not to worry about the lawyer from West Virginia.

As Paul began the deposition at 9:04 that morning, he tuned out the rest of the room. There was only him and the witness.

"Good morning," he said to Hartle.

In the early questioning, Paul tried to shake Hartle, and the attorney soon saw a wave of anxiety cross the executive's face. Paul also saw in Hartle's eyes an openness to answer honestly, something not often encountered when deposing a witness.

For seven hours, Paul walked Hartle through the elements of his case: The Controlled Substances Act of 1970. The "closed" distribution system Congress created to prevent diversion of drugs to the black market. The addictive nature of opium. The Masters ruling, confirming the requirement for distributors like McKesson to detect, report, and stop the shipment of suspicious orders of controlled substances.

Paul showed Hartle the 1910 congressional testimony by Donald McKesson, an early executive of the company. He had told members of Congress that his company was opposed to habit-forming drugs and that if they received orders from suspicious people, they would report them to law enforcement for prosecution.

He asked Hartle to read a section of the 1970 Controlled Substances Act: "The illegal importation, manufacture, distribution, and possession and improper use of controlled substances have a substantial and detrimental effect on the health and general welfare of the American people."

"Does McKesson acknowledge and agree with those findings?" Paul asked.

"Yes," Hartle said.

"And McKesson is engaged in the distribution business, agreed?" Paul asked.

"We are," Hartle replied.

"And that if they do not follow the law as provided by the U.S. Code and the *Code of Federal Regulations*, it has a substantial and detrimental effect on the health and general welfare of the American people, agreed?"

"Yes," Hartle said.

Paul continued. "Does McKesson acknowledge that it has a duty to maintain effective control against diversion of opium pills as mandated by Congress?"

"We do," Hartle said.

Paul asked Hartle to read a statement by the chairman of a House Energy and Commerce subcommittee at the start of a 2001 congressional hearing: "According to the DEA, the number of oxycodone-related deaths has increased 400 percent since 1996, the same time period in which the annual number of prescriptions for OxyContin has risen from approximately 300,000 to almost 6 million."

How, Paul asked, did these pills get from the maker of OxyContin, Purdue Pharma, to the pharmacies?

Hartle said they were sent by distributors.

"Right," Paul said. "So, between 1996 and the year 2001, the number of prescriptions went from 300,000 to almost 6 million. So, the OxyContin business was booming, wasn't it?"

"It increased significantly," Hartle replied.

"And McKesson was amongst the distributors that were delivering the pills from Purdue Pharma to the pharmacies?" Paul asked.

"We were," Hartle said.

Paul asked Hartle to read the section of the Controlled Substances Act that said the price for participating in illicit drug trafficking schemes should be "prohibitive," or excessively high. "It just makes sense, right?" Paul said. "If you're going to punish somebody and the punishment isn't very severe, they're likely to what?"

"To do it again," Hartle said.

"Why?" Paul asked.

"There's no penalty or accountability," Hartle replied.

"Let's say that a speeding ticket is a dollar. What would happen across America if a speeding ticket was a dollar?" Paul asked.

"It wouldn't hold the same weight," Hartle said. "It may not deter people from speeding."

"What if the speeding ticket was a million dollars?" Paul asked. "What would that do?"

"I'm just guessing, but likely people would not speed," Hartle said.

"Like, not to be cute, but McKesson was fined $13 million in 2008 and then was fined again in 2017, $150 million," Paul said. "Do you think that the second fine was intended to be more prohibitive than the first fine?"

"I believe so," Hartle replied.

Paul produced a copy of McKesson's operations manual from 2000 that laid out its suspicious monitoring program and how controlled substances should be handled. He asked Hartle to read a paragraph that detailed the DEA's definition of suspicious orders: "Suspicious orders include orders of unusual size, orders deviating substantially from a normal pattern, and orders of unusual frequency."

Paul asked him to read another sentence: "Recent cases indicate that DEA will seek large penalties from distributors who fail to comply with this regulation."

"You got to follow the law?" Paul asked.

"Right," Hartle said.

"And if McKesson doesn't follow the law, that makes its conduct unlawful?" Paul asked.

"Yes," Hartle said.

Paul reminded Hartle that he was not there as an individual, but as a representative of the company—known in legal parlance as a 30(b)(6) witness. Paul thought that Hartle was exhausted after hours of questioning and hundreds of objections by his defense lawyer. He was hoping Hartle might let his guard down. He posed his most important question of the day:

"Do you think McKesson is partly responsible for the societal costs of prescription drug abuse in America?" he asked.

"There's a lot of people involved," Hartle said. "It's a very complicated and multi-faceted issue."

"I want to talk about McKesson," Paul said. "This is your opportunity to accept partial responsibility for the societal costs of prescription drug abuse in America: Yes or no?"

"So again, it depends on—it depends," Hartle said.

"Back to the McKesson Corporation, which is you sitting in a chair today," Paul said. "Knowing about your past conduct, knowing about the past interactions with the DEA, I'm going to ask you again: Does McKesson Corporation accept partial responsibility for the societal costs of prescription drug abuse in America?"

"We're part of the closed system, so we're responsible for preventing diversion," Hartle said.

"So, the answer is?" Paul asked.

"I think we're responsible for something," Hartle said. "I don't know how you define all societal costs. I still believe it depends on different circumstances."

"So, I don't want to put words in your mouth because it's got to come out of your mouth. So, the answer is yes, or no?"

"I would say, yes, partially," Hartle said.

Paul walked out of the conference room. He felt like he was a Major League pitcher, stepping off the mound and heading to the dugout after striking out one of the most important batters on the other team. He also felt that he was just as good as, maybe better than, any of the other lawyers in the MDL.

Chapter 41

The Digital Detectives

New Orleans, Louisiana, July 2018

For weeks on end in 2018, Anthony Irpino rarely left his spacious law office on the second floor of a grand Victorian in the Garden District of New Orleans. In front of a floor-to-ceiling brick fireplace on one side of the office stood a statue of Sun Tzu, the author of *The Art of War*. Irpino downed bottles of Coke and chewed wads of Kodiak dipping tobacco as he studied spreadsheets referencing hundreds of thousands of drug company documents. The empty Coke bottles served as spittoons and littered his desk. An adjoining office with a couch became his bedroom.

The veteran plaintiffs' trial attorney was impressed by how enormous the opioid litigation had become. The two dozen drug companies being sued had turned over nearly 20 million documents during discovery. Cardinal had produced 1.8 million records alone, burying the plaintiffs' attorneys in paper. Lawyers for the companies were arguing that they didn't need to disclose the contents of 250,000 other documents, claiming that the information contained in them was protected by attorney-client privilege or the result of attorney work product. They designated another 10 million documents as "confidential," arguing that only the lawyers on the case could see them. If the documents became public, the defense argued, they would violate the privacy of the corporations or their employees. Irpino was hired to coordinate the hunt for the hottest documents in the piles deemed off-limits or restricted. It was like trying to find flecks of gold buried in a deep, dark mine shaft.

Of all the positions on the plaintiffs' two-hundred-member legal team, Irpino's role was the most arcane and one of the most important. Raised in Skokie, Illinois, outside of Chicago, he had worked as a short order cook before attending the University of Illinois at Urbana-Champaign and then Tulane Law School in New Orleans. He fell for the city and decided to stay.

At forty-seven, Irpino, who looked like he could be related to Robert De Niro, was in charge of what's known in the civil litigation world as "privilege and confidentiality." It's a high-stakes legal game of hide-and-seek, and its outcome can determine the success or failure of a case. Were the 250,000 documents—emails, memos, PowerPoint presentations, internal audits—truly protected by attorney-client privilege or work product, or were the companies using those designations as a ruse to shield them from the plaintiffs? Were the 10 million documents really "confidential," or did they merely contain embarrassing or damaging information that the public had a right to see?

It was backbreaking work that required many all-nighters and no days off. The work rarely received public recognition. Irpino worked alongside his thirty-six-year-old law partner, Pearl A. Robertson, a tall woman with long blonde hair often pulled back into a ponytail who played basketball in an international league before attending Loyola University College of Law. They might discover one piece of paper that could alter the outcome of a motions hearing or the trajectory of the entire case. Or they might miss a document that could have turned the litigation in their favor. It was difficult to remain focused, triangulating disparate bits of information as they tried to put the puzzle pieces of the privilege documents together. All they had to go on were logs produced by the drug companies that contained the most basic of information: subject lines of emails, names of authors, and dates they were written. Teams of document reviewers and lawyers scanned the metadata and flagged the emails that looked like they might be masking revelatory documents—the ones they would ask the court to compel the companies to turn over.

Irpino and Robertson had teamed up to do the same work on the BP *Deepwater Horizon* case, which resulted in a $20.8 billion settlement in 2016 for the massive oil spill in the Gulf of Mexico. But the opioids case was proving to be far more complicated, with so many defendants—most of them Fortune 500 companies backed by formidable law firms—and more and more cities, counties, towns, and Indian tribal nations filing cases every month.

"This epidemic is such a scourge," Irpino would tell himself. *"Maybe we can make a difference."*

There were times when his thoughts drifted to his brother, who had died in Irpino's home of heart failure after years of substance abuse, which Irpino believed included the use of opioids. He also thought about one of his best friends from college who had become addicted to opioids and leapt from the balcony of his high-rise condominium in downtown Chicago.

When Irpino or a colleague found an inflammatory document, he felt a rush of excitement. "This document is great for us," he'd say. But then his thoughts would quickly turn to his brother and his friend, and the callousness of the companies. *Those fuckers*, he'd say.

On April 11, Judge Polster created a litigation track for the opioid cases. While both sides had made some progress toward a settlement, the judge noted in an order that the plaintiffs and the defendants both believed that setting trial dates might force them to the bargaining table. With the first so-called bellwether trial set to start in Cleveland in October 2019, lawyers for the two sides began to prepare for a monumental courtroom battle. The outcome of that first trial would have enormous consequences. It would help predict how other cases that were waiting for their turn in court might fare before juries. With a trial date pending, Paul Farrell added more lawyers to the hunt for hot documents. He set up what he called "SEAL Team Six," a reference to the Navy's most elite special operations unit.

One of those hot documents surfaced in July 2018. It was discovered by Evan M. Janush, a forty-five-year-old lawyer assigned to the case who had been collaborating with Irpino. Based in New York, Janush was intensely focused and spoke in rapid-fire sentences. He came across emails that had been turned over by Cardinal Health. One of the emails noted that Cardinal had hired an outside auditor in 2007 while the DEA was investigating the company for supplying the internet pharmacies with hydrocodone. But there was no audit attached to the email. At first, Cardinal denied an audit existed. Then lawyers for Cardinal told Janush that they had found the audit in a filing cabinet but claimed it was protected by attorney-client privilege because it had been conducted by a consultant and furnished to a law firm retained by the company. It was one of fifty thousand attorney-client privilege claims asserted by Cardinal. After the plaintiffs complained, a special master assigned to help Polster manage the case, David R. Cohen, ordered Cardinal to produce the January 23, 2008, audit. There was a reason why the company didn't want the plaintiffs to see it. The consultant, Ronald Buzzeo, a retired DEA official, found that Cardinal was filling large and potentially suspicious orders of narcotics and neglecting to report them to the DEA. Later that year, Cardinal paid the $34 million fine to settle the case brought by the DEA and paid another $44 million fine in 2016 for the same allegations. For ten years, Cardinal was able to keep the existence of the internal audit secret.

Janush scored another coup toward the end of that summer. The plaintiffs had loaded the twenty million documents into a search engine platform called Relativity. He began to search under the word "crisis," looking for any emails or documents relating to the opioid crisis. Instead, he found something unexpected.

"If what I have is original—holy shit—that's all I will say for now," Janush wrote to Paul on August 6.

"Dude, you can't leave me hanging," Paul wrote back.

Janush had discovered The Alliance's "Crisis Playbook" produced by APCO Worldwide in 2013 in the face of intensifying DEA investigations into the drug industry. He also found the minutes to an Alliance executive committee meeting during which the Big Three distributors approved filing a friend-of-the-court brief in the Masters Pharmaceutical case. One of the lawyers at the meeting said the DEA no longer wanted to regulate the drug industry but was instead "actually preventing the distribution of controlled substances to licensed dispensers."

"I have a man crush. Evan Janush has discovered two documents which are simply amazing," Paul wrote to the plaintiffs' leadership team the next day. "Pure gold."

Across the country in a Seattle law firm that was part of the litigation, attorneys were searching through documents that had been produced by Mallinckrodt, the generic drug maker. On October 15, 2018, the lawyers were searching through documents Mallinckrodt had turned over to the DEA when one of them found an email chain involving Victor Borelli, the national sales manager for the company. It was the "Doritos" exchange between Borelli and one of his distributor customers that had been written a decade earlier.

The document review team showed the email to Derek W. Loeser, one of the lead lawyers for the Seattle firm of Keller Rohrback. "I can't believe these people said this," Loeser exclaimed. "This is a billion-dollar document."

Paul believed he was on a hot streak. He was more certain than ever that the case—*his case*—was winnable. But he was about to be bigfooted by a famous trial lawyer, and he never saw him coming. In fact, he didn't even know his name.

Chapter 42

The Magician

Houston, Texas, Spring 2019

As the opioid case moved closer to the first trial set for the fall of 2019 in Cleveland, Paul Hanly and his law partner, Jayne Conroy, knew they needed to deploy their secret weapon: a colorful fifty-eight-year-old Texas lawyer who was one of the most successful trial attorneys in America. They hoped to persuade Mark Lanier to be their top litigator in the Cleveland courtroom and convince their partners in the MDL of the wisdom of a move that would instantly demote many of them. Hanly and Conroy, who had worked with Lanier on five previous trials, knew it would be a tough sell on both sides of the maneuver.

Lanier had lots of business, was enormously wealthy, and didn't need to take on a complex case full of competing egos. The Texan lived large on a thirty-five-acre estate about twenty-five miles north of Houston, where he raised chickens, sheep, goats, monkeys, geese, pot-bellied pigs, and llamas on manicured grounds framed by orchards of apples, plums, and peaches. The founder of the Christian Trial Lawyers Association, Lanier was also an ordained minister who taught a TED Talk–style Sunday school class on biblical literacy for hundreds of people at the Champion Forest Baptist Church in Houston—a background that informed his penchant for references to scripture in argument. He collected ancient Hebrew manuscripts and fragments of the Dead Sea Scrolls and had created the Lanier Theological Library on his estate. The seventeen-thousand-square-foot building with soaring windows held one of the country's largest private collections of rare theological documents. Lanier, whose fortune underwrote his eclectic interests, had also built a stone chapel resembling a Byzantine church, along with a replica of an English village with a cobblestone street and a dining hall, where he baked bread and hot cross buns. Running through the property was a narrow-gauge railroad, a tribute to his father, who had worked for the Texas and Pacific Railway.

Lanier liked to indulge himself and those around him. He spent hundreds of thousands of dollars on Christmas galas, inviting lawyers, politicians, judges, church friends, and their families to his estate. The entertainment was always solid gold: Diana Ross, Sting, Bon Jovi, Miley Cyrus, Johnny Cash, and Crosby, Stills & Nash.

The oversized persona aside, Lanier was, in the judgment of his peers, a hell of a lawyer.

"He's a magician," Hanly said. "His mind works as quickly as a computer, and he has a photographic memory. He is the greatest trial strategist."

In preparation for trials, Lanier perfected the art of the deposition. In lieu of the normally staid affairs with a single camera trained on the subject of the deposition, Lanier would set up multiple cameras in the deposition conference room. He would focus one camera on the subject, another on himself, and a third on the screen of an overhead projector. If the deposition was shown in court, the footage could be edited to show different angles, making the screening less monotonous for jurors. He also used an array of Paper Mate colored pens to draw pictures and take notes during important moments and flash them on the screen. At first, the subjects of the depositions and his colleagues were bemused. Before long, they were impressed by the simplicity and brilliance of Lanier's style.

In front of a jury, Lanier played the role of a country lawyer—telling folksy stories, using props and verses from the Bible. His methods sounded gimmicky, but they were wildly successful with those in the box who were the ultimate arbiters. Over the course of his thirty-seven-year career, Lanier, who founded the Lanier Law Firm in 1990, had tried more than two hundred personal injury and product liability lawsuits. He won nearly $20 billion in verdicts against corporations in cases involving asbestos, drugs, and metal hip implants.

Lanier's law firm had joined the litigation as a member of the plaintiffs' executive committee. But after attending a couple of leadership meetings and witnessing the clashing egos, Lanier retreated. Hanly and Conroy—who first met Lanier as courtroom opponents, but later became friends—refused to let him slip away. At a meeting to convince him to come back, Lanier told them that if he signed on, he wanted to be in charge of *everything*: trial strategy, depositions, opening statements, witness examinations, and closing arguments. He was happy to listen to the other attorneys, but the final decisions would be his.

"I'm just going to ruffle feathers and make people mad because I do things my way," he told Hanly and Conroy. "I don't do things by committee. If I'm getting involved, I'm going to do 90 percent of the case."

Hanly and Conroy already had the co-lead of the MDL, Joe Rice, on board. They needed to convince the other lawyers to yield to Lanier's authority. Many of them had already invested huge amounts of time and money in the case. Some of them felt they were just as good as the interloper from Texas. But with many of the lawyers in favor of signing up Lanier, Hanly and Conroy thought they could persuade the holdouts.

"Trial lawyers are like undisciplined thoroughbreds," Hanly said. "They take a lot of grooming and coaxing and whispering to get them to settle down. They want to do things their way and the MDL has a bunch of experienced trial lawyers. And there were people who didn't know Mark well or hadn't seen him try a case."

One of them was Paul Farrell. That spring, Paul met with Hanly, Conroy, and Rice in the Manhattan offices of Motley Rice. They told Paul they wanted Lanier to try the case.

"He's the Michael Jordan of trial lawyers," Hanly said.

"I can try the case," Paul insisted.

"No offense, my young friend," Hanly said. "But you're no Mark Lanier." Hanly had two decades on Paul in both age and trial experience. Hanly knew Lanier was a once-in-a-generation talent.

Paul's respect and affection for Hanly, Conroy, and Rice had only grown over the course of the case. He didn't like what they were recommending; he was skeptical that Lanier was the superstar being depicted. But after a pause to suppress his momentary indignation, he said he could accept Lanier.

"Look, there has not been a single decision that any of us have dissented on. I trust you. I'll do what's best for the case," Paul told them. "But you're going to have a big sell job to get the other lawyers to agree."

One of the biggest obstacles was Hunter Shkolnik, the New York lawyer who had been working on the opioid litigation. He was set to be the lead lawyer for the Cleveland trial. Cuyahoga County was his client, and he dug in. Hanly, Conroy, and several of the other lawyers in the MDL spent hours trying to convince him that Lanier was a guarantee of success.

On April 23, 2019, with the trial six months away, Hanly and Conroy gathered the lawyers to listen to Lanier in a makeshift war room the litigation team had set up in Cleveland. Lanier cast the case in biblical terms, a modern-day David versus Goliath. He reminded the lawyers that David was first offered armor and spears and swords to fight Goliath. But David said he would only go into battle with the weapon he trusted, his slingshot.

"One of the lessons I draw out of that story is, I don't want to go into battle with armor and weapons I haven't tested," Lanier told the lawyers. "I know what works for me. I know which trial scientists to use, which jury consultant to use. I know what type of an opening works. I know how to put on the witnesses. I know the order of witnesses that I put on and why I put them on in that order. I've got rules for all of this, that I've honed over hundreds of cases that I've tried. And I know what works for me. I'm not saying some things don't work for other people. I'm not saying it's good that my way is the only way that works. I'm saying I know my way works."

Lanier was charming and persuasive as he described how he would tackle the case, and his hard-nosed confidence was evident to the group of seasoned litigators. ·

"If I'm coming in, I'm not going to risk something of this magnitude, experimenting with other weapons and other approaches," Lanier continued. "So, y'all can say, 'Great, let's do it.' Or y'all can say, 'No.' And I'm fine, whichever one you choose, but y'all make that choice, y'all fight about it, y'all politicize it, y'all do what y'all need to do. And then let me know. And if it's mine, great. If it's not, I'll do anything I can to help whoever's doing it. But I'm not going to do it unless I do it with weapons that I know."

"I'm only agreeable with certain terms," Shkolnik said.

Shkolnik wanted to put on all of his witnesses. He wanted to deliver part of the opening statement and part of the closing argument.

"Hunter, if things work out well, then I'll give you a little bit of the opening," Lanier said. "And if things work out well, I'll give you one or two of your witnesses, but not all of them. And I just don't know until I see who the jury is, until I see how the trial's setting up. And I will make that decision and you will have to abide by my decision."

"No," Shkolnik said.

Lanier looked around the war room.

Hanly and Conroy had convinced just about everyone else in the room that Lanier was the right choice.

"Mark, it's yes," Hanly said. "Hunter's just not realizing it's yes."

Chapter 43

The 60 Minutes Man

Washington, D.C., May 2019

Joe Rannazzisi wasn't feeling well on the morning of May 15, 2019, as he took a seat at the conference table inside Williams & Connolly, the D.C. firm known for representing some of the biggest names in corporate America, many of them leaders in the pharmaceutical field: Pfizer, AstraZeneca, Eli Lilly, and Cardinal Health.

He wasn't nervous, even though he was staring at a dozen drug company lawyers seated across from him at the firm's headquarters. Joe was looking forward to telling his story during the deposition set for that morning. But two and a half years out from open-heart surgery, he had never fully recovered. He tired easily. His hands trembled. He suffered from migraines. One moment he felt feverish, the next he was shaking with chills.

Joe had decided to leave his job with the software company and accept the offer from attorney Richard Fields to work on behalf of the Cherokee Nation in its lawsuit against the drug industry. For the first time, Joe was now a paid consultant in a suit that had been folded into the MDL. Drug company defense attorneys were lining up to take a shot at one of the most important witnesses for the plaintiffs, hoping to undermine his credibility and neutralize him as a threat.

This was Joe's second appearance at Williams & Connolly. Enu Mainigi, the lawyer assigned to represent Cardinal, had subpoenaed

Joe to appear for a deposition at her firm a month earlier. Mainigi and other drug company lawyers spent an entire day hammering Joe that April, trying to get him to admit that the DEA was partially to blame for the opioid epidemic and he could have done more to work with the drug industry to stop the carnage. The plaintiffs assigned their most talented trial attorney to rehabilitate Joe on the morning of May 15 during the redirect portion of his deposition, when attorneys on his side were able to ask additional questions.

"Mr. Rannazzisi, thank you for your time today. My name is Mark Lanier. You and I have not met before you sat down here just a few minutes ago. Is that right?"

"That's correct," Joe said.

Lanier placed a piece of cardstock on his overhead projector for the room full of lawyers to see. On the card, he had drawn a road that ended at a photograph of Joe in the upper left-hand corner. Along the side of the road were colorful billboards that read "60 Minutes Man Rd.," "Background," "60 Minutes," and "Follow-up."

Lanier began with Joe's background. On another card, he jotted down his education, his degrees in pharmacology and law, and the positions he had held at the DEA.

"Spoiler alert," Lanier said. "Are you still with the DEA?"

"No, I retired," Joe said.

Lanier was in his full-on just-a-country-boy mode as he walked Joe through his responsibilities at the DEA, how he ran Redrum, the drug-related murder task force in Detroit, and how he knocked over meth labs as the chief of the dangerous chemicals section at the agency. Joe told Lanier he became a DEA special agent in 1988.

"Is that when you get the badge?" Lanier asked.

"Yes, sir."

"Did you, like, carry a gun and stuff?"

"Yes, sir."

"Did you ever arrest anyone or do any of that stuff?" Lanier asked.

"Yes, sir," Joe said with a smile.

Lanier put his road map back on the overhead projector. "I want to move to the next stop on the road. It's what I call the *60 Minutes* stop," he said, placing the *60 Minutes* logo on the card. He asked Joe to explain the Controlled Substances Act and the distributors' responsibility to monitor suspicious orders. He then repeated something Joe had said during his October 17, 2017, appearance on *60 Minutes*.

"Was it an industry, based on your experience and opinion, that was out of control?" he asked Joe.

"Yes, sir."

"Explain what you mean by that, please."

"We tried to push them, force them into compliance, but they just wouldn't comply," Joe said. "When they decided they didn't want to comply, they just used influence to create a law or to change a law. So, yeah, I pretty much believed that they were out of control."

Lanier asked Joe to explain the regulations for drug distributors, that they have a responsibility to stop orders when they are of an unusual size or frequency or substantially deviate from normal ordering patterns.

"Does it have to be all three of those?" Lanier asked.

"No," Joe said.

"Two of them?"

"It could be just one," Joe said.

Lanier put another card on the projector and wrote, "Don't ship suspicious orders w/o full due diligence. Resolve suspicion."

On another card, he jotted down the full quote from Joe's *60 Minutes* appearance: "This is an industry that is out of control. What they want to do is what they want to do and not worry about what the law is. And if they don't follow the law in drug supply, people die. That's just it. People die."

"What," Lanier asked, "did you base that opinion on?"

Lanier walked Joe through the letters he had sent to the drug companies. The multimillion-dollar fines the companies paid for noncompliance. The promises the companies made to the DEA that they would do better. The extraordinary volume of pills they shipped after they were fined. The ever-increasing numbers of overdose deaths.

"The last part of your statement here: 'If they don't follow the law in drug supply, people die. That's just it. People die.' Explain what you meant."

"When you have diversion and these drugs are going out into the community and they're getting into the wrong hands, the drugs are being used without supervision, the drugs are being abused; it causes overdoses. It causes death," Joe said. "We were losing people left and right. That's what I meant by people died."

Lanier then turned to the cases the DEA had made against Cardinal Health, McKesson, and AmerisourceBergen. He pulled out the settlement McKesson had signed in 2017 with the DEA and highlighted a passage that said the company had engaged in the same behavior in 2008 and signed a similar settlement with the agency.

"This is not, as we would say in Lubbock, not their first rodeo," Lanier said.

Joe started to laugh before he caught himself.

Lanier then flashed the road map back on the screen and ticked through the defenses the drug industry had used in the litigation. He took out a green Paper Mate pen and wrote down the names of each of the drug company defendants in the case.

"I want to ask you about some explanations and excuses that have been used by the defendants in this case and give you a chance to explain them. Okay?"

Excuse number 1: The drug companies didn't have access to ARCOS, the DEA did, Lanier said. The agency could have stopped suspicious orders of painkillers.

Joe said the companies reported their own sales data to the DEA and had all the information they needed to halt suspicious-looking drug orders. The drug companies saw the sales transactions in real time; ARCOS had a four- to six-month lag time.

Next excuse, Lanier said: The amount of raw material to make opioids increased during Joe's tenure. Joe said the DEA's production quota was based on requests from the manufacturers and the scientific community and corresponded to the number of prescriptions that were being written. Joe said Congress set the standards.

Next excuse: "Pain is undertreated in America."

"I'm not a medical doctor," Joe said.

Lanier then noted that the distributors, the manufacturers, and the pharmacy chains had said that they were confused about their responsibilities under the law.

"They just didn't know what they were supposed to do," Lanier said. "Would that be acceptable in your mind?"

"No," Joe said.

"Is it the DEA's job to give legal advice to the companies?"

"No."

"Have the companies been able to hire people from the DEA and actually bring them inside their companies?" Lanier asked.

Joe said the industry had hired numerous DEA officials, including many from the division that regulated the prescription drug industry. "All of the companies have many avenues to try to get their questions answered," he said.

The final tack: The DEA was partly responsible.

"Who is this gentleman named Mr. Rosenberg?" Lanier asked, referring to the former acting DEA administrator Chuck Rosenberg. "Mr. Rosenberg supposedly said the DEA was part of the problem. Do you believe the DEA was part of the problem?"

"I do not believe the DEA was part of the problem," Joe said. "The DEA was trying to stop diversion."

Lanier presented Joe with a hypothetical. "Do you drive a car?" he asked.

"Yes, sir."

"You are aware of speed limits?"

"Yes, sir."

"You are aware that sometimes there are school zones, where the speed limit is reduced?" Lanier asked. "If someone speeds through the school zone, a police officer might be there with a radar gun, might catch them, might write them a ticket. That's something you could foresee happening, fair?"

"Yes, sir."

"If a person speeds through a school zone and the police officer doesn't happen to be there that day with a radar gun and doesn't catch that person, does that mean that person is innocent?"

Joe smiled and shook his head. "No," he said.

"Can the person blame the cop because the person sped through the school zone and the cop wasn't there?"

"No."

"If the companies aren't diverting or allowing diversion of their product, then the DEA's job gets a whole lot easier, doesn't it?"

"Absolutely," Joe said.

Paul Farrell had been on the fence about Lanier when Paul Hanly, Jayne Conroy, and Joe Rice lobbied to make him the lead trial lawyer. But whatever doubts he harbored about Lanier disappeared by the end of the day. Through the simplest of brushstrokes, one on top of another, Lanier had created a devastating portrait of companies wholly indifferent to their responsibilities.

Paul was starting to realize that he might not be the best lawyer in the room, that there were more skilled mass tort litigators. He had once thought that it was time for the old legal lions to leave the veld, but he was beginning to understand how much he had to learn from the experience of lawyers like Lanier, Hanly, and Conroy. After the deposition, several plaintiffs' attorneys headed over to Joe Rice's D.C. office. Paul walked into a conference room, a look of incredulity on his face. He stared at Hanly, who had come into town to be with the team.

"Oh my God, I'm a total believer," Paul told Hanly. "I have never seen anything like that."

Chapter 44

A Lone Lawyer

Akron, Ohio, Summer 2018

The call came out of nowhere.

"Good afternoon, Karen Lefton speaking." Lefton was at her desk in her small third-floor law office in Akron when she saw the *Washington Post* come up on her caller ID. Must be someone from the newspaper's circulation department to say that her digital subscription had lapsed, she thought. Lefton was a solo practitioner. If the phone rang, she answered it.

"This is Jim McLaughlin, the deputy general counsel of the *Washington Post*," said the man on the line. It was June 21, 2018, and McLaughlin got to the point: Would Lefton be willing to represent the *Post* in its effort to obtain a secret DEA database called ARCOS that was part of the opioid litigation unfolding in U.S. district court in Cleveland?

Lefton quickly Googled McLaughlin to see if he really worked at the *Post*. She wanted to make sure the call wasn't someone's idea of a joke. She had never heard of ARCOS. And lawyers like her didn't get hired by the *Post*.

McLaughlin explained how ARCOS worked and that Judge Polster had ordered the DEA to turn the database over to the plaintiffs as part of the pretrial discovery process following protracted negotiations. But the judge had placed the database under a protective order, preventing it from being released to the public. Polster had also put hundreds of thousands of company documents under seal.

Post investigative reporters wanted access to the secret data, McLaughlin explained, and he believed they were entitled to it because Polster had already provided the information to the lawyers representing hundreds of towns, cities, and counties suing the industry.

The *Post* and the *Charleston Gazette-Mail* of West Virginia had decided to sue for the database and the company documents. Polster had just granted the *Post* the right to intervene in the case, and McLaughlin was facing a looming deadline to file a legal brief.

Lefton was thrilled with the idea of representing the *Post*, but she was certain that every media lawyer in America—and even those with no media experience—would want to work with McLaughlin. Why was he calling her?

Lefton was not McLaughlin's first choice. The *Post* had tried to hire an outside law firm in Washington. Williams & Connolly, often retained by the *Post*, was representing Cardinal and declined to take the case. The other major D.C. law firms he called also were already representing other defendants. McLaughlin told Lefton he had tried firms in Cleveland and Cincinnati, but they too had conflicts. Several of the lawyers in the Ohio firms passed along the name of Lefton. They said she was the obvious choice to handle a media case in the state.

Lefton, sixty-one, with shoulder-length blonde hair and a penchant for wearing colorful suits, never planned on being a lawyer. Her passion was journalism. She started her career in 1980 at the *Akron Beacon Journal*, covering courts and local governments. After nine months, she decided to attend law school part-time at the University of Akron. She thought a law degree would help her become a better reporter. After she passed the bar, she rose through the ranks of the newsroom, where she held several editing positions, including city editor. She eventually became the *Journal*'s general counsel.

The *Journal*, like so many other newspapers, hit hard times and began to cut staff. Lefton decided to leave in 2008. She joined a local law firm, and then set up her own practice. It was a lean operation near a shopping mall in an Akron suburb. She didn't have a secretary. She drove a 2009 Toyota Camry. She was leading the simple life of a local lawyer. She served as outside general counsel to Ohio companies and nonprofits that didn't have an attorney on staff. At times, she also represented the *Beacon Journal*. The offer from the *Post* opened a door to her first passion. She didn't hesitate.

Lefton had dreamed about a case like this. *It's so significant*, she thought. There was another motivating factor for her: She had two good friends whose children had died from opioid overdoses.

Lefton was excited and anxious. She knew that none of her other cases could have the national impact of a lawsuit filed by the *Post*. She also felt the weight of an immense responsibility. As a general business lawyer, she had represented local companies, resolving conflicts between vendors and suppliers and handling disputes between employers and their workers. Her other media cases dealt with local public records requests and access to public meetings. She had never represented a national media organization or taken part in litigation that involved the deaths of so many people. She was now representing the *Post* in a case with novel and challenging legal issues. She was about to go up against the DEA, the Department of Justice, and some of the most prominent and well-known law firms in the country.

On July 9, 2018, Lefton filed a brief on behalf of the *Post* asking the court to disclose the ARCOS database and the documents. "The public interest in the opioid epidemic far outweighs any interest in secrecy sought to be protected by the Department of Justice and the Drug Enforcement Administration and the pharmaceutical manufacturers and distributors," she wrote in her brief.

She submitted an affidavit from Jeff Leen, the investigations editor of the *Post*. He had run the unit since 1999 and edited or helped to supervise eight Pulitzer Prize–winning investigations. He also edited the *Post*'s opioid investigation. "Because of the sprawling breadth and complexity of the opioid problem," Leen wrote in his affidavit, "the *Post*'s newsroom made a strategic decision to dedicate enormous resources to it." He described the *Post*'s reporting on the opioid epidemic as "accountability journalism—that is journalism that seeks to hold powerful companies and high-ranking government officials accountable for their action (or in some cases, inaction) on matters of great public importance."

The ARCOS database would enable the public to see for the first time which U.S. communities had been hit the hardest by the epidemic, Leen wrote. They could also see whether there were obvious red flags that should have alerted drug companies to suspicious orders and which manufacturers, distributors, and pharmacies knew or should have known that their pills were being diverted to the black market.

As an example of the data's usefulness, Leen pointed to the stories the *Charleston Gazette-Mail* published that were based on the ARCOS data it had obtained. The disclosure of the data, Leen said, did not result in "genuine commercial or proprietary harm." Instead, he said that "disclosure was an enormous public service."

The DEA and the defendants fought back. The DEA, represented by Justice Department lawyers, took the lead. As they had before, the government lawyers argued that the release of the data would compromise ongoing investigations and that the information was proprietary. Seventeen days later, Polster denied the requests by the *Post* and the *Gazette-Mail*, declining to lift his protective order. He sided with the Justice Department lawyers, ruling that the data was confidential business information and could compromise DEA investigations.

Lefton was disappointed, but not surprised. "Unfortunately, his mind appears to have been closed back in February," when he had put the database under a protective order, she wrote to McLaughlin in an email. "There is no indication that he even considered, much less weighed, the immense public interest." Polster, she thought, was using the threat of its release as a sledgehammer to induce settlement.

Lefton and lawyers for the *Gazette-Mail* appealed Polster's ruling to the Sixth U.S. Circuit Court of Appeals in Cincinnati. Lefton traveled to Cincinnati for oral arguments before the appellate panel on May 2, 2019. She arrived before anyone else. She always wanted to be the first one inside to get a feel for the courtroom. In the silent space, she thought, *This is not for me. This is not for the* Post. *This is for all my friends and so many other people who have lost their kids.*

Suddenly the courtroom exploded with chatter as a parade of lawyers streamed through the doors. As they took their seats, Lefton nervously looked over at the large group of Justice Department attorneys sitting with out-of-town lawyers representing the drug industry on the other side of the room. Lefton's sister came to the courtroom and sat behind her for support.

Lefton stepped to the lectern. "I'm here today representing the *Washington Post*," she began, looking up at the three-judge panel. Her voice was shaky at times, but she remained clear during the hourlong argument.

"There is a database of information that is underlying this whole case," Lefton said. "And it is being withheld, we believe improperly... We have received none of it. It is not accessible to us or to the public as it should be."

After the argument, Lefton thought of all the points and pithy quotes she had rehearsed and had forgotten to use. But it was over. She had done her best and needed to wait for the court's decision. She went to her sister's house, put on her golf clothes, played a round, and tried not to think about her court appearance. She knew that it could be months before the panel issued its ruling.

Seven weeks later, on June 20, 2019, Lefton was at a luncheon for about three hundred people given by the nonprofit Akron Roundtable, a community forum that brought in speakers from around the world. Lefton had been asked to sit at the head table because she served on the board. As one of the speeches began, she glanced down at her phone. The Sixth Circuit had reached a decision.

Her heart pounded. Her hands shook. She had to read it.

The appellate panel, by a vote of two to one, sided with the *Post* and HD Media, the owners of the *Gazette-Mail*. In a forceful thirty-four-page decision, the panel ruled that the defendants had failed to show how releasing the data would cause them harm. The panel reversed Polster, saying that his decision was "bizarre" and he had acted "irrationally." The judges ordered him to lift the protective order sealing the data and the documents.

By now, the MDL had become a leviathan, growing more and more tentacles that were threatening to strangle the litigation. What began with just two hundred cases had grown tenfold. There were now about five hundred lawyers on each side, though no one was quite sure exactly how many. They had filed hundreds of motions, traded millions of documents during discovery, and Polster seemed to be losing control of the sprawling litigation. It had been eighteen months since he urged the two sides to settle all of the cases and they were no closer to a global deal than on the day he had first gathered them in his courtroom. Now he had been overruled by the appeals court and forced to relinquish one of the few weapons he had to compel a settlement: the threat of releasing the ARCOS data and the internal corporate emails and documents.

Writing for the majority, U.S. circuit judge Eric L. Clay said that "the reporting on the ARCOS data that [HD Media] received from the West Virginia attorney general resulted in no demonstrated commercial harm to defendants and no demonstrated interference with law enforcement interests, but this reporting did result in a Pulitzer Prize, a congressional committee report and a broader public understanding of the scope, context and causes of the opioid epidemic."

Tears streamed down Lefton's face as she sat at the roundtable. Those around her started to stare. She worried that they wondered whether something was wrong. She forwarded the decision to the *Post*.

"Total victory!!! Please see attached," Lefton wrote at 1:05 p.m.

Polster unsealed the data from 2006 through 2012. It was three months before the start of the first trial for Summit and Cuyahoga counties. On July 16, the *Post* published the first of a series of stories based on the material—five hundred million transactions, tracing the path of every pain pill in America, from manufacturers to distributors to pharmacies. The database was so large, Steven Rich, the *Post*'s database editor for investigations, convinced senior editors to purchase a new high-speed computer. Leen's investigative team and reporters across the newsroom combed through the data, along with hundreds of drug company documents, emails, and internal corporate reports that Polster unsealed.

"America's largest drug companies saturated the country with 76 billion oxycodone and hydrocodone pain pills from 2006 through 2012 as the nation's deadliest drug epidemic spun out of control, according to previously undisclosed company data released as part of the largest civil action in U.S. history," read the lead paragraph of the first story by Scott Higham, Sari Horwitz, and Steven Rich.

When two more years of data were released by Polster in January, that number climbed to 100 billion pills.

The database revealed that just six companies distributed 75 percent of the pills from 2006 through 2012: McKesson Corporation, Walgreens, Cardinal Health, AmerisourceBergen, CVS, and Walmart—companies that Joe Rannazzisi and his investigators had tried so hard to stop. Three companies manufactured 88 percent of the opioids: SpecGx, a subsidiary of Mallinckrodt; Actavis, a subsidiary of Teva Pharmaceuticals; and Par Pharmaceutical, a subsidiary of Endo Pharmaceuticals. Purdue Pharma ranked fourth on the list of manufacturers, with about 3 percent of the market.

The reporters also found that death rates from opioids had soared in the towns, cities, and counties that were saturated with the billions of pain pills. The highest per capita death rates during those seven years were in an opioid belt stretching from West Virginia through southern Virginia to Kentucky.

Joe Manchin, the Democratic senator from West Virginia, was infuriated by the numbers. "What they did legally to my state is criminal," he told the *Post*. "The companies, the distributors, were unconscionable. This was not a health plan. This was a targeted business plan. I cannot believe that we have not gone after them with criminal charges."

The documents Polster unsealed included some of the most incendiary emails sent between executives in the drug companies: Victor Borelli's "Doritos" email; Kristine Atwell's message to her bosses at Walgreens asking how pharmacies could possibly be ordering so many bottles of pain pills; and the "Crisis Playbook" that The Alliance had commissioned to repair its image and blame the DEA for not doing enough to stop the epidemic.

The *Post* lifted its paywall, making the documents and the data available to readers, researchers, and other media organizations. Anyone could search down to the county level to see how many pills were distributed, which companies manufactured and distributed the pills, and which pharmacies dispensed how many pills. More than a hundred news organizations across the country used the data to publish their own stories.

At 5 a.m. on the day the first *Post* story was published, Lefton read it on her iPad while she lay in bed. Her husband was still sleeping. She woke him up. The contents of ARCOS were as new to her as to every other reader that morning. She was shocked as she read about the billions of pills the companies had poured into communities.

Lefton's name was included in that story and subsequent stories in other papers that highlighted the underdog lawyer who had forced the federal government to release its secret database. It was a moment to savor—the perfect marriage of her two careers.

The most powerful people in pharmaceutical America didn't want it released, she thought that morning. *A lot of the most powerful people in the Department of Justice didn't want it released. Aside from that, it was a walk in the park.*

Chapter 45

My Cousin Vinny

Washington, D.C., Spring 2019

Paul Farrell was something of a worrying puzzle to his colleagues. He could be warm and charming and wonderfully erudite. Few people were as well-read, and he peppered his speech and legal briefs with historical references from the Roman campaigns to World War II. He was a serious student of *The Art of War*; he had a dozen different translations. And he studied his Bible and the Western philosophers, from Plato to Rousseau, with equal fervor.

Paul could also be obnoxious and crass. He seemed to pride himself on being the outsider, but he frequently failed to read the room and what he thought of as tactical aggression others viewed as belligerence. His behavior was sometimes unrestrained—and problematic.

Paul sent long sarcastic emails to the defense. "Dear Purveyors of Opium Pills," he wrote at the top of one communication sent to every member of the defense team. In court, he theatrically twisted his face in disapproval or rolled his eyes when a judge or a defense lawyer made a point he didn't like. He couldn't help himself. After the executive committee selected Mark Lanier to be the lead trial counsel in the Cleveland case, Paul appeared in the war room wearing the jersey of New England Patriots star cornerback Malcolm Butler. Moments before the start of the Super Bowl against the Philadelphia Eagles in 2018, Patriots coach Bill Belichick had unceremoniously benched Butler. The Patriots would wind up losing the game.

"I've been benched," Paul said as he walked around the war room in Butler's jersey.

Paul Hanly was growing tired of the antics, which he viewed as self-defeating. In the end, Hanly thought, they need to reach a deal with the defense, so there was no advantage in needlessly antagonizing their opponents. Better to try to understand their bottom line.

"Why are you using such aggressive language?" he asked Paul.

"Because they're a bunch of sleazeballs," Paul replied.

"Okay, but the way to get ahead is not by getting in the gutter," Hanly said. "It's to try to find a way to move our clients' cases forward."

Some of the younger members of Paul's team enjoyed the antics. They thought they lightened the room, injecting humor into the drudgery of the nonstop legal work. But Hanly, Jayne Conroy, and the other veterans of the team worried that Paul's escapades might backfire one day.

On May 16, they did—risking the wrath of the special master whose decisions had a major impact on the course of the litigation.

Paul was at the Washington Plaza Hotel in downtown D.C., where he and Mike Fuller were preparing to take a deposition in the case. It was after nine in the evening. Documents were spread across the beds, on the window shelves, on the cabinets and the floors of the room. A young associate at Williams & Connolly, who was representing Cardinal, had written to David Cohen, the special master assigned to help Judge Polster manage the litigation. The associate, Suzanne Salgado, sought to limit the scope of the deposition, and Fuller wrote to Cohen asking him to reject her argument, saying it "does not hold water."

Paul recalled a scene from one of his favorite comedies, *My Cousin Vinny*. Joe Pesci plays an incompetent, wisecracking lawyer from New York City. His cousin and his friend have been wrongly accused of murder in Alabama. Pesci's character heads south with his fiancée,

played by Marisa Tomei, to defend the two young men. In the cli-
mactic courtroom scene of the movie, Pesci's character realizes that
his fiancée holds the key to winning the case. He calls her to the witness stand, her dark hair tossed and teased, a galaxy of metallic studs
splashed across her dress.

"Does the defense's case hold water?" Pesci's character asks her.

"No! The defense is wrong!" she says, beaming.

Ten minutes after Fuller replied to Cohen, Paul emailed a photograph of Tomei from the movie to every lawyer on the defense and
plaintiffs' teams. Someone complained to Cohen, accusing Paul of
being misogynistic. Whoever complained apparently hadn't seen *My
Cousin Vinny*, but they did notice a resemblance between Tomei and
the Williams & Connolly associate.

Within an hour, Cohen called Paul.

"You can't do that," the special master told him. "This is a different world. You can't be making derogatory comments."

"I'm not making derogatory comments," Paul said. "It's from *My
Cousin Vinny*."

"Well, apparently there are some people who haven't seen the
movie and they thought you were making derogatory, misogynist
comments."

"But she was the hero of the movie," Paul offered.

"Paul, I'm telling you right now, you need to send an apology."

At 2:55 the next morning, Paul wrote to Cohen and the defense
team. "I was making the not-so-funny point that Cardinal Health's
argument does not hold water with a picture of the actress gloat-
ing," Paul wrote. "Please accept my sincere apologies. [Special Mas-
ter] Cohen reminded me there is no place in this litigation for snarky
humor. This case and its implications are too important."

Some members of his trial team were amused, but others thought
it was a juvenile move. It was embarrassing to be schooled like a child
by a special master. For all his smarts, Paul could be his own worst
enemy. It wouldn't be the last time.

Chapter 46

RICO

Cleveland, July 2019

Two months after the *My Cousin Vinny* episode, Paul Farrell and his team made a bold move. They filed a blockbuster brief accusing the drug manufacturers and distributors of engaging in a civil RICO. The Racketeer Influenced and Corrupt Organizations Act, designed to take down criminal organizations, had been on the books for years. Congress created the law in 1970 to dismantle the Mafia. RICO was later successfully deployed against corporate con artists, inside traders, and motorcycle gang members. By charging multiple defendants engaged in the same ongoing enterprise, prosecutors were able to wipe out criminal organizations and secure long federal prison terms for the participants. In more recent years, plaintiffs' lawyers trained RICO's civil statutes on the corporate world: financial services firms and the corporations behind large-scale environmental disasters like the BP oil spill in the Gulf of Mexico.

For several years, Mark P. Pifko, a thirty-nine-year-old lawyer at Baron & Budd, one of the key plaintiffs' firms, had been using the civil RICO statutes to sue major corporations. They included Takata, the Japanese manufacturer that produced 4.5 million defective air bags, and the auto companies that installed them despite the flaws. He urged his allies in the opioid litigation to use RICO—initially to much skepticism.

On June 5, 2017, Pifko, a soft-spoken Southern California native, first told Paul Farrell on a conference call that he believed the drug companies had been engaged in an ongoing enterprise to expand the market for opioids and conspired to protect their supply lines from the DEA. "Maybe we can file a RICO," he suggested.

Paul groaned at the suggestion. "Seems like a reach," he told Pifko. "When I think of RICO, I think of the Mafia. What are you talking about?"

Paul had never filed a RICO case and knew little about the complex statute. As he listened to Pifko, he became marginally interested. If the plaintiffs prevailed at trial, they would be entitled to collect triple damages, and they would be able to recover their legal fees from the defendants. But proving a RICO case could turn into a costly slog. The plaintiffs would need to show that the drug companies had participated in a pattern of racketeering activity; that they had created an "enterprise" to pursue the racketeering activities; that the companies were responsible for injuries; and that those injuries resulted from their racketeering activities.

Paul had already read the 2016 *Post* investigative series that documented Joe Rannazzisi's battle with the drug companies and the crafting of the Marino-Blackburn bill. He then saw the joint investigation by the *Post* and *60 Minutes* in October 2017 that recounted how the companies had worked together to launch a carefully orchestrated influence campaign on Capitol Hill. He wondered if Pifko might be on to something.

When attorney Evan Janush discovered The Alliance's "Crisis Playbook" a year later, in June 2018, Paul was convinced. He put out an all-points bulletin to the lawyers, giving them the go-ahead to serve The Alliance with subpoenas for emails, internal memos, and any other material that might form the foundation of a RICO filing. The Alliance was fair game because several of its members were defendants in the case.

In return, the lawyers received a cache of documents: internal strategies and communications designed to push back against the DEA; emails detailing how to orchestrate congressional hearings; messages coordinating friend-of-the-court legal briefs to be filed on behalf of drug distributors facing DEA enforcement actions; and minutes of meetings between executives of the Big Three distributors as they plotted a course to combat the aggressiveness of Joe and his team at the agency.

Paul now saw The Alliance as part of a conspiracy. It was not a traditional D.C. trade group. He understood Pifko's point and began to believe that the drug companies, The Alliance, and other trade organizations were akin to the Commission that ran the Mafia families in New York between the 1930s and the 1980s. Some of the plaintiffs' lawyers thought the analogy was a stretch, but for Paul, his opponents were running a criminal enterprise. There was, he believed, no better analogy.

The lawyers started to braid together thousands of other emails and documents they had obtained from the drug companies through their discovery demands. Their work culminated in a 138-page brief filed on August 12, 2019, three months before the landmark trial was set to start in Cleveland.

First, they claimed that the manufacturers, including Purdue, Mallinckrodt, Johnson & Johnson, and Teva, launched an aggressive public relations and marketing campaign to change the prescribing behavior of doctors, setting the alleged conspiracy in motion. Together, they made opioids more acceptable to the medical community and the American public. A Purdue executive told sales reps in 2000 that the goal was to "raise awareness of undertreated pain" and "to make the whole pie bigger, not only for us but for our competition as well." To help accomplish the goal, drug manufacturers teamed up with pain patient advocacy groups, subsidizing their operations and serving on their boards. With innocuous-sounding names like the Pain Care Forum, the groups made it appear as though the pain treatment movement had the widespread support of both doctors and patients around the country. Purdue executive Robin Hogen wrote in a 2000 memo that if one of the pain advocacy groups working with his company wanted "our bucks (and they honestly cannot survive without industry support), they are going to have to learn to live with 'industry' reps on their board. I don't think they can expect huge grants without some say in governance." A U.S. Senate investigation later revealed that drug manufacturers had given the groups nearly $9 million during a five-year period.

The plaintiffs also wrote in their RICO brief, "The Manufacturer Defendants joined together to promote those false messages through direct partnerships, through organizations that they themselves created for precisely that purpose, through numerous experts and third-parties, and through organizations that set medical standards for practicing physicians. For competitors who should have been at each other's throats to gain market share, the record reveals that, instead, they partnered with each other to grow the opioid market."

The manufacturers and distributors also watched out for each other as the DEA's regulatory enforcement actions became more intense during Joe's tenure. The plaintiffs cited several emails in their motion, including the one between Purdue compliance chief Jack Crowley and his counterpart at Cardinal Health: "I'm sorry that DEA is being so aggressive with this suspicious order stuff," he wrote in 2007. "I wish there was something I could do to help in this situation—we are all in the same boat."

The plaintiffs also argued that the distributors capitalized on the expanded opioid market. They alleged that the companies acted together to broaden their market shares, avoid compliance with the law, shield their operations from the DEA, and undermine the agency. Joe's crackdown on the industry, beginning in 2005, gave the companies a "common purpose to engage in a course of conduct," a key element to proving a RICO case. The distributors, through The Alliance, shared information about whether to comply with the law or change it, collaborated on legal filings to defend drug companies in trouble with the DEA, and actively sought ways to stop the agency from regulating the industry. The plaintiffs cited internal Alliance emails and minutes of board meetings that outlined how the industry could combat the DEA and deflect attention away from the industry as the epidemic raged. They included the email Alliance executive Anita Ducca wrote in 2007, urging her colleagues to develop a strategy to push back against the agency. They cited the creation of the "Crisis Playbook," which Alliance executives noted "protects and enhances the reputation of the industry." The distributors ignored outside legal advice to pay closer attention to complying with the law rather than trying to change it. The plaintiffs included the statement that the Alliance president made at the height of the group's influence campaign on Capitol Hill: "Exhaust all efforts" to pass the Marino-Blackburn bill.

The pharmacies, through their trade organization, the National Association of Chain Drug Stores, also worked closely with The Alliance and collaborated with the Pain Care Forum during the Marino-Blackburn lobbying effort. The plaintiffs also noted that two major drug manufacturers—Purdue and Endo—helped to "influence the language" in the final version of the Marino-Blackburn bill "to make it more favorable for them" while making it less effective for the DEA.

"The Manufacturer, Distributor, and Pharmacy Defendants all gamed the system to avoid compliance with the Controlled Substances Act; purposefully misled DEA that they would cooperate with DEA's enforcement efforts to stave off enforcement actions; and coordinated to 'gang up on the DEA' to make enforcement even more difficult," the plaintiffs wrote. "This was not an innocent or independent activity geared towards maximizing profits within the confines of the law." Instead, they said the defendants "made the decision to band together to protect their commercial interests above all else, by making sure that sales were not disrupted by legitimate federal regulation."

Lawyers for the drug companies scoffed at the allegations in their motion to dismiss the RICO and conspiracy claims. They said there was no evidence that they had worked with each other to "achieve any unlawful common purpose." Attorneys for the drug distribution companies added that any lobbying activity by The Alliance or any other group was protected under the First Amendment. They also argued that communications between drug distributors and drug makers were being blown out of proportion by the plaintiffs. "These 'routine business relationships' between certain Distributors and Manufacturers fall far short of establishing the existence of a RICO enterprise," they wrote. They also noted that the drug distributors reported all of their sales of narcotics to the DEA and had also reported suspicious orders to the agency. "There is a complete failure of proof" that the distributors were engaged in any ongoing enterprise to evade the law, they argued.

As both sides prepared for the first bellwether trial of the MDL, set to start October 21 in Cleveland, Judge Polster's ruling on the RICO and conspiracy motions loomed large. If he permitted the plaintiffs to put on evidence of an alleged conspiracy, drug company attorneys would be forced to defend the case on two fronts—public nuisance and RICO.

On September 3 and September 10, Polster handed down a pair of rulings. In the first, he said that the plaintiffs' claims that the companies were engaged in a conspiracy could move forward. In the second, he allowed the allegations that the companies engaged in a racketeering enterprise to be heard by a jury. Both were devastating blows to the drug industry.

Paul was delighted. It put even more pressure on the companies, forcing them to defend the case on yet another front. The rulings also could be used as a cudgel to convince the companies to settle the cases.

It's more blood in the water, Paul thought.

Some drug company lawyers were not overly concerned. Plaintiffs' attorneys frequently folded multiple causes of actions into their cases, hoping some would stick. Kaspar Stoffelmayr, who represented Walgreens, wondered whether the racketeering claims would hold up during a trial or on appeal. He saw the RICO claims as part of the "kitchen sink" approach to mass tort litigations; toss everything in and see what happens.

On September 14, lawyers for seven drug companies, including the Big Three distributors and CVS, Walgreens, and Walmart, asked Polster to recuse himself. The lawyers said Polster had overstepped his authority and created the appearance of a bias against the companies. They cited statements he had made early in the case encouraging a settlement so money for drug treatment and other services could go to communities reeling from the epidemic.

"Defendants do not bring this motion lightly," the drug company lawyers wrote in their motion. "Taken as a whole and viewed objectively, the record clearly demonstrates that recusal is necessary."

Lawyers for the manufacturers steered clear of the motion. Several had already settled their cases or were close to settling. But lawyers for the distributors and the pharmacies believed they had nothing to lose. The judge had repeatedly ruled against them in a series of critical pretrial motions. Their relationship with Polster, they thought, couldn't get any worse.

In the two decades of defending major corporations, Stoffelmayr had never joined a motion requesting a judge to step down from a case. Polster, he believed, was too sympathetic to the plaintiffs. Still, he worried about the implications of launching a risky attack against a powerful figure. *"You take a shot at the king, you better not miss,"* he thought.

Polster rejected their request. The defense attorneys took their argument to the Sixth U.S. Circuit Court of Appeals in Cincinnati. On October 10, the appellate panel sided with Polster, ruling that judges in complex cases are encouraged to pursue settlements to avoid costly and time-consuming trials. But they warned the judge to watch what he said about the case going forward. The defense attorneys had taken their shot and missed.

Within eleven days, both sides would be back before Polster in his eighteenth-floor courtroom for the start of the first trial in the landmark case.

Chapter 47

"We Have a Deal"

Cleveland, October 2019

Across the street from the Carl B. Stokes U.S. Courthouse in Cleveland, the plaintiffs' lawyers had set up a war room in rented office space. The bleary-eyed, caffeinated crew worked around the clock in preparation for the case brought on behalf of Ohio's Cuyahoga and Summit counties. The lawyers were a week away from the October 21 trial date.

The vast war room was crammed with copy machines, boxes of documents, whiteboards, hastily erected cubicles, and walls plastered with World War II–era propaganda posters telegraphing the need for secrecy. Lawyers were not beneath trawling for inside information.

"Careless Talk Costs Lives," read one.

"Keep Mum," read another.

Someone had stenciled a message on the wall: "If In Doubt, Don't Ship It Out."

Joe Rice, the trial lawyer from South Carolina, was trying to negotiate a settlement with the defense. Jayne Conroy and other attorneys pored over thousands of potential trial exhibits. Mark Lanier was preparing his opening statement, while Paul Farrell and Paul Hanly were working every corner of the case.

Hanly was warming to Paul, appreciating his drive and his willingness to adapt and learn as the litigation evolved. "In the MDLs that

Joe and I and Jayne have litigated, we ultimately settled for billions of dollars," Hanly would tell Paul. "You have to be a good litigator, but you have to be a dealmaker."

Paul's early arrogance, which Hanly always read as a form of insecurity, had slowly started to abate. Hanly told him there was no upside to boorish behavior, such as sending insulting emails to defense attorneys. He told him that he needed to understand what motivated his opponents, what the companies wanted in the end. Paul began to pepper Hanly and Conroy and Rice with questions about case law, jury selection, and strategies for taking depositions and arguing before judges. He stopped describing opposing counsel as "sleazeballs" and began to treat them with a little more respect. He no longer sulked and made faces when a judge ruled against him.

In the MDL hothouse, Paul and Hanly were becoming unlikely allies.

Along with helping Paul manage the litigation teams, Hanly tried to shield Lanier from the settlement talks and the in-house infighting, including who would get to sit at the counsel table with the Texan in Polster's courtroom.

Lanier, as he had promised, followed his own preparation formula. He surrounded himself with attorneys and experts from his own firm, including his in-house jury psychologist. In the run-up to the trial, he invited different sets of plaintiffs' lawyers to his Texas estate to present the results of their investigations of each drug company. Each team was given an hour for a PowerPoint presentation.

Lanier was impressed by the members of the trial team, particularly Paul. He hadn't previously heard of the lawyer from West Virginia but came to value his acumen and dedication and how he had developed the basis of the case against the distributors. "I love Paul to death," he told other lawyers.

Lanier and his team next met in Cleveland with potential witnesses to determine which ones would be best on the stand. The lawyers spent time listening to the stories of people who had seen the epidemic unfold on the ground: A medical examiner who had watched the bodies pile up. A man once addicted to opioids who now ran a rehab program. A woman who oversaw a foster care program who explained how difficult it was to find new homes for all the children who had been removed from their addicted parents, or who had lost one or both parents to the epidemic. Some kids, she said, risked years in group homes or institutions.

James Rafalski, the former DEA investigator who worked on some of the agency's biggest cases, was on deck to testify. Lanier planned to show the jury the deposition he took of Joe Rannazzisi. The lawyers planned to call James Geldhof, the former DEA supervisor in Detroit, to testify in a later trial. Finally, Lanier secluded himself and focused on how he would explain the sprawling case to a jury. He always used props, and this trial would be no different. He planned to hold up a three-thousand-year-old Sumerian poppy jar that he had taken from his own theological library to explain how the ancients had revered opium and respected its powers. He had also acquired a first edition of *The Wonderful Wizard of Oz* by L. Frank Baum, published in 1900. By bringing a first edition to court, he would make the jury feel the age of the book, and he planned to illustrate the long-known dangers of opium by reading the section where Dorothy falls asleep in the poppy field.

Lanier was ready.

"Ladies and gentlemen of the jury, it's a great honor to get to stand in front of you and try this extremely important case," he said as he practiced his one-and-a-half-hour opening before his team. "It's an important case to you. It's an important case to me. It's an important case to my clients, Cuyahoga and Summit counties. It's an important case to the judge, to the judicial system. It's important to our state of Ohio. It's important to the United States of America. I daresay it has global implications. And so as we stand here, I ask myself this question: Where do we put this into some order or sense for us? See, this is a case about the distribution of opioids, not just in Ohio, but in the entire United States. And it's about the resulting crisis within our community that's come about through the way these opioids have been distributed. Your job as jurors is to figure out what went wrong, why we have this crisis, how it's damaged the communities. And so as you come here, I provide you initially a road map for the trial. My opening statement is pretty simple. It's just, here's what you can expect as we travel this journey together through this trial."

He had drawn his road signs: "DEA." "Controlled Substances Act." "The Supply Chain." "The Drug Company Defendants." And the final stop: "Cuyahoga and Summit Counties."

On October 16, the lawyers began selecting a jury. Complicating the proceedings were four state attorneys general—from North Carolina, Tennessee, Texas, and Pennsylvania—a group that Paul dubbed "the four bullies." They had just tried to persuade Polster to delay the trial, contending that they were close to their own settlement with the drug companies.

While the cities and counties were filing lawsuits, many states had brought their own cases and were trying to take the lead in a national settlement. Their move on the eve of trial highlighted an intense power struggle between the state attorneys general and the cities and counties in their states. The attorneys general, politicians who hold elected office, had been pushing to settle and take home a win to their constituents. Some of the plaintiffs' lawyers representing the cities and counties wanted to bring the cases before juries and let them decide whether the companies should be held accountable and how much they should pay.

Some of the state attorneys general argued that they had also worked on their own opioid cases for years. They said that the plaintiffs' attorneys, who were mostly in private firms, were partly motivated by the substantial fees they were likely to receive from a settlement or a jury verdict.

Paul Geller, the plaintiffs' lawyer from Florida, compared the move by the attorneys general to the 1980 Boston Marathon. That year, runner Rosie Ruiz was declared the winner of the women's race. Her title was stripped eight days later when it was discovered that she hadn't run the entire race, but instead had entered a half mile before the finish line. It was the plaintiffs' lawyers who had done all the hard work on the case.

They didn't take the depositions, they didn't review the documents, and then all of a sudden they announced they crossed the finish line and said we have a deal, Geller thought. *It's bullshit.*

On Friday, October 18, three days before the trial was set to start, Polster summoned everyone—the attorneys general, the drug company executives, and the lawyers for the twenty-four hundred cities, counties, and Indian tribes now in the MDL—to his eighteenth-floor courtroom to figure out if a last-minute global settlement could be reached. The state attorneys general said they were crafting an $18 billion deal with the companies that would be spread out over eighteen years. They needed the MDL lawyers to agree. The cities, counties, and tribes weren't interested. They thought it would give the states too much control over the payout and not enough money would reach their communities. The plaintiffs' lawyers summoned five officials from some of the hardest-hit areas to tell Polster how their communities had been devastated by opioids. The mayor of Huntington, West Virginia, Steve Williams, said his town experienced twenty-six overdoses in one five-hour period. The corporation counsel for Milwaukee County, Margaret Daun, said, "We need the money now. And the local governments like the one I represent need control over the money. We don't want saving people's lives to be hijacked by party politics." A Muscogee (Creek) Nation official rose to speak of the ruination of Indian country. "We are, without a question, the most severely impacted of all communities in the United States," Muscogee Nation attorney general Kevin Dellinger told Polster. "This devastation comes on top of centuries of displacement, oppression, and neglect, all of which together make addressing the opioid epidemic in our remote communities that much more challenging."

Paul fumed, telling Polster that the communities he and the other plaintiffs' attorneys represented were not on board. The judge responded that he wanted a settlement. He asked Paul to meet with the attorneys general, who were huddled in a courtroom two floors below. Paul barged into the room, grabbed a chair, and sat down.

"Who are you?" Texas attorney general Ken Paxton asked.

"I'm Paul Farrell. I'm co-lead of the national litigation and I happen to be from West Virginia." Paul accused Paxton and the other attorneys general of undermining the MDL and shortchanging West Virginia. Because the attorney general for West Virginia had already settled with Cardinal and AmerisourceBergen for $36 million in 2017 and recently struck a deal with McKesson for another $37 million, Paxton told Paul his state was not going to be included in the $18 billion proposal.

"Well, son," Paxton said, "it sounds like you need to go and talk to your attorney general."

Paul was furious. Neither Huntington nor any of the other towns, cities, and counties had received any of the settlement money. And just because his state's attorney general settled with the distributors didn't mean Paul's clients had given up their rights to sue the companies.

Paul wanted to punch the Texan. Instead, he turned and walked away.

By the end of Friday, settlement talks had collapsed. A jury would be seated Monday. On Saturday, tensions ran high in the war room. At 3:30 a.m. Sunday, they boiled over. Conroy and the others had run into a computer glitch that caused all the exhibit stamps on the plaintiffs' documents to obscure the text. They couldn't figure out how to fix the problem, and several people in the room started yelling—and then they started to cry.

"It was a terrible night," Conroy said. "We have literally been up for days and we're dealing with trial strategy. We're dealing with examinations that we're trying to prepare. But the thing that is absolutely killing us is this ridiculous exhibit issue. And we have to get this right. And I have a lot of people crying."

On Sunday afternoon at about 3 p.m., Conroy and her team met with lawyers for the defendants in the courthouse for the final decision by one of Polster's special masters, David Cohen, about which exhibits would be allowed in. Conroy and her team resolved the computer glitch. There were several documents on Conroy's list of two hundred exhibits for the first week that she desperately wanted to get in, including several critical to Lanier's opening. One was a video of five drug distribution company executives holding their right hands in the air as they were sworn in to testify before a House Energy and Commerce oversight panel on May 8, 2018. When the Republican chairman of the panel, Gregg Harper of Mississippi, asked whether any of them accepted responsibility for the epidemic, four of them said, "No": John Hammergren of McKesson; George S. Barrett of Cardinal Health; J. Christopher Smith, former president and CEO of H.D. Smith Wholesale Drug; and Steven H. Collis, chairman of AmerisourceBergen. Only one said, "Yes": Joseph Mastandrea, the chairman of Miami-Luken, a midsized distributor based in Ohio. While Barrett said his company bore no responsibility for the epidemic, he did issue a partial mea culpa about the shipments to the CVS stores in Sanford, Florida. "With the benefit of hindsight, I wish we had moved faster and asked a different set of questions," Barrett said.

It was a powerful, cinematic moment and Conroy wanted jurors to see it. But Cohen sided with defense objections, ruling that the C-SPAN video of the testimony was hearsay and couldn't be admitted because the plaintiffs hadn't properly authenticated it with an official congressional transcript. It was a blow for the plaintiffs. Lanier would not be able to use an important piece of evidence for his opening statement and Conroy was upset that she had let the trial team down.

The other exhibit was the damning *Austin Powers* spoof that had been created by Cephalon in 2007. The company had since been acquired by Teva, a defendant in the lawsuit. Cohen ruled that the jury could watch that video. Conroy saw that as a crucial win. Lanier could now use *Dr. Evil* in his opening.

That night, Paul took his wife, Jacqueline, to dinner at Butcher and the Brewer in downtown Cleveland, where a wood-fired ribeye could be had for $45. Paul was ebullient. He was sure the trial would begin the next morning because Lanier's mother, who attended every one of his opening statements, had just flown into Cleveland. But that evening, inside a glass-walled office in the war room, Rice and Hanly were still trying to reach a settlement with two defense lawyers negotiating on behalf of the Big Three: Jeffrey M. Wintner and Thomas J. Perrelli, a former associate attorney general during the Obama administration. For hours, the two sides traded proposals and counterproposals during a series of phone calls. There was no discussion of the relevant strengths and weaknesses of their cases. These negotiations for just two counties, Cuyahoga and Summit, were about dollars: how much should the defendants pay versus how much they were willing to pay. It was just the beginning of negotiations to settle thousands of other cases waiting in line for their turn in court. Each one had to be negotiated separately, unless the two sides could reach a global settlement.

Perrelli told Hanly and Rice, "I can't get any more than this."

"Well, that's not gonna be enough," Hanly and Rice responded.

"You've got significant liability issues. And what do you think the markets are going to do when all these documents come out?"

By 8 p.m., the defendants began offering more money. Rice poured himself a Canadian Club whiskey on the rocks. Before midnight, he gave Perrelli a final number: $215 million for the two Ohio counties. Teva had agreed to settle in exchange for $20 million in cash over three years and a donation of another $25 million worth of Suboxone, a drug used to treat opioid addiction.

Rice gave the defense lawyers an ultimatum. "This is getting ridiculous," he told them. "This is what I'll do. I will stay by this phone for twenty minutes. If I don't hear from you, I'm turning it off and going to bed. Mark will open at nine."

Rice thought that might tip the negotiations. He sensed their desire to settle. He also knew they feared Lanier.

Fifteen minutes later, Perrelli called back. Paul had returned from dinner and was in the war room. Rice motioned for him to come into the office. He put the call on speaker so Paul and Hanly could hear.

"Okay, we have a deal," Perrelli said.

Hanly called Lanier in his hotel room. He thought he might be up. The Texan was too wired for sleep.

Like all of his nights before trial, Lanier was feeling like a Viking, ready for battle. *I want to pillage and plunder a village*, he was thinking before the call.

While Lanier wasn't surprised—he felt cheated—victory by default.

"Okay, I'll pack up my stuff and go," Lanier told Hanly.

Paul returned to his hotel room. Hanly and Rice finished their drinks and turned off the lights in the war room. "Another great Joe Rice victory," Hanly said to his colleague as they walked back to their rooms at two that morning.

————

Five hours later, a line of lawyers and reporters began to form outside Polster's courtroom, hoping for a chance to see the trial's opening statements. At 9:01, Polster entered the packed chamber. The room fell silent as he announced what had just been leaked to the news media: The parties had reached a settlement. The Big Three had agreed to pay $215 million to the two counties. Teva had also agreed to settle. In the months before the trial date, drug manufacturers, including Johnson & Johnson and Mallinckrodt, had also settled, pushing the final amount to more than $300 million.

Paul was thrilled by the amount of money the two counties would receive, even though he hadn't played the central role in the litigation he had once anticipated. *A no-brainer settlement*, he thought. He knew he would get the chance to try his own case against the distributors in a West Virginia courtroom. All he needed now was a trial date.

Outside the courthouse, reporters and television cameramen surrounded the plaintiffs' lawyers.

"What was the sticking point last night?" one reporter asked.

"Money," Rice said. "They wanted to pay less and I wanted them to pay more."

"Is there an admission of wrongdoing?" another asked.

"No, but common sense tells me that they paid over $323 million to these two counties. One might say that's a pretty good admission," Rice said.

Cuyahoga County executive Armond D. Budish, standing next to Summit County executive Ilene Shapiro, told the reporters that the infusion of cash would bring immediate and much-needed funds to the people of their counties. But, Budish added, "The settlement does not bring things to an end."

No one knew that better than Hanly, Conroy, Rice, and Paul. They would allow themselves celebratory drinks at a bar with the team later that night, but the next day they would be back at it. They had only reached a deal for two of their clients; there were nearly twenty-four hundred others waiting for big payouts.

A crowd of reporters surrounded Lanier. He described some of the props he had planned to use during his opening statement. He excitedly gave them a taste. He told them about the Sumerian opium jar dating back to 1000 BC that he had brought to Cleveland. Poppies would be rubbed against it, he said, "to extract the liquid to get high."

He then held up his first edition of *Oz*. He read from the passage in the poppy field.

"'If we leave her here she will die,' said the Lion. 'The smell of the flowers is killing us all.'"

Chapter 48

"This Can't Be Real"

Huntington, West Virginia, May 2020

At first, Paul Farrell thought someone had pranked him. As he read through case files at his home in Huntington on May 6, 2020, an email popped up on his laptop. It was from Mark Pifko, the attorney from Baron & Budd in Los Angeles, writing to say that a young lawyer at his firm had just found a parody of the theme song from the 1960s sitcom *The Beverly Hillbillies*. Executives at AmerisourceBergen had jokingly emailed it to each other in the spring of 2011 at the height of the epidemic.

"See attached document," Pifko wrote. "Callous disregard for the problem they were feeding."

Paul began to read the parody.

"Come and listen to a story about a man named Jed / A poor mountaineer, barely kept his habit fed . . ."

Paul saw that the vice president in charge of regulatory affairs for AmerisourceBergen, Chris Zimmerman, had emailed the parody to Julie Eddy, a government affairs director for the company.

Paul wrote back to Pifko. "Bullshit," he said. "This can't be real."

Pifko assured him that it was. Another lawyer at his firm, Alex Sherman, discovered the email while searching through millions of drug company documents. He had decided to enter the search term "pill w/2 mills." The "Pillbillies" email popped up. The phrase "pill mills" was in the last stanza.

There's something else, Pifko told Paul. Sherman had discovered another incendiary email.

"Not done yet here," Pifko wrote to Paul two hours later. AmerisourceBergen, he said, "knows how to make some southern friends. See attached."

In 2012, the Kentucky General Assembly had been considering a series of regulatory changes to crack down on pill mills and overprescribing. They included a prescription drug monitoring program to prevent drug users and dealers from filling multiple opioid prescriptions at different pharmacies.

On September 13, 2012, Steve Mays, senior director of regulatory affairs at AmerisourceBergen, forwarded an email listing the legislative initiatives to Cathy Marcum, a regional director for regulatory affairs at the company. "FYI, Looks like KY has been busy," Mays wrote.

Marcum responded, "One of the hillbilly's [*sic*] must have learned how to read." She closed her email with a smiley face emoji.

AmerisourceBergen and the other defendants were supposed to have produced emails and documents to the plaintiffs before the October trial date in Cleveland. But the "Pillbillies" email was in a large cache of tens of thousands of documents that AmerisourceBergen didn't turn over to the MDL plaintiffs until months later. Sherman stumbled upon the email while combing through the newly produced documents.

The day after learning about the emails, Paul sent a letter to the lawyers for AmerisourceBergen. "Dear AmerisourceBergen," it began. "We will be addressing your late disclosure and lack of candor in a separate letter." He closed by writing, "In April of 2011, the month the ['Pillbillies'] email was circulated to your senior staff, you sold 291,400 pills of hydrocodone and oxycodone into Cabell County, West Virginia."

Paul fired off a series of emails to his colleagues. Why wasn't the "Pillbillies" email turned over to the MDL plaintiffs before the October 21, 2019, Cleveland trial date? AmerisourceBergen's lawyers said the document was initially withheld because it was covered by attorney-client privilege and didn't need to be turned over. They then said it was "erroneously not produced." Anthony Irpino and Pearl Robertson began to document a pattern of other emails that the company should have turned over before the trial date.

The plaintiffs' lawyers asked Judge Polster to sanction AmerisourceBergen for violating discovery rules. The "Pillbillies" email, along with the others they found, could have strengthened their bargaining position on the eve of the Cleveland trial. Polster sanctioned AmerisourceBergen, ordering it to produce all documents that it had wrongly withheld. He also said the plaintiffs could force several top AmerisourceBergen officials to sit again for hours-long depositions.

Polster had continued to push for a global settlement. After the Cleveland settlement in October 2019, the judge decided to set up a new slate of bellwether cases to be sent back, or remanded, to federal courts across the country. "Resolution of substantial portions of the Opiate MDL will be speeded up and aided by strategic remand of certain cases at this time," the judge wrote in his November 2019 order.

He sent one case to San Francisco, another to Chicago, and a Cherokee Nation case to Oklahoma. Early in 2020, he selected two of Paul's West Virginia distributor cases—one filed by Cabell County and the other by the city of Huntington—to be sent back to federal court in Charleston, West Virginia, where they would be tried before senior district judge David A. Faber.

Polster also scheduled another trial in Cleveland that he would preside over, pitting two other Ohio counties, Lake and Trumbull, against the national pharmacy chains, including CVS, Walmart, Rite Aid, and Walgreens. The trial was originally scheduled for the fall of 2020 but was pushed to the fall of 2021 because of the Covid pandemic that shut down all the opioid trials. Nothing in the "Pillbillies" email surprised Paul. He had heard the same tired jokes about West Virginians in college.

At Notre Dame, his classmates called him "Cooter," a reference to a backwoods character from the hit TV show *The Dukes of Hazzard*. They teased him incessantly about his roots. Paul brushed off the bad jokes, and these emails were equally unfunny. When he saw the names of the corporate executives on the "Pillbillies" email, he realized that some of them worked for the division responsible for ensuring that pain pills were not being diverted to the black market. *And they're mocking the suffering of the people in Appalachia,* Paul thought. *These are the people that have been entrusted by AmerisourceBergen to protect my community and they're making fun of us.*

To Paul, the "Pillbillies" email was providence. Surfacing in the middle of the pandemic, he saw it as a sign. There would be a reckoning, he believed, as soon as he could get his case into a West Virginia courtroom.

Chapter 49

"Every Nineteen Minutes"

Cleveland, July 2020

Eric Kennedy thought he could hold it together as he prepared to take the deposition on July 30 of a key figure in the upcoming trial in Charleston, West Virginia. He would question the longtime president of The Alliance, John Gray, while still coping with his own grief. Eleven months earlier, Kennedy had lost his only son to an accidental fentanyl overdose. The twenty-seven-year-old had snorted cocaine, unaware it had been laced with the deadly synthetic opioid.

The memories of that day kept returning in shards: The emergency call. The doctor asking him if he wanted to see his son's body at the hospital. Later, the eulogy he gave to six hundred people who had gathered on the verdant grounds of the Cleveland Botanical Garden for the memorial service for Robert Jacque Kennedy, known as Jackson, a painter with a degree from the School of the Art Institute of Chicago.

Kennedy, a bespectacled and bald litigator whose work spanning forty years had earned him a spot in the Ohio Trial Lawyer Hall of Fame, wasn't angry with Gray, The Alliance, or any of the drug companies it represented. Since the day his son died, he had been too lost in his own sorrow to muster much other emotion. The deposition was scheduled to last about four and a half hours and it was an important moment in the litigation, the first and perhaps the only time that the plaintiffs would be able to question Gray about the conduct of The Alliance and the companies he represented.

Kennedy wasn't sure if Gray knew about his son. Even if he did, Kennedy knew what Gray would say: Drug distributors shipped prescription pills and had nothing to do with illicit fentanyl, much of it manufactured in China and Mexico and smuggled into the United States.

While Gray would be technically correct, Kennedy also knew that the explosion in heroin and fentanyl overdoses was a direct outgrowth of the opioid epidemic. The DEA's crackdown on the companies had decimated the black market for pain pills. Opioid users searched for other options, setting off two more cataclysmic waves of death. In 2015, heroin overdoses surpassed the number of deaths from pills. Two years later, the third wave of the epidemic swept through communities across the country. Many victims were unaware that fentanyl had been laced into their heroin, cocaine, or other drugs to make them more potent and more addictive.

Fentanyl is the deadliest drug to ever hit U.S. streets. It is fifty times more powerful than heroin, a hundred times more powerful than morphine, its chemical cousin. It is so powerful that just a few flecks of the white powder, the size of grains of salt, can cause rapid death. The fast-acting opioid kills a person by shutting down the part of the brain that controls respiration, causing breathing to slow and then stop.

In a series of missed opportunities, oversights, and half-measures, federal officials in the Obama administration failed to grasp how quickly fentanyl was creating another, far more deadly wave of the opioid epidemic. Between 2013 and 2017, more than 67,000 people died of synthetic opioid–related overdoses. In 2017, synthetic opioids were to blame for 28,869 of the overall 47,600 opioid overdoses, a 46.4 percent increase over the previous year.

Fentanyl deaths continued to soar under the Trump administration. After the failed nomination of Tom Marino as his drug czar,

Trump tapped White House adviser Kellyanne Conway to take charge of combating the opioid epidemic. While Trump said the crisis was a top priority, people in communities across the country continued to die in record numbers from fentanyl and health officials struggled to provide treatment for tens of thousands more. Throughout his tenure, Trump's drug office failed to devise a cohesive antidrug strategy. In 2020, as the Covid pandemic gripped the nation, nearly 93,000 people died from drug overdoses—the largest number ever recorded by the CDC. The prime culprit: fentanyl.

As one of the leading trial lawyers in Ohio, Kennedy had secured a spot on the plaintiffs' executive committee for the MDL. He was assigned to investigate CVS, McKesson, and The Alliance, and to work on Paul Farrell's upcoming trial in Charleston. Paul knew about Kennedy's son and wanted to give him a larger role in the litigation. He asked Kennedy if he would depose Gray. To prepare, Kennedy read every email and memo Gray had written, along with the minutes of every Alliance board meeting he had ever attended. He knew that Gray had presided over the group, formally called the Healthcare Distribution Alliance, or HDA, since 2004. Gray held a law degree from the University of Virginia and an MBA from Wharton. He had just announced his retirement. The year after the Marino-Blackburn bill became law in 2016, Gray was paid $2.9 million.

With the country in Covid lockdown and the trials put on hold, Kennedy took the deposition remotely. He was in a conference room in his Cleveland law firm; Gray in his house in Great Falls, Virginia. Six defense attorneys for Gray and the drug companies dialed into the videotaped deposition that morning.

Kennedy began by asking Gray about a series of events in 2012, a time when Joe Rannazzisi's team was on a war footing with the drug industry. That year, the DEA had suspended the registrations of Cardinal, CVS, and Walgreens, and served subpoenas on McKesson for its drug shipment records and other internal documents.

"The HDA on behalf of its members was so concerned about the DEA that you personally organized a meeting with a Washington, D.C., law firm, Williams & Connolly. Do you remember organizing that meeting, sir?" Kennedy asked.

"Yep."

"You organized a meeting, sir, in 2012 with this Washington, D.C., law firm to try to figure out what to do with the DEA and its enforcement of the law against distributors. That's why that meeting was put together, true?" Kennedy asked.

"It was an attorney-client relationship," Gray said. "I don't feel I should answer any of that."

Kennedy then referenced an email Gray had written to seven members of the executive committee of The Alliance, including the Big Three, after meeting with two top Washington attorneys at Williams & Connolly, Robert B. Barnett and Richard M. Cooper. Barnett was a well-known lawyer in the city who had negotiated multimillion-dollar book deals for Barack Obama, Laura Bush, and Bob Woodward, among many others.

Kennedy read Gray's email: "Given their experience and knowledge of the political and legal aspects of dealing with DEA, we updated them on the industry's recent concerns with DEA's latest efforts to thwart drug diversion and abuse." Alliance representatives told Barnett and Cooper that they were considering a legislative approach to address the growing tension with the DEA. Kennedy read a memo that Gray had attached to the email: "Mr. Barnett and Mr. Cooper felt that new legislation to specifically address our concerns with DEA was highly unlikely to be successful due to limited momentum in that direction. Moreover, elected officials tend to steer away from controversy during an election year." Instead of challenging the DEA, the attorneys told The Alliance that it "may be better off averting DEA actions by taking even stronger compliance measures."

"Here's what's important," Kennedy told Gray. "They felt that [you] may be better off averting DEA actions by taking even stronger compliance measures. Is that what they told you?"

"You know, if I wrote that at the time, it must have been my impression," Gray said. "I can't specifically recall."

"You want to avert DEA actions. They said maybe your distributors should take even stronger compliance measures. That's what you wrote," Kennedy said.

"Okay."

"I mean, sir, it was pretty simple advice, wasn't it? They were kind of saying to you and the distributors: If you want to stop getting arrested for robbing banks, maybe you ought to just stop robbing banks. Pretty straightforward, simple, commonsense advice from your lawyers, right?" Kennedy said.

"That's fine. That's your interpretation," Gray said.

Also in 2012, the attorney general in West Virginia sued Cardinal, AmerisourceBergen, and other drug companies in state court. That year, The Alliance had hired APCO Worldwide to start work on its public relations strategy and the "Crisis Playbook," paying the company an initial $250,000. The Alliance also considered hiring the RAND Corporation, a well-known research organization, to examine the opioid epidemic and propose possible solutions. Kennedy asked Gray why The Alliance had considered hiring RAND. Members of RAND, including analyst Daniel Ellsberg, were famously part of a study team that produced the Pentagon Papers. Ellsberg leaked copies of the papers to the *New York Times* and the *Washington Post* in 1971.

Gray said he couldn't recall engaging RAND.

"You don't recall that they wanted you folks to fund a study that would actually look for solutions and answers to this real crisis, the opioid epidemic?" Kennedy asked.

"No. I remember we talked with them, but I do not remember the specifics of what was going to be the scope and the direction of the study."

Kennedy then produced a July 11, 2012, email Gray had written to a senior vice president at Cardinal that outlined the scope of the proposed RAND study. Kennedy again read Gray's words back to him.

"Another important aspect of the project is the organizing of an expert advisory panel, both to provide primary input on a range of questions related to drug abuse and diversion," Gray wrote. "I am sitting on this until we hear from the attorneys with respect to the West Virginia litigation to determine what role [HDA] can or cannot play in that effort. We will have to decide whether or not the RAND initiative will be too little too late and whether or not it helps or hinders the West Virginia matter. Furthermore, will [HDA's] resources be better applied to a much larger PR effort concerning both West Virginia and the rest of the states' attorneys generals to prevent the West Virginia litigation from spreading to other jurisdictions?"

"Is that what you said to the Cardinal folks?" Kennedy asked.

"That's what it looks like," Gray said.

"So, sir, you're questioning whether to fund the study that might find answers, might save lives, you're questioning that because it might hurt Cardinal's position in a lawsuit? Is that what you're suggesting?" Kennedy asked.

"No. No, we're not saying that at all," Gray said. "That—that wasn't the point of this memo."

The Alliance eventually decided against retaining RAND.

"Why did you not fund it?" Kennedy asked.

"Well, because it was not clear whether it was going to be useful," Gray said. "It was too little too late because their timeline was too long and we thought by the time it would come out, the litigation would have moved on and it would be irrelevant."

"Sir, this is 2012 when you state this, right?"

"Correct."

"Too little too late in 2012?" Kennedy asked. "Do you know how many more people died in West Virginia after 2012?"

"This was strictly with respect to the trials," Gray replied.

Kennedy then showed Gray an email he had written to an executive vice president at McKesson, discussing the RAND proposal. Again, Kennedy read: "Upon reviewing their draft contract, we became concerned about the ironclad language with respect to the publication of the study and our ability to control content," Gray wrote. "I think the key here is when we can stop the report from being published, assuming it reaches conclusions not favorable to our industry. Our outside counsel is currently evaluating this situation. I would like to have your thoughts about this effort since we have not yet committed to anything."

If the study was unflattering for the industry, Gray wanted to make sure it never saw daylight.

Kennedy continued to read from Gray's email: "I see the possible value in a study like this if we can prevent final publication of a study unfavorable to our purposes; however, it also falls in the old adage of never ask a question you do not already know the answer to," Gray wrote.

"Was that your email to McKesson, sir?" Kennedy asked.

"That's the email." Gray said it was the way Washington worked. "We do that with all our studies," he said. "If we get to the point we don't find it's useful or helpful or it misrepresents, then we want to be able to push back on the consultants and say, 'Look, this is not accurate, not fair, whatever.' And that's, again, standard procedure we've done with all our—all our studies about any subject."

Rather than hire RAND, The Alliance paid APCO another $265,000 to complete its work on the "Crisis Playbook" and other public relations projects for the group. The Alliance also retained lobbyists and law firms to work on its behalf on Capitol Hill and in statehouses around the country.

For years, The Alliance and its members had complained that the DEA would not provide the distributors with access to ARCOS. Each distributor only knew how much it had shipped to a particular pharmacy. Without access to ARCOS, the companies said they did not have the full picture of what was happening on the ground in communities they served with opioids. Having only limited information, they argued, they could not be accused of bearing responsibility for the epidemic.

Gray, The Alliance, and its members had lodged this complaint about not having access to ARCOS in multiple forums—in its press materials, on its website, and in testimony before Congress.

Kennedy showed Gray an email that Anita Ducca, the Alliance executive, had written to a lobbyist for the group in 2016. Ducca, by then making $245,000 a year, said she was preparing a list of questions for the then–DEA administrator, Michele Leonhart.

Kennedy read: "I don't know if you want to add this, given some of the sensitivities about whether or not we truly want ARCOS data shared after all," Ducca wrote to the Alliance lobbyist, Patrick Kelly. "If we got it, what would we do with it?"

"This is a year before you told Congress how critical this was, true?" Kennedy asked.

"Uh-huh."

"Let me finish," Kennedy said. He showed Gray an Alliance fact sheet from 2013. "This is your publication. This says, 'National Epidemic: Prescription Drug Abuse.' Do you see that?"

"Uh-huh."

"And it says, 'The Centers for Disease Control and Prevention reports that one person dies every nineteen minutes in the United States from prescription drug abuse,'" Kennedy said.

"Uh-huh."

"This is 2013. Do you see that?"

"Uh-huh."

"So, for context purposes, when the HDA decided to launch a PR program instead of becoming more compliant with the law, they knew that one American was dying every nineteen minutes from an overdose of a prescription drug, right?" Kennedy asked.

"That's not correct."

"Every nineteen minutes. They knew it. Is that correct?" Kennedy said as he began to feel his own anguish for the first time in the deposition.

"That's not necessarily correct," Gray said.

Kennedy then asked Gray about an Alliance board meeting that was held at The Greenbrier, a popular destination for Washington's elite.

"Sir, let me ask you this: In September of 2013, the HDA held meetings at The Greenbrier in West Virginia."

"Uh-huh."

"Do you know how many pills the Big Three distributed in West Virginia while you were at that meeting? Did you know it?" Kennedy asked.

"I can't recall whether I knew or not."

"I've got nothing further," Kennedy said. "Thank you, Mr. Gray."

Kennedy stood up from his conference table in Cleveland. The screen went blank. He stared out the window as tears streamed down his face.

"My son is gone," he said. "What a mess."

He gathered himself and walked into the hallway of his firm, his legal assistant for forty years, Donna Rozman, at his side. She was like Jackson's second mother. She hugged Kennedy as he began to cry again.

"Great job," she said, gathering him in her arms.

Chapter 50

"We're Going to Trial"

Charleston, West Virginia, May 3, 2021

Few places in America were hit harder by the opioid epidemic than Cabell County and the city of Huntington. Over the past decade, there had been seven thousand overdoses and eleven hundred deaths—all in a community of just a hundred thousand. In the tiny towns that lined the Ohio River on the western edge of West Virginia, there were few or no degrees of separation between the living and the dead. Everyone, it seemed, knew someone who had died from prescription opioids. The torrent of pills that poured into the region put unimaginable pressure on paramedics and police officers, foster care workers, nurses and doctors—everyone working on the front lines.

The living and the dead were Paul Farrell's friends and neighbors, and he was growing impatient. He didn't want to wait any longer to go to trial. Cabell and his hometown of Huntington were two of his earliest and most important clients. It had been four years since he filed his public nuisance suit on their behalf against the drug companies and he was no closer to seeing the inside of a courtroom than he was in 2018, when Judge Polster held the first MDL hearing in Cleveland. After the distributors and one manufacturer, Teva, settled the first test case in Cleveland on the eve of trial in 2019, paying two Ohio counties $260 million, Paul thought it was his turn to try one of the

MDL cases against McKesson, Cardinal, and AmerisourceBergen. He asked Polster to transfer his case back to Judge Faber in Charleston, West Virginia. He then made a risky—and potentially fateful—move. He asked Polster if the case could be tried before Faber, not a jury. In a bench trial, as it's called, a judge presides over every aspect of the case and hands down the verdict on his own.

Paul thought he could secure a trial before a judge far faster than one before a jury, even though there are clear advantages to bringing an emotionally charged case before residents of a community hit so hard by the epidemic. But unless the companies were staring at a trial date, Paul believed his case would drag on for years. With a date certain, he thought his opponents just might fold, pay up, and walk away from a court fight.

If the companies didn't settle, Paul still calculated that Faber might be a sympathetic ear. Even though the judge was a lifelong Republican and was seen as a business-friendly, by-the-book jurist, Paul knew that he was above all else a proud Mountaineer. Faber was born in Charleston and attended high school not far from his chambers at the Robert C. Byrd U.S. Courthouse, an imposing seven-story neoclassical building that occupies an entire city block and is named for the longest-serving U.S. senator in American history. A graduate of Yale Law, Faber had served as the U.S. attorney for the Southern District of West Virginia before President George H. W. Bush appointed him to the bench in 1991.

Paul and Faber shared a love for their state—for its people, for fly fishing its streams and rivers, and for cheering on college baseball teams. They also shared a love for history. The judge, seventy-eight, held a doctorate in history from the University of Cambridge, a degree he earned when he was seventy-one.

Like Paul, the judge had seen how prescription pain pills hollowed out Charleston—the state capital, a once-bustling industrial and government hub. Now it looked broken. Abandoned businesses faced empty streets. Gaunt drug users lurked in the city's parks.

The lawyers for the drug distributors told Polster they weren't ready for a trial in West Virginia. They needed to draft more discovery demands, take more depositions, file more motions.

Paul was so eager to secure a trial date scheduled in his home state that he made another risky move: He told the defense lawyers that he would be willing to waive punitive damages, which are designed to punish companies for their conduct above the actual damages they had inflicted, if they consented to a nonjury trial before Faber. Paul also consented to a request by Polster to drop his RICO claims. The companies quickly agreed to a bench trial. Paul thought that in the end, punitive damages would be a moot point. The drug distributors would settle—just as they had in Cleveland hours before Mark Lanier was scheduled to deliver his opening statement. If the case did go to trial, Paul planned to ask for $2.5 billion. If the companies wanted to settle, Paul would be willing to take $200 million, maybe less. He kept that card in his back pocket in case he needed to play it.

While most of the plaintiffs' lawyers sided with Paul's strategy, not everyone agreed. Jayne Conroy was deeply troubled by the idea of giving Faber so much power in the most important case to reach a courtroom in the MDL. Juries brought fat judgments; judges brought jurisprudence. *Not a good idea*, she thought.

Unlike Paul, Conroy believed there was no need to hurry. Any hiatus would provide the plaintiffs with more time to find damaging documents and sharpen their lines of attack. A delay would also give them more time to prepare their witnesses for what was sure to be an onslaught of attacks during cross-examinations conducted by some of the finest civil defense lawyers in the nation. Adding to Conroy's anxiety was that no one really knew whom this judge held responsible for the epidemic. Maybe he thought it was the fault of drug users or corrupt doctors, or both. Maybe he thought the distributors were simply filling legitimate pain pill orders.

More than anything, she believed the trial team would be far better off with jurors deciding the case—men and women from a community that had been crushed by prescription opioids. Many of its residents wanted a reckoning. Conroy also believed it was easier to read jurors—and change tack accordingly—during a lengthy trial. Are they engaged or bored? Are they taking notes or nodding off? Which witnesses are resonating with the jurors? Which ones are failing to connect? With each read of the jury, the lawyers could readjust their strategy and hone their arguments. In Conroy's experience, judges were far more difficult to decipher. The emotional appeal of the case might mean nothing to Faber. The judge, she worried, could wind up being a foe, not an ally.

Paul remained undeterred. It was his case, his call. As the trial approached, he thought about how history might judge him if he lost—the fool who waived a jury trial in favor of putting his case in the hands of a pro-business judge. The guy who lost the case for his hometown. *A Shakespearean tragedy,* he thought. But Paul also believed he needed to trust his instincts. They had taken him this far. If he couldn't convince a judge from West Virginia with an advanced degree in history of the significance of what had happened to the state and the role of the drug distributors, then he wouldn't be able to convince anyone. If he won, he would establish a record of what took place in the Ohio River valley during the worst drug epidemic in U.S. history. The success of his public nuisance theory, he imagined, would be studied by litigators and law students for generations to come.

The case was scheduled to start on August 31, 2020. But with the Covid-19 pandemic raging that March, Faber pushed the trial to October 19 and then again to January 4, 2021. The defense sought yet another postponement until the fall, but the judge ruled that the trial could proceed that spring by putting social-distancing measures in place and closing the fifth-floor courtroom to the public and the news media. They could watch on a live feed piped into a courtroom on the floor above.

On May 2, 2021, the eve of trial, Paul sat in his hotel room at the Embassy Suites in Charleston, putting the final touches on his opening statement. The plaintiffs' lawyers had rented out most of the rooms on the third floor of a downtown hotel a short walk from the courthouse; the defense team for Cardinal took up the entire seventh floor. Signs posted in the elevators read, "The 7th floor is closed to public access." The defense lawyers for the two other companies camped out at the Charleston Marriott Town Center and the Courtyard by Marriott, both of which were also within walking distance of the courthouse. Paul's room, 315, was littered with sheaves of paper and boxes of documents. Cases of orange Gatorade Zero and diet Mountain Dew lined one of its walls. The lawyers working with him sat around in sweats or shorts and ball caps, assembling the last documents Paul needed for his opening statement.

By now, Paul had lost all hope of securing a settlement. Amid the Covid shutdown and the trial delays, the ground had shifted. Months of secret negotiation sessions between the drug companies and the MDL plaintiffs had produced a proposed $26 billion global settlement with the three thousand towns, cities, and counties suing the industry. Under the deal, those plaintiffs would receive payouts from the drug companies over eighteen years. The dollar amount seemed like a lot, but when it was divided up under a complex formula, places like Huntington would receive next to nothing. Paul carved his case out of the proposed settlement.

It's terrible for West Virginia, Paul thought. He wanted to do more for his clients and the people of his hometown. They had been hit harder than anyone else in the nation. With the proposal pending, he knew the distributors would never settle with Huntington and Cabell for hundreds of millions, while the other cities, towns, and counties around the country would receive a fraction of that amount. If the companies settled with Paul, why would the other municipalities agree to sign on to a deal that would pay them so much less?

Paul believed he had one option: take his chances at trial before Faber. *We're going to have a reckoning in West Virginia, county by county by county,* he thought.

The next morning at 9:30, Paul stepped confidently to the lectern in Faber's courtroom to deliver his opening statement. He wore a dark gray suit and a baby blue tie, along with a tie pin and colorful socks Paul Hanly had given him for his opening. Certain of his own bona fides as a student of history, he hoped to appeal to Faber's avocation—in language no lawyer would ever use before a jury. "Despite its complexity, the law of parsimony or Occam's philosophical razor suggests the simplest explanation is usually the right one," Paul began. "Judge, we intend to prove the simple truth that the distributor defendants sold a mountain of opium pills into our community, fueling the modern opioid epidemic.

"I've told my clients you are a student of history, so perhaps this analogy is apt," he continued. "Patrick Henry and John Marshall were contemporaries. They were both lawyers. One was known for his power of persuasion, evoking fiery emotion; the other, methodical and convincing. We believe our aim in these proceedings is to follow the path of the latter, to be methodical and convincing. I believe that we will show you facts upon which you will record in the permanent record as the historian. We will present direct evidence from primary sources, as well as firsthand accounts of what happened here, and seek the truth in this forum."

Faber remained as stone-faced as ever as he stared down from the bench, wisps of white hair combed over his balding head.

The trial team had positioned a large white posterboard on an easel in the courtroom. It was a color-coded fever chart, its lines chronicling the ever-increasing numbers of pain pills the Big Three distributors shipped into Huntington and Cabell between 2006 and 2014—eighty-one million doses, Paul told the judge. The chart looked like a mountain, rising dramatically as more and more pills poured into the towns and hollers of West Virginia. At each elevation, he tacked small black flags his team had fashioned out of cardstock onto the poster they nicknamed "Pill Mountain." Each flag, Paul told the judge, signified a moment in time that should have put the drug companies on notice about the damage the drugs were doing to the community.

He explained that his public nuisance case against McKesson, Cardinal, and AmerisourceBergen rested on four pillars: the volume of pills; the warnings the companies received about their conduct; the addictive nature of opium; and the epidemic itself.

"Through transparency, we can get visibility into the volume and into the conduct. Through transparency, once we establish conduct and consequences, we're going to ask you for accountability," he said.

Paul invoked the floods that had periodically devastated West Virginia's communities since the founding of the state in 1863. "We've experienced a new flood. And it's a flood of opium pills into our community," he said. "The data that we intend to present to you will establish a mountain of opium pills sold by the Big Three into Cabell, which resulted in the four horsemen of the epidemic. We will present to you evidence that, in the past ten years, there have been seven thousand overdoses in Huntington-Cabell and one thousand one hundred opioid-related deaths."

Paul told Faber that despite the rising number of overdoses and the drumbeat of warnings from the DEA and the courts, the companies did little to change their behavior. Instead, he said, they enlisted The Alliance and lobbyists and members of Congress to undermine the DEA by changing the law. The industry's response, he said, was akin to the "Empire striking back."

While the companies shipped increasing amounts of pills, some of their executives made fun of the opioid epidemic and the people of Appalachia, Paul told Faber, citing the "Pillbillies" parody. He thought it was a chilling example of how a corporate culture had grown numb to its responsibilities to protect the public.

"With great power comes great responsibility," Paul concluded, "and they blew it."

Paul's co-counsel in the trial, Anne McGinness Kearse, a seasoned litigator for South Carolina-based Motley Rice, with a broad smile and curly red hair, stepped to the lectern. It fell on her to sell Faber on what was called the "Gateway Theory"—the proposition that opioids, once they became more difficult to acquire, inexorably led addicts to heroin and fentanyl. She argued that the costs to local governments from the vast majority of overdoses and deaths, whether from opioids or other drugs, were the responsibility of the distributors. She asked for $2.5 billion to fund an "abatement plan" that would cover the damages to the communities and help them set up treatment programs.

More than anything, their case depended on a central idea: The opioid epidemic was not a separate phenomenon from the explosion of heroin and fentanyl addiction. It was the fuse that ignited the explosives. Even if the plaintiffs convinced Faber that the companies had caused a public nuisance, they could walk away with little in damages if the plaintiffs failed to also persuade the judge of their Gateway Theory.

"A fire was lit by the oversupply of prescription opioids and pills coming into their community and fueled by the illicit drugs, including heroin and fentanyl," Kearse said. "The prescription opioid misuse and use of heroin and illicitly manufactured fentanyl were intertwined and deeply troubling."

Paul felt confident. The table had been set.

Across from him was an all-star team of lawyers the drug companies had assembled for the trial. They included Enu Mainigi, the Williams & Connolly lawyer representing Cardinal; Robert A. Nicholas, a veteran trial attorney for Reed Smith retained by Amerisource-Bergen; and Paul W. Schmidt, one of the top litigators at Covington hired to represent McKesson. They had each notched numerous victories for clients in the financial services and pharmaceutical industries. With his shaved head and intense stare, Schmidt looked like Bruce Willis from *Live Free or Die Hard* dressed in a finely tailored suit. The *National Law Journal* had named him one of the country's top corporate lawyers, earning him the moniker "the Swiss Army Knife of Litigation."

All three defense lawyers made many of the same points during their opening statements. Drug distributors do not manufacture opioids. They do not write prescriptions. They do not dispense drugs. They are logistics companies, nothing more. They also noted that the DEA determines the quantity of narcotics that can be manufactured each year. If the DEA was so concerned, they asked, why didn't the agency cut the production quotas for oxycodone and hydrocodone?

"Why is McKesson in this case?" Schmidt asked the judge. "It's not in this case because it prescribes opioids. It doesn't. It's not in this case because it's a named marketing defendant in the complaint governing this case. It's not. It's not in this case because it approves or sets quotas for opioids. That's the DEA and the FDA. It doesn't dispense opioids. That's pharmacies. And it doesn't approve the doctors and the pharmacists who handle opioids. That's regulators. This is the distribution chain.

"Their lawsuit depends on ignoring almost every part of this chain."

Schmidt, Mainigi, and Nicholas repeated another central theme of their defense: Purdue Pharma and other drug manufacturers changed the narrative in America about the treatment of pain, making the large volumes of pills possible. Treating pain became a priority in the medical community. Doctors were judged on whether they were appropriately addressing the pain needs of their patients, and pain had become recognized as the fifth vital sign by leading medical institutions, the defense attorneys reminded the judge. "Public health organizations and medical groups picked up that view," Schmidt said. "State medical boards around the country picked up on that idea, including here in West Virginia."

Schmidt then produced a copy of a booklet published by the West Virginia Board of Medicine in 2005. In it, the board said, the use of opioids to treat pain was "essential." Three years later, the board published another booklet for physicians. Schmidt read a passage for Faber:

"There is no debate among public health experts about the

under-treatment of pain, which has been recognized as a public health crisis for decades. The cost of under-treated pain in dollars is astronomical, but the cost in human suffering is immeasurable. Turning away from patients in pain simply is not an option."

The booklet was published around the time that Joe Rannazzisi and the DEA started to crack down on the drug companies. The volume of pills coming into Huntington and Cabell wasn't because of the distributors, Schmidt said. "It was because of what doctors were being told by their own board of medicine and how distributors were responding to the decisions that doctors were making in the form of prescriptions."

Schmidt then trained his sights on Joe. He noted that Joe and the DEA had long recognized the importance of drug companies like McKesson.

"This is congressional testimony from Mr. Rannazzisi," Schmidt told the judge. He quoted what Joe said about companies such as McKesson: "It is vital that an adequate and uninterrupted supply of pharmaceutical controlled substances be available for effective patient care."

Each of the three defense attorneys invoked Joe's name during their opening, telling the judge that he was a renegade DEA agent who chose to fight the industry rather than try to solve the opioid epidemic. It seemed as though the defense attorneys couldn't wait for the day when Joe would take the witness stand.

Neither could Joe. He had been waiting for nearly six years.

Chapter 51

Death Threats

Charleston, West Virginia, May 13, 2021

Paul Farrell had thought Judge Faber would be an ally. He'd even persuaded some of the members of his trial team, but his colleagues were no longer sure. Faber began to scoff at key pieces of Paul's evidence and courtroom strategy.

On May 13, the ninth day of the trial, Paul called Chris Zimmerman to the stand. Ten years earlier, the vice president of regulatory affairs for AmerisourceBergen had shared the "Pillbillies" parody email with his colleagues at the company. Even though Zimmerman was a drug company executive, Paul hoped to turn him into a witness to help the plaintiffs. Zimmerman had other ideas.

"The first thing I'd like to identify—I hope I get this right—it's to the tune of *The Beverly Hillbillies,* but it says 'A poor mountaineer.' Do you see that?" Paul asked.

"I see that," Zimmerman said.

"Sir, do you acknowledge that here in West Virginia that we sometimes recognize ourself or refer to ourselves as Mountaineers?"

"Yes."

"Do you know what the mascot for West Virginia University is?"

"Mountaineers."

"And it's making a reference to keeping his habit fed. But what,

what I'm particularly interested in is this last sentence. Will you read that aloud, please?"

"'About pills that is, Hillbilly Heroin'? That one?" Zimmerman asked.

"Yes. Then it says 'OC.' Do you know what OC means?"

"Yeah. The term early on OxyContin, what is also referred—I have seen in several articles as hillbilly heroin, yes."

"So, you'll recognize or acknowledge that at least in 2011, hillbilly heroin and pills, prescription pills, have some reference point to each other?" Paul asked.

"Could you repeat the question, please?"

"Do you know what hillbilly heroin is?"

"I've heard OxyContin referred to as hillbilly heroin, yes."

"So, in common parlance, you understand that there is a connection between the reference in this parody you circulated between hillbilly heroin and prescription opiates?"

"Right, to the government affairs folks I did. That's correct."

Paul had planned to introduce several other incendiary emails that AmerisourceBergen executives passed around during the height of the epidemic. In one, a company investigator forwarded an email titled "Oxycontin for kids" to one of his colleagues. It contained a parody of a Kellogg's Honey Smacks cereal box. Instead, the cereal was called "Smack"—slang for heroin—and the box pictured a cartoon character holding a hypodermic needle in one hand, a spoonful of pills in the other.

He also wanted to introduce the email exchange between Steve Mays, the regulatory affairs director, and Cathy Marcum, the corporate security director, about the Kentucky lawmakers' efforts to tighten pain pill regulations.

"One of the hillbilly's [sic] must have learned how to read," Marcum wrote back, adding a smiley face emoji.

"So, your conduct and your behavior, would you agree with me, has an influence on the corporate culture?" Paul asked.

Zimmerman was ready. "I'm sure you're going to probably show me some more emails. But I can tell you the culture at [Amerisource-Bergen] is of the highest caliber. And if you pick some emails out of hundreds of thousands of emails and millions of pages of documents and some of them, you know, are educational, but some of them, unfortunately, I would have rather they didn't circulate some of the information..."

"These people email back and forth quite a bit. And, you know, I wish they wouldn't send those type of emails. Unfortunately, they did and, you know, I can apologize for that behavior. But it was sent in a joking manner and not as a description of the environment they're under. But, I mean, I'll sit here and you can show me more emails and I'll respond to them."

"But, you know, I think some of the frustration our team...is that we've been working tirelessly—I've been doing it for thirty-one years for the whole reason to keep the supply chain safe and secure. And whether you, whether you—I take it personally when you attack my credibility that way...And, you know, I do apologize to the court for some of the language and some of the things that are contained in them."

Robert Nicholas, the lawyer for AmerisourceBergen, saw his opening. Tall, with salt-and-pepper hair, Nicholas objected to the continued introduction of the emails, arguing that they were not relevant to the public nuisance case, and introducing the same types of emails was redundant—or, in legal terms, cumulative—and grounds to keep them out of the trial.

"I'm going to sustain the objection," Faber ruled.

"Can I ask for the basis of your sustaining the objection, Judge, for the record?" Paul asked.

"It's cumulative. You're showing what you obviously claim to be a cavalier attitude on the part of this defendant towards the drug problem and—isn't that why you're offering it?"

"Yes, Your Honor."

"And this is cumulative to the other documents and I'm not—well, I don't want to comment on the evidence, but I'm not sure how much this proves, you know. People break the stress of their jobs by humor, and this might be tasteless, but I suppose it is relevant to the company's attitude," Faber said.

"That's my point, judge."

"This is cumulative and I'm going to sustain the objection," Faber ruled.

"Judge, for the record, we're trying to prove that it is more than just stress relief," Paul said. "We're trying to establish that it is a pattern of conduct by those people charged with protecting our community. And they're circulating emails disparaging hillbillies."

"Well, I've ruled on this document, Mr. Farrell, and I probably said too much about it."

The ruling on the emails was followed by another setback, keeping out testimony about The Alliance on the grounds that its lobbying activity was protected by the First Amendment. Another plank of Paul's case was gone. The way the trial was playing out, Jayne Conroy thought she might have been right all along. A bench trial was beginning to look like a bad bet.

Following Zimmerman's testimony, the *Mountain State Spotlight*, a West Virginia news organization, published a story about the inflammatory emails with the headline: "As opioid epidemic raged, drug company executives made fun of West Virginians." Other media outlets quickly did their own pieces.

Rex Chapman, a former University of Kentucky basketball phenom and NBA player who was once addicted to opioids, tweeted out the story to his 1.1 million followers. "We addicts are no more than common trash to these drug companies and politicians," Chapman wrote. "They don't give a shit at all about opioid addicts. And THEY hooked us."

He followed that tweet with another. "This is Chris Zimmerman. Senior Vice President—AmerisourceBergen…" Chapman attached four photographs of Zimmerman, one with his wife. The comments on Chapman's feed became increasingly hostile and threatening.

"Sick bastards," one wrote.

"Monsters."

"Time for him to go."

On Monday, May 17, Paul spotted Nicholas standing near the lectern in the courtroom before court convened.

"There's a matter I want to address with the court," Nicholas told him.

"What is it?" Paul asked.

Nicholas glared back. "Death threats have been made against Mr. Zimmerman and his family, and you are adding fuel to the fire," Nicholas said.

"I have no fucking idea what you're talking about," Paul said.

Nicholas asked Faber to cut the live feed to the overflow courtroom on the sixth floor where the journalists and other lawyers were watching the trial. He also asked Faber to seal the official transcript of the courtroom proceedings. Faber agreed.

Nicholas told the judge that Zimmerman and his family had been the subject of death threats and that the stories about his testimony had been posted on the website and the Twitter and Facebook feeds of Paul's law firm. Paul said he had no idea. One of his assistants who handled social media for the firm had posted the article from the *Mountain State Spotlight,* but not Chapman's tweets. Faber summoned the lawyers to his chambers for an off-the-record meeting.

"Your Honor, it is with great regret and hesitancy I have to bring to your attention the fact that the email that was entered into evidence was the subject of strong social media, and death threats have been made on my client and his family and his wife and they fear for their safety," Nicholas said. "Our people are concerned for their physical safety, and Mr. Farrell has a website that is publishing this stuff and that we just think it's unacceptable."

Paul explained that his law firm posted the article, not the tweets.

"Is this something I should get the U.S. Marshals to investigate?" Faber asked.

"Judge, if they're in fear for their physical safety, then yes, you should get the U.S. Marshals to investigate," Paul said. "With all due respect, the emotions that you are seeing on social media, which I haven't seen, the emotions that you're seeing, are because there are a number of families who have lost children to this epidemic. So, while I don't wish violence on anybody, how could you expect to show up in West Virginia with the volume of pills and the devastation that occurred, and the people that are in charge of our safety write that email? How could you not expect there to be a visceral response?"

"Mr. Farrell, it's one thing to have a response, it's another to have death threats," the judge said. "How many more emails like this do you have?"

"I've got several."

"Why do you need them?"

"I'm trying to demonstrate how callous they were in the exercise of their duty."

The judge told Paul he had already ruled. He wasn't going to permit the introduction of any more emails circulated by Amerisource-Bergen executives. He ordered the lawyers back into the courtroom. Paul's plan to portray Zimmerman as a heartless corporate executive had backfired.

Eleven days later, on the morning of May 24, at nine o'clock sharp, Faber took his seat on the bench.

"Are we ready to go, Mr. Farrell?" he asked.

"Yes, if I may have a moment, Judge," Paul said as he stood at the lectern.

Two days earlier, Paul Hanly died at his home in Miami Beach, surrounded by his family and Jayne Conroy. He had been diagnosed with anaplastic thyroid cancer five months earlier, a rare and aggressive form of cancer. The tumor in his throat slowly suffocated him. He was seventy.

"We mark the passing of Mr. Paul Hanly Jr.," Paul said. "Mr. Hanly was one of the founding fathers of this litigation and served as its co-lead. He was our colleague, our friend, and my mentor. He was loved and will be missed."

"Thank you, Mr. Farrell," Faber said. "Your comments will be included in the records of the court."

Several defense lawyers in the courtroom walked over to Paul and his team to express their condolences. They also called and emailed Conroy with stories about how Hanly had treated them with respect and how much they admired his commanding and calm demeanor.

In Cleveland, Judge Polster told a reporter that Hanly was "an excellent lawyer, a consummate professional" in what had probably been "the most complicated constellation of litigation that's come to the federal court in my tenure.

"He fought hard. He fought fairly. And that's what you want from a lawyer, from an advocate," Polster said.

The plaintiffs' trial team was devastated—no one more so than Conroy. She had bought a second home in Miami down the street from Hanly shortly before he was diagnosed. The day of his death, she sent an email to the team. "Paul was a trail blazer in the legal industry," she wrote. "He was a brilliant, gifted trial lawyer with a near photographic memory. His prowess in the courtroom was rivaled only by the boldness of his wardrobe. As one of the first lawyers to file a lawsuit nearly 20 years ago against opioid manufacturers for their roles in the opioid epidemic, it is this fight that will stand as his life's work and legacy."

A few months earlier, Paul Farrell and his wife, Jacqueline, had traveled to Miami to see Hanly. Paul brought a six-pack of Beck's, Hanly's favorite beer. Even though he had trouble speaking, Hanly dressed for the occasion—a white Cuban guayabera shirt, a floral ascot wrapped around his neck. They talked and laughed.

After thirty minutes, Hanly asked if he could break off the conversation. He was growing fatigued.

"You have taught me so much," Paul told him. "I've tried to follow through with what you've taught me."

"You still have a ways to go," Hanly deadpanned.

The two hugged each other and said goodbye.

"I love you," Paul said.

Chapter 52

"A Stunning Claim"

Charleston, West Virginia, May 26, 2021

For months, attorney Mike Fuller had been working with James Rafalski, the veteran investigator who retired in 2017 after thirty-nine years in law enforcement, the last thirteen with the DEA. Rafalski was preparing to appear before Judge Faber as an expert witness—the opening act before Joe Rannazzisi—and air the frustrations of the DEA agents and investigators battling the epidemic on the ground. Rafalski wrote up extensive notes and memorized dates and shipping information on all three distributors. He had prepared a 122-page report analyzing the distributors' pill shipments. To the trial team, he was an important building block in the case against the distributors.

It was a big moment for Rafalski. He saw the ravages of the opioid crisis first-hand and testified scores of times about his big drug cases. But he had never testified as an expert witness. He finally had the opportunity to confront the companies he had pursued for years—the chance to hold them accountable in the first trial of the massive MDL litigation.

Rafalski was a methodical investigator, the kind of guy who created a plan and then locked on to it. As his court date approached, he felt that he was ready. But the week before Rafalski was scheduled to testify, Paul Farrell announced that he was switching gears. He would handle the direct examination, not Fuller. Two days out, Paul told Rafalski that he was ditching Fuller's strategy. Instead of burrowing into the details of Rafalski's report, Paul wanted to stay at sixty thousand feet and talk about the investigator's broad conclusions. Rafalski felt uneasy.

On May 26, he took the stand. Paul walked him through his long law enforcement career, first in a Michigan sheriff's office, then as a police officer and head of a special investigation's unit in Romulus, Michigan, and finally, at age forty-eight, to the DEA, where he worked on fifty major cases, including the Harvard, Masters, and Mallinckrodt investigations. Rafalski testified that he was asked by the plaintiffs to examine the records of the Big Three distributors in the West Virginia trial in the same way he would have as a DEA investigator.

The defense attorneys from all three drug distribution companies objected and asked the judge to bar him from testifying. They argued that Rafalski had relied on faulty methodology, and the findings in his report were opinion, not fact. Not included in his report was how doctors and manufacturers had contributed to the opioid epidemic. His conclusions were incomplete, based only on what the plaintiffs' attorneys had asked him to examine, to the exclusion of mitigating evidence. This was not expert testimony but the flawed ruminations of a witness hostile to their industry.

"I thought I would go ahead and hear the testimony," Faber told Paul. "If I agree with the defendants, then it all goes out the window. But I think I'll hear it and give you a chance to put it in before I make that decision."

Rafalski testified that he determined the distributors failed for more than a decade to prevent pills from reaching the black market. The companies did not design adequate systems to investigate and block suspicious orders—orders that he said could "fall into illicit hands." Their negligence was a "systemic" and "widespread" failure. "I did not find any indication in the review of the material that I had that they were specifically monitoring distributions into the geographic area of Cabell County or the City of Huntington, West Virginia," Rafalski testified.

Rafalski worked with Craig McCann, the owner of a securities litigation firm in Virginia who had analyzed the ARCOS data for the plaintiffs. Rafalski laid out six different methodologies that the companies developed to identify suspicious orders of oxycodone and hydrocodone from pharmacies. He explained that he applied those methodologies to the shipments to Huntington and Cabell. For example, Cardinal and AmerisourceBergen used a system that was triggered when an opioid order came in that was three times the twelve-month average of orders.

It was complicated, but Paul told Faber it was essential to walk through Rafalski's analysis to understand how pain pills flooded West Virginia. Paul said that by using all six different algorithms in his analysis, Rafalski was trying to illustrate that "whatever metric they want to run shows that the transactions should have lit up like a Christmas tree."

Paul tried another metaphor: No matter what suspicious order monitoring system was used, these huge orders were triggering "fire alarms." But nobody at the companies was investigating or conducting "due diligence" with the pharmacies to see what was causing the fire.

"Let's assume that no due diligence is done and that the alarm, for lack of a better word, the fire alarm, never gets turned off. What should happen with all of the *subsequent* orders until the fire alarm is turned off?" Paul asked Rafalski.

"They should not be shipped," Rafalski said.

In the case of Huntington and Cabell, Rafalski testified that there was a wide range of the number of pain pills that should have been flagged and halted—20 to 99 percent of all orders—depending on which of the methodologies was employed.

Using one of the methodologies, Rafalski said that Amerisource-Bergen should not have shipped *90.6 percent* of its oxycodone pills from 2002 through 2018.

It was a remarkable number. Rafalski explained why: Once the first suspicious order of pain pills was red-flagged, the company should have stopped all subsequent orders until it figured out why that initial order was so unusual.

Rafalski testified that the companies should have reported those orders to the DEA. Instead, from 2007 through 2018, he noted that AmerisourceBergen logged 77,398 transactions with pharmacies in Huntington and Cabell—but only reported 45 of them as suspicious. Cardinal reported only one suspicious order from 1996 through 2011. McKesson reported none out of 18,862 transactions from 1996 through 2012. It reported five as suspicious in 2013.

When Farrell finished, Paul Schmidt, the attorney representing McKesson, stepped to the lectern to cross-examine Rafalski. He asked him about the role of doctors in the opioid epidemic.

"You recognize that doctors and other prescribers are responsible for determining medical need when they write prescriptions for opioids?" Schmidt asked.

"That's one of the requirements for a physician," Rafalski replied.

"The DEA does not expect distributors to second-guess the legitimate medical judgments of prescribers. True?" Schmidt asked.

"Well, I would agree with that, in general terms unless they were to know some information or observe something way outside of the normal," Rafalski replied.

"There's no determination—no requirement in the regulations that distributors have to affirmatively determine that prescribing decisions are legitimate, is there?" Schmidt asked.

"I'd agree with that," Rafalski said.

Schmidt then asked Rafalski if he agreed with a DEA statement in 2006 that the overwhelming majority of American physicians who prescribe controlled substances do so for legitimate medical purposes.

"I agree with that," Rafalski said.

With that admission in hand, Schmidt brought up Joe Rannazzisi.

He asked Rafalski if he was aware that Joe had once testified that "99 percent of doctors prescribe opioids for legitimate medical purposes."

Yes, Rafalski said.

"You agree that the medical community bears some responsibility for the opioid crisis, correct?" Schmidt asked.

"I believe that probably everybody bears some responsibility for the opioid crisis," Rafalski replied. "I don't think that anyone can sit here today that took a role in trying to combat it would ever say they did everything perfectly."

"Does that include the DEA?"

"That includes the DEA," Rafalski said.

"Does that include Joe Rannazzisi, former head of the Office of Diversion Control of the DEA?" Schmidt asked.

"I guess Mr. Rannazzisi would speak for himself," Rafalski said.

"I'm asking your view, sir," Schmidt said.

"I've already stated I think everybody, if they were able to look back and look at what they did, I don't think there's anybody in America that could say, 'I did everything perfect,'" Rafalski said.

"Does that include Mr. Rannazzisi in your view?" Schmidt pressed him.

"If I make a statement like that, I guess I would hope that he could look back and feel the same way," Rafalski said.

Schmidt circled back to his original question about doctors. "Do you agree that doctors bear some responsibility for the opioid crisis?" he asked.

"I believe they do," Rafalski said.

Why hadn't Rafalski included in his report the responsibility of others, such as doctors, pharmacies, other distributors, or manufacturers? Schmidt asked. Rafalski said his report did not go outside of the scope of what he was asked to do by the plaintiffs' lawyers—examine the role of the three distributors.

Schmidt then showed Rafalski a document from a DEA program

launched in 2017 that identified factors contributing to the opioid crisis in West Virginia. It included the "over-prescribing of opioids." The DEA document did not mention distributors.

Schmidt zeroed in and asked Rafalski if he knew of any distributors that sent pain pills to Huntington and Cabell that had not been requested by a licensed health care provider and dispensed by a DEA-licensed pharmacy.

Rafalski said he didn't.

"You're aware that there are all kinds of circumstances when an order can be of unusual size, pattern, or frequency, but not be diverted?" Schmidt asked.

"That's a correct statement," Rafalski said.

"Do you know if you take the body of suspicious orders that have occurred over time how many of them are actually diverted?" Schmidt asked.

"I don't know that, no, sir," Rafalski replied.

"Do you know if it's above or below 5 percent, 10 percent?" Schmidt asked.

"I don't know," Rafalski said.

"Can you point to any action DEA took on any suspicious order that McKesson, Cardinal, or ABDC made for Cabell County or Huntington?" Schmidt asked.

"I cannot," Rafalski said.

Schmidt then began attacking the methodology in Rafalski's expert report that had flagged tens of millions of suspicious orders that should have been stopped. "You have claimed that every one of those tens of millions of orders were likely to be diverted?" Schmidt asked.

"More likely than not, yes, sir," Rafalski said.

"You didn't actually review any of the orders flagged by your methodologies, correct?"

"I did not," Rafalski said.

"In terms of these orders that you claim were likely diverted, you don't know how many of those orders went to fill legitimate medical need, correct?" Schmidt asked.

"I do not."

"You don't know whether it's 99 percent of the flagged orders that went to legitimate medical need, 1 percent, or some other number?"

"I do not know," Rafalski said.

"And I believe you said in your direct examination at one point that 90 percent of the pills should not have been shipped. Do you remember saying something to that effect?"

"Yes," Rafalski said.

"Now, if that view were followed, how many cancer patients would have been deprived of medication?"

"Well..."

"How many, sir, do you know?" Schmidt asked.

"I do not," Rafalski said.

"Do you know how many patients recovering from surgery would be deprived of medication if your opinions were followed?"

"I do not," Rafalski said.

"Do you know how many patients receiving end-of-life care would be deprived of medications if your opinions were followed?"

"I do not," he said.

"Do you know how many doctor prescriptions for legitimate medical need would not be filled if your opinions were followed?"

"I do not," he said.

"Do you know how many of these tens of millions of orders should have been reported to the DEA as suspicious?"

"No, I do not," Rafalski said.

"DEA never used these methodologies that you present in your report, correct?" Schmidt asked.

"Not that I'm aware of, no," Rafalski replied.

"And you never used them while you were at DEA, correct?"

"I did not," Rafalski said.

"Instead, you created these methodologies for the first time for litigation, correct?" Schmidt asked.

"Yes, sir," Rafalski said.

Finally, Schmidt pointed out to Rafalski that since 2007 and 2008, the three distributors had blocked pill orders that went above a certain number.

"How many have they blocked?" Schmidt asked.

"I don't recall," Rafalski said.

"Do you recognize it's hundreds of thousands nationwide?" Schmidt asked.

"I didn't look at nationwide," Rafalski said.

"Do you know how many it is in West Virginia?"

"I do not," Rafalski said.

"Do you know how many it is in Huntington-Cabell?"

"In the totality, I do not."

At the end of his testimony, Rafalski left the courtroom. Schmidt and the other defense attorneys urged Faber to strike him as an expert witness.

"The claim he made is staggering on its face, that by running these magic numbers that are simple and that no one has ever done before and that ignore everything happening in the real world, you can automatically identify 90 percent of pills that should not be shipped," Schmidt told the judge. "That's a stunning claim on its face. And when we dig into it, we see why it's stunning. No one has done it and it's divorced from any indicia of methodology or reliability."

"Yeah," Faber replied. "To be frank with you, Mr. Farrell, I was shocked when he came up with the 90 percent number."

Faber said he would admit Rafalski's testimony for now. He would consider whether Rafalski met the standards of an expert and decide later if his opinions should be admitted as evidence.

The plaintiffs' team had just watched a master class in how to destroy a witness. Several team members regretted that they hadn't better prepared Rafalski for Schmidt's searing cross-examination.

Rafalski left the courthouse and headed to the Embassy Suites. He was exhausted, so stressed that he had lost ten pounds during the three weeks he spent in Charleston preparing for his day in court. As he packed up his white 2013 Ford Explorer, he flashed back on all the cases he had made against the drug companies and how his long career may have come to a brutal end.

Mike Fuller and a few other attorneys from the trial team tried to make him feel better as he stood in the hotel lobby. "You were great," Fuller told him.

Rafalski didn't believe him. He knew his time on the stand had not gone well. He remembered glancing over at Faber several times during his testimony and seeing a pained look on his face. As he began the long drive home to Michigan, he knew that he had lost the judge.

Chapter 53

"Are You Ready?"

Charleston, West Virginia, June 8, 2021

Joe Rannazzisi couldn't wait to take the witness stand. Ever since the day he was declared persona non grata by the DEA in 2015, he wanted to testify in a courtroom and tell the story of the opioid epidemic. How he tried to rein in renegade companies. Stop their mind-boggling pill shipments. How the industry ignored his warnings and accepted the flurry of Justice Department fines as a cost of doing business. The companies' political prowess in Washington and how they were able to neutralize the most potent weapon the DEA had in its arsenal against the industry. Their indifference to the heartbreaking suffering on America's streets.

After a six-hour drive from his home near Washington, Joe stepped out of his Ford Excursion in the parking lot of the Embassy Suites, checked into his room, and walked down the block to the Charleston Town Center, a down-on-its-luck mall where the plaintiffs' trial team had set up its war room in an abandoned PacSun clothing store. It was Sunday, June 6, two days before he was scheduled to testify. Joe sat down with Linda Singer, the Motley Rice trial attorney who was assigned to prepare him for his testimony. As the two huddled in a corner, Paul Farrell pulled up a chair beside the veteran DEA agent whose work had inspired him to take on the opioid industry. He and Joe had met briefly during Joe's deposition by Mark

Lanier at the Washington offices of Williams & Connolly two years earlier, but they never had a chance to talk.

Singer, with dark curly hair and a quick temper, was in no mood for Paul's interventions. "Don't hijack this," she snapped. "We're working on his direct."

"I'm just sitting down to listen," Paul said.

Everyone was on edge, keenly aware of Joe's importance to the case, particularly after the drubbing James Rafalski had taken ten days earlier. Joe needed to turn in a star performance.

"Are you ready?" Paul asked him.

Joe stared back. "I've been ready," he said.

The night before his testimony, Joe spent the evening holed up in his hotel room. He read and reread several sections of the *Code of Federal Regulations* and the Controlled Substances Act. The arcane passages, he knew, were the keys to the case. He wanted to be able to recite each section and subsection by heart. He knew that the defense lawyers would argue that the regulations do not specifically say their clients had to stop shipping suspicious orders of narcotics. He turned to CFR Section 1301 and then 1306. He reviewed CSA Section 823. Read together, the sections required the companies to maintain "effective controls" over their drugs and set up suspicious order monitoring programs. If the companies shipped suspicious orders, they were in violation of the "effective controls" provision of the statute.

Joe ironed his white shirt and laid out the clothes he planned to wear the next day, a dark gray suit and a gold-colored tie. At nine that night, he turned out the lights. The next morning, June 8, he was up at 4:45. He wasn't anxious. He wasn't nervous. He thought his time on the stand might be contentious, but for him, it would be easy. *It's only hard when you're not telling the truth,* he told himself. *Everything is documented.*

Just before three that afternoon, Joe stepped into Judge Faber's austere wood-paneled courtroom, its jury box occupied by members of the U.S. Marshals Service. He had testified in criminal cases as an agent and on Capitol Hill as a senior DEA official—so many times he had lost count. But this was different. He was going up against some of the best defense lawyers in the business. By now, their strategy couldn't be clearer: Everyone was to blame for the epidemic except the drug distributors. Drug company marketeers pushed pain pills on the public and the medical community. Doctors overprescribed. The DEA failed to reduce the quota for the volume of opioids that could be manufactured each year. The drug distributors, their lawyers argued, were simply logistics companies, delivering products ordered by DEA-licensed pharmacies to fill prescriptions written by DEA-registered doctors. Who were they to question the judgment of America's medical community?

Singer began her examination of Joe by pulling several pages from Lanier's folksy playbook, using a road map to help explain his journey through the DEA and his experiences with the companies. As she established his credentials as a lawyer, a pharmacist, a DEA diversion investigator, an agent, and then a supervisor, Faber seemed engaged. The plaintiffs' attorneys were relieved. The judge tended to drift off during these afternoon sessions. But not on this afternoon. He scribbled notes as Joe spoke and paid close attention to the veteran DEA man.

Singer asked Joe to explain the closed system of drug distribution. "What happens if drugs escape from the closed system?"

"You get diversion," Joe said.

"And what happens when drugs are diverted?"

"People become addicted, people overdose, and people die," Joe said.

Singer then asked why it was important that the companies police themselves. "Now, help us understand," she said. "At DEA, you have warrants, better than subpoenas. You have guns. Why do you need participants in the closed system to do that job?"

"Our resources are limited," Joe said. "The Controlled Substances

Act was set up so a supply chain could police itself all the way down to the doctor and pharmacy level."

Joe was barely ten minutes into his testimony when Paul Schmidt, the lawyer representing McKesson, raised the first of scores of objections that he and the other defense lawyers would lodge that afternoon and over the next two days.

"Your Honor, I don't think he's an expert on why the Controlled Substances Act was set up," Schmidt said. "I'll move to strike that testimony and ask that he be limited to his understanding and his role."

Faber overruled Schmidt. He appeared eager to hear Joe's story.

When the trial resumed the next morning, Singer asked Joe to tell Faber about his meeting at DEA headquarters with the McKesson executives fifteen years earlier. She wanted to establish that the companies had been repeatedly warned about their shipments but took few steps to stop the flood of pills. She also wanted to establish that the companies had settled DEA enforcement cases by paying fines and promising to monitor suspicious orders of opioids from their customers. Joe recounted how he had asked McKesson executives during the January 3, 2006, meeting to explain why the company had shipped another two million pills to six online pharmacies in Tampa after being warned that pills were being siphoned off to the black market. In one eleven-day period, the company had shipped 520,000 doses to one of those pharmacies.

Instead of offering an explanation, Joe recalled that one of the executives said, "Well, I guess you got us."

"What happened after that?" Singer asked.

"I was floored by that statement. You know, they said, 'We can't tell you why. We don't know.' And it upset me. It really upset me."

"And why did it upset you?"

"In eleven days, a pharmacy got 520,000 hydrocodone tablets? Doing the math, you know, that's just a crazy number," Joe said. "It would be over 500 hydrocodone prescriptions a day. That's insane. There's no legitimate reason to have that much."

Singer then tried to advance one of the plaintiffs' key arguments—that drug users eventually migrated to heroin because pain pills were becoming harder to find on the street. The DEA's crackdown and the wall-to-wall press coverage of opioids had eventually spooked doctors around the country, and they started to limit the number of prescriptions they penned. Heroin abuse had ravaged Huntington and Cabell. If Singer could use Joe to document the "Gateway Theory," it might help the plaintiffs secure more money from the defendants to abate the costs of the follow-on epidemic of heroin if they won the case.

"Mr. Rannazzisi, during your tenure at DEA, both before and during your service as deputy assistant administrator, did you have a chance to form any observations with respect to use of opioids and its relationship to heroin?" she asked.

The defense immediately objected. "Your Honor, this is pure expert testimony," Schmidt said. "They have experts to cover this. Mr. Rannazzisi is not an expert on this. I don't believe this was ever covered at his trial deposition. So it's outside the scope as well as improper expert testimony."

Robert Nicholas, the lawyer for AmerisourceBergen, jumped in. "Outside the scope," he barked.

"I'll sustain the objection," Faber ruled.

Singer pivoted and tried to blunt one of the major defenses raised by the companies, that the production quota of opioids, which is set by the DEA, skyrocketed during Joe's tenure. He could have done something to reduce the volume of opioids reaching the black market. Instead, the defense lawyers said, he did nothing.

"Now, did [the] quota for oxycodone and hydrocodone increase significantly during your tenure?" Singer asked.

"Absolutely," Joe said.

"And why was that?"

Quota levels, he said, are based on the number of prescriptions written and filled, the volume of opioids dispensed at hospitals and hospice centers, and the amounts requested by the scientific and research communities. "As that number kept going up, we would have to adjust the quota every year to ensure that there was enough quota for patients," Joe said. "So, the way it worked was, if more prescriptions were going out of pharmacies, if more patients in hospitals were getting more drug, that quota was going to increase because we have to meet the needs of the patient population."

"So, Mr. Rannazzisi, as the opioid epidemic and opioid diversion grew, why didn't DEA lower quota?"

"You can't just lower quota. It doesn't work that way," Joe said. "And I know people have said this over and over again. Quota, it's a scientific and mathematical exercise to ensure that there's enough drug in the system. I always think of it this way: If you have a hundred people and all of those people are trying to get oxycodone and some of them are drug seekers who shouldn't have it and some of them are legitimate patients that need it, maybe they're [in] palliative care, maybe they're [in] chronic pain, but they need that drug. The quota is established so they will get their drug. But if I come in and say, 'You know what, I'm just going to cut it by 20 percent,' then that's 20 percent less. But the patient population and those drug seekers are competing for 20 percent less. And that's how shortages occur."

What would have kept opioids off the black market? Singer asked.

"Compliance with the Controlled Substances Act at every level of the distribution chain," Joe said. "That's what stops drug-seeking behavior, because if they can't get the drug, if they can't go into the pharmacy to get the drug, they're shut off."

Singer wanted to make one more point before Faber—that Joe tried to persuade the opioid industry to change its behavior. Rather than comply with the law, the industry fought back with every weapon it had.

"Did you ever say publicly that you were at war with industry?" she asked.

"Yes, I did."

"And what did you mean?"

Joe began to recount his battle with Cardinal over the massive amounts of pills it was shipping from its warehouse in Lakeland, Florida. "I was called over to the [Justice] Department and they were just trying to circumvent me and what we were trying to do," Joe said.

"I'll object to the witness purporting to say what the company was intending to do," said Jennifer G. Wicht, a lawyer representing Cardinal.

"Yeah, same objection," Schmidt said. "I think the witness obviously has strong views, but they don't form facts."

Singer tried a different tack. "Mr. Rannazzisi, I know the judge directed us to stick to the facts. So, what did you observe?"

"I observed that they were not complying and they continued to not comply," Joe said. "And, so, we just continued to do what we were doing, which was enforcing the law."

"Objection to the legal conclusion, Your Honor," Wicht said.

"I'll overrule the objection," Faber said.

"And, so, Mr. Rannazzisi, when you said you were at war with industry, who started the war from your perspective?" Singer asked.

"Objection, Your Honor," Wicht said.

"Objection. Your Honor, the witness—" Schmidt began to say.

"Yeah, this line has gone far enough, Ms. Singer," Faber said. "You made your point and I'll sustain that objection."

As Singer ended her direct examination and made her way back to the plaintiffs' table, Schmidt strode to the lectern. There seemed to be no doubt that he had been waiting for this day, just like Joe.

Schmidt started off by attacking Joe and arguing that the DEA didn't follow up on the suspicious order reports the drug distributors did file. That Joe could have cut the production quota for opioids. That he testified before Congress that 99 percent of the drug companies were obeying the law, and nearly all prescriptions had been written for legitimate medical needs.

The exchanges between the two soon turned rancorous. This

confrontation had been in the making for years. The two Type-A warriors were ready to fight it out.

Schmidt asked Joe to recall the meeting he had with the McKesson executives in his office fifteen years earlier. He said there was no evidence that anyone ever said "you got us" during the meeting. If he was so concerned that a pharmacy had ordered 520,000 doses of hydrocodone within eleven days, why didn't he shut it down?

"Sir, did you cut them off immediately after that?" Schmidt asked.

"I couldn't because of due process," Joe said. "Obviously, you know about due process. Due process means that I have to do my investigation in line to ensure that it's done appropriately, and I have enough evidence to shut them down."

Schmidt turned to Faber. "Your Honor, I think the witness is pretty clearly arguing with me," he said. "I'd ask him just to answer the questions."

"He can explain his answer," Faber said. "Go ahead and ask him the next question."

"My reaction was just to, you know, the due process," Schmidt said. "I recognize I'm dealing with a lawyer as a witness, but I'm trying to keep it polite."

He really wasn't. The following day, Joe's third on the stand, the warring continued. Schmidt began strafing Joe with a barrage of questions, barely allowing him time to respond but making sure he was scoring points with the judge. Even the plaintiffs' lawyers had to admire his command of the complicated material, the precision of his questions, the strategy he had devised for his cross-examination.

Schmidt must have known that Joe had a temper when he was at the DEA; he kept prodding him, trying to get Joe to blow up, like he did on the call with the congressional staffers. But Joe was wise to the tactic. He provided short, narrowly tailored answers to Schmidt's questions while occasionally smiling at his inquisitor. Schmidt asked if any of the warehouses the DEA had shut down served Huntington or Cabell. They did not, Joe said. He asked Joe if he was aware of any drug distributors that had violated the law in Huntington or Cabell. Joe said he was not.

"Are you aware of any distributor in this case that distributed opioids in Huntington or Cabell that were not approved by the FDA?" Schmidt asked.

"I'm not aware of any."

"Are you aware of an instance where the DEA ever told a distributor in this case not to do business with the DEA-registered manufacturer?"

"I don't have any information on that."

"Distributors aren't authorized to write prescriptions, correct?"

"That's correct," Joe said.

"They don't evaluate a patient's legitimate medical need for opioids in terms of deciding whether the opioids are appropriate for that patient, correct?"

"That's correct."

"They can't second-guess legitimate medical decisions by prescribers, correct?"

"I don't understand when they would be questioning a legitimate medical prescription."

"And they don't have access to individual patient medical records because of privacy laws, correct?"

"They wouldn't have access to that."

Schmidt then tried the strategy he had used so effectively with Rafalski. He wanted Joe to admit fault, that the DEA was to blame for the opioid epidemic, not the drug companies.

"You've taken issue with manufacturers in your work, correct?" Schmidt asked.

"Yes."

"You've taken issue with chain pharmacies in your work, correct?"

"Yes."

"You blamed independent pharmacies, correct?"

"Yes."

"In terms of you, you had ultimate authority of the Office of Diversion Control for ten years during the opioid crisis, correct?"

"Yes."

"There was an opioid crisis the entire time that you were the head of DEA's Office of Diversion Control, correct?"

"That's correct, yes."

"It worsened during your tenure, correct?"

"It did increase, yes."

"Including here in West Virginia, correct?"

"Yes," Joe said.

"Across the country?"

"Yes."

"You were the senior most law enforcement official at DEA responsible for pharmaceutical diversion, correct?"

"That's correct, yes."

"And despite the issue you've taken with others, am I right that you take no responsibility for the opioid crisis?"

"I don't take any responsibility for the opioid crisis, no," Joe said.

"Zero percent?"

"Yes, zero percent."

"In fact, I've had the chance to ask you questions about your fulfillment of these responsibilities, and you've told me when it comes to registration, with the powers available to you, you believe you were perfect?"

"We did registration in line with what the law allowed us to do, yes."

"Registration of doctors and pharmacies, given the powers you had, did you execute those powers perfectly?"

"We executed them according to the law," Joe said. "So, if we're dealing with the law, yes, we did it as far as the law would allow us to do."

"Given the powers you had to investigate doctors and pharmacies, you exercised those perfectly. True?"

"Yes, within the resources we had and within the law, we did, yes."

"Given the powers you had regarding quotas, you believe you executed those powers perfectly, correct?"

"Again, we were required to follow the statutes and the laws related to quota and we did so appropriately, yes."

"You believe you did so perfectly, given the powers you had regarding quotas?"

"We did the best we could do within the confines of the law, yes."

"You wouldn't do anything differently in terms of how you approached the opioid crisis while you were at the DEA, correct?" Schmidt asked.

Joe sensed that Schmidt had just committed a cardinal sin in the legal profession. He had asked a question without knowing the answer. Joe had been considering that question—and his answer—for a long time.

"Would you do things differently?" Schmidt asked. "Just 'yes' or 'no.'"

"It's not a 'yes' or 'no' question," Joe said.

At that moment, Joe saw Schmidt's eyes widen. Perhaps the seasoned litigator realized that he may have asked one question too many. Joe was about to answer when Schmidt suddenly withdrew his question. "I'll move on," Schmidt said.

After Joe returned to his room at the Embassy Suites that night, he thought about what he would have said had Schmidt let him answer: *Executives in handcuffs. Billions in fines. Tens of thousands of lives saved.*

He wondered what Faber would have thought. Maybe his words would have resonated with the judge. Maybe the judge would have come to see the drug companies the same way Joe saw them.

They were working together, Joe would have told Faber. *They had the knowledge. They had the intent. And once you have knowledge and intent, you're no longer a corporation. You're a cartel.*

Chapter 54

"Magic or Tragic"

Charleston, West Virginia, July 27, 2021

For many members of the plaintiffs' trial team, the summer-long stay at the Embassy Suites felt like a stint in prison. They couldn't wait for their long, tortuous sentences to end. It had been thirteen weeks since the trial began on May 3, and they were tired of seeing the same faces in the hotel atrium, eating the same food at the Tidewater Grill and Soho's, walking by the same street people as they trudged past the Charleston Town Center, the Outback Steakhouse, and the sketchy city bus stop on their way to the federal courthouse. There were few respites from the twenty-hour workdays. On some mornings and evenings, the attorneys sought refuge on the Sunrise Carriage Trail, strolling beneath its canopy of trees, past the site where two Civil War Union spies were executed and up the gently sloping switchbacks to the grounds of the old governor's mansion overlooking the Kanawha River and the once-grand capital city.

After nearly three months in the courtroom and the testimony of forty witnesses, Paul Farrell knew that the outcome of his case was far from certain. Judge Faber had handed down several unfavorable rulings and made some worrisome remarks from the bench. None was more troubling than when he told the plaintiffs' attorneys that he thought their evidence on the Gateway Theory was "kind of thin."

On the morning of Tuesday, July 27, the importance of the

plaintiffs' closing arguments—split between Paul and Anne Kearse, the trial lawyer from Motley Rice, couldn't have loomed larger. A successful close, tying together the months of often tedious testimony into a convincing narrative, might favorably tip the case. A poorly constructed argument that failed to confront the formidable defenses raised by the company's lawyers could be ruinous.

More than the outcome of this case was on the line. If the plaintiffs couldn't win in West Virginia, could they win anywhere?

At precisely nine that morning, Paul stepped to the lectern.

"Eighty-one million pills distributed to a community of a hundred thousand people or less isn't a substantial factor in the opioid epidemic. It *will* cause an opioid epidemic. I want to start with that premise," Paul told the judge. "There is no one who will stand up and has testified in this court that the number eighty-one million is wrong."

Paul, idiosyncratic again in his approach, told Faber that he had drawn up a mock jury verdict form to help guide his closing argument and frame the case. The first question he posed: Is there an opioid epidemic in Huntington and Cabell County? He reminded Faber of the number of people who had died during the past decade in a community of one hundred thousand people.

"One thousand, one hundred, and fifty-one lost souls to the opioid epidemic," he said.

Paul next asked: Did the epidemic have an impact on the health and safety of the community? He recounted several pieces of testimony: Joe Rannazzisi asserting that the industry created an imminent danger by failing to maintain effective controls over its drugs. Nate Hartle, McKesson's vice president for regulatory affairs and compliance, conceding that his company was "partially" responsible for prescription drug abuse. Chris Zimmerman, who held the same position at Amerisource-Bergen, agreeing that the opioid epidemic had a devastating impact.

"The heroin and opioid epidemic is one of the great public health problems of our time. Period," Paul said. "That's a fact."

He turned to another question: Did the diversion of prescription drugs give rise to the epidemic? He pointed out that Joe had repeatedly warned the distributors that the diversion of their drugs from the closed supply chain had dangerous and potentially lethal consequences. He said Hartle conceded that the likelihood that drugs would be siphoned off to the black market increased as distributors shipped more and more pills around the nation.

"We have put on sufficient evidence for this court to find that nobody can dispute that diversion is a substantial factor in the opioid epidemic in Huntington–Cabell County, in West Virginia, and in the United States," Paul said.

With each question, Paul settled into a rhythm, confident that his closing was coming together. He asked the judge: Do drug distributors have a duty to maintain effective controls over their opioids? And did the lax distribution lead inevitably to a subsequent heroin epidemic when opioids became more difficult to acquire for users?

"What do you think is going to happen anywhere in America if you dump eighty-one million pills of pharmaceutical-grade heroin into a community of one hundred thousand?" Paul asked, his voice rising in the courtroom. "How can anybody say that heroin is too remote of a consequence after dumping eighty-one million pills of the same molecule into a community?"

Paul acknowledged that he and his team had spent part of the trial taking Faber down a "rabbit hole" into the confounding world of suspicious-order monitoring systems. "This is a point that we probably tested your patience with, but it was necessary for a very important reason. The systems the defendants were using were nationwide," Paul said. "What that means is that there was a corporate headquarters policy. There was a single system and it applied to every distribution center in America."

The drug distributors set thresholds or limits for how much oxycodone and hydrocodone their pharmacy store clients could order, he said. But if those clients ordered more drugs, exceeding the thresholds, the companies simply raised the limits and shipped more doses.

"It's undisputed in the record: Once the system was flagged, they were under an obligation to freeze the account," Paul said.

By not taking that step, he said, and by continuing to ship, the result was entirely predictable—more people would become addicted, and their communities would ultimately be devastated by overdoses and destroyed families.

"This is the foreseeable life cycle when you open Pandora's box and you let out the opium. It has consequences," Paul said. "What their arguments are, are remoteness, that it's not foreseeable that dumping eighty-one million pills into a community of less than one hundred thousand is going to have adverse consequences. We don't believe that this is credible. The second thing that they do is they're going to say, 'Okay, if we are responsible for the entire opioid epidemic, so are a bunch of other people.' And they blame the manufacturers, and bad doctors, and good doctors, and pharmacies, and the State of West Virginia, or the Board of Pharmacy, the Board of Medicine, PEIA [the West Virginia Public Employees Insurance Agency], the FDA for approving the daggone stuff, and the DEA."

Paul asked Faber to hold the distributors accountable for their specific role in the epidemic and award enough money to help Huntington and Cabell County abate the damage—2.5 billion over fifteen years.

It was Kearse's turn. She opened by hammering home the urgency of the case. They weren't just talking about something that had happened in the past—the city of Huntington and Cabell County were still in the midst of an opioid epidemic.

Kearse reminded the judge of testimony by several city and county officials, including police and fire chiefs, first responders, and the mayor of Huntington, Steve Williams. They said they watched in horror as the people they served, already addicted to prescription pills, started to shoot and snort heroin. Their go-to drug, whether it was oxycodone or hydrocodone, had become too scarce and too expensive to acquire on the street.

"Many people who have developed opioid addictions due to abuse of prescription medication turn to heroin," Kearse told the judge. "This is from the folks on the ground seeing this. It's not expert testimony, but what they're seeing in their community. Many people who have developed opioid addictions due to abuse of prescription medication turn to heroin due to the lower price, thirty to eighty dollars for a prescription pill compared to twenty to twenty-five for a dosage unit of heroin."

It was unclear if Faber still thought the argument "thin." He sat expressionless as Kearse concluded.

Each defense attorney was given two hours for their closings. Robert Nicholas, the attorney for AmerisourceBergen, went first and began with a simple argument that those who followed would echo: Licensed physicians dealt with pain in Huntington and Cabell by prescribing opioids, and 99 percent of them did so in good faith, using their professional judgment and the medical standards of the day. Licensed pharmacies dispensed the opioids that the doctors prescribed. The distributors did not second-guess those judgments by stopping shipments and withholding medicine.

"They weren't qualified to do that," Nicholas told the judge. "It wasn't their place to do that."

He noted that the plaintiffs took six weeks to present their case, but they never produced evidence of unreasonable conduct by the distributors.

"They shipped medicine to licensed pharmacies pursuant to lawful prescriptions of an FDA-approved medication written by licensed doctors and the distribution numbers and the prescription numbers lined up almost exactly 1:1 because prescribing drove distribution," he argued. "Remember, distributors don't see individual prescriptions. They don't see patient information. They don't communicate with doctors. They're shipping orders in bulk."

If the companies cut off the supply, a random group of patients with opioid prescriptions written by DEA-registered doctors—patients in hospice care or battling debilitating pain—would be unable to get their medicine, Nicholas said.

AmerisourceBergen, like the other distributors, followed the suspicious order monitoring requirement. Nicholas said his client reported suspicious orders of pills to the DEA. But the definition of what constituted a suspicious order had never been defined by the agency, and the requirement to withhold such orders was never enshrined in federal regulations, he said.

Nicholas then attacked the testimony of former DEA investigator James Rafalski. "This expert looked at you and everyone with a straight face and he testified that these distributors should have blocked 90 percent of the opioid medications to Cabell and Huntington during all of the years in issue," Nicholas said. "That was outrageous, and it was preposterous. It was outrageous because it would have had the absurd and heartless effect of depriving almost everyone in the county and in the city from medicine to treat their pain as prescribed by doctors. It was preposterous because it assumed that almost all of the doctors in the county and in the city didn't know what they were doing or had bad intentions. Mr. Rafalski should be afforded no credibility."

Nicholas then went after Joe Rannazzisi. He noted that Joe had made the same argument that the distributors were making—if the DEA cut the volume of opioids drug manufacturers were permitted to produce, legitimate pain patients would suffer. The same was true for the distributors, he said. If they blocked shipments, real pain patients would be unable to obtain their medicine.

"This may be the most frustrating testimony in the entire case," Nicholas told the judge. "Because this is a perfect statement of our position as well, and it's what we've been saying all along. If we arbitrarily limit the supply, people who need their medication will not receive it. They will be without it. We have to be very careful when blocking shipments because we have no way of knowing or controlling who would have access to the limited supply and who would be left empty-handed."

It was "an erroneous oversimplification" for the plaintiffs to claim that the way to lower the volume of pills was to simply block opioid shipments. "To borrow the words of Mr. Rannazzisi, 'It doesn't work that way,'" Nicholas said.

On the afternoon of Wednesday, July 28, Paul returned to the podium to deliver the final words of the trial. He had made another unilateral and risky move, scuttling a thirty-two-slide rebuttal laying out the key elements of the case and scheduled to last an hour, and replacing it with eight slides and a story he wanted to share with Faber that would last just twenty-six minutes. But before he began, Paul had some scores to settle.

"Over the past several hours, it's been difficult to sit by and listen to some of my colleagues. On behalf of the City of Huntington and the Cabell County Commission, we take great offense at some of the misrepresentations," Paul told the judge. "This isn't a high school debate where we're trying to keep a scorecard of points. But there are a couple of individual points that I do want to bring to this court's attention."

He said the defense lawyers never mentioned the ruling in the Masters case and the responsibilities it laid out for the drug distributors of the nation. They never mentioned their duty to maintain effective controls over narcotics and the evidence that supply does drive demand when it comes to drugs.

"We're talking about opium. To pretend that the supply of opium doesn't create addiction and demand totally ignores the entire premise of why we've regulated this drug," he said. "It is a metastasized cancer in our body politic and will continue to grow. Opium has been around since the Byzantine era. It has toppled governments because it, by its very nature, is addictive. You can't get opioid addicts without a supply of opium."

Paul then defended Rafalski. "I want to take a brief minute and make a comment about James Rafalski because he's a good man and I think his credibility has been disparaged by the defendants," Paul told the judge. "What Mr. Rafalski's testimony is and what his common sense is, that if you get an order for 180,000 pills, somebody should probably stop and check and make sure that this isn't a mistake because it seems like it's a clerical mistake."

Paul turned his attention back to the judge and said he had been thinking about what he wanted to say to Faber at the close of the trial. He asked his trial team to pull up the first slide in his abbreviated rebuttal. It was a photograph of a fly fisherman, casting his line across a river.

"So, I like to fish, and I understand that you may have, too," Paul said. He told Faber that he and his wife used to travel to a little town named Barnum, West Virginia, near the Maryland border. It's on the south fork of the Potomac River, near the Jennings Randolph dam.

"I know it well, Mr. Farrell," Faber said.

Paul told the judge that he used to monitor the subtle changes in the water levels there, coming to understand that small changes can portend big things.

"That, to me, is what I hear when I hear the defendants talk about their monitoring and the subtle changes in the practice of medicine," he said. "But this isn't what happened in Huntington–Cabell County, West Virginia. What happened was something different."

Another photograph then appeared on the screen in the courtroom—the opening of the floodgates of the Summersville Dam on the 105-mile-long Gauley River in West Virginia. Three gigantic plumes of water blasted out of the dam, dwarfing the spectators watching from the banks of the river and above the dam.

Faber sighed, burying his head in his hands.

"So, here—here's kind of the metaphor that I want to draw about what the defendants are saying," Paul soldiered on. "The defendants are the dam and they're standing up on top of the bridge there. They're standing up above the water and they're looking down. And the volume of water that comes out is under their control. Now, this isn't an issue of the safety valve failed. This volume of water here at the—at the bottom, at the bottom of Summersville Lake here, some-body turned it on. It's not an accident. They had to turn it open."

Not only are the companies supposed to monitor the subtle changes in the drug distribution world, Paul told the judge, they're also required to prevent blowouts.

"And that's what we had in this case, was we had a blowout. We had eighty-one million pills that came flooding into our community, and it wasn't by accident, Judge. Somebody delivered those pills here and it was the distributors. Their argument that they were all prescriptions written by doctors is insufficient to immunize them or [provide] a safe harbor for their regulatory responsibilities. If they don't want to be responsible for controlling the volume of prescription opioids, they should get out of the business. The reason they don't want to get out of the business is they don't want to lose the bigger accounts. This is a component of their job, to watch for, to monitor—design, moni-tor, and to block orders that are suspicious. And if the number of pills that came into Huntington–Cabell County, West Virginia, isn't sus-picious, I don't know what is."

Paul told the judge he wanted to close with the biblical tale of the ten lepers, a tale he often told to anyone who would listen—lawyers, journalists, government officials.

"Leprosy didn't define them as lepers, it's what they were suffer-ing from. And this distinction makes a lot of difference in the mission that we have because we have human souls that are suffering from addiction," Paul said. "So, you see, I have not lost faith that we can cleanse our community, Judge, but faith alone may be insufficient. What we need to do is a lot of work. And after four years, my work is now done, and I truly believe in my heart that I have done all that I can, and now we entrust this work to your capable hands.

"It's either going to be magic or tragic."

As the lawyers and members of the news media made their way out of the courthouse, a group of defense lawyers headed to a nearby parking garage. Once inside, they began celebrating, high-fiving each other. On the steps of the courthouse, Paul stood by himself. His trial team had scattered. He was surrounded by a small group of reporters, most of them from local news outlets. He told them he had done the best he could for his community. He appeared chastened, no longer confident he had defeated his opponents and won the case.

Paul slowly walked away from the courthouse, past the Charleston Town Center, and into the Embassy Suites for one final stay in the city. He knew Faber's decision could be months away.

Paul recalled the last words he said to Faber in his closing: *"It's either going to be magic or tragic."*

Epilogue

When Rich Bishoff graduated from the Pittsburgh Institute of Mortuary Science with high honors in 1987, he thought he was prepared for a life comforting the families of the dead. He learned how to embalm bodies and make them appear at peace and full of grace for wakes. He learned how to orchestrate church services and coordinate funeral processions. Most important, he learned how to care for the heartbroken people left behind. It was never easy, but he believed he had chosen one of the highest callings in any community—helping family members in the aftermath of death, from cancer, car crashes, heart attacks, and freak accidents. Every moment in life mattered, he told them, and this moment of profound sorrow, like all others, would one day pass.

Bishoff, bald with a round face, graying mustache, and soft blue eyes, began his career as a funeral home apprentice in Charleston, West Virginia. He met the woman he would marry, Janie, in South Charleston. They raised two daughters in the bucolic South Hills neighborhood overlooking the Kanawha River and the capital city built along its banks. Originally from Oakland, Maryland, near the West Virginia border, Bishoff fell for the charms of Charleston. He joined the River Ridge Church. He served on the board of the city's hospice care center. He presided over the Kanawha City Lions Club and coached the Horace Mann Middle School girls' softball team. He found himself at West Virginia's epicenter of culture, commerce, and politics. He also found himself in the company of some of the hardest-working people he had ever known.

But by the 1990s, the Kanawha Valley, like many regions of West Virginia, had descended into despair. The state's coal industry, which once employed nearly eight hundred thousand people in the 1920s, had collapsed. Today, about twelve thousand work in the industry. Jobs at the chemical plants that lined the valley—Union Carbide, Dow Chemical, Bayer—disappeared as the companies scaled back or shuttered their operations. By the 2000s, Charleston suffered another crippling blow as hundreds of thousands of doses of oxycodone and hydrocodone began to pour onto the streets of the city and the surrounding communities. Soon, West Virginia had the nation's highest drug addiction rate, the lowest life expectancy, and the largest number of deaths from opioid overdoses.

Two decades into his career, Bishoff realized that no amount of training could have prepared him for the grief that was strangling his community. A new way of life and death had taken hold in Charleston. The calls came at all hours, nearly every day—corpses found in bathrooms, in parking lots, on kitchen floors. Many families couldn't afford to pay for the funerals. The state's burial benefits department had run out of money. Bishoff told the grieving and the impoverished they had one option: direct cremation. Family members looked back with blank expressions, unable to fathom what he had just told them. He explained that he would take the corpses of their loved ones directly to the crematorium and return their ashes. Direct cremations had become the modern-day potter's field of Charleston.

Bishoff, himself a father of two, had trouble finding the right words for the families. *How do I console parents who lost a child to an overdose?* he wondered. *What do I say to a child or a teenager whose father or mother is gone?* Steadying families and supporting them as they dealt with their losses to opioids became increasingly difficult. He compared the epidemic to a never-ending tornado, tearing through lives, families, the entire community. But there was no Federal

Emergency Management Agency rolling into town with cash to help people rebuild. All that was left behind was the debris of lives lost and the seething anger that suffocated their survivors.

The anger was first directed at the users and then, slowly but with growing intensity, at the companies that many of the families came to believe were responsible—like the Big Three distributors on trial in Charleston during the summer of 2021. Some of the families Bishoff consoled didn't care about the trial, the fines the companies had paid in the past, or the verdict that might send millions to communities ravaged by the epidemic. They wanted to know why no executives were behind bars. As they saw it, that was the true crime.

During a break in a funeral at the Blessed Sacrament Catholic Church in South Charleston that summer, Bishoff spoke for the living, articulating the deep seam of frustrated rage that cuts through his community. Even if Paul Farrell prevailed in his case before Judge Faber and secured hundreds of millions of dollars for Huntington and Cabell County, no corporate executives would pay for their actions. For many in West Virginia, that's the bottom line. That's the lost promise of the justice system.

"The families want someone to serve time, real time, the kind of time they're serving," Bishoff, now sixty, said inside the church that summer evening. "Their lives have been destroyed. They've lost their children. They've lost their parents. They've lost people close to them. They're going to deal with that the rest of their lives. People who were in a position to make those decisions and sent those drugs into our community should do real time."

By April 2022, as the manuscript of this book was headed to the printer, there was still no word from Faber about when he would hand down his verdict in the Charleston trial. It had been nine months since Paul and the lawyers for the drug distributors delivered their closing arguments. But there was nothing but silence from Faber's chambers. *Another indignity*, Bishoff thought. *Another sign that justice remains elusive for the poor and powerless.* "It's more pain for the people who have suffered a loss," he said. "It's just one more slap in the face."

While Paul and the plaintiffs and the defendants waited for a verdict, there was a flurry of developments in the MDL and other cases pending in state courthouses around the country. Some of the developments were cheered by the plaintiffs; others were seen as setbacks. The biggest development came on February 25, 2022, when the distributors, along with Johnson & Johnson, announced that they had agreed to settle the more than four thousand cases pending against them in the MDL in exchange for $26 billion. The distributors would pay the communities $21 billion over eighteen years; Johnson & Johnson, $5 billion over nine years. It was a historic settlement, rivaled only by the tobacco company payouts of the 1990s. The drug companies accepted no responsibility for the epidemic and denied any wrongdoing. The announcement of the settlement didn't damage the stock prices of the Fortune 500 companies. In fact, they rose that day for each of the companies by 3 percent or more.

None of the money will go to the families of the dead. Most of it will fund opioid addiction treatment and prevention efforts and other community-based programs. The size of the payouts, scheduled to start flowing in the spring of 2022, depends upon a complicated allocation formula worked out by each state. The formulas factor in the population of the communities, how many people had been diagnosed with opioid use disorder, and how many died from an overdose. An independent clearinghouse will be set up to oversee where and when the companies ship their opioids. In many ways, it's too little, too late. Doctors are now loath to write prescriptions for narcotics, and the pill mills are long gone, leading the companies to dramatically scale back their opioid operations. Johnson & Johnson has removed itself entirely from the U.S. opioid trade. More than one hundred plaintiffs' law firms will split up $1.6 billion in legal fees. Another $350 million will go to law firms hired by the attorneys general, and another $200 million will be set aside to cover data processing and other costs associated with the litigation. A judicial panel will determine how to divide the money. It could be another year before the panel sorts out all of the payments.

It took nearly two years to reach the deal. Peter Mougey, the tall, bespectacled partner of Florida-based Levin Papantonio Rafferty, was one of four attorneys who led the plaintiffs' negotiations team. With the country in Covid lockdown, Mougey first met with negotiators for the defendants during a Zoom call in 2020. One of the lawyers leading the negotiations for the distributors was Thomas Perrelli, the former associate attorney general under Obama who had helped to craft the deal that settled the Cleveland case on the eve of trial in 2019. As the lockdowns began to ease during the spring and summer of 2021, the negotiators met at the offices of a corporate law firm in New York City considered to be among the most profitable in the world. Midtown Manhattan was a ghost town. While some hotels had begun to open, most of the city's restaurants, bars, offices, and gyms remained shuttered. The offices at Wachtell, Lipton, Rosen & Katz were empty. Mougey felt as though he and the other negotiators were the only ones working in the thirty-eight-story skyscraper, known as Black Rock, home to CBS Corporation.

Leery of flying back and forth to their homes during the pandemic, the lawyers spent weeks holed up in Manhattan, gathered around the same conference table on the twenty-eighth floor of Black Rock. The negotiations were painful. Mougey compared them to "pulling out the hair on your legs one by one with a tweezer." At several points, he worried that the lawyers representing both sides would walk. But as the negotiations ground on, often late into the evenings, the opponents began to forge unexpected friendships. Some of the sharpest legal minds in the mass tort world began to craft a complex formula for how the money could be divvied up between the communities in the MDL. The lawyers for the defendants also demanded that any deal would shield their clients from future lawsuits.

On July 21, the distributors and Johnson & Johnson announced a tentative agreement to settle the cases for $26 billion—with a caveat. They said the vast majority of the more than four thousand cities, counties, and towns—and their states—had to sign on to the agreement. Without a critical mass of communities in agreement, the deal was off and the cases could drag on for years in the courts. The companies set a deadline: January 26, 2022.

Mougey and other plaintiffs' lawyers, including Jayne Conroy, worked fifteen-to-twenty-hour days as they tried to persuade several states that were holding out for more money to join the settlement. It was mind-numbingly complicated. Every state had to devise an allocation formula for how much money each community would receive and then convince the local officials and their lawyers to agree. If Missouri, for instance, wanted to receive money under the settlement, its attorney general had to persuade the locals in nearly every community to sign on. State officials across the country argued bitterly about how the money should be parceled out and whether they were getting their fair share.

To keep track of every community that had filed suit and how much money they might receive, Mougey managed a massive spreadsheet. Each day, he emailed progress—or lack of progress—reports to the nearly one thousand lawyers involved in the litigation. He was constantly on the phone. On many mornings, he would wake up at six after catching just a few hours of sleep and start making more rounds of calls. Eventually, more than 90 percent of the local governments that had sued signed onto the deal.

In a separate deal, hundreds of Native American tribes also agreed to settle their suits against the distributors and Johnson & Johnson for $665 million. Opioids hit Indian country hard. At the height of the epidemic, Native Americans overdosed and died at a rate that rivaled some of the most devastated regions in Appalachia. Lloyd Miller, a lead attorney representing a third of the tribes, called the settlement epic. "A real turning point in history," he said, noting that Indian nations had historically been ignored in mass torts. In the tobacco litigation, for instance, they were completely cut out.

Paul's case in Charleston was not included in the $26 billion deal. Figuring his hometown would not receive what it deserved, he had decided to take his chances in court, asking Judge Polster to carve his case out of the settlement negotiations. He has since created a new law firm with Mike Fuller and moved to San Juan, Puerto Rico, which has become a tax haven for high-net-worth individuals. Also not included in the settlement are the chain pharmacies and some opioid manufacturers, who continue to fight the cases in court. A pair of rulings in 2021 gave the companies hope that they might ultimately prevail.

The public nuisance theory that forms the basis of many of the opioid cases has had a rough ride through the judicial system. In back-to-back wins for the opioid industry, judges in state courts in California and Oklahoma tossed out the nuisance claims as 2021 came to a close. On November 1, Orange County Superior Court judge Peter Wilson announced he would rule in favor of Johnson & Johnson, Teva, Endo, and Allergan, a division of AbbVie Inc., and reject a public nuisance case brought by Linda Singer, the Motley Rice lawyer who had handled Joe Rannazzisi's testimony in Charleston. It marked the first win by any of the two dozen defendants who were being sued as part of the national MDL and in state courthouses around the country.

During the non-jury trial, plaintiffs for Santa Clara, Los Angeles, and Orange counties, along with the city of Oakland, argued that the drug manufacturers aggressively marketed opioids for a wide range of maladies while downplaying the risks of addiction. They asked Wilson to award the counties $50 billion to cover the costs of the public nuisance the companies had allegedly created. The judge ruled that the plaintiffs failed to tie the conduct of the companies to prescriptions that were not medically necessary.

"There is simply no evidence to show that the rise in prescriptions was not the result of the medically appropriate provision of pain medications to patients in need," Wilson wrote in his ruling, which spanned more than forty pages. "Any adverse downstream consequences flowing from medically appropriate prescriptions cannot constitute an actionable public nuisance."

Just over a week later, on November 9, the Oklahoma Supreme Court overturned a $465 million verdict against opioid manufacturer Johnson & Johnson. The court found that the trial judge who handed down that verdict in 2019 misinterpreted the state's public nuisance law. "In reaching this decision, we do not minimize the severity of the harm that thousands of Oklahoma citizens have suffered because of opioids," the judges wrote in their 5–1 ruling. "However grave the problem of opioid addiction is in Oklahoma, public nuisance law does not provide a remedy for this harm."

Johnson & Johnson applauded the ruling.

"Today the Oklahoma State Supreme Court appropriately and categorically rejected the misguided and unprecedented expansion of the public nuisance law as a means to regulate the manufacture, marketing, and sale of products, including the Company's prescription opioid medications," a company statement read.

The twin rulings rattled members of the plaintiffs' bar. While the lawyers overseeing the MDL publicly stated that state court rulings had little bearing on their larger national civil action, some were privately worried that more adverse rulings could be coming their way. Jayne Conroy was in the middle of a state opioid trial on Long Island when the rulings were announced. She was arguing alongside MDL attorney Hunter Shkolnik, the New York lawyer who was one of the earliest attorneys to join the opioid litigation. Their case rested entirely on the public nuisance theory.

"It was a big blow," Conroy said. "Around the country, as people were trying to pull together the global settlement, it was not a good fact for us."

Within weeks, though, the plaintiffs won a reprieve, scoring successive courtroom victories, both delivered by juries, not judges. Mark Lanier finally got to argue one of the MDL cases before a jury in Cleveland. He served as the lead counsel, along with co-counsel Peter

H. Weinberger, in the first trial involving three of the nation's largest pharmacy chains—CVS, Walgreens, and Walmart. Joe Rannazzisi was one of his star witnesses. At the conclusion of the six-week trial in Polster's courtroom in the fall of 2021, Lanier told the jurors in closing arguments that the pharmacies made money "off every pill they sell." But they didn't make a thing "off a refusal to sell."

On November 23, 2021, after deliberating for nearly six days, the twelve-member panel ruled against the pharmacies. The jurors found that the companies contributed to the explosion of opioid overdoses and deaths in Lake and Trumbull counties in northeastern Ohio, and their conduct had created a public nuisance. Polster will hold hearings to determine how much the companies will pay to cover the damages in the two Ohio counties. After the trial, Lanier interviewed members of the jury. They told him Joe was one of their favorite witnesses. "They loved him," Lanier said.

Just after Christmas, the plaintiffs received more good news. On December 30, jurors in Conroy and Shkolnik's Long Island case ruled that drugmaker Teva and its subsidiaries had created a public nuisance in Nassau and Suffolk counties by flooding the region with opioids and downplaying their risks while thousands died. The six-month-long trial began in June with more than two dozen defendants from every link in the opioid supply chain—manufacturers, pharmacies, and distributors. It was the first case in the nation to bring them all together in one courtroom.

During the trial, the Big Three settled for $1 billion; Johnson & Johnson for $230 million; drug maker Allergan for $200 million; and CVS, Walgreens, Rite Aid, and Walmart for $26 million. In the end, only Teva and its subsidiaries remained. The jurors finally got to see the *Dr. Evil* salesforce video that had been produced fourteen years earlier. It took them nine days to return their verdict, finding that the drug manufacturer violated New York's public nuisance statutes. The case, like the others based on the public nuisance theory, is headed to the appellate courts. It could be years before those cases are resolved and the communities see any money from the verdicts, assuming they withstand legal challenges that could reach the U.S. Supreme Court.

While Conroy savored the victory on Long Island, it was tinged with sadness. Her law partner, Paul Hanly, was supposed to be by her side as the co-lead counsel in the case. He died a month before opening statements. "It's just awful not having him to bounce things off of, to be the better person to take a witness or deliver an argument," Conroy said. "I don't think I can express it well enough. I go to bed every night thinking, 'Wow, if only he were here,' and then I wake up, and I realize I have to do it without him."

After spending some time on Cape Cod with her family for Christmas, Conroy went back to work. Her daughter, Mildred Conroy, also an attorney, is working on the litigation, along with Lanier's daughter, Rachel Lanier. Polster has sent five more bellwether cases back to their original jurisdictions for trials involving the pharmacy chains. Conroy's firm has two of those cases—one in Cobb County, Georgia, and the other in Santa Fe, New Mexico. Lanier will lead another trial in Tarrant County in his home state of Texas. The defendants include CVS, Rite Aid, Walgreens, and Walmart, along with several smaller pharmacy chains. Conroy had a trial scheduled for April 2022 in San Francisco against several manufacturers and pharmacies, including Teva, Walgreens, Allergan, Endo, and Par.

Polster's prediction in 2017 that the MDL could drag on for years unless the two warring sides settled the case has come to pass—at least in part. The plaintiffs continue to fight it out with the pharmacy chains and some of the drug makers. Behemoths in the business world, the pharmacy chains have some of the deepest pockets in the litigation and the most to lose.

The litigation has become a morass, said Elizabeth Chamblee Burch, a professor at the University of Georgia School of Law and an expert on multidistrict litigation. She questioned whether MDLs like the one created for the opioid litigation are the best way to bring justice to thousands of victims across the country, many of whom feel no connection to the massive litigation, citing a study she co-authored.

"It's just like the Wild West," Burch said. "You have the high stakes and you have the big personalities and the key players and lawyers who are disconnected from their clients. And then you just throw it all in a big pot and you let 'em go at it. So, for me, the concern is how the plaintiffs ultimately fare in all of this. And I think the answers that we've been coming up with from a study that we did over the last couple of years is not very well."

While many of the companies are trying to settle their way out of the chaos and unpredictability of the MDL, others have taken a page from an age-old playbook in the corporate world. When facing financial ruin, file for bankruptcy. Purdue Pharma filed in 2019 in the face of the thousands of lawsuits that accused the company of setting off the opioid epidemic by marketing OxyContin as a less-addictive painkiller than others on the market. The company has denied those allegations. On October 21, 2020, the Justice Department announced that Purdue would plead guilty to felony charges of fraud and violating anti-kickback laws and pay more than $8 billion in fines. Under the settlement, members of the billionaire Sackler family, which owned and operated the company, will pay $225 million in civil penalties.

Under a separate bankruptcy plan, Purdue agreed to settle the lawsuits with the plaintiffs in the MDL by contributing $4.5 billion to abatement funds in communities damaged by the epidemic. In exchange, U.S. Bankruptcy Court judge Robert D. Drain in White Plains, New York, granted the Sacklers broad protection from current and future litigation. The bankruptcy plan was appealed in federal court by the U.S. Trustee, the Justice Department branch that monitors bankruptcy cases. Nine states and the District of Columbia, which had opposed the plan, also appealed. On December 16, 2021, Judge Colleen McMahon of the U.S. District Court for the Southern District of New York rejected the bankruptcy plan, finding that it improperly released the Sacklers from civil liability.

"The bankruptcy court did not have the authority to deprive victims of the opioid crisis of their right to sue the Sackler family," Attorney General Merrick B. Garland said.

On January 3, 2022, Drain ordered the company and the nine states and the District of Columbia into mediation talks.

Two months later, on March 3, the Sacklers and their company reached an agreement with the states to contribute up to $6 billion to resolve the lawsuits. More than one hundred thousand individual victims and survivors of the opioid crisis would share $750 million of the funds in the agreement, which is still subject to Drain's approval. A cache of confidential documents detailing the internal workings of the company will be made publicly available. The Sacklers did not acknowledge wrongdoing or personal responsibility. Under the agreement, they will be protected from any civil opioid litigation. They could still face criminal prosecution.

"While the families have acted lawfully in all respects, they sincerely regret that OxyContin, a prescription medicine that continues to help people suffering from chronic pain, unexpectedly became part of an opioid crisis that has brought grief and loss to far too many families and communities," the Sacklers said in a statement.

As part of the deal, members of the Sackler family were required to attend a March 10, 2022, court hearing and listen to heartbreaking stories from the front lines of the epidemic. Twenty-eight people—some former drug users, some who lost family members, others caring for opioid-addicted babies—finally got their long-awaited chance to speak to the Sacklers directly. As more than four hundred people listened to the virtual hearing, Kristy Nelson played audio of the chilling 911 call she made after she found her only son, Bryan, dead in his bed from an opioid overdose.

"Four thousand eight hundred and four. That is how many days have gone by since I made that horrifying phone call—a call that I never ever dreamed of making," Nelson said to David and Theresa Sackler, who were on a video feed, and Richard Sackler, who was listening in on the hearing. "A call that I would not have had to make if it weren't for your unlawful behavior and obsessive greed."

Nelson then told the Sacklers that her son would have turned thirty-four in twelve days and she planned to mark his birthday at his grave.

"I understand today's your birthday, Richard," she said. "How will you be celebrating? I guarantee it won't be in the cemetery."

She concluded: "You are scum of the earth."

Ed Bisch lost his eighteen-year-old son Eddie to an overdose in 2001. He said the Sacklers should be in criminal court, not in bankruptcy court.

"I'm not sure I know of any family in America that is more evil than yours," he said.

Mallinckrodt, which manufactured more pain pills than any other drugmaker, followed Purdue's example. In February 2020, the Ireland-based company filed for bankruptcy for its generic drug division, SpecGx. Mallinckrodt announced that it would settle the lawsuits pending against its company for $1.6 billion to be paid out over eight years to communities reeling from the epidemic. The company itself filed for bankruptcy in October 2020. As part of the bankruptcy proceedings, Mallinckrodt agreed to make its internal emails and documents available to the public but admitted no wrongdoing.

Since testifying in Charleston and Cleveland, Joe Rannazzisi has been helping several other plaintiffs prepare their cases for trial as a paid expert, and he expects to be called as a witness in the remaining cases. He's hopeful that some communities will finally get financial help. But he's also haunted by what happened to key members of his team at the DEA. He knows the ruination of their careers is not his fault, but he feels responsible and wishes he could have done something to protect them. Mimi Paredes successfully sued the DEA for removing her from her job and giving her a do-nothing assignment when she returned from maternity leave. She and Ruth Carter, the DEA investigator who worked the CVS and Cardinal Health cases in Florida, are helping local communities as they prepare to take their cases to trial against several drug makers and pharmacy chains.

David Schiller, the lead DEA agent in the McKesson case, has retired from the agency and co-founded a drug disposal company called NarcX. Discussing his days at the DEA brings back bad memories. "I just don't talk about it anymore," Schiller said recently. "It's all about money. I've learned that the hard way. People don't care about death. I've learned more about people not caring about death in the three years I spent investigating McKesson than I did my thirty years with DEA. It's all about how much money am I going to make. It's not about how many people are dying."

It's been six years since Jim Geldhof retired from the DEA. He has been advising plaintiffs preparing to sue the opioid industry and appeared in a 2021 *Vice* video that explored the epidemic. He was on deck to be called as a witness in Paul's case but was asked at the last minute to stand down. Faber had ordered the lawyers to pare their witness lists, and Geldhof lost his chance to confront the companies he had pursued for so many years. While he was disappointed, he was more upset by how the plaintiffs' lawyers presented the case in Faber's courtroom. He believed they should have tied the volume of pills into Huntington and Cabell County to specific cases of diversion to the black market, linking the companies to pharmacies that were breaking the law and to criminal activity and deaths from drug overdoses. Instead, he said, the case got bogged down in a numbers game by focusing on the volume of pills that poured into Huntington and Cabell and the responsibilities the companies had to stop the shipments.

"Don't turn a dope case into a math problem," he said.

Since retiring from the DEA, James Rafalski divides his time between his home outside of Detroit and his lake retreat on the Lower Peninsula of Michigan.

"When I first met with all of the attorneys, I realized it was the right thing to do," Rafalski said of his participation in the litigation. "I still think it was the right thing to do, and I don't regret doing it."

Rafalski said he never openly questioned the strategy of the Charleston case and doesn't harbor any animosity toward any members of the litigation team for how his testimony went. He still wonders whether Paul should have waited for a jury trial. He also believes the strategy Lanier used in the chain pharmacy trial of connecting the companies to the diversion of drugs to the black market might have played better in front of Faber.

When Joe reflects on the cases he made against the companies, he always thought that a corporate executive might have come forward to say they were sorry for what had happened to the nation. Even when some of the companies settled the cases against them, few accepted responsibilities in the agreements they signed. "They still don't get it. They don't understand that what they did was horrible," Joe said. "They're never going to concede to anything, and they're going to continue to operate this way because they're very powerful and they have a lot of resources and they can do whatever they want. I said it before and I'll say it again: They do what they want to do, regardless of what the law is, and that's the truth. It's never going to change unless we get somebody who's serious enough to prosecute someone.

"A kid slinging crack off a corner goes to jail, because he has a gun, for five or ten years or whatever. But a corporation that's involved with the distribution of drugs that are killing people all over the country—the illegal distribution of these drugs—why did they not get prosecuted?

"The answer is power and influence."

Acknowledgments

This book would not have been possible without the work and the camaraderie of our colleagues at the *Washington Post*. We must first thank Jeff Leen, the *Post*'s investigative editor. He has edited nearly every investigative story the *Post* has published about the opioid epidemic and the conduct of the drug companies since 2016. He also edited our year-long investigative project, "The Opioid Files," marshalling the considerable firepower of the *Post*'s newsroom and training it on this important topic. He also read the manuscript for our book, providing us with indispensable edits and advice. We have worked with Jeff for more than two decades on multiple projects and we feel fortunate to have been guided by the best investigative editor in the business. We also thank Dave Fallis, the deputy editor of the investigative unit. He too was intimately involved in every aspect of the *Post*'s coverage of the epidemic and "The Opioid Files" project, coordinating massive amounts of data and documents and turning them into revelatory investigative pieces. (He also begged us to stop buying food from the newsroom vending machines, encouraging us to eat healthier while we worked with our colleagues deep into the night.)

We are extremely grateful for the masterful editing and endless encouragement by the *Post*'s national security editor, Peter Finn. He was an invaluable partner in this endeavor, and we thank him for his patience, impeccable judgment, and sage advice.

We owe our heartfelt thanks to Marty Baron, the *Post*'s former executive editor, managing editor Cameron Barr, former managing editor Emilio Garcia-Ruiz, and managing editor Steven Ginsberg. They threw their support behind our reporting, often in the face of intense pushback from the drug companies, and assigned dozens of talented journalists from staffs across the newsroom to the project. Emilio purchased a high-powered computer so the investigative unit could turn the data we obtained into a public-facing database, enabling our readers to follow the path of every pain pill manufactured, distributed, and dispensed in the United States.

Thank you to *Post* attorneys Jim McLaughlin, Jay Kennedy, and Kalea Clark and outside counsel Karen Lefton for their legal advice and for filing (and winning) a lawsuit to obtain the confidential Drug Enforcement Administration's ARCOS database and thousands of previously confidential company documents.

The *Post*'s superb investigative database editor, Steven Rich, undertook the herculean task of sorting through 500 million drug company transactions contained in the DEA database. Steven, along with investigative data editor Andrew Ba Tran and former investigative data reporter Aaron Williams, created the public database documenting which companies manufactured, distributed, and dispensed 100 billion pain pills between 2006 and 2014.

Thank you to our publisher, Fred Ryan, for his unwavering support of our work and for giving us the time to write this book. And thank you to managing editor Tracy Grant for cheering us on and permitting us to extend our leaves from the *Post* when we needed more time.

We are also indebted to the tenacious and hard-working Meryl Kornfield. She was a key reporter on "The Opioid Files" project and helped us tremendously with research, reporting, and fact-checking for this book. Another valued colleague, *Post* staff writer Manuel Roig-Franza, generously agreed to read our manuscript and gave us innumerable editing suggestions. He is a rare talent.

Thank you to members of the investigative unit and editors and reporters across the *Post* newsroom for their collaboration, particularly

Lenny Bernstein, Katie Zezima, and Joel Achenbach. We are especially indebted to Lenny for finding a DEA agent named Joe Rannazzisi and realizing before anyone else his importance and the magnitude of the story. We are also grateful for the excellent work by our colleagues Jenn Abelson, Amy Brittain, Shawn Boburg, Debbie Cenziper, Alice Crites, Aaron C. Davis, Carol Eisenberg, Robert O'Harrow Jr., Colby Itkowitz, Jennifer Jenkins, Beth Reinhard, Eric Rich, and Julie Tate. Our thanks also to the incomparable video journalists Dalton Bennett, Alice Li, and Joyce Koh.

We have so many people to thank in our newsroom, one of the finest in the world: Reem Akkad, Chris Alcantara, Jeremy Bowers, Andrew Braford, Ziva Branstetter, Matt Callahan, Ricky Carioti, Annabeth Carlson, Brian Cleveland, Jake Crump, Robert Davis, Sarah Dunton, Maria Sánchez Diez, Armand Emamdjomeh, Ann Gerhart, Salwan Georges, Jon Gerberg, MaryAnne Golon, Sarah Hashemi, Jason Holt, Tom Justice, Courtney Kan, Nick Kirkpatrick, Joanne Lee, Brian Malasics, Greg Manifold, Melina Mara, Brittany Renee Mayes, Elizabeth McGehee, Tim Meko, Jesse Mesner-Hage, Laura Michalski, Robert Miller, Nick Miroff, Atthar Mirza, Charles Mostoller, Ted Muldoon, Melissa Ngo, Annaliese Nurnberg, Coleen O'Lear, Tyler Remmel, Danielle Rindler, Christopher Rowland, Ric Sanchez, Kevin Schaul, Leslie Shapiro, Whitney Shefte, Nora Simon, Madison Walls, Will Van Wazer, Josh White, Peter Whoriskey, Michael Williamson, and Kanyakrit Vongkiatkajorn. A special thanks to Julie Vitkovskaya, a remarkable producer of investigative work and special projects. We'd also like to thank Kristine Coratti Kelly, Molly Gannon, Shani George, and Katherine O'Hearn, for promoting our journalism.

We wouldn't have written this book without Gail Ross, our close friend and agent extraordinaire, who believed in the importance of this project from the beginning. Thank you also to Howard Yoon and Dara Kaye of the Ross Yoon Agency for their invaluable help on our book proposal.

We were fortunate to have had the excellent team of Kristina Orrego, Malka Roth, and Dema Al-Kakhan, who helped us organize and transcribe the interviews for this book.

At Twelve Books, we could not have a better publisher than Sean Desmond, whose graceful and deft editing made this a far better book and whose humor, kindness, and frequent movie suggestions sustained us through nearly two years of reporting, writing, and editing, much of it during Covid lockdown. Thank you also to Megan Perritt-Jacobson, Zohal Karimy, and Estafania Acquaviva for their creative efforts to promote our work. We are so grateful for the outstanding editing by Bob Castillo, Rachel Kambury, and Roland Ottewell. We'd also like to thank Albert Tang for his powerful book jacket design.

We were also honored to work with documentary filmmaker Alex Gibney, as well as producers Sarah Dowland, John Jordan, Stacey Offman, and Svetlana Zill, editor Andy Grieve, and Nancy Abraham and Lisa Heller at HBO, for their gripping documentary *The Crime of the Century*.

There has been a lot of revelatory reporting about the opioid epidemic. Each body of work builds upon the other, revealing a more fulsome and accurate portrait of the culpability of the drug companies and how so many Americans became addicted to opioids and died from overdoses. We are indebted to the courageous reporters and their ground-breaking books that came before us, especially *Pain Killer: An Empire of Deceit and the Origin of America's Opioid Epidemic*, by Barry Meier; *Empire of Pain: The Secret History of the Sackler Dynasty*, by Patrick Radden Keefe; *Dreamland: The True Tale of America's Opiate Epidemic*, by Sam Quinones; *Dopesick: Dealers, Doctors and the Drug Company That Addicted America*, by Beth Macy; *Death in Mud Lick: A Coal Country Fight against the Drug Companies That Delivered the Opioid Epidemic*, by Eric Eyre; *Drug Dealer, MD: How Doctors Were Duped, Patients Got Hooked, and Why It's So Hard to Stop*, by Anna Lembke; and *The Opioid Epidemic: What Everyone Needs to Know*, by Yngvild Olsen and Joshua M. Sharfstein.

Thank you to the talented team at *60 Minutes*: Bill Whitaker, Ira Rosen, Sam Hornblower, Jeff Fager, and Bill Owen. Thanks as well to Jan Hoffman and the relentless reporters at the *New York Times*, the *Los Angeles Times*, Reuters, the *Wall Street Journal*, Bloomberg News, STAT, the Associated Press, NPR, and Law360 for their incisive and insightful work on the epidemic and the opioid industry. We would also like to thank Carol Leonnig and Philip Rucker for their invaluable advice.

From Scott: I would like to thank my family for their steadfast support and constant encouragement: Craig Higham, Derek Higham, and Jack Higham, my son and my North Star in all things. I would also like to thank Bonnie Rothman for her love, her companionship, and her always smart edits and sound advice. I don't know where I would be without my friends for always being there, no matter what, no matter how far. And I wish my parents, Barbara and Lee Higham, could be here to see the publication of this book. I know they would be proud.

From Sari: I want to thank the loves of my life: my husband, Bill Schultz, and our daughter, Rachael Schultz, both of whom gave me many smart editing suggestions. Bill also took care of me during the writing of this book, and he makes my life fun, joyous, and exciting. I know of no one with better judgment—or who is a better lawyer. I am so proud every day of Rachael for her kind, caring, and compassionate values and her hard work to make the world a better place. I am beyond thankful for my loving parents, William and Zella Horwitz, who inspired me to pursue my dream to be a writer. And I am grateful for the love, support, and encouragement of my sisters, Heidi Horwitz and Wendy Greenwald.

Finally, we would both like to thank all of the people who participated in this book, for their trust, their faith, and, above all else, their courage to share their deeply personal stories.

A Note on Sources

This is a work of narrative nonfiction that took two years to report and write. All the interviews for this book were on-the-record. They were conducted with those working on the front lines of the opioid epidemic—Drug Enforcement Administration investigators, agents, and lawyers; plaintiffs' attorneys; Justice Department officials; state, city, county, local, and tribal authorities; drug rehabilitation workers; drug users; and experts in the fields of addiction and treatment. Some of these interviews were done while we were reporting on the epidemic for the *Washington Post*. That newsroom-wide effort culminated in a 2019 investigative series called "The Opioid Files."

For this book, we conducted more than 160 hours of additional interviews with the DEA agents, investigators, and staff attorneys assigned to investigate the opioid industry, as well as the plaintiffs' lawyers retained by the more than four thousand cities, towns, counties, and Indian tribes that sued two dozen drug manufacturers, distributors, and chain pharmacy stores. We requested the opportunity to speak with attorneys representing the main defendants in the lawsuits; they either declined to discuss the case or did not return our written requests for interviews. Only one defense attorney we contacted consented to an interview. Over the years, the companies and their trade associations have issued numerous statements defending their activities. We have published a representative sample of these statements online, which can be found here: americancartelbook.com.

In addition to the interviews, this book relies on thousands of government records. They include Immediate Suspension Orders and Orders to Show Cause issued by the DEA against the companies; settlement agreements and memorandum of understanding between the companies and the Justice Department and the DEA; and court records and transcripts of hearings and proceedings held in federal and state courts and before DEA administrative law judges. The book also relies on thousands of internal government and company emails, documents, memorandum, and reports, along with a *Washington Post* analysis of 500 million transactions contained in the DEA's ARCOS database, which tracks the path of every pain pill in the United States, from manufacturer to distributor to pharmacy. The records and the database were obtained following a year-long legal battle waged by the *Post* and the owner of the *Charleston Gazette-Mail*. Many of the records and the database can be accessed through the *Post*'s website. Hundreds of thousands of additional records that have been disclosed in numerous court proceedings and government investigations can be accessed through an opioid document repository managed by Johns Hopkins University and the University of California, San Francisco. It is our hope that these documents and the database, along with this book and the other groundbreaking books and projects documenting the conduct of the companies, will help the public better understand how the nation became addicted to opioids and who should be held to account for the deadliest drug epidemic in American history.

Prologue

> *This chapter is based on interviews with Joe Rannazzisi and Paul T. Farrell Jr., along with articles in the* Charleston Gazette-Mail *by Eric Eyre.*

3   *Late on his last day as a DEA agent:* Interview with Joe Rannazzisi.

3   *Almost everyone had already cleared out:* The Drug Enforcement Administration website.

3   *It was an unusual feeling:* Interview with Joe Rannazzisi.

4   *Joe's friends had known for months:* Interview with Joe Rannazzisi.

4   *The shape of that reckoning:* Interview with Joe Rannazzisi.

4   *In Huntington, West Virginia:* Interview with Paul Farrell.

4   *A local news story:* Eric Eyre, "Drug Firms Poured 780M Painkillers into WV amid Rise of Overdoses," *Charleston Gazette-Mail*, December 17, 2016.

4   *Paul's family had lived in Huntington:* Interview with Paul Farrell.

5   *Paul's younger brother:* Interview with Patrick Farrell.

5   *By 2018, this sprawling coalition:* In Re: National Prescription Opiate Litigation, MDL No. 2804.

6   *A modern-day opium war:* Centers for Disease Control and Prevention website.

6   *Over time, it became apparent to Paul:* Interview with Paul Farrell.

6   *They aren't, Joe would say one day:* Interview with Joe Rannazzisi.

Chapter 1: Joe Rann

This chapter is based on interviews with Joe Rannazzisi and DEA agent Matt Murphy; a DEA memorandum documenting the January 3, 2006, meeting between the Office of Diversion Control and the McKesson executives; the Memorandum of Agreement between the DEA and McKesson; and articles about John H. Hammergren in the Wall Street Journal, *the* New York Times, *and the* Daily Beast.

7   *Joseph T. Rannazzisi was furious:* Interview with Joe Rannazzisi.

7   *Headquartered in San Francisco:* McKesson Corporation annual reports.

7   *The firm had been shipping:* DEA memorandum about McKesson meeting, January 3, 2006.

7   *As the chief of the DEA's Office of Diversion Control:* Interview with Joe Rannazzisi.

8   *Euphoria-inducing, heroin-like pain pills:* CDC website.

8   *almost as many as the U.S. military:* National Archive Vietnam War U.S. Military Fatal Casualty Statistics.

8   *Joe's job was to make sure:* Interview with Joe Rannazzisi.

8   *Three distributors—companies that purchase the pills:* Russ Britt, "Growing Share of 'Big Three' Gets Federal Attention," MarketWatch, May 30, 2007.

8   *Joe had summoned the executives:* Interview with Joe Rannazzisi.

9   *Joe and his team sat down:* Interview with Joe Rannazzisi; LinkedIn profiles.

9   *Hammergren was a quarry far different:* Interview with Joe Rannazzisi.

10 *A life in law enforcement:* Interview with Joe Rannazzisi.

11 *But now kiddie dope was killing:* Interview with Joe Rannazzisi.

11 *DEA leadership expected:* Interview with Joe Rannazzisi.

12 *He had sent every drug company:* DEA communications; interview with Joe Rannazzisi.

12 *Four months earlier:* DEA communications; interview with Joe Rannazzisi.

13 *By the end of the year:* Interview with Joe Rannazzisi.

Chapter 2: Dr. Evil

This chapter is based on interviews with Joe Rannazzisi, a 2003 GAO report on Purdue and its marketing campaign, interviews that the Associated Press *and* NPR *conducted with Hershel Jick, articles in the* Washington Post, *a copy of the* Austin Powers *video,* Pain Killer: An Empire of Deceit and the Origin of America's Opioid Epidemic *by Barry Meier, and* Dreamland: The True Tale of America's Opiate Epidemic *by Sam Quinones.*

15 *Inside a Dallas conference hall:* Exhibits in MDL No. 2804.

15 *It was about 9 a.m.:* Exhibits in MDL No. 2804.

15 *The voice of comedian Mike Myers:* Exhibits in MDL No. 2804.

16 *The company had introduced Fentora:* Sari Horwitz, Scott Higham, Dalton Bennett, and Meryl Kornfield, "Inside the Opioid Industry's Marketing Machine," *Washington Post*, December 6, 2019.

16 *Dr. Evil said he was unhappy:* MDL exhibits.

16 *Fentora had been approved:* Fentanyl Buccal Tablets Information, FDA website.

16 *"Tell the Street," Dr. Evil said:* MDL exhibits.

16 *The use of opium to relieve pain:* The Drug Enforcement Administration Museum, History of Opium; Barry Meier, *Pain Killer: An Empire of Deceit and the Origin of America's Opioid Epidemic* (Random House, 2003).

16 *In 1914, the federal government:* History, DEA website.

16 *During congressional hearings:* "Importation and Use of Opium Hearings," House Committee on Ways and Means, January 11, 1911.

17 *Ten years later, the use of heroin:* "History of Heroin," United Nations Office on Drugs and Crime website.

17 *Even though opioids were heavily regulated:* Meier, *Pain Killer.*

17 *But it was the pharmaceutical company Purdue Pharma:* Meier, *Pain Killer*; A. Van Zee, "The Promotion and Marketing of OxyContin: Commercial Triumph, Public Health Tragedy," *American Journal of Public Health* 99, no. 2 (2009).

18 *The 104-word note was written:* H. Jick and J. Porter, "Addiction Rare in Patients Treated with Narcotics," *New England Journal of Medicine* 302, no. 2 (1980).

18 *In interviews more than thirty years later:* Taylor Haney and Andrea Hsu, "Doctor Who Wrote 1980 Letter on Painkillers Regrets That It Fed the Opioid Crisis," NPR, June 16, 2017; Marilynn Marchione, "Painful Words: How a 1980 Letter Fueled the Opioid Epidemic," *Associated Press*, May 31, 2017.

18 *At one point,* Time *magazine:* Sarah Zhang, "The One-Paragraph Letter from 1980 That Fueled the Opioid Crisis," *The Atlantic*, June 2, 2017.

18 *But the real rate of addiction:* National Institute on Drug Abuse website.

19 *The companies paid doctors:* Horwitz et al., "Inside the Opioid Industry's Marketing Machine."

19 *The Joint Commission:* Horwitz et al., "Inside the Opioid Industry's Marketing Machine."

19 *They also showered them with little gifts:* U.S. General Accounting Office. *OxyContin Abuse and Diversion and Efforts to Address the Problem.* GAO-04-110. Washington, D.C., 2003.

19 *The companies dangled big bonuses:* Horwitz et al., "Inside the Opioid Industry's Marketing Machine."

19 *Between 1996 and 2001:* U.S. Congress, *Congressional Record*, 110th Cong., 1st sess., 1997, vol. 153.

20 *Drug manufacturers also paid movie stars:* Horwitz at al., "Inside the Opioid Industry's Marketing Machine."

20 *Joe Rannazzisi was incensed:* Interview with Joe Rannazzisi.

Chapter 3: Lightning Strike

This chapter is based on interviews with Joe Rannazzisi, along with the Memorandum of Agreement between the DEA and McKesson, SEC filings by AmerisourceBergen and the DEA Order to Show Cause issued against Cardinal Health. It is also based on a Washington Post *analysis of Automation of Reports and Consolidated Orders System (ARCOS) data obtained through a lawsuit filed by the* Post *and HD Media, the owner of the* Charleston Gazette-Mail, *in MDL 2804, National Prescription Opiate Litigation.*

21 *When his warnings to executives:* Interview with Joe Rannazzisi.

21 *He decided to deploy:* Memorandum of Agreement between U.S. Department of Justice and McKesson Corporation, May 2, 2008.

21 *McKesson's executives pleaded:* Interview with Joe Rannazzisi.

21 *Agents and investigators shut down:* Interview with Joe Rannazzisi.

22 *Joe's teams struck five other McKesson warehouses:* Interview with Joe Rannazzisi.

22 *On April 24, 2007:* "DEA Suspends Orlando Branch of Drug Company from Distributing Controlled Substances," DEA press release.

22 *Within five months:* "AmerisourceBergen Signs Agreement with DEA Leading to Reinstatement of Its Orlando Distribution Center's Suspended License to Distribute Controlled Substances," Amerisource-Bergen press release.

23 *Joe next trained his sights:* September 30, 2008, Memorandum of Agreement between U.S. Department of Justice and Cardinal Health.

23 *In Florida, pharmacies typically dispensed:* September 30, 2008, Memorandum of Agreement.

23 *Maybe they'll finally get the message:* Interview with Joe Rannazzisi.

24 *That same year, Mallinckrodt:* ARCOS data analysis by the *Washington Post.*

24 *It costs drug makers pennies:* Drug Information Database, Drugs.com.

25 *But for now, Joe wanted:* Interview with Joe Rannazzisi.

Chapter 4: The Alliance

This chapter is based on interviews with Joe Rannazzisi, along with the July 30, 2020, deposition of Healthcare Distribution Alliance president John Gray, and internal Alliance and drug company emails and memos that are now part of MDL 2804, National Prescription Opiate Litigation.

25 *Top corporate officers:* Healthcare Distribution Alliance memos; Deposition of HDA president John Gray.

26 *Joe viewed The Alliance:* Interview with Joe Rannazzisi.

26 *On September 25, 2007:* Interview with Joe Rannazzisi.

26 *Before joining The Alliance:* Anita T. Ducca, HDA website.

26   *"Develop a strategy for outreach":* Ducca emails now part of MDL 2804, National Prescription Opiate Litigation.

26   *Two and a half weeks earlier:* Ducca emails.

27   *Under AmerisourceBergen's system:* June 22, 2007, Memorandum of Agreement between the DEA and AmerisourceBergen.

28   *On December 7:* Jack Crowley, "Our Friends at DEA," email now part of MDL 2804, National Prescription Opiate Litigation.

28   *For nearly thirty-one years:* Jack Crowley LinkedIn profile.

28   *"I see our friends are at it again":* Crowley emails.

Chapter 5: "We Will Not Get Fined Again!"

   This chapter is based on internal Alliance and drug company emails and memos that are now part of MDL 2804, National Prescription Opiate Litigation. It is also based on the Memorandum of Agreement between the DEA and the McKesson Corp.

29   *In 2008, Congress shut down:* Ryan Haight Online Pharmacy Consumer Protection Act, S 980, 110th Cong., 2nd sess., Congressional record 154, pt. 4: 4632–4635; Mary Pat Flaherty and Gilbert M. Gaul, "Experimentation Turns Deadly for One Teenager," *Washington Post,* October 21, 2003.

29   *As one major source for illicit drugs:* Interview with Joe Rannazzisi.

30   *Long lines of customers lingered in parking:* Leonora LaPeter Anton, "The Pain Clinic Next Door," *Tampa Bay Times,* May 30, 2010; Pat Beall, "How Florida Spread Oxy across America," *Palm Beach Post,* July 6, 2018.

30   *As Joe's teams raided:* Interview with Joe Rannazzisi.

30   *Inside the drug companies:* Jack Crowley, "DEA and Suspicious Orders," email, 2008.

31   *On March 20:* Kristen Freitas, "DEA Strategy Document and FDA Update," email, 2008.

31   *Over the years:* Congressional campaign finance reports.

32   *Freitas began her career:* Healthcare Distribution Alliance website; LinkedIn.

32   *Most of the questions:* DEA strategy update email.

32   *Two months later:* May 2, 2008, Memorandum of Agreement between U.S. Department of Justice and McKesson Corporation.

32 *"By failing to report suspicious orders":* May 2, 2008, Department of Justice press release.

33 *Joe was not pleased:* Interview with Joe Rannazzisi.

33 *Nineteen days after the settlement:* May 21, 2008, McKesson communications.

Chapter 6: The Blue Highway

This chapter is based on internal DEA documents, along with articles in the Washington Post *and the* Palm Beach Post *and a* Washington Post *analysis of ARCOS data obtained by a lawsuit filed by the* Post *and HD Media, the owner of the* Charleston Gazette-Mail, *in MDL 2084, National Prescription Opiate Litigation.*

34 *The route between the pill mills:* Interviews with DEA agents and investigators.

35 *With the internet pharmacies decimated:* Beall, "How Florida Spread Oxy"; interviews with DEA agents and investigators.

35 *Founded in 1867 in St. Louis:* Mallinckrodt website.

36 *By 2008, Mallinckrodt was manufacturing:* ARCOS data analysis by the *Washington Post.*

36 *Members of the Sackler family, who controlled Purdue:* Sarah Cascone, "In a Landmark Move, the Metropolitan Museum of Art Has Removed the Sackler Name from Its Walls," Artnet.com, December 9, 2021.

Chapter 7: "Just Like Doritos"

This chapter is based on a November 29, 2018, deposition of Victor Borelli and articles in the Washington Post *and the* Sun-Sentinel *of Fort Lauderdale. It is also based on settlement documents between the DEA and Mallinckrodt and internal company emails that are now part of MDL 2804, National Prescription Opiate Litigation.*

37 *Victor Borelli was a driven national salesman for Mallinckrodt:* Deposition of Victor Borelli, November 29, 2018, in Baltimore, Maryland; Scott Higham, Sari Horwitz, and Steven Rich, "Internal Drug Company Emails Show Indifference to Opioid Epidemic," *Washington Post*, July 19, 2019.

37 *In May 2008, Borelli sent an email:* Victor Borelli, email, 2008, In Re: National Prescription Opiate Litigation, MDL No. 2804.

37 *In another email:* Victor Borelli, "Re: Oxy 30," email, 2009.

37 *By age forty-six:* Borelli deposition.

38 *And then, in 2005:* Borelli deposition.

38 *Borelli's drive for sales:* Brenda Rehkop, "RE: Sunrise Wholesale," email, 2008, In Re: National Prescription Opiate Litigation, MDL No. 2804.

39 *Another executive forwarded the email:* Cathy Stewart, "RE: Sunrise Wholesale," email, 2008, In Re: National Prescription Opiate Litigation, MDL No. 2804.

39 *Sunrise Wholesale was sending oxycodone:* Draft Partial Excerpt of Complaint, July 10, 2015; Lenny Bernstein and Scott Higham, "The Government's Struggle to Hold Opioid Manufacturers Accountable," *Washington Post*, April 2, 2017; Bill Whitaker, "Who's Responsible for the Opioid Epidemic? Doctors or Pharmaceutical Companies?" *60 Minutes*, September 30, 2018; Marc Freeman, "Former Doctor Who Overprescribed Pain Pills Gets 157 Years in Prison," *Sun Sentinel*, July 31, 2018.

39 *In 2009, an executive at Mallinckrodt:* Borelli deposition.

40 *In the seven years:* Borelli deposition.

40 *On a single day in 2010, KeySource ordered:* Brenda Rehkop, "RE: Item#85300," email, 2010.

Chapter 8: Follow the Pills

This chapter is based on interviews with Jim Geldhof and James Rafalski, along with the June 15, 2010, DEA Order to Show Cause and Immediate Suspension filed against Harvard Drug. It is also based on the federal indictment of the George brothers, the U.S. attorney's office prosecution memo in the case against Mallinckrodt, and the Memorandum of Agreement between the DEA and Mallinckrodt.

41 *In the fall of 2010:* Interview with Joe Rannazzisi.

41 *Jim Geldhof, the supervisor:* Interview with Jim Geldhof.

43 *One of them was James Rafalski:* Interview with James Rafalski.

43 *Harvard Drug was based:* Interview with James Rafalski; ARCOS data analysis by the *Washington Post*.

44 *The twins had recruited doctors:* Thomas Francis, "How Florida Brothers' 'Pill Mill' Operation Fueled Painkiller Abuse Epidemic," NBC News, May 7, 2012; Bob LaMendola, "How the George Brothers Made Millions with Pill Mills," *South Florida Sun Sentinel*, August 25, 2011; Michael LaForgia, "Twin Kingpins behind Some of the Most Brazen Pain Clinics in South Florida," *Palm Beach Post*, March 31, 2012.

44 *On June 10, 2010, Rafalski:* Francis, "How Florida Brothers' 'Pill Mill' Operation Fueled Painkiller Abuse Epidemic"; LaMendola, "How the George Brothers Made Millions with Pill Mills"; LaForgia, "Twin Kingpins behind Some of the Most Brazen Pain Clinics"; DEA Order to Show Cause, Immediate Suspension of Registration, Harvard Drug Group, June 15, 2010.

Chapter 9: "Pillbillies"

This chapter is based on internal drug company emails now part of MDL 2804, National Prescription Opiate Litigation, and a Washington Post *analysis of ARCOS data obtained by a lawsuit filed by the* Post *and HD Media, the owner of the* Charleston Gazette-Mail, *in the litigation.*

46 *The parody was of the theme song:* "RE: Saw This And Had To Share It..." email, 2011; Meryl Kornfield, "Drug Distributor Employees Emailed a Parody Song about 'Pillbillies,' Documents Show," *Washington Post*, May 23, 2020.

47 *In 2011, nearly sixteen thousand people:* Centers for Disease Control and Prevention website.

47 *That year alone, AmerisourceBergen distributed:* ARCOS analysis by the *Washington Post*.

47 *One of the world's largest pharmaceutical service companies:* "Fortune 500: AmerisourceBergen," CNN Money, May 23, 2011.

47 *AmerisourceBergen was one of the companies:* DEA Settlement and Release Agreement, AmerisourceBergen, June 22, 2007.

48 *The legislation required companies:* HB 7095: Prescription Drugs, 2011 session, Florida House website.

48 *On April 21, 2011, Ann Berkey:* Ann Berkey, "Florida Pill Mill," email, 2011.

48   *The lobbyist for AmerisourceBergen:* Rita Norton, "RE: Florida Pill Mill," email, 2011.

48   *The push to kill the legislation:* "Florida Governor Signs 'Pill Mill' Bill," Associated Press, June 3, 2011.

48   *There was an element of karma:* "Pillbillies" email, Exhibits in MDL No. 2804.

Chapter 10: Broward County North

This chapter is based on interviews with Jim Geldhof, Lisa Roberts, and Kathy Chaney, and articles in the Cleveland Plain Dealer, *the* Washington Post, *and the* New York Times, *along with* Dreamland: The True Tale of America's Opiate Epidemic *by Sam Quinones.*

50   *On a warm June night in 2011:* Interview with Jim Geldhof.

50   *One by one:* Video provided by Lisa Roberts and SOLACE.

50   *People sitting in the rows:* Interview with Jim Geldhof.

50   *The Appalachian city of 20,000:* "Portsmouth, Ohio," Ohiohistorycentral.com.

51   *Located almost as far south:* Interview with Lisa Roberts; Sam Quinones, *Dreamland: The True Tale of America's Opiate Epidemic* (Bloomsbury, 2015).

51   *Residents, many on disability:* Interview with Lisa Roberts; Quinones, *Dreamland*.

51   *The hardened DEA supervisor:* Interview with Jim Geldhof.

51   *Chaney was crying:* Interview with Kathy Chaney.

51   *Portsmouth was 90 percent White:* U.S. Census; Noel King, "Why Is the Opioid Epidemic Overwhelmingly White?" NPR, November 4, 2017.

51   *Addiction experts theorized:* Gina Kolata and Sarah Cohen, "Drug Overdoses Propel Rise in Mortality Rates of Young Whites," *New York Times*, January 16, 2016.

52   *One of the speakers that night:* Interview with Lisa Roberts.

52   *One of the most notorious in Portsmouth:* U.S. Attorney's Office, Southern District of Ohio, "Scioto County Doctor Sentenced to 7 Years in Prison for Role in Pill Mill," November 13, 2019; Lenny Bernstein, David S. Fallis, and Scott Higham, "How Drugs Intended for Patients Ended Up in the Hands of Illegal Users: 'No One Was Doing Their

Job,'" *Washington Post*, October 22, 2016.; John Caniglia, "'Unfathomable': How 1.6 Million Pills from a Small-Town Doctor Helped Fuel the Opioid Crisis in Ohio," Cleveland.com, September 1, 2019.

53 *Vying with Temponeras:* U.S. Attorney's Office, Southern District of Ohio, "Chicago Physician Receives Four Life Sentences for Illegally Distributing Pills That Led to Deaths of Four People," February 14, 2012.

53 *When the town hall ended:* Interview with Jim Geldhof.

Chapter 11: "Game, Set, Match"

This chapter is based on DEA settlement documents with Harvard Drug, KeySource Medical, Masters Pharmaceutical, and Mallinckrodt, and the Decision and Order issued by the DEA in its case against Masters Pharmaceutical. It is also based on DEA PowerPoint presentations documenting pill distribution patterns in Florida, draft complaints against Mallinckrodt and settlement documents prepared by the U.S. attorney's office in Detroit, and interviews with Jim Geldhof, James Rafalski, and Barbara Boockholdt.

54 *The bodies were piling up:* Declaration of Joseph Rannazzisi, U.S. District Court for the District of Columbia, *Cardinal Health, Inc. v. Eric H. Holder Jr., et al.*

54 *It was clear from the DEA's pill-tracking ARCOS database:* ARCOS data analysis by the *Washington Post*; Interview with Jim Geldhof.

54 *Geldhof saw that one of the worst offenders:* Interview with Jim Geldhof.

54 *Masters was already well known:* "Masters Pharmaceutical Fined by DEA," FDA News, May 5, 2009.

54 *But it was clear to Geldhof:* Interview with Jim Geldhof.

54 *Poring over documents the DEA had collected:* Interview with James Rafalski.

55 *He discovered that between 2009 and 2010:* Interview with James Rafalski.

56 *On August 23, 2011:* DEA PowerPoint presentation, Mallinckrodt, August 23, 2011.

56 *Barbara Boockholdt, chief of the DEA's regulatory division:* Interview with Barbara Boockholdt.

56 *Rafalski sat in silence:* Interview with James Rafalski.

57 *It was a rare 5.8-magnitude earthquake:* John Hopewell, "Remembering the 2011 Virginia Earthquake That Rocked the Eastern U.S.," *Washington Post*, 2016.

57   *Rafalski tried to lighten the mood:* Interview with James Rafalski.

57   *Three weeks later:* Aaron C. Davis, Shawn Boburg, and Robert O'Harrow Jr., "Little-Known Makers of Generic Drugs Played Central Role in Opioid Crisis, Records Show," *Washington Post*, July 27, 2019.

57   *The subpoena delivered a gold mine:* Interviews with Jim Geldhof and James Rafalski.

57   *"This is game, set, match":* Interviews with Jim Geldhof and James Rafalski.

Chapter 12: A Betrayal

This chapter is based on interviews with Joe Rannazzisi and Imelda L. "Mimi" Paredes and articles in the Indianapolis Star, *the* Washington Post, *and the* New York Times.

58   *Joe Rannazzisi called her:* Interview with Joe Rannazzisi.

58   *At her desk inside DEA headquarters:* Interview with Mimi Paredes.

59   *In 1993, three years after he graduated:* Isabel Wilkerson, "3 Promising Naval Officers Leave Tears and Disbelief," *New York Times*, December 7, 1993; Mark Fitzhenry, "Ex-Navy QB Grizzard, Runner O'Neill Killed," *Washington Post*, December 2, 1993.

59   *Paredes was devastated:* Interview with Mimi Paredes.

60   *Barber was cool:* Interview with Mimi Paredes.

60   *Like Paredes, Barber had served:* Interview with Mimi Paredes; Amy Lynch, "Army Past Helps Quarles & Brady Partner Provide Real-World Advice," *Indianapolis Star*, February 13, 2015.

60   *As serious as he could be:* Interview with Mimi Paredes.

60   *Barber at times:* Interview with Mimi Paredes.

60   *He joined a law firm, Quarles & Brady:* Scott Higham and Lenny Bernstein, "The Drug Industry's Triumph over the DEA," *Washington Post*, October 15, 2017.

61   *Paredes felt betrayed:* Interview with Mimi Paredes.

61   *Joe understood that these former civil servants:* Interview with Joe Rannazzisi.

Chapter 13: Cardinal Knowledge

This chapter is based on interviews with Joe Rannazzisi, along with court documents and motions filed as part of Cardinal Health, Inc. v. Eric H. Holder

Jr. *in U.S. district court, sworn declarations by Rannazzisi and Ruth Carter filed in that case, and the June 8, 2012, decision in the DEA's case against CVS by DEA chief administrative law judge John J. Mulrooney II.*

63 *The phone calls haunted Joe Rannazzisi:* Interview with Joe Rannazzisi.

64 *It was so bad:* "State Surgeon General Declares Public Health Emergency," Florida Department of Health, July 1, 2011.

64 *Joe dispatched one of his best investigators:* Interview with Joe Rannazzisi.

64 *Joe had one drug company fixed firmly:* Interview with Joe Rannazzisi; Declaration of Joseph Rannazzisi, U.S. District Court for the District of Columbia, *Cardinal Health, Inc. v. Eric H. Holder Jr., et al.*

64 *Cardinal had a banner year:* Cardinal Health annual report, 2011.

65 *The numbers in the DEA's ARCOS database:* Interview with Ruth Carter; "Sanford History," sanfordfl.gov; Declaration of Ruth A. Carter, U.S. District Court for the District of Columbia, *Cardinal Health, Inc. v. Eric H. Holder Jr., et al.*

65 *Two CVS pharmacies in Sanford:* Interview with Ruth Carter.

65 *"I knew it was bad":* Interview with Ruth Carter.

66 *On October 18, 2011:* Interview with Ruth Carter.

66 *Between 2008 and 2011, the company sold more than 5 million pills:* Interview with Ruth Carter.

66 *Material turned up in the search:* Interview with Ruth Carter.

66 *Ten days after serving the warrants:* Interview with Ruth Carter.

66 *Cardinal had sold that store 2.2 million oxycodone tablets:* Interview with Ruth Carter.

67 *Carter interviewed the pharmacist-in-charge:* Interview with Ruth Carter.

67 *Time to shut these motherfuckers down:* Interview with Ruth Carter.

Chapter 14: "Because I'm the Deputy Attorney General"

This chapter is based on interviews with Joe Rannazzisi and Imelda L. "Mimi" Paredes, along with emails written by Jamie Gorelick, Craig Morford, and Randolph Moss to Justice Department officials, which were obtained pursuant to a lawsuit filed by the Washington Post *under the Freedom of Information Act.*

68 *On November 22, 2011:* Interview with Joe Rannazzisi.

68 *James H. Dinan headed:* LinkedIn profile.

68 *"Joe, what are your guys doing in Florida?":* Interview with Joe Rannazzisi.

69 *The agency determined: Cardinal Health, Inc. v. Eric H. Holder Jr.,* 846 F. Supp. 2d 203 (D.D.C. 2012).

69 *Dinan cautioned Joe:* Interview with Joe Rannazzisi.

69 *Craig S. Morford, who served:* Memo from Craig Morford to DEA administrator Michele Leonhart.

70 *The implication was clear:* Interview with Joe Rannazzisi.

70 *Several hours earlier, Jamie Gorelick:* Jamie Gorelick, "Time-Sensitive Correspondence," email, 2011; WilmerHale website; "Gorelick to Leave Justice Department," Justice Department, January 15, 1997.

71 *Joe thought the outside pressure:* Interview with Joe Rannazzisi.

71 *The previous night:* Jamie Gorelick, email, 2012.

71 *Like Gorelick, Moss had served:* "District Judge Randolph D. Moss," U.S. District Court District of Columbia website.

72 *Moss sent an email to Dinan:* Randolph Moss, Cardinal Health, email, 2012.

72 *Shortly before 2 p.m.:* Interview with Joe Rannazzisi; U.S. General Services Administration website.

72 *Joe took a seat:* Interview with Joe Rannazzisi; U.S. General Services Administration website.

73 *On his drive back to DEA headquarters:* Interview with Joe Rannazzisi; U.S. General Services Administration website; interview with Mimi Paredes.

73 *The companies were going over his head:* Interview with Joe Rannazzisi.

Chapter 15: Imminent Danger

This chapter is based on emails obtained through the Freedom of Information Act, and court documents and hearing transcripts filed in Cardinal Health, Inc. v. Eric H. Holder Jr., et al., *the Order to Show Cause against CVS, and the Justice Department settlement with CVS.*

74 *Joe Rannazzisi kept his word:* Immediate Suspension Orders against CVS and Cardinal Health.

74 *Just before Joe struck:* Jamie Gorelick, "Cardinal/DEA," email, 2012.

75 *That afternoon:* Transcript of Motions Hearing before the Honorable Judge Reggie B. Walton, United States District Judge, February 3, 2012.

75 *Walton, a former public defender:* "Senior Judge Reggie B. Walton," U.S. District Court District of Columbia website.

75 *"These are extremely dangerous drugs":* "Senior Judge Reggie B. Walton," U.S. District Court District of Columbia website.

76 *The DEA had accused Cardinal:* "Cardinal Health, Inc., Agrees to Pay $34 Million to Settle Claims That It Failed to Report Suspicious Sales of Widely-Abused Controlled Substances," U.S. Attorney's Office Colorado, October 2, 2008.

76 *Without hearing from the DEA:* Temporary Restraining Order, *Cardinal Health, Inc. v. Eric H. Holder Jr., et al.*, February 3, 2012.

76 *After the ruling, Gorelick sent Goldberg a told-you-so email:* Jamie Gorelick, "Cardinal Health v. Holder (DDC)—TRO," email, 2012.

76 *"Thanks Jamie":* Stuart Goldberg, "RE: Cardinal Health v. Holder (DDC)—TRO," email, 2012.

76 *That afternoon, the DEA agents:* Interviews with Joe Rannazzisi and Ruth Carter.

76 *The company was free to ship pain pills:* Transcript of Motions Hearing before the Honorable Judge Reggie B. Walton, United States District Judge, February 29, 2012.

77 *Walton began the hearing:* Transcript of Motions Hearing before the Honorable Judge Reggie B. Walton, United States District Judge, February 29, 2012.

79 *Walton had heard enough:* Transcript of Motions Hearing before the Honorable Judge Reggie B. Walton, United States District Judge, February 29, 2012; Memorandum Opinion, *Cardinal Health, Inc. v. Eric H. Holder Jr., et al.*, March 7, 2012.

80 *The Alliance, on behalf of its thirty-four members: Cardinal Health, Inc., v. Eric H. Holder*, U.S. Court of Appeals, Amicus Curiae Brief of Healthcare Distribution Management Association, March 6, 2012.

80 *But less than three months after Walton's ruling:* Administrative Memorandum of Agreement, between Cardinal Health and the DEA, May 15, 2012; "Cardinal Health Brings Resolution to Litigation with DEA Settlement," Cardinal Health, May 15, 2012.

80 *CVS, headquartered in Woonsocket: Cardinal Health, Inc., v. Eric H. Holder*, U.S. Court of Appeals, Appellees' Opposition to Appellant's Emergency

Motion for Injunction Pending Appeal, March 7, 2012; "CVS Caremark CEO Merlo's 2012 Pay Jumps 44%," MarketWatch, March 29, 2013.

80   *"A pittance":* Interview with Joe Rannazzisi.

Chapter 16: "At the Corner of Happy & Healthy"

This chapter is based on interviews with Joe Rannazzisi and former Oviedo police chief Jeffrey Chudnow, along with the Settlement and Memorandum of Agreement between the DEA and Walgreens, internal Walgreens emails now part of MDL 2804, National Prescription Opiate Litigation, and articles in the Washington Post.

81   *On March 15, 2011, Jeffrey Chudnow:* Interview with Oviedo Police Chief Jeffrey Chudnow; Letters from Chudnow to executives, March 15, 2011.

81   *Chudnow got no response:* Interview with Oviedo Police Chief Jeffrey Chudnow.

82   *Chudnow also wrote formal letters:* Interview with Oviedo Police Chief Jeffrey Chudnow.

82   *Joe Rannazzisi and his team:* Interview with Joe Rannazzisi.

83   *The Oviedo pharmacies were among:* Robert Reed, "Walgreens Leaves 'the Corner of Happy and Healthy' behind with New Slogan," *Chicago Tribune*, December 1, 2017.

83   *Between 2006 and 2012, Walgreens sat atop:* Jenn Abelson, Aaron Williams, Andrew Ba Tran, and Meryl Kornfield, "At Height of Crisis, Walgreens Handled Nearly One in Five of the Most Addictive Opioids," *Washington Post*, November 7, 2019.

83   *On April 4, 2012, the DEA launched:* Settlement and Memorandum of Agreement, June 10, 2013; ARCOS data analysis by the *Washington Post*.

83   *On January 10, 2011, Kristine Atwell:* Kristine Atwell, "High Quantity Stores 68297," email, 2011.

84   *The month after Atwell raised her alarm:* Walgreens Order to Show Cause and Immediate Suspension of Registration, Department of Justice, September 13, 2012.

84   *In September 2012, the DEA shut down the Jupiter warehouse:* Walgreens Order to Show Cause and Immediate Suspension of Registration.

84 *That practice seemed to come in conflict:* "Oath/Promise of a Pharmacist," International Pharmaceutical Federation.

84 *Executives there began formulating a pharmacy store survey:* Rick Gates, "Florida Focus on Profit (Svihra)," email, 2011.

85 *In June 2013, Walgreens agreed to pay:* "Walgreens Agrees to Pay a Record Settlement of $80 Million for Civil Penalties under the Controlled Substances Act," Drug Enforcement Administration, Miami, June 11, 2013.

85 *That year, Walgreens posted $72 billion in revenue:* Walgreens annual report, 2013.

Chapter 17: "Crisis Playbook"

This chapter is based on drug industry documents and emails unsealed in MDL 2804, National Prescription Opiate Litigation, as well as documents made public as part of the lawsuits filed against the tobacco industry.

86 *To turn things around:* "Proposed Plan for the Public Launching of Tassc," APCO Associates, September 30, 1993; "Crisis Playbook: An Interactive Guide to Crisis Communications, HDA"; "APCO Holdings, Revenue, Growth, & Competitor Profile," incfact.com.

86 *In 1993, APCO took on a damaged brand:* "Proposed Plan for the Public Launching of Tassc," APCO Associates, September 30, 1993; "Crisis Playbook: An Interactive Guide to Crisis Communications, HDA"; "APCO Holdings, Revenue, Growth, & Competitor Profile," incfact.com.

87 *For $515,000, The Alliance:* HDMA Executive Committee Meeting, June 2, 2013.

87 *"Who's to blame?":* HDMA Executive Committee Meeting, June 2, 2013.

87 *APCO also created talking points:* "HDMA-APCO Stakeholder Research and External Positioning Project," June 2, 2013.

87 *In phase two of the project:* "HDMA-APCO Stakeholder Research and External Positioning Project."

88 *The playbook proposed responses:* "HDMA-APCO Stakeholder Research and External Positioning Project."

88 *Six months after the Orlando meeting:* Tom Twitty, "DEA Strategy Task Force Meeting Update," email, 2013.

Chapter 18: Marsha and Tom

> *This chapter is based on internal Healthcare Distribution Alliance emails and lobbying strategy documents, along with Justice Department and DEA emails, the Pennsylvania Crime Commission report on organized crime in the state, and congressional campaign finance and lobbying reports. It is also based on articles in the* Patriot News *of Harrisburg, Pennsylvania, the* Associated Press, *the* Morning Call *of Allentown, Pennsylvania,* The Atlantic, *the* Daily Item *of Sunbury, Pennsylvania, and* The Hill *newspaper in Washington, D.C.*

90   *Marsha Blackburn was a former beauty queen:* Kris Kitto, "Understanding the Beauty-Queen Politician," *The Hill,* September 15, 2008; U.S. Senate Biographies, "Marsha Blackburn"; Blake Farmer, "Several Famous People Held This Trying Summer Job," NPR, July 15, 2011; "Best & Worst of Congress," *Washingtonian,* September 1, 2004.

91   *Lobbyists for The Alliance:* HDA minutes.

91   *"Rep. Marino's office is very open to feedback":* Jewelyn Cosgrove, "Ensuring Patient Access and Effective Drug Enforcement Act," email, 2013.

91   *Marino was a second-term congressman:* Biographical Directory of the United States Congress; Candy Woodall, "Did Tom Marino's Controversial Past Force Him out of the Running for Trump's Drug Czar?" *Penn Live,* May 5, 2017; "Organized Crime in Pennsylvania: A Decade of Change," Pennsylvania Crime Commission, 1990 Report; Francis Scarcella, "Tom Marino Defeats Chris Carney in the 10th District," *Daily Item,* November 3, 2010; Russell Berman, "The Class of 2010 Heads Home," *The Atlantic,* February 22, 2016.

92   *The average cost of running a successful House campaign:* "American Government," Open Secrets.

92   *The three-page bill did nothing:* H.R. 4709—Ensuring Patient Access and Effective Drug Enforcement Act of 2014.

93   *The legislation was the brainchild:* Jill Wade Tyson, "DAG Diversion Enforcement Meeting," email, 2014.

93   *In 2013, as they pushed:* House campaign finance reports.

94   *Patrick Kelly, The Alliance's executive vice president in charge of lobbying:* "Chronology of HDMA/HDA Executive Committee and Board of

Directors' Drug Abuse and Diversion Discussions at Meetings/Conference Calls," HDA, January 2, 2018.

94 *"This is all so sensitive":* Kristen Freitas, email, 2013.

94 *Thorsen agreed:* Carlyle Thorsen, email, 2013.

Chapter 19: Playing Games

This chapter is based on interviews with Joe Rannazzisi; emails and internal documents now part of MDL 2804, National Prescription Opiate Litigation; the transcript and video of the April 7, 2014, House of Representatives Energy and Commerce Committee hearing; and articles in the Washington Post.

95 *On April 7:* Interview with Joe Rannazzisi.

95 *Members of Congress took their seats:* Transcript and video recording from House Energy and Commerce Subcommittee on Health hearing, April 7, 2014.

95 *The industry smoothed the way:* Campaign finance records.

96 *Joe delivered his opening statement:* Hearing transcript.

96 *The Alliance had already identified:* Higham and Bernstein, "The Drug Industry's Triumph"; Scott Higham, Sari Horwitz, Steven Rich, and Meryl Kornfield, "Inside the Drug Industry's Plan to Defeat the DEA," *Washington Post*, September 13, 2019.

96 *"Sometimes it seems that":* Hearing transcript.

96 *The question, almost word for word:* Higham et al., "Inside the Drug Industry's Plan"; Deposition of Patrick M. Kelly, "Potential Hill Questions for DEA," Exhibit in MDL No. 2804.

97 *Joe briefly answered:* Hearing transcript.

97 *"We were looking for a little bit":* Hearing transcript.

97 *Blackburn moved quickly:* Hearing transcript, Higham et al., "Inside the Drug Industry's Plan."

98 *Paredes was appalled:* Interview with Mimi Paredes.

98 *Joe looked up at the dais:* Interview with Joe Rannazzisi.

Chapter 20: "Tom Marino Is Trying to Do That?"

This chapter is based on interviews with Joe Rannazzisi, along with internal Justice Department emails and memos obtained by the

Washington Post *under the Freedom of Information Act. It is also based on transcripts and videos of congressional hearings, and articles in the* Washington Post.

99 *It was an early afternoon:* Interview with Joe Rannazzisi.

99 *The DEA had already warned in a memo:* Higham and Bernstein, "The Drug Industry's Triumph."

100 *Five minutes before the hearing ended:* Transcript and video recording from House Judiciary Committee hearing, April 8, 2014.

100 *Holder had announced:* Jerry Markon, "Holder Calls Deaths from Heroin Overdoses an 'Urgent and Growing Public Health Crisis,'" *Washington Post*, March 10, 2014.

100 *Actor Philip Seymour Hoffman:* Markon, "Holder Calls Deaths from Heroin Overdoses."

100 *"I was troubled by some language":* Hearing transcript.

101 *Marino followed up three weeks later:* Rep. Tom Marino letter to Attorney General Eric H. Holder Jr., April 30, 2014.

101 *On June 4, Bill Tighe:* Bill Tighe, "DAG Diversion Enforcement Meeting," email, 2014, obtained under a Freedom of Information request made by the *Washington Post*.

101 *"Linden Barber used to work for DEA":* Jill Wade Tyson, email, obtained under a Freedom of Information request made by the *Washington Post*.

101 *In 2001, in one of the earliest lawsuits:* Civil Action No. 01-C-137-S.; Debbie Cenziper, Emily Corio, Kelly Hooper, and Douglas Soule, "They Looked at Us Like an Easy Target," *Washington Post*, October 18, 2019.

102 *Despite that connection:* Interview with Joe Rannazzisi.

102 *The attorney general was juggling:* Sari Horwitz, "Eric Holder Says Republicans Have Made Him a 'Proxy' to Attack President Obama," *Washington Post*, July 2, 2012.

102 *Joe knew Holder couldn't be expected to know:* Interview with Joe Rannazzisi.

Chapter 21: "Be Zen"

This chapter is based on interviews with Joe Rannazzisi, Imelda L. "Mimi" Paredes, Eric Akers, and John Partridge, as well as lobbying reports filed in the U.S. House and Senate, internal drug industry emails, and the invitation for the Marino luncheon, which were unsealed as part of MDL 2804, National Prescription Opiate Litigation.

103   *On June 24, 2014:* Rita Norton, "Rep. Marino Lunch," email, 2014.

103   *It was the continuation of the money flowing:* Campaign finance and lobbying reports.

104   *A week after the Marino fund-raiser:* Interviews with Joe Rannazzisi, Mimi Paredes, and Eric Akers.

104   *Paredes could see Joe's eyes narrow:* Interview with Mimi Paredes.

105   *"What problem are you trying to address":* Interviews with Joe Rannazzisi, Mimi Paredes, and Eric Akers.

105   *Paredes could almost feel the heat:* Interview with Mimi Paredes.

105   *"Wait a minute":* Interviews with Joe Rannazzisi, Mimi Paredes, and Eric Akers.

105   *"Oh, fuck":* Interview with Eric Akers.

105   *Joe didn't regret what he said:* Interview with Joe Rannazzisi.

105   *She told Paredes not to worry:* Interview with Mimi Paredes.

105   *Tyson and Akers tried to clean up:* Interview with Eric Akers.

Chapter 22: "You're Being Paranoid"

This chapter is based on interviews with Joe Rannazzisi and Imelda L. "Mimi" Paredes, along with congressional testimony, the letter Representatives Tom Marino and Marsha Blackburn wrote to Justice Department inspector general Michael Horowitz, former Attorney General Eric Holder's public remarks about the Marino-Blackburn bill, and articles in the Washington Post.

106   *At a daylong law enforcement conference:* "Attorney General Holder Announces Plans For Federal Law Enforcement Personnel To Begin Carrying Naloxone," Department of Justice, July 31, 2014.

107   *Joe couldn't have been happier:* Interview with Joe Rannazzisi.

107   *The Ensuring Patient Safety and Effective Drug Enforcement Act:* Congressional record.

107   *One afternoon that summer:* Interviews with Joe Rannazzisi and Mimi Paredes.

107   *A few weeks later:* Interview with Mimi Paredes.

108   *On September 18:* Transcript and video recording from House Crime, Terrorism, Homeland Security, and Investigations Subcommittee, September 18, 2014.

108   *A week later, on September 25:* Reps. Marsha Blackburn and Tom Marino, letter to Inspector General Michael Horowitz, September 25, 2014; Jackie Kucinich, "Two House Republicans Accuse DEA official of Intimidation," *Washington Post*, September 29, 2014.

108   *Paredes now understood:* Interview with Mimi Paredes.

Chapter 23: "The Best Case We've Ever Had"

This chapter is based on interviews with David Schiller, Jim Geldhof, Jim Rafalski, and Imelda L. "Mimi" Paredes, along with internal DEA and Justice Department emails, settlement agreements between the federal government and McKesson, and documents and briefs filed with the U.S. Court of Appeals in Washington, D.C.

109   *David Schiller was a rock star:* Lenny Bernstein and Scott Higham, "'We Feel Like Our System Was Hijacked': DEA Agents Say a Huge Opioid Case Ended in a Whimper," *Washington Post*, December 17, 2017; Bill Whitaker, "Whistleblowers: DEA Attorneys Went Easy on McKesson, the Country's Largest Drug Distributor," *60 Minutes*, December 17, 2017.

109   *But none of those cases:* Interview with David Schiller.

109   *As the assistant special agent in charge:* Interview with David Schiller; Bernstein and Higham, "'We Feel Like Our System Was Hijacked.'"

110   *Schiller and his lead investigator:* Interviews with David Schiller and Helen Kaupang.

110   *DEA lawyers from headquarters:* "Registration Consequences for McKesson Corporation for Violations of the Controlled Substances Act," DEA memo, November 4, 2014.

110   *Schiller couldn't get a straight answer:* Interview with David Schiller.

110   *McKesson first appeared on Schiller's radar:* Interview with David Schiller; Bernstein and Higham, "'We Feel Like Our System Was Hijacked.'"

111 *A grand jury indicted Clawson:* People of Colorado v. Robin Steinke et al.; grand jury indictment.

111 *As he did with every investigation:* Interview with David Schiller.

111 *The timeline began in 2008:* Interview with David Schiller; U.S. Department of Justice Memorandum of Understanding with McKesson, January 5, 2017.

112 *Schiller contacted other DEA field offices:* Interview with David Schiller; U.S. Department of Justice Memorandum of Understanding with McKesson, January 5, 2017.

112 *Schiller called Joe Rannazzisi:* Interview with David Schiller; U.S. Department of Justice Memorandum of Understanding with McKesson, January 5, 2017; interview with Joe Rannazzisi.

113 *A week before Christmas in 2014:* Interview with David Schiller; U.S. Department of Justice Memorandum of Understanding with McKesson, January 5, 2017; interview with Joe Rannazzisi.

113 *As Schiller waited to pass through security:* Interview with David Schiller; U.S. Department of Justice Memorandum of Understanding with McKesson, January 5, 2017; interview with Joe Rannazzisi.

114 *Joe had decided to shun the sit-down:* Interview with Joe Rannazzisi.

114 *Partridge, an unflappable twenty-five-year veteran:* Interview with John Partridge.

114 *In Detroit, Jim Geldhof:* Interview with Jim Geldhof.

115 *Geldhof traced the start of the problem:* Interview with Jim Geldhof; Lenny Bernstein and Scott Higham, "Investigation: The DEA Slowed Enforcement while the Opioid Epidemic Grew Out of Control," *Washington Post*, October 22, 2016.

116 *One of those lawyers:* Interview with Jonathan P. Novak.

116 *"What are you doing":* Interview with Jim Geldhof.

116 *In Washington:* Quarterly reports from the Chief Administrative Law Judge John J. Mulrooney II obtained through a Freedom of Information Act request; Bernstein and Higham, "Investigation."

117 *On the final day of March 2015:* David Schiller and Mimi Paredes, "RE: McKesson," emails, March 2015.

118 *It got worse:* Interviews with David Schiller and Mimi Paredes.

118   *But Hobart, McKesson's attorney:* Bernstein and Higham, "'We Feel Like Our System Was Hijacked.'"

118   *Paredes was unsympathetic:* Interview with Mimi Paredes; Paredes, "MCK Settlement Position on Outstanding Terms," email, 2015.

Chapter 24: The Mushroom Treatment

This chapter is based on interviews with Joe Rannazzisi and Imelda L. "Mimi" Paredes, along with articles in the Washington Post *and internal emails from the Healthcare Distribution Alliance and drug companies that are now part of MDL 2804, National Prescription Opiate Litigation.*

120   *At the end of August:* Interview with Joe Rannazzisi.

120   *Three months earlier:* Sari Horwitz, "Top FBI Official Is Appointed to Take Helm at the DEA," *Washington Post*, May 13, 2015.

120   *One DEA official warned Joe:* Interview with Joe Rannazzisi.

121   *When Rosenberg first arrived:* Jack Riley, *Drug Warrior: Inside the Hunt for El Chapo and the Rise of America's Opioid Crisis* (Hachette, 2019).

121   *Soiles met Joe outside an elevator:* Interview with Joe Rannazzisi.

122   *After thirty years at the DEA:* Interview with Joe Rannazzisi.

122   *He also had to introduce the man named:* Interview with Joe Rannazzisi; Del Quentin Wilber, "A DEA Agent, an Undercover Sting, and 'The Merchant of Death,'" *Washington Post*, September 5, 2012.

123   *The latest version of the bill:* Interview with Joe Rannazzisi; Del Quentin Wilber, "A DEA Agent"; "Ensuring Patient Access and Effective Drug Enforcement Act of 2016," 114th Congress, 2nd Session; Higham et al., "Inside the Drug Industry's Plan."

123   *Within days of Joe submitting:* HDA Board of Directors Meeting, September 28, 2015.

Chapter 25: An Expensive Speeding Ticket

This chapter is based on interviews with Jim Geldhof, James Rafalski, and Brien O'Connor, along with settlement agreements between the federal government and McKesson and Mallinckrodt, and prosecution memos prepared by the U.S. attorney's office in Detroit.

124 *By September 25, 2015:* U.S. Securities and Exchange Commission, McKesson Form 8-K.

124 *The fine was $50 million more:* U.S. Securities and Exchange Commission, McKesson Definitive Proxy Statement "McKesson Revenue & Profit," Macrotrends.net.

124 *Jim Geldhof was in his office:* Interview with Jim Geldhof.

125 *Masters had appealed the agency's decision:* United States Court of Appeals, *Masters Pharmaceuticals, Inc. v. DEA.*

125 *Rafalski's other big case:* Interview with James Rafalski.

126 *"We will argue that thousands of orders":* McKesson prosecution memo, August 7, 2014.

126 *On July 10, 2015:* Leslie Wizner, "Subject to FRE 408 Settlement Negotiations," letter, 2015.

127 *She also asserted that Mallinckrodt knew:* Wizner, "Subject to FRE 408 Settlement Negotiations."

127 *O'Connor countered that there was nothing:* Interview with Brien T. O'Connor.

127 *By the fall, Geldhof was losing his patience:* Interview with Jim Geldhof.

Chapter 26: Banjo

This chapter is based on interviews with Joe Rannazzisi and Jim Geldhof, and the transcript of the oral arguments in United States v. Moore, *October 7, 1975.*

129 *There is a long-standing tradition:* Interview with Joe Rannazzisi.

129 *"Why don't you come over":* Interview with Joe Rannazzisi.

130 *Joe's friend Jimmy Soiles:* Interview with Joe Rannazzisi.

130 *The next day:* Interview with Joe Rannazzisi.

131 *Over and over, he listened:* Interview with Joe Rannazzisi; "United States v. Moore," No. 74-759, Transcript of oral arguments, October 7, 1975.

131 *Joe was struck by how Marshall seemed to anticipate:* Interview with Joe Rannazzisi.

132 *That question also haunted Jim Geldhof:* Interview with Jim Geldhof.

Chapter 27: A Public Nuisance

This chapter is based on interviews with Paul T. Farrell Jr. and the 2016 investigation into the opioid industry by the Charleston Gazette-Mail, *which was awarded the Pulitzer Prize for Investigative Reporting. It is also based on Joe Rannazzisi's sworn declaration filed in* Cardinal Health, Inc. v. Eric H. Holder Jr., *the friend-of-the-court briefs crafted by the Healthcare Distribution Alliance, known at the time as the Healthcare Distribution Management Association, and notes and documents from Farrell's meeting with* Washington Post *reporters Lenny Bernstein and Scott Higham.*

135 *On February 10, 2017:* Interview with Paul Farrell.

136 *Two months before Paul's trip:* Interview with Paul Farrell; Eric Eyre, "Drug Firms Poured 780M Painkillers into WV amid Rise of Overdoses," *Charleston Gazette*, December 17, 2016.

137 *Paul thought the amount:* Interview with Paul Farrell; Eyre, "Drug Firms Poured 780M Painkillers."

138 *Sometimes it seemed like there were as many Farrells:* Interview with Paul Farrell; Eyre, "Drug Firms Poured 780M Painkillers."

139 *He even beat Hillary Clinton:* Mingo County election records; Rick Holmes, "On the Road with Rick Holmes: The Battles of 'Bloody Mingo,'" *Hannibal Courier Post*, December 13, 2018.

139 *The day after his brother's challenge:* Interview with Paul Farrell.

139 *It gave county commissioners the power:* West Virginia Code of Ordinances, Chapter 91: Nuisances.

140 *Paul started poring over cases:* Interview with Paul Farrell.

140 *That's when he spotted:* Interview with Paul Farrell, *Cardinal Health, Inc. v. Eric H. Holder Jr.*

140 *Paul also found the case:* Interview with Paul Farrell, *Cardinal Health, Inc. v. Eric H. Holder Jr.; Masters Pharmaceuticals, Inc. v. DEA.*

140 *He downloaded every document:* Interview with Paul Farrell.

141 *Paul had one final stop:* Interview with Paul Farrell.

Chapter 28: "Our Allies"

This chapter is based on interviews with Joe Rannazzisi, Imelda L. "Mimi" Paredes, John Partridge, and Richard W. Fields, along with emails and documents now part of MDL 2804, National Prescription Opiate Litigation. It is also based on Chuck Rosenberg's June 22, 2016, testimony before the Senate Judiciary Committee, congressional lobbying reports, federal campaign finance records, an article by DEA chief administrative law judge John J. Mulrooney II in the Marquette Law Review, *and articles in the* Washington Post.

142 *There was a reason Joe didn't call Paul Farrell:* Interview with Joe Rannazzisi.

142 *One day, after he began his new job:* Interviews with Joe Rannazzisi and Richard Fields.

143 *On his last night:* Interview with Joe Rannazzisi.

144 *His senior deputy, John Partridge:* Interview with John Partridge.

144 *His most trusted legal counsel:* Interview with Mimi Paredes.

144 *He felt that he was to blame:* Interview with Joe Rannazzisi.

144 *On March 17, 2016:* U.S. Congress, *Congressional Record*, 114th Cong., 2nd sess., 2016, vol. 163.

144 *A senior DEA official said:* Higham and Bernstein, "The Drug Industry's Triumph."

145 *It passed by unanimous consent:* S.483—Ensuring Patient Access and Effective Drug Enforcement Act of 2016, 114th Congress.

145 *The drug industry had spent $60 million:* Campaign finance records.

145 *The night the House approved:* Burt Rosen, "S. 483 (Ensuring Patient Access and Effective Drug Enforcement Act)," email, 2016.

146 *On June 22, Rosenberg testified:* Transcript and video recording from Senate Judiciary Committee hearing, June 22, 2016.

146 *Joe was watching the hearing:* Interview with Joe Rannazzisi.

Chapter 29: "They're Gonna Get Hammered"

This chapter is based on interviews with Paul T. Farrell Jr. and James Rafalski, along with the transcript of the January 12, 2017, hearing in Masters Pharmaceuticals, Inc. v. DEA. *before the U.S. Court of Appeals in Washington, D.C., and the June 30, 2017, ruling by the U.S. Court of Appeals in the Masters case. It is also based on the amicus briefs filed in the Masters case by the Healthcare Distribution Alliance, the National Association of Chain Drug Stores, and the Generic Pharmaceutical Association; the DEA's decision and order in its case against Masters; and the 2009 Memorandum of Understanding between Masters and the DEA.*

148   *Paul Farrell settled into his windowless law office:* Interview with Paul Farrell.

148   *Richard T. Lauer, an attorney: Masters Pharmaceutical, Inc. v. DEA,* No. 15-1335, Court of Appeals for the D.C. Circuit, Audio of oral arguments, January 12, 2017.

149   *It was still early:* Interview with Paul Farrell.

149   *Masters had paid a $500,000 fine:* Masters Pharmaceutical, Inc., Memorandum of Agreement with the DEA.

149   *But a year after paying the fine:* James Rafalski report.

150   *Lauer tried to stay on message:* Audio of January 12, 2017, hearing.

150   *The attorney representing the Justice Department:* Audio of January 12, 2017, hearing.

151   *Listening to the hearing at his office:* Interview with Paul Farrell.

Chapter 30: On the Road

This chapter is based on interviews with Paul T. Farrell Jr. and Michael J. Fuller Jr., along with local news accounts of the DuPont and nursing home cases and settlements, and a Washington Post *analysis of ARCOS data obtained by a lawsuit filed by the* Post *and HD Media, the owner of the* Charleston Gazette-Mail.

152   *The commissioners in Mingo County:* Interview with Paul Farrell.

152   *Mingo County had become a hot spot:* ARCOS data analysis by the *Washington Post.*

152   *To meet the demand:* ARCOS data analysis by the *Washington Post.*

152   *Paul Farrell sat in the back:* Interview with Paul Farrell.

153   *At first the commissioners were skeptical:* Interview with Paul Farrell.

154   *On March 9, 2017, he filed his first suit: Cabell County Commission v. AmerisourceBergen Drug Corp. et al.,* Complaint.

154   *That spring, he ran into a lawyer:* Interviews with Paul Farrell and Michael Fuller.

154   *Paul, as always, wouldn't take no for an answer:* Interviews with Paul Farrell, Michael Fuller, and Amy J. Quezon.

155   *Fuller suggested they team up:* Interviews with Paul Farrell, Michael Fuller, and Amy J. Quezon; "DuPont, Chemours Agree to Settle Teflon Cases for $671M," *Law360,* February 13, 2017.

155 *Paul began to imagine the possibilities:* Interview with Paul Farrell.

Chapter 31: Field of Dreams

This chapter is based on interviews with Mark Zban and Paul T. Far-rell Jr., along with articles about Zban's sports career in the Charleston Gazette *and the* Charleston Daily Mail.

156 *Fifteen-year-old Paul Farrell:* Interview with Paul Farrell.

157 *His uncle had played football at Marshall:* Interview with Mark Zban.

157 *For Paul, it was a slow-motion, cinematic experience:* Interview with Paul Farrell.

158 *Paul's family knew Zban's family:* Interviews with Paul Farrell and Mark Zban.

158 *By the time he reached his early thirties:* Interview with Mark Zban.

158 *Paul was heartbroken:* Interview with Paul Farrell.

158 *As his addiction deepened:* Interview with Mark Zban.

159 *A year after his release:* Interview with Mark Zban.

159 *"Looks like you're doing well":* Interview with Paul Farrell.

159 *Zban remarried:* Interview with Mark Zban.

159 *Watching Zban's life unravel:* Interview with Paul Farrell.

160 *"This is the true essence of the epidemic":* Interview with Paul Farrell.

Chapter 32: "The Hunt Is On"

This chapter is based on interviews with James Rafalski, Jim Geldhof, and Paul T. Farrell Jr., along with the June 30, 2017, ruling handed down by the U.S. Court of Appeals in Masters Pharmaceuticals, Inc. v. DEA.

161 *One week into his retirement:* Interview with James Rafalski.

161 *"I've got some good news":* Interviews with James Rafalski and Jim Geldhof.

161 *In a scathing thirty-eight-page opinion:* U.S. Court of Appeals, District of Columbia Circuit Court, *Masters Pharmaceuticals, Inc. v. DEA.*, No. 15-1335, Decision, June 30, 2017.

161 *Rafalski had spent nearly seven years:* Interview with James Rafalski.

162 *The ruling was unanimous:* D.C. Circuit Court decision.

162 *In Huntington, West Virginia:* Interview with Paul Farrell.

Chapter 33: "Make Them Pay"

This chapter is based on interviews with James Rafalski, Jim Geldhof, Michael J. Fuller Jr., Paul T. Farrell Jr., and Jim Peterson.

163 *The dining room was in the secluded Italianate mansion:* Interview with Jim Peterson.

163 Damn, *Rafalski thought:* Interview with James Rafalski.

163 *Rafalski, along with Jim Geldhof:* Interviews with James Rafalski and Jim Geldhof.

164 *But Paul pressed him:* Interviews with James Rafalski and Paul Farrell.

164 *Rafalski figured he could combine:* Interview with James Rafalski.

164 *Joining Paul and the partners:* Interviews with Paul Farrell and Michael Fuller.

165 *"This is a chance to make them pay":* Interview with Paul Farrell.

Chapter 34: Legal Titans

This chapter is based on interviews with Paul J. Hanly Jr., Jayne Conroy, and Paul T. Farrell Jr., along with obituaries in the New York Times *and the* Washington Post.

166 *At 11 a.m. on November 15:* Interviews with Paul Farrell and Paul Hanly.

166 *Between 1999 and 2017:* North Carolina Attorney General Josh Stein website.

166 *The scion of a colorful political family:* Interview with Paul Hanly.

166 *Hanly grew up admiring Kenny:* Robert Hanley, "Ex-Mayor John V. Kenny of Jersey City Dies at 82," *New York Times,* June 3, 1975.

167 *Hanly had been working opioid cases:* Interviews with Paul Hanly and Jayne Conroy.

167 *Like Hanly, she dressed stylishly:* Interview with Jayne Conroy.

167 *Conroy grew up sailing:* Interview with Jayne Conroy.

167 *For years afterward, Conroy and Hanly:* Interviews with Paul Hanly and Jayne Conroy; National Trial Lawyers Top 100 website.

168 *On the day after Christmas:* Interview with Paul Hanly.

168 *They reached out to John Simmons:* Interviews with Paul Hanly and Jayne Conroy.

169 *Simmons grew up in nearby East Alton:* Conroy interview; John Simmons biography, Simmons Hanly Conroy website.

169 *Conroy and Hanly laid out their case:* Interviews with Paul Hanly and Jayne Conroy.

170 *In 2007, Purdue settled the lawsuits:* Interviews with Paul Hanly and Jayne Conroy.

170 *The department brought its own case:* Barry Meier, "In Guilty Plea, Oxy-Contin Maker to Pay $600 Million," *New York Times*, May 10, 2007.

170 *In his Manhattan office:* Interviews with Paul Hanly and Jayne Conroy.

170 *By this time, Hanly had a personal experience:* Interview with Paul Hanly.

171 *About a year after meeting with Bizzarro:* "Simmons Hanly Conroy Files Suffolk County, N.Y., Lawsuit against Drug Companies over Opioids Epidemic and Addiction," Simmon Hanly Conroy website, August 31, 2016.

171 *He told the* Wall Street Journal *in December:* Thomas Catan and Evan Perez, "A Pain-Drug Champion Has Second Thoughts," *Wall Street Journal*, December 17, 2012.

171 *In a video cited by the* Journal*:* Video by Physicians for Responsible Opioid Prescribing.

171 *Hanly compared his lawsuit:* Interview with Paul Hanly.

172 *Son of a bitch:* Interview with Paul Farrell.

172 *Hanly looked at Paul:* Interview with Paul Hanly.

Chapter 35: The Drug Czar

This chapter is based on drug industry documents and emails unsealed in MDL 2804, National Prescription Opiate Litigation, and the Mar-quette Law Review *article written by DEA chief administrative law judge John Mulrooney. It is also based on an NPR story about Tom Marino, the transcript of Senator Orrin Hatch's floor remarks addressing the joint investigative report into the Ensuring Patient Access and Effective Drug Enforcement Act by the* Washington Post *and* 60 Minutes, *and a 2018 investigation by the Senate Homeland Security and Governmental Affairs Committee into pain patient advocacy groups titled "Exposing the Financial Ties between Opioid Manufacturers and Third Party Advocacy Groups."*

173 *Shortly after Donald Trump:* Ed O'Keefe, "Tom Marino Set to Serve as White House Drug Czar," *Washington Post*, April 11, 2017.

173 *To confront the impending public relations crisis:* "Key Facts about Opioid Regulation," Healthcare Distribution Alliance.

173 *The prospect of a damning joint report:* Gabe Weissman, "Re: 60 Minutes update from NACDS," email, 2017.

174 *Five days later, on Sunday, October 15:* Higham and Bernstein, "The Drug Industry's Triumph."

174 *That evening:* Bill Whitaker, "Ex-DEA Agent: Opioid Crisis Fueled by Drug Industry and Congress," *60 Minutes,* June 17, 2018.

174 *Since retiring, he had been reluctant:* Interview with Joe Rannazzisi.

175 *Several members of Congress:* Nancy Cordes, "'All of Us Were Fooled': Opioid Report Reverberates across Political World," CBS News, October 16, 2017.

175 *The joint* Washington Post/60 Minutes *investigative report:* Higham and Bernstein, "The Drug Industry's Triumph"; Whitaker, "Ex-DEA agent."

176 *Manchin told reporters:* Cordes, "'All of Us Were Fooled.'"

176 *Two days after the report appeared:* Bill Chappell, "Tom Marino, Trump's Pick as Drug Czar, Withdraws after Damaging Opioid Report," NPR, October 17, 2017.

176 *In the days that followed:* U.S. Congress, *Congressional Record*, 115th Cong., 1st sess., 2017, vol. 163.

176 *A group calling itself the Academy of Integrative Pain Management:* Archive of Sen. Hatch press releases; campaign finance records.

Chapter 36: Jumped the Gun

This chapter is based on interviews with Paul J. Hanly Jr., Paul T. Farrell Jr., Jayne Conroy, and Joe Rice, along with the transcript of the November 30, 2017, Judicial Panel on Multidistrict Litigation hearing and the December 12, 2017, MDL transfer order.

178 *Paul Hanly was walking:* Interview with Paul Hanly.

178 *They were among the lawyers:* John Schwartz, "Ron Motley, Who Tackled Big Tobacco, Dies at 68," *New York Times*, August 22, 2013.

178 *"Paul, did you know about this?":* Interview with Paul Hanly.

179 *To the two veteran litigators:* Interviews with Paul Hanly and Joe Rice.

179 *Paul didn't bother to ask:* Interview with Paul Farrell.

179 *On November 30, 2017:* Judicial Panel on Multidistrict Litigation hearing in St. Louis, Missouri, Transcript, November 30, 2017.

180 *As Conroy approached the courthouse:* Interview with Jayne Conroy.

180 *Conroy didn't know:* Interviews with Paul Farrell and Jayne Conroy.

180 *The multidistrict litigation panel:* Terry Turner, "Multidistrict Litigation," Drugwatch.com, September 24, 2021; "MDLS 101: Primer on Multi-District Litigation," Robins Kaplan LLP, November/December 2016.

180 *On November 30:* Multidistrict Litigation panel hearing transcript.

180 *The first to speak:* Multidistrict Litigation panel hearing transcript.

182 *Paul had calculated:* Interview with Paul Farrell; "A Leader in the National Transvaginal Mesh Litigation," Farrell & Fuller website.

182 *Conroy thought Paul had jumped the gun:* Interview with Jayne Conroy.

183 *Paul was willing to take that chance:* Interview with Paul Farrell.

183 *Mark S. Cheffo:* Multidistrict Litigation panel hearing transcript.

183 *Twelve days after the hearing:* Judicial Panel on Multidistrict Litigation, Transfer Order, December 12, 2017.

183 *While Conroy was not happy:* Interview with Jayne Conroy.

183 *But Paul Farrell was deeply disappointed:* Interview with Paul Farrell.

Chapter 37: "This Is Horrific"

This chapter is based on interviews with Paul J. Hanly Jr., Paul T. Farrell Jr., Jayne Conroy, and Joe Rice, along with court filings in MDL 2804, National Prescription Opiate Litigation, and articles by Cleveland 19 News.

185 *Downtown Cleveland was decked:* Dan DeRoos, "The Behind-the-Scenes Story about Cleveland's Christmas Tree," Cleveland 19 News, November 14, 2017.

185 *Jayne Conroy had seen her share:* Interview with Jayne Conroy.

186 *Judge Polster had ordered:* In Re: National Prescription Opiate Litigation, Order, December 14, 2017.

186 *"This is an epidemic unlike anything":* Interviews with Jayne Conroy and Paul Farrell.

186 *Paul was unimpressed:* Interview with Paul Farrell.

187 *Shortly before Christmas:* Interviews with Paul Hanly, Jayne Conroy, and Paul Farrell.

187 *On Christmas Eve:* Interview with Paul Hanly.

188 *Hanly scoffed at the suggestion:* Interview with Paul Hanly.

188 *For Paul, it had become personal:* Interview with Paul Farrell.

188 *With the litigation slate set:* Interviews with Paul Hanly, Jayne Conroy, and Paul Farrell.

189 *Hanly still wasn't completely happy:* Interview with Paul Hanly.

Chapter 38: "Tear Each Other Up"

This chapter is based on interviews with Paul T. Farrell Jr., Judge Dan Aaron Polster, and Kaspar J. Stoffelmayr, along with the transcript of the January 9, 2018, proceeding before Polster and a March 5, 2018, New York Times *article about Polster by Jan Hoffman.*

191 *On the morning of January 9:* In Re: National Prescription Opiate Litigation, Transcript of Proceedings, January 9, 2018.

191 *Polster began his meeting by noting:* In Re: National Prescription Opiate Litigation, Transcript of Proceedings.

192 *"I don't think anyone":* In Re: National Prescription Opiate Litigation, Transcript of Proceedings.

193 *Paul Farrell couldn't believe:* Interview with Paul Farrell.

193 *The judge had grown up in Cleveland:* Jan Hoffman, "Can This Judge Solve the Opioid Crisis?" *New York Times*, March 5, 2018.

193 *Polster told the lawyers:* In Re: National Prescription Opiate Litigation, Transcript of Proceedings.

194 *One by one, the key lawyers:* In Re: National Prescription Opiate Litigation, Transcript of Proceedings.

195 *Like many lawyers:* Interview with Kaspar Stoffelmayr.

196 *As the lawyers left:* Hoffman, "Can This Judge Solve the Opioid Crisis?"

Chapter 39: A Perry Mason Moment

This chapter is based on interviews with Paul T. Farrell Jr. and the transcript of the February 26, 2018, ARCOS hearing held before U.S. district judge Dan Aaron Polster.

197 *On February 26 at three:* Interview with Paul Farrell.

197 *Lawyers for the drug companies:* In Re: National Prescription Opiate Litigation, Transcript of Proceedings, February 26, 2018.

198 *James R. Bennett II:* LinkedIn profile.

198 *He stepped to the podium:* In Re: National Prescription Opiate Litigation, Transcript of Proceedings.

198 *Paul was tired:* Interview with Paul Farrell.

198 *"The important thing":* In Re: National Prescription Opiate Litigation, Transcript of Proceedings.

199 *Paul had already studied:* Interview with Paul Farrell.

199 *"I don't mean to interrupt":* In Re: National Prescription Opiate Litigation, Transcript of Proceedings.

200 *Paul felt like he was in a scene:* Interview with Paul Farrell.

200 *"With the Privacy Act concerns":* In Re: National Prescription Opiate Litigation, Transcript of Proceedings.

202 *He ordered the DEA:* In Re: National Prescription Opiate Litigation, Protective Order Re: DEA's ARCOS Database, March 6, 2018.

202 *"Nothing is going to be revealed":* In Re: National Prescription Opiate Litigation, Transcript of Proceedings.

Chapter 40: The Death Star

This chapter is based on interviews with Paul T. Farrell Jr., along with the July 31, 2018, deposition of Nathan Hartle.

203 *Covington & Burling:* "Firm History," Covington & Burling LLC website; Jonathan O'Connell, "Covington & Burling Set to Move Headquarters to CityCenterDC," *Washington Post*, May 16, 2012.

203 *On July 31, 2018:* Interview with Paul Farrell.

204 *As Paul began the deposition:* Interview with Paul Farrell.

204 *For seven hours:* Deposition of Nathan Hartle, July 31, 2018.

Chapter 41: The Digital Detectives

This chapter is based on interviews with Anthony Irpino, Pearl A. Robertson, Evan M. Janush, Paul T. Farrell Jr., and Derek W. Loeser, along with the January 23, 2008, audit of Cardinal's compliance program by Cegedim Dendrite Compliance Solutions. It is also based on Judge Dan Aaron Polster's April 11, 2018, litigation track order; Victor Borelli's January 27,

2009, email exchange with Steve Cochrane, vice president of sales for Key-Source Medical; and internal emails between Janush and Farrell.

209   *For weeks on end in 2018:* Interview with Anthony Irpino.

210   *It was backbreaking work:* Interviews with Anthony Irpino and Pearl Robertson.

211   *"This epidemic is such a scourge":* Interview with Anthony Irpino.

211   *On April 11:* In Re: National Prescription Opiate Litigation, Case Management Order One, April 11, 2018.

211   *Paul Farrell added more lawyers:* Interview with Paul Farrell.

212   *One of those hot documents:* Interview with Evan Janush.

212   *There was a reason why:* Ronald W. Buzzeo, "Cardinal Healthcare's Suspicious Order Monitoring (SOM) System," January 23, 2008.

212   *Janush scored another coup:* Interview with Evan Janush; Evan Janush, "Have You Seen the 'HDMA Crisis Playbook'?" email, 2018.

213   *"I have a man crush":* Paul Farrell, "[Opioid-MDL-Leadership] Superstar Evan Janush," email, 2018.

213   *Across the country in a Seattle law firm:* Interviews with Anthony Irpino and Derek Loeser.

213   *Paul believed he was on a hot streak:* Interview with Paul Farrell.

Chapter 42: The Magician

This chapter is based on interviews with Mark Lanier, Jayne Conroy, Paul J. Hanly Jr., and Paul T. Farrell Jr., along with articles in the New York Times, *Reuters and the* American Lawyer.

214   *As the opioid case moved closer:* Interviews with Paul Hanly and Jayne Conroy.

214   *Lanier had lots of business:* Interviews with Paul Hanly, Jayne Conroy, and Mark Lanier.

214   *The founder of the Christian Trial Lawyers Association:* Interview with Mark Lanier; Champion Forest Baptist Church website.

215   *He collected ancient Hebrew manuscripts:* Interview with Mark Lanier; Lanier Theological Library website.

215   *He spent hundreds of thousands of dollars:* Interview with Mark Lanier; Jonathan D. Glater, "A Houston Holiday: Barbecue, Al Green, and 5,000 Guests," *New York Times*, December 13, 2003.

215 *In preparation for trials:* Interview with Mark Lanier.

217 *That spring, Paul met with Hanly:* Interviews with Jayne Conroy, Paul Hanly, and Paul Farrell.

217 *On April 23, 2019:* Interviews with Paul Farrell, Mark Lanier, Jayne Conroy, and Paul Hanly.

Chapter 43: The 60 Minutes Man

This chapter is based on interviews with Mark Lanier, Joe Rannazzisi, Paul T. Farrell Jr., Paul J. Hanly Jr., and Jayne Conroy, along with the transcript of the May 15, 2019, deposition of Rannazzisi.

220 *Joe Rannazzisi wasn't feeling well:* Interview with Joe Rannazzisi.

220 *Joe had decided to leave his job:* Interviews with Joe Rannazzisi and Richard Fields.

221 *"Mr. Rannazzisi, thank you":* Joe Rannazzisi deposition, May 15, 2019.

223 *Joe started to laugh:* Joe Rannazzisi deposition; interview with Joe Rannazzisi.

223 *"I want to ask you":* Joe Rannazzisi deposition.

225 *Paul Farrell had been on the fence:* Interview with Paul Farrell.

Chapter 44: A Lone Lawyer

This chapter is based on interviews with Karen Lefton, along with articles in the Washington Post. *It is also based on federal court briefs and judicial orders, including the July 9, 2018, Brief in Support of Disclosure of ARCOS Data; the Affidavit of Jeff Leen,* Washington Post *investigations editor; Judge Dan Aaron Polster's July 26, 2018, Court Order Denying Relief re ARCOS Data; the audiotape of Lefton's May 2, 2019, oral argument before the Sixth Circuit Court of Appeals; and the Sixth Circuit's ruling in the case.*

226 *The call came out of nowhere:* Interview with Karen Lefton.

226 *"This is Jim McLaughlin":* Interviews with Karen Lefton and Jim McLaughlin.

226 *Lefton quickly Googled McLaughlin:* Interview with Karen Lefton.

226 *McLaughlin explained how ARCOS worked:* Interviews with Karen Lefton and Jim McLaughlin.

227 *Lefton was not McLaughlin's first choice:* Interviews with Karen Lefton and Jim McLaughlin; Joel Achenbach, "How an Epic Legal Battle

Brought a Secret Drug Database to Light," *Washington Post*, August 2, 2019.

228 *On July 9, 2018:* U.S. District Court of Northern District of Ohio, Brief in Support of Disclosure of ARCOS data, July 9, 2018.

228 *She submitted an affidavit:* U.S. District Court of Northern District of Ohio, Affidavit of Jeffrey Leen, July 9, 2018.

229 *The DEA and the defendants fought back:* U.S. District Court of Northern Ohio, Brief in Response to Washington Post Company's Motion for Access to the Unredacted Brief in Support of Objections, July 9, 2018.

229 *Seventeen days later, Polster:* In Re: National Prescription Opiate Litigation, Opinion and Order, July 26, 2018.

230 *Lefton and lawyers for the* Gazette-Mail*:* U.S. Circuit Court of Appeals in Cincinnati, Appeal.

230 *Lefton stepped to the lectern:* U.S. Circuit Court of Appeals in Cincinnati, Audio and Transcript of Oral Arguments, May 2, 2019.

230 *After the argument:* Interview with Karen Lefton.

230 *Seven weeks later:* Interview with Karen Lefton; U.S. Circuit Court of Appeals in Cincinnati, Opinion, June 20, 2019.

231 *"Total victory!!!:* Karen Lefton, "Fwd: 18-3839 In re: Nat'l Prescription Opiate Lit. 'opinion and judgment filed' (1:17-md-02804)," email, 2019.

232 *On July 16:* Scott Higham, Sari Horwitz, and Steven Rich, "76 Billion Opioid Pills: Newly Released Federal Data Unmask the Epidemic," *Washington Post*, July 16, 2019.

232 *When two more years of data were released:* Steven Rich, Scott Higham, and Sari Horwitz, "More than 100 Billion Pain Pills Saturated the Nation over Nine Years," *Washington Post*, January 14, 2020.

232 *The reporters also found that death rates from opioids had soared:* Sari Horwitz, Steven Rich, and Scott Higham, "Opioid Death Rates Soared in Communities Where Pain Pills Flowed," *Washington Post*, July 17, 2019.

233 *Joe Manchin, the Democratic senator:* Horwitz et al., "Opioid Death Rates Soared."

233 *The* Post *lifted its paywall:* "Drilling into the DEA's Pain Pill Database," *Washington Post*, July 16, 2019.

233 *At 5 a.m. on the day the first* Post *story was published:* Interview with Karen Lefton; "How an Epic Legal Battle Brought a Secret Drug Database to Light."

Chapter 45: My Cousin Vinny

This chapter is based on interviews with Paul T. Farrell Jr., Paul J. Hanly Jr., and Jayne Conroy, and emails between Farrell, Special Master David Cohen, and members of the defense and plaintiffs' teams.

234 *Paul Farrell was something of a worrying puzzle:* Interviews with Paul Hanly, Paul Farrell, and trial team members.

235 *But Hanly, Jayne Conroy, and the other veterans:* Interviews with Paul Hanly, Paul Farrell, and trial team members.

235 *Paul was at the Washington Plaza Hotel:* Interviews with Paul Farrell and Michael J. Fuller Jr.

236 *Ten minutes after Fuller replied:* Paul Farrell, email.

236 *Within an hour:* Interview with Paul Farrell.

236 *At 2:55 the next morning:* Paul Farrell, email.

Chapter 46: RICO

This chapter is based on interviews with Paul T. Farrell Jr., Mark P. Pifko, and Kaspar J. Stoffelmayr, along with articles in the Washington Post, *and the plaintiffs' RICO motions and defense motions to exclude RICO from the case. It is also based on Judge Dan Aaron Polster's September 3 and September 10, 2019, rulings allowing the conspiracy and RICO allegations to proceed, defense motions to disqualify Polster from the case, and the Sixth U.S. Circuit Court of Appeals ruling rejecting the defense motions to disqualify Polster.*

237 *Two months after the* My Cousin Vinny *episode:* In Re: National Prescription Opiate Litigation, Plaintiffs' Consolidated Memorandum in Opposition to Defendants' Motion for Summary Judgment on Plaintiffs' Civil Conspiracy, RICO and OCPA Claims, August 12, 2019.

237 *The Racketeer Influenced and Corrupt Organizations Act:* Racketeer Influenced and Corrupt Organizations Act—Hardly a Civil Statute (From RICO—Expanding Uses in Civil Litigation, P 3-59, 1984, Arthur F. Mathews, ed.—See NCJ-95991), Office of Justice Programs, U.S. Department of Justice.

237 *For several years:* Interview with Mark Pifko.

238 *Paul groaned at the suggestion:* Interview with Paul Farrell.

239 *Paul now saw The Alliance as part of a conspiracy:* Interview with Paul Farrell.

239 *Their work culminated in a 138-page brief:* In Re: National Prescription Opiate Litigation, Plaintiffs' Consolidated Memorandum in Opposition to Defendants' Motion for Summary Judgment on Plaintiffs' Civil Conspiracy, RICO and OCPA Claims.

240 *The plaintiffs also argued that the distributors capitalized:* In Re: National Prescription Opiate Litigation, Plaintiffs' Consolidated Memorandum.

241 *The pharmacies, through their trade organization:* In Re: National Prescription Opiate Litigation, Plaintiffs' Consolidated Memorandum.

241 *Lawyers for the drug companies scoffed:* In Re: National Prescription Opiate Litigation, Manufacturers' Motion for summary judgment on Plaintiffs' RICO and OCPA Claims, July 19, 2019.

242 *Attorneys for the drug distribution companies added:* In Re: National Prescription Opiate Litigation, Distributors' Motion for summary judgment on Plaintiffs' RICO and OCPA Claims, July 19, 2019.

242 *On September 3 and September 10:* In Re: National Prescription Opiate Litigation, Order Regarding Defendants' Motions for Summary Judgment on Civil Conspiracy Claims, September 3, 2019; In Re: National Prescription Opiate Litigation, Opinion and Order Regarding Defendants' Summary Judgment Motions on RICO and OCPA, September 10, 2019.

242 *Paul was delighted:* Interview with Paul Farrell.

242 *Kaspar Stoffelmayr, who represented:* Interview with Kaspar Stoffelmayr.

243 *On September 14, lawyers for seven drug companies:* In Re: National Prescription Opiate Litigation, Order Regarding Defendants' Motions for Summary Judgment on Civil Conspiracy Claims, Motion to disqualify Judge Pursuant to 28 U.S.C. § 455(a), September 14, 2019.

243 *In the two decades of defending major corporations:* Interview with Kaspar Stoffelmayr.

243 *Polster rejected their request:* In Re: National Prescription Opiate Litigation, Opinion and Order denying Defendants' Motion to Disqualify Judge, September 26, 2019.

243 *The defense attorneys took their argument:* U.S. Court of Appeals for the Sixth Circuit, Case No. 19-3935, Petition for Writ of Mandamus, October 1, 2019.

243 *On October 10, the appellate panel sided with Polster:* U.S. Court of Appeals for the Sixth Circuit, Case No. 19-3935, Order, October 10, 2019.

Chapter 47: "We Have a Deal"

This chapter is based on interviews with Mark Lanier, Paul J. Hanly Jr., Paul T. Farrell Jr., Paul J. Geller, Jayne Conroy, Michael J. Fuller Jr., and Joe Rice, along with articles in the Washington Post *and the* New York Times.

244 *Joe Rice, the trial lawyer:* Interviews with Joe Rice, Paul J. Hanly Jr., Jayne Conroy, and Paul Farrell.

245 *Lanier, as he had promised:* Interview with Mark Lanier.

246 *"Ladies and gentlemen of the jury":* Lanier mock opening.

247 *Complicating the proceedings were four state attorneys general:* Interview with Paul Farrell; Lenny Bernstein, Scott Higham, Sari Horwitz, and Aaron C. Davis, "State AGs Dangle $18B Potential Settlement, but Fail to Delay Federal Opioid Trial," *Washington Post*, October 15, 2019; Lenny Bernstein, Sari Horwitz, Scott Higham, and Aaron C. Davis, "High-Profile Talks to Avert Landmark Opioid Trial Break Down," *Washington Post*, October 18, 2019.

247 *Paul Geller, the plaintiffs' lawyer:* Interview with Paul Geller.

248 *On Friday, October 18:* Bernstein et al., "High-Profile Talks to Avert Landmark Opioid Trial Break Down."

248 *A Muscogee (Creek) Nation official:* "Muscogee (Creek) Nation Presents Statement in Consolidated Opioid Suit in Federal Court in Cleveland, OH," Muscogee Nation website.

249 *Paul fumed, telling Polster:* Interview with Paul Farrell.

249 *Because the attorney general for West Virginia:* Eric Eyre, "2 Drug Distributors to Pay $36M to Settle WV Painkiller Lawsuits," *Charlston Gazette-Mail*, January 9, 2017; Lenny Bernstein, "West Virginia Reaches $37 Million Opioid Settlement with Drug Shipper McKesson," *Washington Post*, May 2, 2019.

249 *Paxton told Paul his state was not going to be included:* Interview with Paul Farrell.

249 *On Saturday, tensions ran high:* Interview with Jayne Conroy.

250 *One was a video of five drug distribution company executives:* Katie Zezima and Scott Higham, "Drug Executives to Testify before Congress about Their Role in U.S. Opioid Crisis," *Washington Post*, April 12, 2018.

250 *The other exhibit was the damning* Austin Powers *spoof:* Exhibit in MDL No. 2804.

251 *That night, Paul took his wife:* Interview with Paul Farrell.

251 *But that evening:* Interviews with Paul Farrell, Joe Rice, and Paul Hanly.

252 *Five hours later:* Lenny Bernstein, Scott Higham, Sari Horwitz, and Aaron C. Davis, "Last-Ditch Opioid Settlement in Ohio Could Open Door for Much Larger Deal," *Washington Post*, October 21, 2019.

252 *Paul was thrilled by the amount of money:* Interview with Paul Farrell.

Chapter 48: "This Can't Be Real"

This chapter is based on interviews with Paul T. Farrell Jr. and Mark P. Pifko, along with emails between Farrell and Pifko, and emails between executives at AmerisourceBergen that are now part of MDL 2804, National Prescription Opiate Litigation.

254 *At first, Paul Farrell thought someone had pranked him:* Interview with Paul Farrell; Mark Pifko, email, 2020.

255 *On September 13, 2012, Steve Mays:* Email exchange between Steve Mays and Cathy Marcum.

255 *The day after learning about the emails:* Paul Farrell, email.

256 *Polster had continued to push:* Polster, court order.

257 *Nothing in the "Pillbillies" email surprised Paul:* Interview with Paul Farrell.

Chapter 49: "Every Nineteen Minutes"

This chapter is based on interviews with Eric Kennedy; the transcript of the deposition of John M. Gray taken on July 30, 2020; and articles in Law360 *and the* Cleveland Plain Dealer.

258 *Eric Kennedy thought he could hold it together:* Interview with Eric Kennedy; Deposition of John Gray.

259 *Kennedy wasn't sure if Gray knew:* Interview with Eric Kennedy; Deposition of John Gray.

259 *In 2015, heroin overdoses surpassed:* CDC website.

259 *In a series of missed opportunities:* Scott Higham, Sari Horwitz, and Katie Zezima, "The Fentanyl Failure," *Washington Post*, March 13, 2019; Sari Horwitz, Scott Higham, Steven Rich, and Shelby Hanssen, "Trump Administration Struggles to Confront the Fentanyl Crisis," *Washington Post*, May 22, 2019; Sari Horwitz and Scott Higham, "The Flow of Fentanyl: In the Mail, over the Border," *Washington Post*, August 23, 2019; Katie Zezima and Colby Itkowitz, "Flailing on Fentanyl," *Washington Post*, September 20, 2019.

259 *Fentanyl deaths continued to soar:* Higham et al., "The Fentanyl Failure"; Horwitz et al., "Trump Administration Struggles"; Horwitz and Higham, "The Flow of Fentanyl"; Zezima and Itkowitz, "Flailing on Fentanyl."

260 *In 2020, as the Covid pandemic gripped the nation:* CDC website.

260 *Paul knew about Kennedy's son:* Interview with Paul Farrell.

260 *Kennedy began by asking Gray:* John Gray deposition.

261 *Kennedy read Gray's email:* John Gray deposition.

262 *That year, The Alliance had hired:* Healthcare Distribution Alliance communications.

262 *Gray said he couldn't recall engaging RAND:* John Gray deposition.

264 *Rather than hire RAND:* HDA communications.

265 *Kennedy showed Gray an email:* John Gray deposition.

266 *Kennedy stood up from his conference table:* Interview with Eric Kennedy.

Chapter 50: "We're Going to Trial"

This chapter is based on U.S. district court trial transcripts, articles in Law360, and interviews with Paul T. Farrell Jr. and Jayne Conroy.

267 *Few places in America were hit harder:* City of Huntington v. Amerisource-Bergen Drug Corporation, et al., No. 3:17-cv-01362, Trial transcripts.

267 *The living and the dead were Paul Farrell's friends and neighbors:* Interview with Paul Farrell.

268 *Paul thought he could secure a trial:* Interview with Paul Farrell.

268 *Even though the judge was a lifelong Republican:* Emily Field, "Judge with 'West Virginia Grit' Takes on 1st Opioid MDL Trial," *Law360*, April 28, 2021.

268 *Paul and Faber shared a love for their state:* Interview with Paul Farrell.

269 *Paul was so eager to secure a trial date:* Interview with Paul Farrell.

269 *Jayne Conroy was deeply troubled:* Interview with Jayne Conroy.

270 *Paul remained undeterred:* Interview with Paul Farrell.

270 *The case was scheduled to start: City of Huntington v. AmerisourceBergen Drug Corporation, et al.,* No. 3:17-cv-01362, Docket.

270 *On May 2, 2021:* Interview with Paul Farrell.

272 *The next morning at 9:30:* Charleston trial transcripts.

272 *"I've told my clients you are a student of history":* Charleston trial transcripts.

274 *All three defense lawyers made many of the same points:* Charleston trial transcripts.

276 *Neither could Joe:* Interview with Joe Rannazzisi.

Chapter 51: Death Threats

  This chapter is based on U.S. district court trial transcripts, the Twitter feeds of Rex Chapman and Eric Eyre, and interviews with Paul T. Farrell Jr. and Jayne Conroy.

277 *Paul Farrell had thought Judge Faber:* Interview with Paul Farrell; Charleston trial transcripts.

278 *Paul had planned to introduce several other incendiary emails:* Interview with Paul Farrell; Charleston trial transcripts.

280 *The way the trial was playing out:* Interview with Jayne Conroy.

280 *Following Zimmerman's testimony:* Lucas Manfield and Lauren Peace, "As Opioid Epidemic Raged, Drug Company Executives Made Fun of West Virginians," *Mountain State Spotlight*, May 13, 2021.

280 *Rex Chapman, a former University of Kentucky basketball phenom:* Rex Chapman's Twitter account.

281 *On Monday, May 17:* Interview with Paul Farrell.

281 *Nicholas told the judge:* Interview with Paul Farrell.

282 *Eleven days later:* Charleston trial transcripts.

282 *Two days earlier, Paul Hanly died:* Charleston trial transcripts; interviews with Jayne Conroy and Paul Farrell.

283 *Several defense lawyers in the courtroom walked over:* Interviews with Jayne Conroy and Paul Farrell.

283 *In Cleveland, Judge Polster told a reporter:* Katharine Q. Seelye, "Paul J. Hanly Jr., Top Litigator in Opioid Cases, Dies at 70," *New York Times,* May 22, 2021.

283 *The plaintiffs' trial team was devastated:* Interview with Jayne Conroy.

283 *A few months earlier:* Interview with Paul Farrell.

Chapter 52: "A Stunning Claim"

This chapter is based on U.S. district court trial transcripts and interviews with James Rafalski, Paul T. Farrell Jr., and members of the plaintiffs' trial team.

285 *For months, attorney Mike Fuller:* Interview with James Rafalski.

286 *On May 26, he took the stand:* Interviews with James Rafalski and Paul Farrell; Charleston trial transcripts.

293 *He was exhausted:* Interview with James Rafalski.

Chapter 53: "Are You Ready?"

This chapter is based on U.S. district court trial transcripts and interviews with Joe Rannazzisi, Paul T. Farrell Jr., and plaintiffs' trial team members.

294 *Joe Rannazzisi couldn't wait:* Interview with Joe Rannazzisi.

294 *As the two huddled in a corner:* Interviews with Joe Rannazzisi and Paul Farrell.

295 *The night before his testimony:* Interview with Joe Rannazzisi.

296 *Singer began her examination of Joe:* Charleston trial transcripts.

297 *When the trial resumed the next morning:* Charleston trial transcripts.

300 *Schmidt started off by attacking Joe:* Charleston trial transcripts.

304 *At that moment, Joe saw Schmidt's eyes widen:* Charleston trial transcripts; interview with Joe Rannazzisi.

Chapter 54: "Magic or Tragic"

This chapter is based on U.S. district court trial transcripts and interviews with Paul T. Farrell Jr. and plaintiffs' trial team members.

305 *For many members of the plaintiffs' trial team:* Interviews with plaintiffs' trial team members.

305 *After nearly three months:* Interview with Paul Farrell.

306 *At precisely nine that morning:* Interview with Paul Farrell; Charleston trial transcripts.

308 *It was Kearse's turn:* Interview with Paul Farrell; Charleston trial transcripts.

309 *Each defense attorney was given two hours:* Interview with Paul Farrell; Charleston trial transcripts.

313 *Once inside, they began celebrating:* Interview with *Mountain State Spotlight* reporter Eric Eyre.

314 *Paul slowly walked away:* Interview with Paul Farrell.

Epilogue

    This chapter is based on interviews with Rich Bishoff, Paul Farrell, Jayne Conroy, Anthony Irpino, Pearl Robertson, Peter Mougey, Joe Rice, Mark Lanier, Mike Fuller, Joe Rannazzisi, Jim Geldhof, James Rafalski, Mimi Paredes, David Schiller, and Elizabeth Chamblee Burch, along with U.S. district court trial transcripts; state court rulings and verdicts in opioid trials in California, Oklahoma, and New York; the jury verdict against the pharmacy chains in federal court in Ohio; and court proceedings in the Purdue Pharma and Mallinckrodt bankruptcy cases.

315 *When Rich Bishoff graduated:* Interview with Rich Bishoff; Snodgrass Funeral Homes website.

316 *The state's coal industry:* James A. Haught, "A Short History of Mining—and Its Decline—in West Virginia," *Register Herald*, March 30, 2017; Eric Scheuch, "Life after Coal: The Decline and Rise of West Virginia Coal Country," Columbia Climate School's State of the Planet, August 7, 2020.

316 *Two decades into his career:* Interview with Rich Bishoff.

318 *The biggest development came on February 25, 2022:* Meryl Kornfield, "Major Drug Distributors and J&J Finalize Opioid Settlement, Launching Nationwide Funding," *Washington Post*, February 25, 2022.

318 *More than one hundred plaintiffs' law firms:* Interview with Peter Mougey.

319 *It took nearly two years:* Interview with Peter Mougey.

319 *On July 21, the distributors and Johnson & Johnson:* Meryl Kornfield and Lenny Bernstein, "Drug Distributors, Johnson & Johnson Reach $26 Billion Deal to Resolve Opioid Lawsuits," *Washington Post*, July 21, 2021.

320 *Mougey and other plaintiffs' lawyers:* Interviews with Peter Mougey and Jayne Conroy.

320 *Every state had to devise:* National Opioids Settlement, nationalopioidsettlement.com; Opioid Litigation Global Settlement Tracker, www.opioidsettlementtracker.com/globalsettlementtracker.

320 *In a separate deal, hundreds of Native American tribes:* Meryl Kornfield, "Native American Tribes Reach Landmark Opioid Deal with Johnson & Johnson, Drug Distributors for up to $665 Million," *Washington Post*, February 1, 2022.

320 *At the height of the epidemic:* Sari Horwitz, Debbie Cenziper, and Steven Rich, "As Opioids Flooded Tribal Lands across the U.S., Overdose Deaths Skyrocketed," *Washington Post*, June 29, 2020.

321 *Paul's case in Charleston was not included:* Interview with Paul Farrell.

321 *On November 1, Orange County Superior Court judge Peter Wilson:* Nate Raymond, "California Judge Delivers Drugmakers 1st Trial Win in Opioid Litigation," Reuters, November 2, 2021; Robert Jablon and Donald Thompson, "Orange County Judge Rules in Favor of Drugmakers in California Opioid Crisis Lawsuit," Associated Press, November 2, 2021.

322 *Just over a week later, on November 9:* Meryl Kornfield and Lenny Bernstein, "Oklahoma Supreme Court Overturns Historic Opioid Ruling against J&J," *Washington Post*, November 9, 2021.

322 *"It was a big blow":* Interview with Jayne Conroy.

323 *On November 23, 2021:* Meryl Kornfield and Lenny Bernstein, "CVS, Walgreens, and Walmart Are Responsible for Flooding Ohio Counties with Pain Pills, Jury Says," *Washington Post*, November 23, 2021.

323 *At the conclusion of the six-week trial:* Jan Hoffman, "CVS, Walgreens, and Walmart Fueled Opioid Crisis, Jury Finds," *New York Times*, November 23, 2021.

323 *After the trial, Lanier interviewed:* Interview with Mark Lanier.

324 *While Conroy savored the victory:* Interview with Jayne Conroy.

324 *The litigation has become a morass:* Interview with Elizabeth Chamblee Burch.

325 *On October 21, 2020, the Justice Department announced:* "Justice Department Announces Global Resolution of Criminal and Civil Investigations with Opioid Manufacturer Purdue Pharma and Civil Settlement with Members of the Sackler Family," Justice Department announcement, October 21, 2020; Meryl Kornfield, Christopher Rowland, Lenny Bernstein, and Devlin Barrett, "Purdue Pharma Agrees to Plead Guilty to Federal Criminal Charges in Settlement over Opioid Crisis," *Washington Post*, October 21, 2020.

325 *On December 16, 2021:* Meryl Kornfield, "Judge Overturns Deal Giving Purdue Pharma's Sackler Family Civil Immunity from Opioid Claims," *Washington Post*, December 16, 2021.

326 *"The bankruptcy court did not have the authority":* Statement by Attorney General Merrick B. Garland regarding Purdue Pharma Bankruptcy, Justice Department, December 16, 2021.

326 *On January 3, 2022:* Steven Church, "Purdue Judge Gives Sacklers until Jan. 14 to Negotiate New Deal," Bloomberg, January 3, 2022.

326 *Two months later, on March 3:* Meryl Kornfield, "Sackler Family Members to Contribute up to $6 Billion in Latest Agreement to Resolve Opioid Claims," *Washington Post*, March 3, 2022.

326 *As part of the deal:* Meryl Kornfield, "Opioid Victims Confront Purdue Pharma's Sackler Family: 'It Will Never End for Me,'" *Washington Post*, March 10, 2022.

327 *In February 2020, the Ireland-based company:* Katie Zezima and Katie Mettler, "Drug Manufacturer Mallinckrodt to Pay $1.6 Billion to Settle Opioid Claims," *Washington Post*, February 25, 2020.

327 *Since testifying in Charleston and Cleveland:* Interview with Joe Rannazzisi.

327 *Mimi Paredes successfully sued:* Interview with Mimi Paredes.

328 *David Schiller, the lead DEA agent:* Interview with David Schiller.

328 *It's been six years since Jim Geldhof retired:* Interview with Jim Geldhof.

328 *Since retiring from the DEA, James Rafalski:* Interview with James Rafalski.

329 *When Joe reflects on the cases:* Interview with Joe Rannazzisi.

Index

"abatement plan," 274
Academy of Integrative Pain
    Management, 176–177
Activa, 36, 232
The Advancement of Sound Science
    Coalition, 86–87
Akers, Eric, 105
Akron Beacon Journal, 227–228
Alliance. *See* "The Alliance"
American Pharmacists Association,
    93
American Society of Hospital
    Pharmacists, 143
AmerisourceBergen Corp.
    ARCOS data on, 232
    background, 8
    crisis communication strategy of,
        88–89
    DEA compliance strategy, 26–28
    distribution warehouses, 22, 200
    Farrell's discovery of, 140
    on investigative reporting
        by *Washington Post* and *60
        Minutes*, 173–174
    lobbying strategies, 25–27, 48,
        92, 103
    Mallinckrodt communications, 57
    "Pillbillies" email, 46–47,
        254–256, 277–279
    public nuisance bench trial
        closing arguments, 305–314
    public nuisance bench trial
        proceedings, 271–276,
        286–293, 296–304
    public nuisance suit filed against,
        154, 164–165
    public nuisance suit representation,
        181–182, 201
    public nuisance suit RICO
        rulings, 243
    on responsibility for opioid crisis, 250
    settlements and fines paid by, 137,
        249, 262
    settlement talks, 189, 251–253
    Walgreens and, 83
anti-anxiety drugs, 52–53
APCO Worldwide, 86–89, 213,
    262, 264
ARCOS (Automation of Reports
    and Consolidated Orders
    System) database
    access to, 88, 135–137, 197–202,
        223–224, 226–233, 264–265
    analysis of, 287–288
    background, 43–44, 54
    Florida distribution numbers, 56,
        65, 83
Arnold & Porter, 86

attorney generals, xi–xii. *See also
    specific attorney generals*
attorneys, xii. *See also specific
    attorneys*
Atwell, Kristine, 83–84, 233
Auburn (Washington), 23
Aurora (Colorado), 111–112
Austin Powers spoof, 15–16, 250

Banjo (dog), 130–131
Barber, D. Linden, 60–62, 93, 94,
    101, 126
Barnett, Robert B., 261
Baron & Budd, 155, 181, 237,
    254
Barrett, George S., 65, 250
Bartlit Beck, 195
Baum, L. Frank, 246, 253
Bayer, 17
Belichick, Bill, 235
Bennett, James R., II, 198–200
benzodiazepine pills, 156
Berkey, Ann, 48
Beverly Hillbillies parody, 46–47, 49,
    254–257, 273, 277–279
Bizzarro, Lynne A., 171
Blackburn, Marsha
    background, 90–91
    campaign contributions for,
        93–94, 145
    congressional hearing questions,
        96–98, 107
    legislation backpedaling, 175
    legislation introduced by, 95, 99.
        See also Marino-Blackburn bill
    Rannazzisi investigation request,
        108
Blue Highway, 34–36, 47, 65–66,
    125
Boggs, Gary, 13, 113

Boockholdt, Barbara, 56–57
Borelli, Victor, 37–40, 44, 55, 57,
    125–126, 213, 233
Boston Marathon analogy, 247–248
Brighton (Colorado), 110–112
"Broward County North," 50–53
Brown, Dennis, 170
Brownlee, John L., 23–24
Budd, Russell W., 155, 156, 179,
    187–188, 189
Budish, Armond D., 253
Bureau of Narcotics and Dangerous
    Drugs, 41
Burgess, Michael C., 94, 96
Butler, Malcolm, 234–235
Buzzeo, Ronald, 212

Cabell County (West Virginia),
    47, 154, 255–256, 267–276,
    287–292, 294–304, 305–314
Cabraser, Elizabeth J., 189
*Cardinal Health, Inc. v. Eric H.
    Holder Jr.*, 77–80, 140
Cardinal Health, Inc.
    ARCOS data on, 232
    background, 8
    Barber's connection to, 93
    crisis communication strategy,
        88–89
    DEA compliance strategy, 26–28
    distribution warehouses, 22, 23,
        64–67, 199–200
    Immediate Suspension Orders
        for, 68–71, 74–80
    internal audits, 212
    on investigative reporting
        by *Washington Post* and *60
        Minutes*, 173–174
    lobbying strategies, 25–27, 48,
        103, 104

Mallinckrodt communications, 57
public nuisance bench trial
closing arguments, 305–314
public nuisance bench trial
proceedings, 271–276,
286–293, 296–304
public nuisance suit depositions,
235–236
public nuisance suit filed against,
154, 164–165, 189
public nuisance suit
representation, 181–182, 201,
220–221
public nuisance suit RICO
rulings, 240–242, 243
RAND study proposal and,
263–264
on responsibility for opioid
crisis, 250
settlements and fines paid by, 80,
136–137, 212, 249, 262
settlement talks, 251–253
temporary restraining order
requested by, 75–76
Walgreens and, 83
Carter, Ruth, 64–67
Cephalon, 15–16, 18, 88, 171, 250
Chaney, Kathy, 50–51, 53, 163,
164–165
Chapman, Rex, 280–281
"chargeback" program (rebates), 45,
56, 57, 127
Charleston (West Virginia),
154–155, 163–164, 182, 256,
260, 268, 305
Charleston Gazette-Mail, 4,
136–137, 227, 229–231
Cheffo, Mark S., 183, 195
Cherokee Nation, 142–143, 220,
256

Chillicothe (Ohio), 53
Chrysler, Dick, 32
Chu, Judy, 94
Chudnow, Jeffrey, 81–82
Clawson, Jeffrey, 111
Clay, Eric L., 231
Cleveland (Ohio), 183, 185–190,
193, 217, 244, 256–257,
258–266
closed system of drug distribution,
207–208, 296–299
Cochrane, Steve, 37, 57
Code of Federal Regulations, 205, 295
Cohen, David R., 212, 235–236, 250
Colder, Karl, 135–136, 137, 198
Cole, James M., 68, 70–73,
74, 140
Collis, Steven H., 47, 250
Colorado, 84, 110–112, 117
Congress, cast of characters,
xiii–xiv. See also specific members
of Congress
Conroy, Jayne
background, 167–171, 183
on Farrell's decisions, 182–183,
185–186, 269–270, 280
on Farrell's theatrics, 180, 235
on Hanly, 283
at Hanly's deathbed, 282–283
on Lanier, 214, 216–219
public nuisance suit roles,
188–189, 244–245, 249–250
on settlements, 253
Controlled Substances Act (1970),
8, 17, 84, 99, 127, 131, 136,
204–206, 222, 241, 295–299
Conway, Kellyanne, 260
Cooper, Richard M., 261
Cosgrove, Jewelyn, 91
Cote, Larry P., 78

court cases. *See also* multidistrict
　　litigation; *specific cities, counties
　　and states*
　attorney generals, xii–xiii
　defense attorneys, xii. *See also
　　specific attorneys*
　drug distributors, xiii. *See also
　　specific drug distributors*
　drug manufacturers, xiii. *See also
　　specific drug manufactures*
　judges, xiv. *See also specific judges*
　pharmacies, xiii. *See also specific
　　pharmacies*
　plantiffs' attorneys, xii. *See also
　　specific attorneys*
Covid pandemic, 256–257, 260, 270
Covington & Burling, 101–102,
　　113, 123, 203–204
Craig, Dustin, 143
Craig, Jimmy, 142
"Crisis Playbook," 87–89, 213, 233,
　　238, 241, 262, 264
Crowley, Jack, 28, 30–31, 240
Cuyahoga County (Ohio), 244,
　　251–253
CVS pharmacies
　ARCOS data on, 232
　lobbying strategies, 93, 104, 145
　public nuisance suit filed against,
　　154, 164–165, 243, 256–257,
　　260
　Sanford, Florida case, 65–67, 69,
　　74–75, 78, 80, 140, 250
　Walgreens comparison, 83

Dallas, Baron & Budd, 155
Daun, Margaret, 248
defense attorneys, xii. *See also specific
　　attorneys*
Dellinger, Kevin, 248

DeNaples, Louis, 91
Denver (Colorado), 109–112, 117
Department of Justice, cast of
　　characters, xi–xii. *See also
　　specific attorney generals*
Detroit (Michigan), 8, 9, 11,
　　41–44
Dilaudid, 42
Dinan, James H., 68–69, 71–72, 74
"Doritos" email, 37, 57, 125,
　　213, 233
Drug Enforcement Administration
　　(DEA), xi, 17, 26–28, 41. *See
　　also specific DEA agents*
drug industry
　closed system of drug
　　distribution, 207–208, 296–299
　drug distributors, xiii. *See also
　　specific companies*
　drug manufacturers, xiii. *See also
　　specific companies*
　historical regulation of, 16–17
　lawsuits, xii–xiv. *See also
　　multidistrict litigation; specific
　　attorney generals, attorneys,
　　companies, and judges*
　legislation. *See* Controlled
　　Substances Act; Harrison
　　Narcotics Tax Act; Marino-
　　Blackburn bill; Ryan Haight
　　Online Pharmacy Consumer
　　Protection Act
　pharmacies, xiii. *See also specific
　　pharmacies*
Ducca, Anita T., 26–27, 241, 265
Duft, Patricia, 56

Eddy, Julie, 46–47, 48, 254
Ellsberg, Daniel, 262
Emch, Alvin L., 201

Endo Pharmaceuticals, 171,
241–242
Englewood Specialty Pharmacy,
150–151
Ensuring Patient Safety and
Effective Drug Enforcement
Act, 92–94, 103–105, 107. *See
also* Marino-Blackburn bill
Eyre, Eric, 136–137

Faber, David A., 256, 268–276,
277–283, 285–293,
295–304, 305–314
Farmer, Frank, 64
Farrell, Charlene, 5, 137–138,
251
Farrell, Farrell & Farrell, 138
Farrell, Jacqueline, 251, 283
Farrell, Patrick, 5
Farrell, Paul, Sr., 138, 157–158
Farrell, Paul T., Jr.
background, 4–5, 6, 135–141,
157–158, 159, 165
on Faber, 268, 277
Hanly and, 244–245, 272,
283–284
Lanier and, 217, 225, 245
on Master's case ruling, 162
personal qualities, 234–236,
244–245, 260
on "Pillbillies" email, 254–257
public nuisance bench trial
closing argument, 305–314
public nuisance bench trial
preparation, 269, 270–271
public nuisance bench trial
proceedings, 272–276,
277–283, 285–293
public nuisance bench trial
request, 268–270

public nuisance bench trial
witness preparation, 294–295
public nuisance multidistrict
litigation, 178–184, 186–187,
244–245, 249, 251–252,
267–268
public nuisance suit ARCOS data
base argument, 197–200
public nuisance suit depositions,
203–208
public nuisance suit document
discovery process, 211–213
public nuisance suit filed by, 154,
159–160
as public nuisance suit leader,
159–160, 187–190
public nuisance suit map, 156
public nuisance suit partnerships,
154–156
public nuisance suit pitch,
152–154, 166, 171–172
public nuisance suit witness list,
163–165
research for litigation possibility,
148–151
RICO filing by, 237–243, 269
on settlements, 193, 196,
252–253
Federal Register, 136, 141
fentanyl use, 15–16, 18, 258–260,
274
Fentora (fentanyl), 15–16, 18
Fields, Richard W., 142–143, 220
"Fifth Vital Sign," 19
Florida
ARCOS distribution numbers
for, 56, 65, 83
distribution companies in, 21–23,
38–40, 41–44, 55–57, 82,
112, 300

Florida (*Continued*)
  legislation on pill mills, 47–48
  pain management clinics in,
    29–33, 35, 39, 44–45, 47–48
  pharmacies in, 64–67, 69, 74–75,
    78, 80, 81–85, 140, 250
  public health emergency in, 39,
    54, 64
Florida Department of Health, 39,
    48
flyfishing metaphor, 312–313
Fort Pierce (Florida), 84
Freedom of Information Act
    requests, 137
Freitas, Kristen, 31–32, 94
Friedman, Paul L., 131
Fuller, Michael J., Jr., 154–156, 164,
    189, 235–236, 285–286, 293

Garre, Gregory G., 125
"Gateway Theory," 100–101, 274,
    298, 305–309
Geldhof, James
  background, 41–43, 50–53
  as expert witness, 163,
    164–165, 246
  Masters case and, 54–55, 57,
    148, 161
  McKesson case and, 114–117
  on Rannazzisi, 42–43
  retirement of, 132
  on settlements, 124–125,
    127–128
Geldhof, Matt, 132
Geller, Paul J., 189, 247–248
George, Christopher and Jeffrey,
    44–45, 55
Giuliani, Rudy, 24, 70
Goldberg, Stuart M., 71–73, 74, 76
Gorelick, Jamie, 70–71, 74, 76

Gray, John, 94, 123, 258–266
Grey, Jennifer, 20
Grizzard, Alton, 59

Hammergren, John H., 9, 33,
    114, 124, 250
Hanly, Jake, 170
Hanly, Paul J., Jr.
  background, 166–172, 178–179,
    183, 187
  death of, 282–284
  Farrell and, 244–245, 272, 283–284
  on Farrell's theatrics, 235
  on Lanier, 214–219, 225
  public nuisance suit roles,
    187–190, 194–195, 244–245
  settlement talks, 251–253
Hanly Conroy, 168
Harper, Gregg, 250
Harrison Narcotics Tax Act (1914),
    16–17
Hartle, Nathan J., 204–208,
    306–307
Harvard Drug, 43–45, 55, 57, 127
Hatch, Orrin G., 31, 145—146,
    176
H.D. Smith Wholesale Drug, 88,
    154, 250
health care access demographics,
    51–52
Healthcare Distribution Alliance.
    See "The Alliance"
Heimlich, William Joseph, 167
Henn, Emily Johnson, 204
heroin use, 8, 11, 17, 100–102,
    106–107, 259, 274, 298,
    306–308
Higham, Scott, 232
Hill, Peterson, Carper, Bee &
    Deitzler, 155, 156, 163–164

Hobart, Geoffrey E., 110, 118
Hoffman, Philip Seymour, 100
Hogen, Robin, 239–240
Holder, Eric H., Jr., 99–102, 106,
    107, 123, 146
"the Holy Trinity," 52–53
Horowitz, Michael E., 108
Horwitz, Sari, 232
House Energy and Commerce
    Subcommittee on Health,
    90–91, 94, 95–98, 205, 250
Huntington (West Virginia), 4–5, 35,
    138, 153, 157–159, 187, 248–249,
    256, 267–276, 287–292,
    294–304, 305–314
Hurley Drug Company, 152
Hyman, Phelps & McNamara, 9

Immediate Suspension Orders
    (ISOs)
    for AmerisourceBergen, 22–23
    for Cardinal Health, Inc., 68–71,
        74–80
    legislation against, 93, 95–98,
        102, 107, 145, 175–177
    for Masters Pharmaceutical, 125
    for McKesson Corporation,
        112–113
    pushback against use of, 71–73,
        74–80, 112–116
    for Walgreens, 84
In Re: National Prescription Opiate
    Litigation, 180–181
internet opioid sales, 47
Irpino, Anthony, 209–211, 256

Janush, Evan M., 212–213, 238
Jick, Hershel, 18–19
Johnson & Johnson, 171,
    239–242, 252

Joint Commission on Accreditation
    of Healthcare Organizations, 19
Jonas, Tracy, 33
judges, xiv. See also Faber, David A.;
    Polster, Dan Aaron; Walton,
    Reggie B.
Jupiter (Florida), 82–84

Kadzik, Peter, 101
Kaupang, Helen, 110
Kearse, Anne McGinness, 273–274,
    306, 308–309
Keller Rohrback, 213
Kellogg's Honey Smacks, 278
Kelly, Patrick, 94, 265
Kennedy, Eric, 258–266
Kennedy, Robert Jacque, 258–259,
    266
Kentucky, 42, 44, 47, 255, 278
KeySource Medical, 37, 40, 55, 57
Kroger, 154

Lake County (Ohio), 256–257
Lakeland (Florida), 21–22, 23,
    112, 300
Landover (Maryland), 112
Lanier, Mark, 214–219, 221–225,
    234, 244–247, 250, 252, 253
Lanier Law Firm, 216
Lauer, Richard T., 148–150, 151
Law360, 179
lawyers, xii. See also specific attorneys
Leen, Jeff, 228–229
Lefton, Karen, 226–231, 233
Leonhart, Michele
    Cardinal case and, 69–70, 75, 77
    on Holder, 101–102
    McKesson case and, 33
    retirement of, 120, 146
    testimony of, 108

Levin Papantonio Rafferty, 155,
    156, 189, 203–204
Library of Congress, 136, 140–141
"Lightning Strike" operation,
    21–22
Livonia (Michigan), 112, 115
Loeser, Derek W., 213
Lynch, Loretta E., 123

Mafia analogy, 237–240, 242
Mainigi, Enu A., 181, 220–221,
    274–276
Main Justice, 68–69, 71–72
Mallinckrodt, Edward, Jr., 36
Mallinckrodt, Edward, Sr., 36
Mallinckrodt Pharmaceuticals
    ARCOS data on, 43–44, 232
    background, 24, 34–36
    case against, 125–128, 131, 132
    "chargeback" program, 45, 56,
        57, 127
    distribution companies tied to,
        55–57, 65, 140, 150
    "Doritos" email and, 37, 57, 125,
        213, 233
    RICO allegations against,
        239–242
    sales force, 37–40, 44, 55, 57,
        125–126, 213, 233
    settlements and fines paid by,
        163–164, 252
    subsidiary of, 232
Manchin, Joe, III, 175, 176, 233
Marcum, Cathy, 255, 278
Marino, Tom
    attorney general overtures by,
        100–102
    background, 91–92
    campaign contributions for,
        93–94, 103–104, 145

drug czar nomination, 173,
    175–176, 177
legislation introduced by, 95,
    99, 101, 102. *See also* Marino-
    Blackburn bill
Rannazzisi investigation request,
    108
Marino-Blackburn bill (S.483)
    DEA's opposition to, 102,
        104–105, 144–146
    Holder on, 106–107
    investigative report on, 173–176,
        238
    lobbying efforts behind, 103–104,
        145, 189, 238, 241, 260
    passing of, 144–146
    reiteration of, 123
    RICO evidence and, 241
Marquette Law Review, 175
Marshall, Thurgood, 97, 131
Maryland, 112
Mastandrea, Joseph, 250
Masters Pharmaceutical, 54–57,
    125, 140, 148–151, 161–162
Mays, Steve, 255, 278
Mazzei, Mark, 129–130
McCann, Craig, 287
McConnell, Mitch, 144
McHugh Fuller, 154–155
McKesson, Donald, 16–17,
    204–205
McKesson Corporation
    ARCOS data on, 136, 232
    background, 16–17
    crisis communication strategy of,
        88–89
    DEA case against, 7–9, 12–14,
        109–119, 132
    DEA compliance strategy,
        26–28

distribution warehouses, 21–22, 200

Farrell's discovery of, 140

fines and settlements paid by, 206, 223, 249

on investigative reporting by *Washington Post* and *60 Minutes*, 173–174

lobbying strategies, 25–27, 48

Mallinckrodt communications, 57

public nuisance bench trial closing arguments, 305–314

public nuisance bench trial preparation, 271–276

public nuisance bench trial proceedings, 286–293, 296–304

public nuisance suit depositions, 204–208

public nuisance suit filed against, 154, 164–165, 260

public nuisance suit representation, 181–182, 189, 204

public nuisance suit RICO rulings, 243

RAND study proposal and, 264

on responsibility for opioid crisis, 250

settlements and fines paid by, 32–33, 124–125

settlement talks, 251–253

Walgreens and, 83

McLaughlin, Jim, 226–227, 229

McNally, Alan G., 81

Menendez, M. J., 117

Merlo, Larry J., 80

Merrill, Jessica, 67

Miami-Luken (distributor), 250

Michigan, 8, 9, 11, 41–44, 84, 112, 115

Milione, Louis J., 122

Mingo County (West Virginia), 152–154, 176

Moore, United States v., 131

Morford, Craig S., 69–70, 77

Moss, Randolph D., 71–72, 75–76, 77–79

Motley, Ron, 178

Motley Rice, 178, 217, 273, 294, 306

Mougey, Peter J., 164, 189

Mountain State Spotlight, 280, 281

Mulrooney, John J., II, 116–117, 147, 175

multidistrict litigation (MDL)
ARCOS database and, 197–202, 226–233

attorneys, xii. *See also specific attorneys*

background, 178–184

bench trial closing arguments, 305–314

bench trial proceedings, 272–276, 277–283, 285–293, 294–304

bench trial request, 267–276

conference for, 185–188

depositions, 203–208, 220–225, 235–236, 246, 258–266

document discovery process, 209–213, 238–239, 254–257

filing by Farrell, 178–184

judges. *See* Faber, David A.; Polster, Dan Aaron

jury selection, 247–248

leadership roles for, 214–219

pre-trial preparations, 244–248

RICO filing, 237–243

settlement instructions from Polster, 191–196, 248–249, 256

settlement talks, 248–253

war plan for, 188–190

muscle relaxers, 52–53
Muscogee (Creek) Nation, 248
"mushroom treatment," 122–123,
    144
My Cousin Vinny (film), 235–236

naloxone, 106
National Association of Chain
    Drug Stores, 31, 32, 93, 103,
    104, 125, 145, 241
National Community Pharmacists
    Association, 93, 103
New England Patriots, 234–235
New York, 84
Nicholas, Robert A., 274–276, 279,
    281–282, 298, 309–311
North Carolina, 166–167, 171–172,
    247–249
Norton, Rita, 48
Novak, Jonathan P., 116

Obama, Barack, 120, 123, 146,
    176, 259
O'Connor, Brien T., 126, 127
Ohio
    Chillicothe, 53
    Cleveland, 183, 185–190, 193,
        217, 244, 256–257, 258–266
    Cuyahoga County, 244, 251–253
    Lake County, 256–257
    Portsmouth, 35, 50–53
    Scioto County, 51–53
    Summit County, 244, 251–253
    Trumbull County, 256–257
    Washington Courthouse, 112, 115
1 percent statistic falsehood, 18–19, 20
organized crime claims, 237–240,
    242
Orlando (Florida), 22
Oviedo (Florida), 81–83

oxycodone and OxyContin. See
    drug industry
"Oxy Express" route, 35, 47

pain, as "Fifth Vital Sign," 19
pain advocacy groups, 31, 239–240
Pain Care Forum, 239–240, 241
pain management clinics, 29–33,
    35, 39, 44–45, 47–48, 51–53
Papantonio, Mike "Pap," 155, 164,
    179, 186–189
Paredes, Imelda L. "Mimi"
    background, 58–61
    demotion of, 144
    on Marino-Blackburn bill,
        104–105
    McKesson case and, 117–119,
        124
    on retirement of Rannazzisi, 122
    support for Rannazzisi, 58, 73,
        96, 98, 107–108
"Partners Against Pain" campaign, 20
Partridge, John, 104, 114, 122, 144
Paxton, Ken, 249
Pennsylvania, 22, 91–92, 104,
    247–248
Perrelli, Thomas J., 251–252
Peterson, Jim, 163
pharmacies, xiii. See also specific
    pharmacies
pharmacist oath, 84
Philadelphia Eagles, 234–235
Philip Morris, 86–87
Physicians for Responsible Opioid
    Prescribing, 171
Pifko, Mark P., 237–239, 254–255
Pillard, Cornelia T. L., 150, 162
"Pillbillies" email, 46–47, 49,
    254–257, 273, 277–279
Pinon, Dwayne, 85

plantiffs' attorneys, xii. *See also specific attorneys*
Platte Valley Pharmacy, 110–112
Polster, Dan Aaron
　on ARCOS database access, 197–202, 226–227, 229–232
　background, 183
　bellwether cases and, 256–257
　conference held by, 186–190
　on document access, 233
　Farrell's bench trial request and, 268
　on Hanly, 283
　litigation track created by, 211–212
　pre-trial summoning by, 248–249
　RICO rulings by, 242–243
　settlement announcement, 252
　settlement instructions by, 191–196, 248–249, 256
Portenoy, Russell, 17, 19, 171
Porter, Jane, 18
Port Richey (Florida), 84
Portsmouth (Ohio), 35, 50–53
Priyadarshi, Paras, 66, 79
Proctor, R. David, 181
Purdue Pharma
　ARCOS data on, 232
　cases against, 167–171
　on DEA's actions, 28
　distributors' implication of, 275
　fall from favor, 34, 36
　lobbying strategies, 145–146
　marketing campaigns, 17–20
　multidistrict litigation representation, 183, 195
　RICO allegations against, 239–242
　settlements and fines paid by, 23–24, 101–102, 170
Pyser, Steven M., 200–201

Quezon, Amy J., 154–155, 164, 189

race and ethnicity, health care access demographics, 51–52
Racketeer Influenced and Corrupt Organizations Act of 1970 (RICO), 237–243, 269
racketeering activity claims, 237–240, 242
Rafalski, James "Ralph"
　background, 43–45
　as expert witness, 163–165, 246, 285–293, 310, 311–312
　Mallinckrodt case and, 54–57, 125–128
　Masters case and, 54–57, 125, 148–151, 161–162
Rafalski, Linda, 165
RAND Corporation, 262–264
Rannazzisi, Gabby, 130
Rannazzisi, Joe
　on The Alliance, 26
　background, 5–6, 7–14
　Barber and, 60, 61–62
　congressional hearing and, 94, 95–98
　deposition by, 220–225, 246
　on distribution companies, 41–43
　distribution warehouse cases, 21–23, 63–67, 68–73, 74–80, 82–85, 112, 113–114, 140, 151
　as drug industry's enemy, 25–26, 91, 107–108, 238, 240–241
　as expert witness, 5, 276, 294–304, 306–307, 310–311
　Farrell's attempt to contact, 141
　health issues, 142, 143–144, 147, 220
　Holder and, 99, 101–102, 106

Rannazzisi, Joe (*Continued*)
  internet sales focus of, 47
  on Marino-Blackburn bill,
    104–105, 145
  on McKesson settlement (2008),
    33
  on misleading marketing, 20
  pain management clinic cases,
    29–33
  Paredes's support for, 58, 73, 96,
    98, 107–108
  personal qualities, 63
  post-retirement job, 142–143
  Rafalski's testimony on, 289
  removal of, 120–122
  retirement of, 3–4, 122–123,
    129–132, 146
  on settlements, 23–24
  as whistleblower, 136, 174–175,
    177, 222
Rannazzisi, Rachel, 130, 132
Rannazzisi, Stephen, 10
Reardon, Stephen J., 27
rebate program ("chargebacks"), 45,
    56, 57, 127
Reed Smith, 274
Reeves, Clifford Lee, II, 78,
    115–116
Rehkop, Brenda, 38, 40
Rendell, Marjorie O., 182
Rice, Joe, 178, 183, 187–188, 189,
    194, 216, 244–245, 251–253
Rich, Steven, 232
RICO (Racketeer Influenced and
    Corrupt Organizations Act of
    1970), 237–243, 269
Riley, Jack, 120–122, 129
Riley, Nicolas Y., 150–151
Rite Aid pharmacies, 154, 256–257
Roberts, Lisa, 52

Robertson, Pearl A., 210–211, 256
Rosen, Burt, 145, 146
Rosenberg, Chuck, 120, 121–122,
    129, 146, 147, 224
Rozman, Donna, 266
Ruiz, Rosie, 248
Ryan Haight Online Pharmacy
    Consumer Protection Act
    (2008), 29

S.483. *See* Marino-Blackburn bill
Sackler family, 17
Salgado, Suzanne, 235–236
Sanford (Florida), 65–67, 74, 78, 250
Sargus, Edmund A., Jr., 182
Scherbenske, John, 144
Schiller, David, 109–114,
    117–118, 124
Schmidt, Paul W., 274–276,
    288–292, 297–298, 300–304
Schultz, Barry, 39, 126
Scioto County (Ohio), 51–53
"Scioto County Cocktail," 53
Scott, Rick, 48–49
"SEAL Team Six," 212
Seeger, Christopher A., 189
Shah, Samir, 45
Shapiro, Ilene, 253
Sherman, Alex, 254–255
Shkolnik, Hunter J., 181, 183,
    217–219
Simmons, John, 168–169
Simmons Hanly Conroy, 170
Simon, Jeffrey B., 181
Singer, Linda, 183, 294–300
60 Minutes, 173–176, 222, 238
Smith, J. Christopher, 250
Soiles, James, 120–121, 130
SOLACE—Surviving Our Loss
    And Continuing Every Day, 52

South Florida Pain Clinic, 44–45
SpecGx, 232
Srinivasan, Sri, 149, 151
Stoffelmayr, Kaspar J., 195–196,
    242–243
Suboxone, 251
Summersville Dam metaphor,
    312–313
Summit County (Ohio), 244,
    251–253
Sunrise Wholesale, 38–39, 55,
    126
Super Bowl (2018), 234–235
Swedesboro (New Jersey), 23

Tellis, Roland K., 181
Temponeras, Margaret, 52–53
temporary restraining order (TRO),
    75–76
Tennessee, 247–249
Teva Pharmaceuticals, 88, 171,
    232, 239–242, 250, 251–253,
    267–268
Texas, 247–249
"The Alliance"
    on ARCOS database access,
        264–265
    background, 25–28
    crisis communication strategy by,
        86–89
    "Crisis Playbook" and,
        87–89, 213, 233, 238, 241,
        262, 264
    DEA strategy, 31, 91–94,
        260–261
    depositions of employees,
        258–266
    Farrell on, 140
    friend-of-the-court brief drafted
        by, 80, 162

on investigative reporting by
    Washington Post and 60
    Minutes, 173–174
lobbying by, 31–32, 96, 104,
    123, 145
Masters case and, 125
public nuisance suit strategy, 189,
    260
RAND study proposal, 262–263
RICO allegations against,
    241–242
subpoenas for, 238–239
"the Holy Trinity," 52–53
Thorsen, Carlyle P., 94
Thorsen French Advocacy, 94
Tighe, Bill, 101
Time magazine, 18–19
Tomkiewicz, Joseph, 46–47
Trumbull County (Ohio), 256–257
Trump, Donald, 173, 176,
    259–260
Tug Valley Pharmacy, 152
Tweel, Clay, 180
Twitty, Tom, 88–89
Tyson, Jill Wade, 101, 105

Unique Pain Management,
    52–53
United States v. Moore, 131

Vance, Sarah S., 181
Vicodin (hydrocodone), 7–8,
    42
Volkman, Paul, 53

Walgreen, Charles, Sr., 83
Walgreens
    ARCOS data on, 232
    Atwell's email and, 233
    lobbying strategies, 104

Walgreens (*Continued*)
 Oviedo (Florida) case, 81–85
 public nuisance suit filed against,
  154, 164–165, 256–257
 public nuisance suit
  representation, 195–196
 RICO allegations against,
  242–243
Wall Street Journal, 171
Walmart, 154, 232, 243, 256–257
Walsh, John, 117
Walton, Reggie B., 75–80
Washington Courthouse (Ohio),
 112, 115
Washington Post, 136, 141, 173–176,
 226–233, 238
Washington University, 35–36
Wasson, Gregory D., 81
Weissman, Gabriel, 173
Welch, Peter, 94
West Virginia, 135–137, 139–140,
 248–249, 262–263. *See also*
 Cabell County; Charleston;
 Huntington; Mingo County

West Virginia Board of Medicine,
 275–276
Whitaker, Bill, 174
White, Mary Jo, 24, 70
Whitehouse, Sheldon, 145
Wicht, Jennifer G., 300
Williams, Steve, 248, 308
Williams & Connolly, 181,
 200–201, 220–221, 227,
 235–236, 261, 274
Williamson (West Virginia),
 152–154
WilmerHale, 70, 71–72
Wintner, Jeffrey M., 251–252
Wizner, Leslie, 56–57, 125,
 126–127, 163–164
The Wonderful Wizard of Oz (Baum),
 246, 253

Xanax, 156

Zban, Mark, 157–160, 187
Zimmerman, Chris, 46–47, 254,
 277–282, 306

About the Authors

Scott Higham is a Pulitzer Prize-winning investigative reporter for the *Washington Post*. He served as a lead reporter on the *Post's* "The Opioid Files" series, which was a Pulitzer Finalist for Public Service in 2020. His investigation into the opioid industry with *60 Minutes* received the Peabody Award, an Emmy, and the duPont-Columbia and Edward R. Murrow awards. Higham is the co-author of *Finding Chandra: A True Washington Murder Mystery*.

Sari Horwitz is a four-time Pulitzer Prize-winning investigative reporter who has been at the *Washington Post* for four decades, where she has covered the Justice Department and criminal justice issues. She was a lead reporter on the *Post's* "The Opioid Files" series, which was a Pulitzer Finalist for Public Service in 2020. Horwitz has authored or co-authored three books: *Finding Chandra: A True Washington Murder Mystery*, *Sniper: Inside the Hunt for the Killers Who Terrorized the Nation*, and *Justice in Indian Country*.